The Ballad and Oral Literature

HARVARD ENGLISH STUDIES   17

The Ballad and Oral Literature

Edited by
Joseph Harris

Harvard University Press
Cambridge, Massachusetts
London, England
1991

Lyrics from "A Hard Rain's A Gonna Fall" (Bob Dylan) © 1963
Warner Bros. Inc. All rights reserved. Used by permission.

This book is printed on acid-free paper, and its binding materials
have been chosen for strength and durability.

Library of Congress Cataloging-in-Publication Data
The Ballad and oral literature / edited by Joseph Harris.
    p. cm.—(Harvard English studies)
  Includes bibliographical references.
  ISBN 0-674-06045-8 (alk. paper)
  ISBN 0-674-06046-6 (pbk.)
  1. Ballads—History and criticism. 2. Oral tradition. 3. Folk
literature—History and criticism. I. Harris, Joseph, 1940– .
II. Series.
PN1376.B28   1991
398.2—dc20   90-24717

Preface

Six of the papers gathered here originated as lectures at a symposium on the Child ballads held at Harvard University in November 1988; these chapters, by Flemming G. Andersen, Hugh Shields, David Buchan, Emily Lyle, Vésteinn Ólason, and Natscha Würzbach, have, however, been considerably reworked for printed presentation here. Two other contributions to the symposium resisted article format and had to be omitted: the excellent lectures by Otto Holzapfel of the Deutsches Volksliedarchiv in Freiburg ("The Concept of European Folk Ballads Today") and Stefaan Top of Leuven ("The Broadside Singers' Tradition in Belgium, 1750–1950"). In compensation I was able to solicit ballad articles from Sigrid Rieuwerts, who had spent 1987–88 at Harvard working especially in the unpublished materials of Houghton Library, and from William B. McCarthy, a paper originally presented at the centennial meeting of the American Folklore Society in Cambridge just after the Child symposium. For the ninth article on ballads I am particularly grateful to Bengt R. Jonsson of Stockholm for contributing despite difficult conditions and being unable to attend the conference. The latter half of the book comprises six articles on oral literature other than the ballad, or more generally on aspects of orality and literacy, solicited from colleagues, permanent or temporary, here at Harvard. Karl Reichl, normally Professor of English at Bonn, was a Visiting Professor in the departments of Near Eastern Languages and Literatures and of Comparative Literature in the spring semester of 1989 and held invited lectures on Turkic oral epic in November 1988 thanks to a grant from the Andrew W. Mellon Foundation. Dwight Reynolds, now Assistant Professor of Arabic Language and Literature in Amherst College, was a Junior Fellow of the Harvard Society of Fellows, 1986–1990.

At the beginning of the enterprise concluded in this volume I profited from consultations with Anne Dhu Shapiro (then of Harvard, now of Boston College), whose study of tune families of traditional folksong, including most Child ballads, is forthcoming from Pennsylvania State University Press. Others who contributed, one way or another to this volume, were Hugh Amory, Lorna Bolkey, Susan Deskis, Linda Morley, Jennifer Snodgrass, and, not least, the Andrew W. Mellon Foundation and the Harvard Faculty of Arts and Sciences with various grants. Trying to shape the volume, and to edit with a modicum of consistency such a variety of contributors and topics, has been, as the saying goes, an education. The goal has been to make specialist work accessible across disciplinary lines; but abbreviations which remain unexplained (MED, EETS, STC, and so on) are standards which seemed to need no gloss. *ESPB* is, of course, *The English and Scottish Popular Ballads,* ed. Francis James Child, 10 pts. in 5 vols. (Boston and New York: Houghton, Mifflin and Co.; London: Henry Stevens Son and Stiles, 1882–1898).

Contents

JOSEPH HARRIS

Introduction

This volume had its origin in a conference in memory of Francis James Child (1825–1896) on the occasion of the centenary of the founding in Cambridge of the American Folklore Society. Child, whose influence on the national institutions of scholarship was immense, was not, in this particular cause, the most active among the original group of scholars, which included Henry Wadsworth Longfellow and W. W. Newell, but they honored him as first president of the new learned society.[1] Child graduated from Harvard in 1846—the year the word "folklore" was coined—and immediately joined the teaching staff; when he died at the age of seventy-one he had taught on the faculty for fifty years. His service to the University and to scholarship is acknowledged by a dark bronze bas-relief roundel on rough-hewn oak showing Child's youthful profile; presented September 27, 1898, it hangs on the east wall of the

1. See Rosemary Lévy Zumwalt, "On the Founding of the American Folklore Society and the *Journal of American Folklore*," in William M. Clements, ed., *100 Years of American Folklore Studies: A Conceptual History* (Washington, D.C.: American Folklore Society, 1988), pp. 8–10; Lee J. Vance, "Folk-Lore Study in America," *The Popular Science Monthly* 43 (1893): 586–598, esp. 595.

Faculty Room of University Hall, the very room where the
organizational meeting of the AFS had taken place on January
4, 1888.[2] Among the many imposing professorial portraits
there, including George Lyman Kittredge in his white suit "like
an egret in a flock of cowbirds,"[3] the inconspicuous medallion
of Child is easily overlooked, despite its position directly behind the traditional seat of the President of the University
when he presides at meetings of the Faculty of Arts and Sciences. Child's greatest scholarly accomplishment was, of
course, his edition of English and Scottish ballads; but he was
also a founder and first president of the American Dialect Society, Harvard's first professor of English, and according to
Gerald Graff, the first American academic to use the "outside
offer" to better his position.[4] Despite his status as founding
father or culture hero, it is remarkable how little Child is invoked outside of ballad study and how little known within the
Harvard of today, even among the generations of students who
study in the Child Memorial Library.[5] He receives three brief
mentions, for example, in a recent history of American folklore studies and about the same attention in Graff's "institutional history" of literary studies; printed accounts of his life

2. The sculptor was Lilia Usher (1859–1955) and the presentation committee was headed by Francis Boott (Harvard class of 1831), according to
helpful information from Louise Ambler, Harvard Portrait Collection. A
copy of the medallion hangs in the Child Memorial Library.

3. B. J. Whiting, "Introduction," in George Lyman Kittredge, *Chaucer
and His Poetry*, 55th anniversary ed. (Cambridge, Mass.: Harvard University Press, 1970), pp. vii–xxxvi; quotation, p. xx.

4. See Louise Pound, "The American Dialect Society: A Historical
Sketch," *Publications of the American Dialect Society* 17 (1952): 3–28.
Gerald Graff, *Professing Literature: An Institutional History* (Chicago and
London: University of Chicago Press, 1987), pp. 40–41. See also Robin
Varnum, "Harvard's Francis James Child: The Years of the Rose," *Harvard
Library Bulletin* 36 (1988): 291–319, esp. 295.

5. On the founding and financing of the Child Memorial Library see
Charles H. Grandgent, "The Modern Languages, 1869–1929," in Samuel
Eliot Morison, ed., *The Development of Harvard University since the In-
auguration of President Eliot, 1869–1929* (Cambridge, Mass.: Harvard University Press, 1930), p. 67, n. 1.

and teaching remained limited and hagiographically toned—
until the recent Marxist critique by Dave Harker.[6] Child's "noble modesty" (in a phrase from Kittredge's radiant appreciation of his "master") and the vast and indecipherable state of
Child's *Nachlass* may be to blame for the fact that no full biography has yet been completed.[7]

A gesture toward redressing the balance seemed overdue.
Part of Harvard's institutional contribution, then, to the centennial of the AFS, which convened in Cambridge in October
1988, was the symposium "Mr Child of Harvard and his Ballads," held on October 24–25, and this resulting volume of
Harvard English Studies. (The quaint title of the symposium
was supposed to evoke the times and the Pickwickian figure of
"Stubby" Child, perhaps as in the famous photo in his rose
garden, or seated on the porch of his house on Kirkland
Street.) Another part was an exhibition in the rotunda of
Widener Library mounted by Hugh Amory of the Houghton
Library and Linda Morley, Associate of the Committee on De-
grees in Folklore and Mythology. This collaboration between

6. Simon J. Bronner, *American Folklore Studies: An Intellectual History*
(Lawrence: University Press of Kansas, 1986); compare the slightly fuller
treatment in Rosemary Lévy Zumwalt, *American Folklore Scholarship: A
Dialogue of Dissent* (Bloomington and Indianapolis: Indiana University
Press, 1988). To the biographical sources listed in the *Dictionary of American Biography* could be added Frank Preston Stearns, *Cambridge Sketches*
(Philadelphia and London: Lippincott, 1905); *The Scholar Friends: Letters
of Francis James Child and James Russell Lowell*, ed. M A. DeWolfe Howe
and G. W. Cottrell, Jr. (Cambridge, Mass.: Harvard University Press,
1952); and Dave Harker, *Fakesong: The Manufacture of British 'Folksong'
1700 to the Present Day* (Milton Keynes and Philadelphia: Open University
Press, 1985).

7. George Lyman Kittredge, "Professor Child," *Atlantic Monthly* 78
(1896): 737–742; rpt. with additions as "Francis James Child" in *The
English and Scottish Popular Ballads*, ed. Francis James Child, vol. 1 (Boston: Houghton Mifflin, 1882; issued with part X [1898] with directions for
binding into vol. 1), pp. xxiii–xxxi. Child's papers were arranged by Kittredge in thirty-odd folio volumes, to be found in the Houghton Library at
Harvard. Linda Morley is at work on a biography of Child based on all
sources.

a scholar of Child and the ballad and a connoisseur of Harvard collections and the book trade was remarkably fruitful, and the international guests and conferees who attended the opening reception found an intriguing mixture of personal and professional aspects of Child on display, including such previously unknown materials as the account books of Child's publisher, Little, Brown, documenting Child's exasperating changes in press. To cap the occasion, Amory surprised everyone with the compilation of Child's complete bibliography in presentation copies for participants in the conference.

For the symposium eight lecturers were invited from among the European ballad scholars whose work would have interested Child himself, and a considerable number of American ballad scholars were also able to participate. The organizer thought the limitation to European speakers was appropriate since Child himself had set a high value on European, especially Scandinavian, ballads and ballad scholarship and had even dreamed of a similar invitation to the famous Danish ballad scholar Svend Grundtvig (1824–1883).[8] A surprising minor theme of the Child-Grundtvig correspondence is money, announced in Grundtvig's first letter (February 17, 1872), where the Danish professor, "with only a small salary," says he cannot afford not to require payment for his services as what we would call a "consultant." Child replied generously (March 26, 1872), and among his ideas for bettering Grundtvig's condition was an invitation to speak at "an institution in Boston called the Lowell Lectures," where the payment for five or six lectures would be "not less than 1500 dollars." Grundtvig welcomed the suggestion, offering the title "Old Northern Language and Literature" though he feared that his English would not be adequate to "the very cream of American literary Society" (June 2, 1872). To "the Eddas" and "the Sagas" of the

8. Sigurd Bernard Hustvedt, *Ballad Books and Ballad Men: Raids and Rescues in Britain, America, and the Scandinavian North since 1800* (Cambridge, Mass.: Harvard University Press, 1930). See also Erik Dal, "Francis James Child and Denmark after the Death of Svend Grundtvig 1883," *Norveg: Folkelivsgransking* 21 (1978; festschrift for Olav Bø): 183–196.

original conception, Child wished to add "the Ballads"; the real purpose, however, would be not the public lectures but discussions between the two scholars: "You would be with me and we could discuss many things which we could not go into in letters. The advantage for me would be incalculable" (August 25, 1872). In this last letter, however, one already senses the obstacles: "With regard to the Lowell lectures, I have strong hopes that that pleasant little scheme of mine will be realized. Mr. Lowell was very glad of the suggestion. He said that he would look over his list of lecturers already engaged, and if he found that he had not already asked too many, would write to you. He is an old man, of very few words, and very much averse to writing. So I know that he will not write to *me*, and I shall hear of his action only through you . . ."

The failure of the "scheme" is reported in a letter of July 1, 1873: "Of Mr. Lowell and my cherished project of having you come over to us I have nothing new to say. He is an odd man, and one whom I do not wish to approach again. Indeed I perfectly understood that you would very much object to my doing more than suggest that if such a course of lectures were *wanted*, you might be willing to give them. I fear now that he will invite you at some time not convenient to you."[9] No invitation, convenient or otherwise, was forthcoming, and Child turned his hopes for a personal meeting with Grundtvig—something that never came about—to a vacation encounter in Switzerland. But it is amusing to note that both gentlemen thought hints more than sufficient for what in our time would be an application to a foundation.[10] In 1988 some of Grundtvig's heirs could at last be invited, with the support of the Andrew W. Mellon Foundation and the University. Their lectures form the core of this volume, which, however follows recent developments in scholarship to situate the ballad in contexts not anticipated by Child, especially in the context of "oral literature."

*   *   *

9. John Amory Lowell (1798–1881), first Trustee of the Lowell Institute.

10. Grundtvig cautions against pushing "the question as a personal one" (June 2, 1872).

For Child, ballads were popular or folk literature; his guiding
spirits were Jacob and Wilhelm Grimm, and Child passed on
their assumptions—"romantic assumptions" as they are apt to
be called now—to his students, especially George Lyman Kittredge (1860–1941), Francis Barton Gummere (1855–1919), and
Fred Norris Robinson (1871–1966).[11] Child was concerned
mainly with the authenticity and age of his ballads and with the
cross-cultural comparisons of content necessary to begin to establish a history of each text; he does not seem to have anticipated, except very sporadically, more modern concerns with
the mechanisms of change or with orality and literacy. In their
place he operated with the assumptions of his day about social
evolution and especially with the German distinction between
Kunstpoesie and *Volksdichtung*—"a distinct and very important species of poetry . . . anterior to the appearance of the
poetry of art."[12] David Bynum has shown very well how, under

11. Since Child had barely begun the theoretical introduction to his edi-
tion at the time of his death, our printed sources for his ideas about ballads
in general are limited to his brief article "Ballad Poetry," in *Johnson's New
Universal Cyclopædia,* ed. Frederic A. P. Barnard et al. (New York: A. J.
Johnson & Son, 1877), vol. 1, pp. 365–368; letters (reprinted chiefly in
Hustvedt, *Ballad Books and Ballad Men,* and in *Letters on Scottish Ballads
from Professor Francis J. Child to W[illiam] W[alker] Aberdeen* (Aberdeen:
Bon-Accord Press, 1930); and the headnotes to individual ballads; as well
as the ideas of his students, especially Kittredge and Gummere. See Walter
Morris Hart, "Professor Child and the Ballad," *PMLA* 21 (1906): 755–807;
rpt. in later printings of *ESPB;* James Reppert, "F. J. Child and the Ballad,"
in Larry Benson, ed., *The Learned and the Lewed: Studies in Chaucer and
Medieval Literature,* Harvard English Studies 5 (Cambridge, Mass.: Har-
vard University Press, 1974), pp. 197–212 (based on Reppert's Harvard dissertation of 1953). The interpretations of Child's ideas by Kittredge, Gum-
mere, Hart, Gerould, and even Louise Pound come in for criticism in
Thelma James, "The English and Scottish Popular Ballads of Francis J.
Child," *Journal of American Folklore* 46 (1933): 51–68; rpt. in Mac Edward
Leach and Tristram P. Coffin, eds., *The Critics and the Ballad: Readings*
(Carbondale: Southern Illinois University Press, 1961), pp. 12–19.

12. Child, "Ballad Poetry," p. 365; cited also by Hart, Bynum, and others. For a brilliant contemporary analysis of Child's conception of the popular and the people, see Michael J. Bell, "'No Borders to the Ballad
Maker's Art': Francis James Child and the Politics of the People," *Western
Folklore* 47 (1988): 285–307.

his chosen successor Kittredge, Child's legacy was "enlarged" to a greater range of folklore that assumed far-reaching educational implications: "The study of oral literature had begun at Harvard as the personal preoccupation of one man, and as such it was one of the oldest *foci* of intellectual effort in the modern University. But after 1890 it became also a major generator of new technical disciplines not only for Harvard but also for higher learning in the nation as a whole."[13] After Kittredge scholarly interest in the ballad and folklore declined in its original home, the English Department, but Hyder Edward Rollins (1889–1958), who goes unmentioned in Bynum's sketch, had influential views on the ballad and played a major role in editing broadsides.[14] (In general one can defer to Bynum's picture of the Harvard connections of literary folkloristics in the late- and post-Kittredge era.) Meanwhile, the new focus on specifically oral literature had already begun with Milman Parry and the "Homeric question" and soon spread back to the English Department.[15]

The term "oral literature" was already being used by Kittredge in his 1896 obituary of Child; the passage was prominently incorporated into the biographical sketch prefixed to the

13. "Child's Legacy Enlarged: Oral Literary Studies at Harvard Since 1856," *Harvard Library Bulletin* 22 (1974): 237–267; quotation, pp. 247–248; rpt. in Publications of the Milman Parry Collection, Documentation and Planning Series 2.

14. Carl Lindahl, "The Folklorist and Literature: Child and Others," in Clements, *100 Years,* pp. 52–54, makes the likely suggestion that the cause of the decline was the growth of esthetic approaches in place of source study in literature. Herschel Baker, *Hyder Edward Rollins: A Bibliography* (Cambridge, Mass.: Harvard University Press, 1960), pp. 35–41, lists Rollins's Ph.D. students; according to my count at least eight (including Samuel Bayard) wrote on ballads of one kind or another.

15. Alongside Bartlett Jere Whiting (b. 1904; ret. 1975), who continued the direct line from Kittredge, flourished Francis Peabody Magoun (1895–1979), who first integrated the theories of Parry and Albert Bates Lord into early English (see Bynum, pp. 18–21). In more recent decades Charles Dunn (Celtic and English) and Morton Bloomfield may be mentioned; see their *The Role of the Poet in Early Societies* (Cambridge, England and Wolfeboro, N.H.: Brewer, 1989).

ballad edition beginning in 1898: "Mere learning will not guide
an editor through [the perplexities of ballad tradition]. What is
needed is, in addition, a complete understanding of the 'popular' genius, a sympathetic recognition of the traits that characterize oral literature wherever and in whatever degree they
exist . . . In reality a kind of instinct, [this faculty] had been
so cultivated [in Child] by long and loving study of the traditional literature of all nations that it had become wonderfully
swift in its operations and almost infallible" (p. xxx). Here the
object of study, traditional literature, was still "popular,"
though the concept is distanced with quotation marks, but
Kittredge speaks prophetically of specific traits that characterize oral literature and implies their cross-cultural comparabil-
ity. Perhaps Kittredge even anticipates other recent topics,
such as "oral residues," by opening the possibility of degrees
of orality ("in whatever degree they exist").

A few years later in his famous essay introductory to the
one-volume edition of Child's ballads, Kittredge was even
more prophetic.[16] Rereading this brilliant piece one finds mistaken certitude—the 305 ballad types "comprise the whole extant mass of this material"—and views confidently asserted in
diametrical opposition to the present consensus, such as:
"Ballad-making, so far as the English-speaking nations are
concerned, is a lost art; and the same may be said of ballad-
singing." Or this on the age of the ballad: "There is ample evidence for the antiquity of popular ballads in England. Nobody
doubts that the Angles and Saxons had them in abundance
when they invaded Britain . . . from the dawn of English history . . . The substance of many Anglo-Saxon ballads may be
preserved in *Béowulf*." The impression of downright error is
heightened by Kittredge's emphatic style though he often
smuggles qualifications to his apodictic statements into the
treatment of individual items covered by the generalizations.
But revisiting Kittredge one can also find traces of a prescient

---

16. *English and Scottish Popular Ballads,* ed. Helen Child Sargent and
George Lyman Kittredge (Boston: Houghton Mifflin, 1904), pp. xi–xxxi.

literary theorist, one who anticipates several developments of
modern times. His ballad poet "improvises orally with his audience before him"; in a direct anticipation of Gerould's concept of "communal recreation," Kittredge comments on variation: "Taken collectively, these processes of oral tradition
amount to a second act of composition, of an inextricably complicated character, in which many persons share . . . [a kind
of] collective composition." Anticipating the dogma of the active audience, Kittredge's ballad audience "even if they kept
silent . . . would still have a share in [the singer's] poetic act,"
at times would even "participate in the process." Perhaps even
anticipating structuralism and its aftermath: "a ballad has no
author . . . We do not feel sure that he ever existed [although
we have to] infer his existence"; "a tale . . . *telling itself,* without the instrumentality of the speaker . . . There are *texts,* but
there is no *text.*" Some of these thoughts are as old as Grimm;
but Kittredge also anticipates the idea of a poetics related to
the living conditions of the literature, that is, an oral poetics.
Even Kittredge's refusal to trivialize that "dark oracle" of
Grimm, "das Volk dichtet," is likely to sound different in the
current situation of the humanities than it did in the positivist
decades, though I cannot see that Kittredge's appreciation
foreshadows modern concepts of supra-individual or collective
representations—oracles perhaps equally dark.[17]

In the midst of all this a shrewd analysis of the role of writing
(p. xii) could be a page out of Ong or Goody, and Kittredge
uses "oral literature" in a thoroughly contemporary way several times in the essay, including this more self-conscious instance: "To this oral literature, as the French call it, education
is no friend." I have not searched for nineteenth-century
French uses of *littérature orale* or for earlier English occur-
rences; the point is simply to establish a respectable age for a

17. The classic overview is D. K. Wilgus, *Anglo-American Folksong
Scholarship since 1898* (New Brunswick, N.J.: Rutgers University Press,
1959). See also Clyde Kenneth Hyder, *George Lyman Kittredge: Teacher
and Scholar* (Lawrence: University of Kansas Press, 1962), pp. 104–105 and
p. 198, n. 17.

phrase and concept tellingly criticized by Walter Ong—criticism ironic in coming from one of the most prolific scholars of orality and literacy, a nexus of interests rapidly assuming the status of an "over-field."

In a section entitled "Did you say 'oral literature'?" Ong objects to the oxymoron he finds in the expression.[18] Of course *literature* is derived from *littera,* so that etymologically literature is something written, and Ong comments that "concepts have a way of carrying their etymologies with them forever." Strictly speaking, I suppose, concepts don't have etymologies, only words do, but Ong's real objection is that the word-shaped concept of literature is saturated with chirographic-typographic modes of understanding:

We (those who read texts such as this) are for the most part so resolutely literate that we seldom feel comfortable with a situation in which verbalization is so little thing-like as it is in oral tradition. As a result—though at a slightly reduced frequency now—scholarship in the past has generated such monstrous concepts as 'oral literature.' This strictly preposterous term remains in circulation today even among scholars now more and more acutely aware how embarrassingly it reveals our inability to represent to our own minds a heritage of verbally organized materials except as some variant of writing, even when they have nothing to do with writing at all. The title of the great Milman Parry Collection of Oral Literature at Harvard University monumentalizes the state of awareness of an earlier generation of scholars rather than that of its recent curators.

As a caveat against "the restless imperialism of writing culture" and a reminder of our difficulty in conceptualizing orality and its (rough) equivalent of literature, Ong's warning is well taken.[19]

The essential problem he avoids, however, is what *is* literature? Surely not just anything in *litterae.* Though we sometimes do use the word very broadly (the present curator of the Parry Collection instances the "literature" about a given

18. Walter Ong, *Orality and Literacy: The Technologizing of the Word* (London and New York: Methuen, 1982), pp. 10–15.

19. Ibid., pp. 11–12. For a different approach, see Robert Kellogg, "Oral Literature," *New Literary History* 5 (1973): 55–66.

model of car)[20] it is obviously the famously indefinable special sense that is intended in "oral literature." Ong rather desperately suggested "voicings" for the oral equivalent of literature but immediately fell back on "purely oral art forms" and "verbal art forms." But none of these solves the problem: everything voiced would not be a "voicing" in the special sense any more than everything in letters would be literature.[21] And the "art" of the periphrases is as difficult to define as "literature" and functions here transparently as a synonym.

Whatever "literature" is, it is not dependent on what linguists call the "channel"—that is, whether it is oral, written, printed, secondarily oral as on radio or television, and so on. Rather, literary theory has in general regarded literature as different from nonliterary discourse *either* because of a use of language that contrasts with ordinary speech (marked vs. unmarked; a subset of the grammar), *or* because of its fictive relation to the world (the poet nothing affirmeth), *or* both. The ethnic-analytic problem, most familiar perhaps from cross-cultural attempts at genre systems but generalizable more or less radically along lines suggested by linguistic relativism, would remain: we could, for example, learn the Chamula discourse spectrum from Gossen's fine Central American ethnographies, but we cannot learn at what point in the gradation from *lo?il k'op* ("Ordinary Speech") to *?antivo k'opetik* ("Ancient Words") what we call literature sets in.[22] Yet this litera-

20. Albert B. Lord, "Words Heard and Words Seen," in R. A. Whitaker and E. R. Sinaert, eds., *Oral Tradition and Literacy: Changing Visions of the World* (Durban: Natal University Oral Documentation and Research Centre, 1986), p. 1.

21. Compare the fallacy in Henry R. Mbarwa's practical schoolbook for African use, *Your Oral Literature* (Kijabe, Kenya: Kijabe Printing Press, n. d.), p. 1, which equates literature with "communication"—a fallacy more apparent than real as the book proceeds to deal with the usual categories of folk literature.

22. Gary H. Gossen, "Verbal Dueling in Chamula," in Barbara Kirschenblatt-Gimblett, ed., *Speech Play: Research and Resources for Studying Linguistic Creativity* (Philadelphia: University of Pennsylvania Press, 1976), pp. 121–146. See Dan Ben-Amos, "Analytical Categories and Ethnic Genres," in Ben-Amos, ed., *Folklore Genres* (Austin: University of Texas Press, 1975), pp. 215–242; originally in *Genre* 2 (1969): 275–301. The prob-

ture is an analytic concept we cannot forgo, as Ong himself, giving away much of his argument, admits: "But [with 'voicings' or something like it] we would still be without a more generic term to include both purely oral art and literature" (p. 14). So if "literature" is possible, "oral literature" is also possible. But in another sense the self-contradictory flavor of the phrase ought to be savored as a reminder of the problematics of literature itself and of the relationships of the oral to the literate.

These relationships are the background against which all the papers in *The Ballad and Oral Literature* are conceived, and specific aspects of the "interface" of orality and literacy constitute an explicit red thread running through much of the book. This theme is chiefly implicit, however, in the three opening papers, which focus on formal and stylistic features of several ballad traditions. Flemming G. Andersen examines the roles of ballad formulas or commonplaces in the creation, transmission, variation, and genre-constitution of classical Child ballads. Using evidence from his fieldwork with contemporary Scottish singers, Andersen alone among the contributors argues for a close concern with distinctions made by those who use ballads ("ethnic" categories), as contrasted with "our" conclusions ("analytic"). His broad and up-to-date paper inducts us into the state of scholarship within Child's special preserve, which Andersen finds so much more complex than his predecessor Kittredge that he concludes by recommending "ballads" over "the ballad" (as in the symposium, but not the book, title). As if in reply, Hugh Shields begins by postulating the generic unity of the Child ballads as the foil for his contrasting exploration of "narrative contingencies" in the inherently lyrical folksongs of France and Gaelic Ireland. Shields's study touches also on "ethnic" understanding but

---

lems of cross-cultural genre systems are evident, for example, in Roger Abrahams, "The Complex Relations of Simple Forms," in *Folklore Genres,* pp. 193–214, and William Bascom, "The Forms of Folklore: Prose Narratives," in Alan Dundes, ed., *Sacred Narrative: Readings in the Theory of Myth* (Berkeley and Los Angeles: University of California Press, 1984), pp. 6–29; originally in *Journal of American Folklore* 78 (1965): 3–20.

seems especially notable for its rich and subtle literary insights on the less downright realizations of narrative in the neighboring ballad traditions. David Buchan also assumes an "analytic" unity, but his purpose is a descriptive analysis of a subgenre, ballads of the supernatural, with all its "minigenres." Structuralist methods and aims continue to be immensely productive in the narratology of folklore, but Buchan makes use of Propp's less well-known theoretical contribution, now called the "talerole."

The next five papers take historical approaches. Sigrid Rieuwerts is completing a thorough study of Child 200, "The Gypsy Laddie," for her Giessen doctorate; her article marshals detailed historical evidence to revise Child's judgment on the age and real historical basis of this ballad. Of all the contributions printed here, Child would have appreciated this one most immediately. William McCarthy argues that some features usually thought of as typical of the sea-changes undergone in America by ballads imported from Scotland actually belonged to the original tradition—if only we had looked more to Southwestern Scotland, the region that actually produced the majority of the early immigrants. His study is exemplified by texts sung for the early collector William Motherwell by Agnes Lyle of Kilbarchan (ca. 1825).[23] Next, Emily Lyle takes another mistaken judgment of Child's as the point of departure for developing a deceptively simple but important contribution to the conceptual tools of historical study, especially of oral literature: it is no safer to say that something (a song) did not exist before its earliest attestation than to say that it did; whether positive or negative, there is a real "parity of ignorance."

Two dense and important essays on the history of the ballad in Scandinavia follow. The Icelander Vésteinn Ólason investigates directly the relationship between the oral and the written in Nordic balladry, beginning with the kind of orality demonstrated by a series of ballads (Icelandic, Faroese, and Norwegian) unequivocally based on Old Norse written literature; the second part of his article expands to a general consideration of

---

23. McCarthy's book *The Ballad Matrix: Personality, Milieu, and the Oral Tradition*, is forthcoming from Indiana University Press.

the subgenres of Scandinavian balladry under the aspect of the argument that "their orality, which is undeniable, is conditioned by a basic reference to a literate culture to such an extent that one is justified in talking about a symbiosis between oral poetry and literature."[24] The wide-ranging and detailed article by Bengt Jonsson is also very extensively concerned with the mutual influences of oral and written literature, especially the relationships between Old Norse sagas and eddic poems and Scandinavian ballads. The oral-written interface is, however, only a part of Jonsson's radical new theory of the origin and early history of the ballad in Scandinavia, a theory in which French impulses are channeled to the court of the Norwegian king Hákon the Old via the British Isles and consolidated around 1300 in the East Norwegian court of Hákon Longleg; the article constitutes a valuable glimpse of a book long in the making.

From symbiosis we pass to the one-way influence of Child's collected and printed folk ballads on some of the classic literary ballads in English. In the volume's last contribution on ballads Natascha Würzbach embeds literary criticism of individual poems within an attempt to map the categories of intertextuality of the literary ballad. With Würzbach's, the essay of Jan Ziolkowski is pivotal in the organization of the volume. It continues the attention to the linguistic and literary pressure of the vernacular and the oral on a literate culture, the culture in question being that of the Latin Middle Ages. Ziolkowski's rich survey suggests and exemplifies dozens of fresh opportunities for the medievalist and ushers in a series of essays that go beyond the ballad to other genres.

The first of these papers, by Gregory Nagy, takes up a topic famously associated with the heirs of Child: namely, choral song and dance, with special reference to Ancient Greek and to Faroese. Veterans of the "ballad wars" will find it intriguing to see what twentieth-century literary theory, anthropology,

24. With these conclusions we might compare American work such as that of a recent Mellon Fellow at Harvard, Diane Dugaw, "Anglo-American Folksong Reconsidered: The Interface of Oral and Written Forms," *Western Folklore* 43 (1984): 83–103.

and especially Jakobsonian linguistics do with a subject so closely associated with Gummere; but though Nagy studiously refrains from evoking the "Harvard communalists," it seems appropriate in a volume of this kind to observe that Gummere's work—much of which casts a *theory* of literature as a *history* of literature—might have a wholly different resonance for our speculative age.[25] Albert B. Lord's paper on an instance of ring composition in the Old English poem *The Battle of Maldon* (with reference also to Ancient Greek) returns to the discussion of oral-literary relations; the rhetorical pattern and the habit of mind the poem displays seem to be "residue" of its origin in a Germanic oral poetics. (In a volume of this kind the contribution of Lord is obviously not confined to a single article but is all-pervasive.) For Middle English romances Karl Reichl pursues complex questions of oral and written—summarized as "minstrel versus hack writer"—with a double method. On the one hand, he provides close studies of variation facilitated by his concordance of tail-rhyme romances; on the other, he relies on his extensive fieldwork in Turkic Inner Asia to supply a fascinating analogy, a school of romance *(dåstån)* with similarly close interrelationships of written and oral tradition.

The nineteenth century and the classic fairytale are represented in our volume by the contribution of Stephen A. Mitchell. Mitchell studies a Swedish version, *Gråkappan,* of the international Cupid and Psyche tale (AT 425) at which conscious artists, popular chapbooks, and traditional tellers were all at work; Mitchell finds that few a priori assumptions survive in the borderland of oral and written, and in particular that the death of traditional oral narrative in the environment of writing has been greatly exaggerated. The final paper of the collection, like the first, concerns a contemporary oral literature. Dwight Reynolds bases his study of the included genres within colloquial Arabic oral epic chiefly on his own fieldwork in Egypt.

---

25. Wilgus's account of the "Ballad Wars" includes an extensive analysis of Gummere's mode of argumentation; consider his aphoristic reduction "In effect, *Gummere's doctrine is an etiological myth which explains the essence of the popular ballad*" (p. 12).

Reynolds has made his paper thoroughly accessible to out-
siders, and it is especially interesting here to see the intersec-
tion of methods that emphasize performance and context with
a textual conception of genre.

Our collection does not deal, except in passing, with the music of the ballads and other sung oral genres, though several of
the contributors do so elsewhere in their writings. Moreover,
despite a good deal of influence—easily recognizable—from
performance-oriented schools of thought, in the present volume, as in Child's work, the text "is the thing": another thread
uniting these papers is the conviction that text exists—unless
it exists as *texts!*[26] The contextual approaches dominant in current folkloristics—whether "slouching towards ethnography"
or not—have two disadvantages from the points of view represented here.[27] First, they allow, in the main, only synchronic
statements; but tradition, whatever else it is, is diachronic.[28]

26. For a brief review of the "performance" direction in recent folkloristics, see Jack Santino, "Folklore as Performance and Communication,"
in Clements, *100 Years,* pp. 21–23. Richard Bauman, *Story, Performance,
and Event: Contextual Studies of Oral Narrative* (London: Cambridge University Press, 1986), gives a fuller exposition and bibliography. See also
D. K. Wilgus, "'The Text Is the Thing,'" *Journal of American Folklore* 86
(1973): 241–252.

27. Some landmarks in the text/context debate: *Journal of American
Folklore* 84 (1971), no. 331, rpt. as Américo Paredes and Richard Bauman,
eds., *Toward New Perspectives in Folklore* (Austin: University of Texas
Press, 1972); Wilgus, "'The Text Is the Thing'"; Steven Jones, "Slouching
Towards Ethnography: The Text/Context Controversy Reconsidered,"
Western Folklore 38 (1979): 42–47; Dan Ben-Amos, "The Ceremony of In-
nocence," ibid., pp. 47–52; Steven Jones, "Dogmatism in the Conceptual
Revolution," ibid., pp. 52–55; Robert A. Georges, "Toward a Resolution of
the Text/Context Controversy," *Western Folklore* 39 (1980): 34–40; Kath-
arine Young, "The Notion of Context," *Western Folklore* 44 (1985): 115–
122.

28. Contrast Reimund Kvideland, "Tradition: Objectivations or Social
Behaviour?" and comments by Kirsten Sass Bak in Rita Pedersen and
Flemming G. Andersen, eds., *The Concept of Tradition in Ballad Research:
A Symposium* (Odense: Odense University Press, 1985), pp. 9–21; see
Vésteinn Ólason's refutation in the same volume ("Tradition and Text,"
pp. 87–96) and my review in *Scandinavian Studies* 60 (1988): 315–317. There
are, of course, any number of discussions of performances within historical
contexts but not many attempts to import historically distant materials into

Historical study of any depth (whether of an early "item" or of a development) relies on text. Second, sans-text approaches are obviously partial when our underlying interest is in orality and literacy; that is, orality/literacy can clearly be interpreted as "behavior," but since the behavior involved is itself focused on text—evanescent in the ear or lasting on the page—a complete account of performance and context would still be notably incomplete. Strange that some contemporary literary theory is busy dilating "text" beyond recognition by the injection of "context," just at a moment when much contemporary folkloristic theory is reducing it to a token in the behavioral context. I find myself closer to the literary position and especially close to Vésteinn Ólason's formulation according to which a ballad is a "concretation of tradition . . . the text speaks with more than one voice; in it other texts are echoed, and in them still other texts. This play of echoes and the systems or codes that make it possible is in fact the phenomenon that appears to us as tradition: our quarry."[29] In any case, the papers collected here reaffirm in several ways the old compact between folklore (in one of its narrow senses) and philology (in its broad senses).

---

the context of performance theory; a notable exception is Richard Bauman, "Performance and Honor in 13th-Century Iceland," *Journal of American Folklore* 99 (1986): 131–150.

29. Ólason, "Tradition and Text," pp. 88 and 92.

FLEMMING G. ANDERSEN

Technique, Text, and Context: Formulaic Narrative Mode and the Question of Genre

It is often lamented that the one person who knew most about the traditional ballads did not live to make a definition of the genre.[1] From the observations scattered throughout the volumes of Francis James Child's *The English and Scottish Popular Ballads,* which have been meticulously identified and succinctly interpreted by James Reppert, and from additional material presented by Walter Morris Hart, we can nonetheless get some idea of what Child found to be the most salient properties of the traditional ballad.[2] Child noted that "the word *ballad* in English signifies a narrative song, a short tale in lyric verse," and pointed out that "the fundamental characteristic of popular ballads is . . . the absence of subjectivity and self-consciousness."[3] This early attempt at a characterization of

1. The point is made, for example, by Matthew Hodgart, *The Ballads* (London: Hutchinson's University Library, 1950), p. 154, and Sigurd Bernhard Hustvedt, *Ballad Books and Ballad Men* (Cambridge, Mass.: Harvard University Press, 1930), p. 13.

2. Reppert, "F. J. Child and the Ballad," in Larry D. Benson, ed., *The Learned and the Lewed: Studies in Chaucer and Medieval Literature,* Harvard English Studies 5 (Cambridge, Mass.: Harvard University Press, 1974), pp. 197–212. Hart, "Professor Child and the Ballad," *PMLA* 21 (1906): 755–807; reprinted as an appendix to vol. V of the Dover edition of *ESPB* (New York, 1965).

3. Quoted in Hart, "Professor Child," pp. 781, 756.

18

the ballads is one which he did not particularly want to have quoted. The term "lyric" is here an acknowledgment that ballads are sung narratives, but otherwise Child was chiefly concerned with the textual features. Ballads are viewed as objective in their manner of narration, as having an artless and homely style, yet not without certain stylistic conventions of their own, such as commonplaces, which Child observes are often "out of place" in "inferior traditional ballads."[4] Finally Child notes that ballads are variable in transmission, and that they often suffer in the process.[5] As Reppert points out, however, Child is not at all clear on this particular point.[6]

In the absence of a clear-cut definition, it has been customary simply to define ballads by example, as songs similar in kind to those in Child's volumes.[7] Child himself seems to have resorted to this approach, for in an appeal for ballad collecting in his own country he gave texts of "The Cruel Sister" and "Sir Hugh" as illustrations of the type of material he was interested in.[8] Over the years, however, scholars have been at pains to find generic characteristics, and have variously pointed out prominent features such as "leaping and lingering," conspicuous configurations of verbal repetition, and conceptual patterning as typical of the narrative structure of the traditional ballad.[9] The focus of interest has gradually shifted

4. *ESPB* IV, p. 426; see Hart, "Professor Child," p. 785.

5. Hart, "Professor Child," p. 805.

6. Reppert, "F. J. Child," p. 207.

7. See, for example, Louise Pound, *Poetic Origins and the Ballad* (New York: Macmillan, 1921), p. 88; Thelma G. James, "The English and Scottish Popular Ballads of Francis J. Child," *Journal of American Folklore* 46 (1933): 59; Albert B. Friedman, *The Ballad Revival* (Chicago: University of Chicago Press, 1961), p. 7. A recent exponent of this view is G. Malcolm Laws: "In the field of balladry, definition by example has often been found more enlightening than abstract verbalizing." *The British Literary Ballad* (Carbondale: Southern Illinois University Press, 1972), p. 1. Strangely, the Child canon looms particularly large in studies of the living ballad tradition; see Herschel Gower and James Porter, "Jeannie Robertson and the Child Ballads," and Ailie Munro, "Lizzie Higgins and the Oral Transmission of Ten Child Ballads," *Scottish Studies* 14 (1970): 35–58, 155–188.

8. See Hustvedt, *Ballad Books*, p. 288n.

9. Francis Gummere, *The Popular Ballad* (Boston: Houghton Mifflin, 1907), p. 91; Gordon H. Gerould, *The Ballad of Tradition* (1932; rpt. New York: Gordian Press, 1974), pp. 105–117; Marga Kühnemund, "Ausdruck

from a classification of the ballad as a poetic subgenre toward an appreciation of ballads as a particular narrative technique, a particular way of telling a story.

This development has coincided with a general move in scholarship away from textual studies into contextual, "functionalist" considerations of the traditional ballad—even to the extent of discarding texts altogether, as some scholars have argued that our investigation should be aimed at the fact that people sing rather than at what they sing.[10] It has generally come to be believed that textual studies alone would give us only one side of the coin, or perhaps not even that. I shall take as my point of departure a purely textual phenomenon, the use of formulaic expressions, and treat it with the express purpose of determining how relevant this primarily analytical concept will be for the traditional ballad seen as an ethnic category.[11]

Within one of the indexes to his edition of the ballads Child included a list of recurrent "commonplaces," but he did not comment on their narrative or stylistic functions in the ballads.[12] Since then formulas (as such phrases are now generally

---

der Intensität durch Quantität in der englisch-schottischen Volksballade" (diss., Marburg, 1933); Flemming G. Andersen, Otto Holzapfel, and Thomas Pettitt, *The Ballad as Narrative* (Odense: Odense University Press, 1982); David Buchan, *The Ballad and the Folk* (London: Routledge & Kegan Paul, 1972). For a recent characterization of the traditional ballad, see D. K. Wilgus and Eleanor Long, "The Blues Ballad and the Genesis of Style in Traditional Narrative Song," in Carol L. Edwards and Kathleen B. Manley, eds., *Narrative Folksong: New Directions; Essays in Appreciation of W. Edson Richmond* (Boulder, Colo.: Westview Press, 1985), pp. 435–482, esp. 437–438.

10. Some recent studies are James Porter, "Ballad Explanations, Ballad Reality, and the Singer's Epistemics," *Western Folklore* 45 (1986): 110–127, and J. Barre Toelken, "Context and Meaning in the Anglo-American Ballad," in D. K. Wilgus, ed., *The Ballad and the Scholars* (Los Angeles: Clark Memorial Library, 1986), pp. 29–52. For an example of study of folksongs in terms of "singing activity" see Reimund Kvideland, "Tradition: Objectivations or Social Behaviour?" in Rita Pedersen and Flemming G. Andersen, eds., *The Concept of Tradition in Ballad Research* (Odense: Odense University Press, 1985), pp. 11–16.

11. On the technical meaning of "ethnic" and "analytic" see Dan Ben-Amos, "Analytical Categories and Ethnic Genres," *Genre* 2 (1969): 275–301.

12. *ESPB* V, pp. 474–475.

called) have come to the fore—primarily, of course, thanks to the pioneering work of two other Harvard scholars, Milman Parry and Albert Bates Lord. Their oral-formulaic theory concerning composition-in-performance by means of formulas and formulaic systems became an important tool for scholars in many fields. Application of this very powerful analytical tool enabled scholars to establish long-sought contexts of composition and transmission for the many songs and epics that had come down to us with little contextual information. Since its initial application to the field of traditional balladry—and the subsequent rebuttals—the theory has inspired investigation into the nature and function of formulaic diction, so far mainly within the framework of ballad narrative technique. In this manner formulas have become part and parcel of generic considerations.[13]

Ballad formulas are recurrent phrases, lines, or stanzas expressing significant narrative ideas; one of their functions is to underline the dramatic unfolding of the ballad narrative. More specifically, formulas participate in all the repetition patterns that can be identified in the narrative structure of traditional balladry—emphatic repetition, causative repetition, and other types.[14] Following hints from the oral-formulaic theory, one is tempted to assume that formulas are also significant in the pro-

13. For the most comprehensive bibliography of oral-formulaic studies, see John Miles Foley, *Oral-Formulaic Theory and Research: An Introduction and Annotated Bibliography* (New York: Garland Publishing, 1985), which also presents an admirable overview of the theory and its applications. For a brief history of the oral-formulaic theory in ballad studies, see Albert Friedman, "The Oral-Formulaic Theory of Balladry: A Re-Rebuttal," in James Porter, ed., *The Ballad Image: Essays Presented to Bertrand Harris Bronson* (Los Angeles: Center for the Study of Comparative Folklore and Mythology, 1983), pp. 215–240. See also Flemming G. Andersen, *Commonplace and Creativity: The Role of Formulaic Diction in Anglo-Scottish Traditional Balladry* (Odense: Odense University Press, 1985), pp. 4–17. One of the earliest attempts at a comprehensive characterization of the formulaic narrative technique in ballads was made by Otto Holzapfel in his "Studien zur Formelhaftigkeit der mittelalterlichen dänischen Volksballade" (diss., Frankfurt, 1969).

14. For a definition of the ballad formulas, see Andersen, *Commonplace and Creativity*, p. 37; for a discussion of the various repetition patterns, see ibid., chap. 6.

cess of oral transmission, and although we cannot very well say that ballads are improvised at each singing, it is equally clear that variations do occur in the process of transmission.[15] Despite their commonplace nature formulas are variable units. Comparative analyses of formulaic diction in a large number of ballads show that the actual wording of the formulaic phrases may differ considerably, whereas the content—the narrative idea—will stay essentially the same; this allows a considerable degree of textual modification of what is perceived as the "same" formula.[16] Because they are time-honored expressions of recurrent ballad acts, formulas facilitate memorial transmission; consequently one should expect that any changes found in the formulaic phrases have been deliberately introduced by the singers. As empirical evidence is so very hard to come by, however, the effect of oral transmission on the formal structure of ballads is usually characterized in rather loose, general terms.

The amount of textual change in ballad transmission varies significantly according to circumstances. In multiple performances of the same ballad by the same singer linguistic variations are very minute indeed, and are consequently best characterized in terms of memorization. In transmission from one singer to another, on the other hand, variations are much more likely to come in, depending on the singers' awareness of the tradition, on what they want to communicate, and so on. It is difficult to gauge the exact contribution made by individual singers in the gradual reshaping of ballad stories that takes place over the years. Ballad singers are individuals, with idiosyncratic worldviews and experiences, which can be expressed in a variety of ways within the balladic form.

15. See Albert Friedman, "The Formulaic Improvisation Theory of Ballad Tradition—A Counterstatement," *Journal of American Folklore* 74 (1961): 113–115; Klaus Roth, "Zur mündlichen Komposition von Volksballaden," *Jahrbuch für Volksliedforschung* 22 (1977): 49–65; Flemming G. Andersen and Thomas Pettitt, "Mrs. Brown of Falkland: A Singer of Tales?" *Journal of American Folklore* 92 (1979): 1–24.

16. See Andersen, *Commonplace and Creativity,* chaps. 5 and 8. Elements other than formulas will of course be affected by variation in transmission.

In another sense ballad singers are very similar: in their attitudes to the technique of storytelling in sung verse. Transmission over generations of singers will inevitably lead to extensive variation, and to the formation of new versions of the story. But from a structural point of view there seems to be method in the madness of variation. Lack of source material makes it next to impossible for us to follow a ballad in a single chain of transmission for more than two or perhaps three generations of singers. In most cases we can make no inference concerning variation in transmission as we do not know the exact relationship between the texts.

Conditions are much better, however, if we turn from the traditional ballad to a related and often underestimated genre, the journalistic broadside ballad. Because we are sometimes able to follow the process of transmission more closely, we may find evidence that has direct bearing on the traditional ballad. In a few cases, when journalistic ballads based on historical facts have caught on in tradition, we have both an original text—the broadsheet version produced immediately after the event—and subsequent oral derivatives taken down many years later. Comparative analysis of the original version of a murdered-sweetheart ballad produced in the 1820s—the horrible murder of Maria Marten—and its oral versions recorded by Cecil Sharp almost a century later demonstrates that in the process of transmission the journalistic broadside ballad becomes more and more like a traditional ballad: it becomes shorter, ridding itself of extraneous material while retaining the "emotional core," and features such as verbal repetition and formulas become structuring principles.[17] Although changes in the cultural meaning of a particular song may be impossible to predict, it seems likely that its form will change in one specific direction over the years. Once that story has

17. See Tristram P. Coffin, "Mary Hamilton and the Anglo-American Ballad as an Art Form," in MacEdward Leach and Tristram P. Coffin, eds., *The Critics and the Ballad* (Carbondale: Southern Illinois University Press, 1961), p. 246; Flemming G. Andersen and Thomas Pettitt, " 'The Murder of Maria Marten': The Birth of a Ballad?" in Edwards and Manley, *Narrative Folksong*, pp. 132–178.

been dressed in a balladic structure, however, it appears that variation will take place within this established framework. The generic implication is that balladic narrative technique is created in the process of oral transmission, and that this occurs irrespective of social context—which seems to be a strong argument in favor of maintaining a textual, structural characterization of the ballad. From this kind of evidence it follows that ballads are oral, but the ballad-shaping process is so gradual that the term "oral" must be understood in its nontechnical, non-oral-formulaic sense. Formulas may serve conservative as well as dynamic functions in transmission: they may be viewed as a stabilizing factor, and at the same time they provide one of the means for linguistic variation, according to circumstances.

Ballad formulas function in yet another area, in which the individual singers come into much more prominence. Over the last decade or so scholars have been increasingly concerned with analyses of the poetic potential of formulaic diction— from the point of view of metaphorical and symbolic language, or in terms of "signifiers," or "epic formulas," or concentrating, as I have done myself, on the verb-centered formulas and their associative, "supra-narrative" function.[18] Appearing in the same kinds of contexts in a large number of ballads the formulas have become imbued with specific overtones, which have bearing on the immediate narrative contexts in which

18. See J. Barre Toelken, "An Oral Canon for the Child Ballads: Construction and Application," *Journal of the Folklore Institute* 4 (1967): 75–101, and "Figurative Language and Cultural Contexts in the Traditional Ballads," *Western Folklore* 45 (1986): 128–142. See also Edith Rogers, "The Moral Standing of the Unkempt," *Southern Folklore Quarterly* 36 (1972): 144–159, and her comprehensive study *The Perilous Hunt: Symbols in Hispanic and European Balladry* (Lexington: University Press of Kentucky, 1980). For "signifiers," see Roger deV. Renwick's groundbreaking *English Folk Poetry: Structure and Meaning* (London: Batsford Academic and Educational, 1980), and "On the Interpretation of Folk Poetry," in Edwards and Manley, *Narrative Folksong*, pp. 401–433. For "epic formulas," see Otto Holzapfel, *Det balladeske: Fortællemåden i den ældre episke folkevise* (Odense: Odense Universitetsforlag, 1980), and "'Graf und Nonne': An Analysis of the Epic-Formulaic Elements in a German Ballad," in Edwards and Manley, *Narrative Folksong*, pp. 179–193.

they are employed. Thus the formulas can serve as a stylistic means of personal characterization employed to portray characters at moments of crisis, outlining their individual responses to the dramatic events. Formulas may also serve as signals of what is to come. Different formula families point to different ways of resolving the conflicts, and consequently produce narrative variation by presaging different kinds of story endings.

The overtones signaled by the various types of formulas are typically found within the semantic fields of Love and Death. Hence formulas are part and parcel of what is often considered the typical ballad story: the domestic love tragedy. Furthermore, my analyses have shown that the distribution of formulas in the text corpora is so consistent that we must assume that many singers have employed formulas deliberately to produce different layers of meaning in the stories. In the performance context of an audience steeped in the ballad tradition the singers will be able to arouse specific expectations by employing specific types of formulas.

Characterization of the ballad formula in terms of structural and stylistic functions may help us delineate what is to be understood by the term "ballad narrative technique," but the validity of the analytical description just offered hinges on the ethnic perspective—on how it relates to the singers' own concept of what they are singing. Fieldwork has demonstrated that singers are indeed aware of the poetic potential of the kinds of phrases that we term formulas, and there seems to be a reasonably large correspondence between the results of textual analyses and the singers' own observations.[19] These findings have significant implications. They demonstrate that singers, on the basis of their knowledge of the traditional language, can—and most of them do—leave their personal stamp on the ballads they sing. Through their particular handling of formulaic material we are able to follow precisely how individuality is achieved in this traditional and allegedly objective narrative form. By choosing certain formulas, or by varying formulas in

19. Andersen, *Commonplace and Creativity,* pp. 293–296.

specific ways, the singers can produce new interpretations of the ballads they sing.[20] Formula analysis, then, will be one of the vehicles for understanding the traditional ballad in a functional context, one of the vehicles for investigating that "cultural meaning of ballads" which has so frequently been called for, most recently by James Porter, who rightly urges us to include "reference to singers and in particular to the singers' concept of meaning" in our analyses of the ballad tradition. We need to complement our textual studies with observations made by the singers themselves, for, as Porter also points out, "good singers are intelligent singers" and can provide invaluable information on the meanings and functions of the ballads they sing.[21]

One such singer is Stanley Robertson of Aberdeen, who is of traveler stock and is a nephew of the famed Jeannie Robertson. He is an extremely knowledgeable singer and storyteller, and superbly conscious of the tradition he is passing on.[22] His repertoire of ballads and songs is one of the largest among the Scottish singers, and like most travelers he is more than willing to talk about his cultural tradition and his upbringing as a ballad singer. What, then, are his attitudes to what we have become accustomed to term the traditional popular ballad?

It is quite evident that singers themselves distinguish among different types of songs in their repertoires; depending on how much contact they have had with collectors and field-workers, they will classify certain kinds of songs as "folk songs," "muckle sangs," "ballads," "classical ballads," "big ballads," "great big ballads," or even "great big heavy ballads." It should come as no surprise, however, that the singers do not have ready-made definitions to present at the scholar's re-

20. New interpretations can also be achieved through other means; see James Porter's discussion of the three stages in the gradual crystallization of an individual's version of a ballad in "Jeannie Robertson's 'My Son David': A Conceptual Performance Model," *Journal of American Folklore* 89 (1976): 14–15.

21. Porter, "Ballad Explanations," pp. 114, 123.

22. He was featured in *Tocher: Tales, Songs, Tradition* 40 (1986): 170–224.

quest. As an ethnic genre the traditional ballad is perhaps best defined by example; although singers are taken aback by the ballad scholar's obsession with abstract theorizing, they can themselves immediately classify individual items in their repertoires.

When prompted to explain in general terms the difference between a song and a ballad Stanley Robertson replied without hesitation: "They feel different"—and then, after a few seconds, "It's funny, I've never really asked myself that question, but I can feel the difference when I'm singing." Once the question is related to specific examples, however, he has no trouble in distinguishing the traits that to him are characteristic of the "big ballads," which form a distinct group in his repertoire. First he emphasizes the notion of story, which "in pure detail" must relate the past, present, and future of the events.[23] In a later interview he added that the big ballads are those sung in slow tempo, with a slow presentation of the narrative, and in terms of style the text would need to be clothed in "deep, powerful imagery."[24] Finally, it should be pointed out that he views the story as more important than the song, and the most important aspect of all is the moral of the ballad, which makes it a "true story."[25]

Most of the points raised by Stanley Robertson will sound familiar to ballad scholars, but it is perhaps surprising that such stress should be laid on the detailed chronological story. This runs counter to the traditional definition of the ballad which emphasizes the brevity of the story, the focus on a single episode, and the narration by leaping and lingering. One ballad which seems to fit the traditional picture of narrative technique is "Lord Lovel" (Child 75), which in the briefest terms tells the story of a young man who is going away "strange countries

23. Private tape recording, 1981. I would like to thank Stanley Robertson for the never-failing enthusiasm with which he has answered my inquiries into the ballad tradition.

24. Compare Jeannie Robertson's category of "big ballads," that is "any ballad which tells a serious or tragic story, and which is sung in slow tempo and in solemn style." Herschel Gower and James Porter, "Jeannie Robertson: The Other Ballads," *Scottish Studies* 16 (1972): 139–159, here 139.

25. Private tape recording, 1985.

for to see." He bids his truelove good-bye, but after a while begins to long for her, and returns home, only to find that she has died. Here is Stanley Robertson's six-stanza version, recorded March 9, 1985:

> Lord Lovat he stands at his stable door
>   He was brushing his milk steed down
> When who should pass by but Lady Nancy Bell
>   She was wishing her lover God speed.
>   She was wishing her lover God speed.
>
> O where are you going Lord Lovat she cried
>   Come promise tell me true
> Far over the seas strange countries to see
>   Lady Nancy Bell I'll come and see you
>   Lady Nancy Bell I'll come and see.
>
> He was nae awa a year or two
>   He had scarcely been awa three
> When a mightiful dream came into his head
>   Lady Nancy Bell I'll come and see you
>   Lady Nancy Bell I'll come and see.
>
> He's passed down through Capelton Church
>   And doun by Mary's Haa
> And the men were all a' dressed in green
>   And the ladies were weeping sore
>   The ladies weeping sore.
>
> Who is dead Lord Lovat he cries
>   Come promise tell me true
> Lady Nancy Bell died for her true love's sake
>   Lord Lovat it was his name
>   Lord Lovat it was his name.
>
> He orders the coffin to be opened up
>   And the white sheets rowd down
> And he's kissed her on the cold clay lips
>   And the tears they came trinkling down
>   And the tears they came trinkling down.

    Asked whether this short and strangely restrained ballad—there is no violent action to speak of—could be said to tell a full story (and consequently to fit his own conception of a "big ballad"), Stanley Robertson vehemently replied: "Oh, yes . . .

the travelers would tell you the story. They would not just sing you the ballad; you would get the story with it."[26] This is the scenario which was provided when he heard the ballad sung to him at the learning stage, and which is present in his mind when he sings the version he calls "Lord Lovat's Lament": According to traveler tradition Lord Lovat was a young knight who was going away on a crusade. As Stanley is at pains to point out, he would be a greater man for going, so his decision to leave his truelove is in no way dishonorable. Nor does she in any way blame him; for, as Stanley observes, the fact that Lady Nancy Bell chances to pass by as he was brushing down his horse is a clear indication that she "did not grudge him going." Before he sets out Lord Lovat promises the girl that he will be back. It is interesting to note that in paraphrasing the story Stanley will occasionally sing lines from the ballad, reflecting—as with other travelers—the manner in which he was originally taught it.[27] The third stanza simply states that after a few years he dreams of her. From our analytical point of view, the repetition of the last two lines of the preceding stanza is a very emphatic reminder of Lord Lovat's promise, but there would seem to be more to this particular stanza than a purely structural function. The reference to the years of absence is a formula known from other ballads, imbued with overtones of imminent disaster, such as an unacceptable love affair, unwelcome pregnancy, or the ultimate disaster, the death of the loved one.[28] Stanley himself offers an explanation along similar lines: he views the span of years as a short time for Lord Lovat, who will have been busily occupied, but as a very long time for Lady Nancy Bell, who has been pining for her lover, in spite of her initial acceptance of his going away.

26. Private tape recording, 1981. The same lack of violent action is true of so popular a ballad as "Barbara Allan" (Child 84); see Christine Cartwright, "'Barbara Allan': Love and Death in an Anglo-American Narrative Folksong," in Edwards and Manley, *Narrative Folksong,* pp. 240–265.

27. This is in line with the observations of another traveler singer, Sheila MacGregor of Blairgowrie, who uses the same mixed presentation when teaching her ballads to children. Private tape recording, 1981.

28. Andersen, *Commonplace and Creativity,* pp. 128–134.

In fact, by now they have both had second thoughts on the whole matter. These ominous overtones, expressed in what Stanley elsewhere refers to as "powerful imagery," are increased by the subsequent reference to a "mightiful dream," which—in Stanley's words—"the travelers say was a premonition that something was wrong."[29]

Stanley Robertson learned the ballad of "Lord Lovat" from his aunt, Jeannie Robertson, and her version follows the same narrative course.[30] But he adds a line to the fourth stanza to make the stanza regular. Jeannie, as does her daughter Lizzie Higgins, sings a stanza of only three lines, relating that Lord Lovat first passed down through Capelton's church, and then down through Mary's hall, where he saw the "ladies were weeping for." Stanley inserts a line before the description of the ladies, which significantly describes the men. In addition to providing a balance between male and female characters this insertion accentuates the theme of mourning. As always Stanley is very conscious of what he is doing to the tradition: "I put in a line because my folks always left it in a three line stanza and it seemed to leave the ballad unfinished . . . My reason for putting in this line is to balance up the ballad, the use of green being an ancient colour of mourning. I think it is affective [sic]."[31]

The person they mourn for is of course Lady Nancy Bell, and this is revealed in st. 5 in a manner echoing her words. "Come promise tell me true" is now Lord Lovat's fearful cry when he sees the men in green and the ladies weeping. As soon as Lord Lovat is told the tragic news he orders the coffin to be opened up (st. 6), which according to Stanley shows that he is still a man of authority and immediate power. Even in this situation he is not so broken-hearted as to let go of his male prerogatives.

29. Private tape recording, 1981.

30. For her version, see Gower and Porter, "Jeannie Robertson," pp. 45–46. Jeannie also taught the ballad to her daughter, Lizzie Higgins, whose early version is almost identical to that of her mother; see Munro, "Lizzie Higgins," pp. 159–161. In the 1975 recording on *Up and Awa wi the Laverock* (Topic 12 TS 260), however, Lizzie dropped the last stanza.

31. Private communication, 1983.

The ballad closes with the picture of Lord Lovat bending over the corpse, kissing the cold clay lips, while "the tears they came trinkling down." "I think this is one of the most touching verses . . . I used to weep myself when Jeannie sang it" is Stanley's characteristic remark on the ending of the ballad, demonstrating the depth of his emotional involvement in the story. For many sensibilities the element of melodramatic sentimentality in this closing scene has seemed absurd, and the song was successfully exploited in the middle of the last century by music-hall comedians, who made travesties out of "Lord Lovel" simply by adding a stanza ridiculing the unheroically weeping protagonist. For example, Sam Crouch sang this stanza: "He laid himself down beside the corpse / Gave a sigh and a shudder and a guggle / Gave three long sighs and shut his eyes / He laid down and died in the struggle."[32] Stanley Robertson, however, is far from condemning the ballad's melodrama. His own sensitivity is instead directed towards the minutest detail of ballad language: he makes a point of noting that the tears are "trinkling" and not "trickling" down, in accordance with family tradition.

Perhaps Stanley Robertson's observations do not drastically change our interpretation of this particular ballad, but they do provide invaluable insight into how singers conceive of their ballads, and should in some degree also influence our concept of the genre.[33] First, it is evident that Stanley can in no way support the dismissal of this ballad as, in the words of Bertrand Bronson, "too too insipid" and "lachrymose," symbolizing "a sentimentality too concerned with itself," and this may serve

32. Compare *Journal of the English Folk Dance and Song Society* (1934): 135. Child presents a slightly different version of this mocking stanza: "Then he flung his self down by the side of the corpse / With a shivering gulp and a guggle / Gave two hops, three kicks, heavd a sigh, blew his nose / Sung a song, and then died in the struggle" (*ESPB* II, p. 213). Willa Muir notes that "Lord Lovel" was performed to an Aberdeen audience in 1850 as a comic song by a favorite comedian, Sam Cowell. *Living with Ballads* (London: The Hogarth Press, 1965), p. 259.

33. Jeannie Robertson's comments on the fratricide in "My Son David" are further removed from the scholar's immediate understanding of what that ballad is about; see Porter, "Jeannie Robertson's 'My Son David.'"

as a useful reminder that singers' attitudes do not always coincide with scholarly interpretation.[34] Second, Stanley's remarks demonstrate that we need to reconsider the terms
"story" and "narrative." In Stanley's ethnic usage they not
only refer to the actual events recounted in the ballad, but also
summon a range of contextual information extending the scenario.

Furthermore, it is apparent that ballads are considered to be
true stories, which makes them immediately appealing to the
singers. Stanley Robertson observes: "I have to re-live a ballad. If I sing a ballad I have to become part of it . . . I see it as
I am directing a film," a very apt metaphor for the dramatic
intensity that the singer experiences while he is singing the ballad.[35] To Stanley ballads are primarily a means of communication, a vehicle for expressing emotion and popular wisdom.
The stories are sung with a definite purpose in mind: "They
were teaching you morals, they were teaching you how to pre-
pare yourself . . . how to get yourself out of certain situations."[36] The ballads have a concrete, practical function; they
are culturally didactic, as it were. The notion of the true story
is of paramount importance to singers. Thus Jeannie Robertson notes, in a manner reminiscent of Stanley's, "When I'm
singing the song . . . I picture it, jeest as if it was really hap-
penin . . . My songs are natural . . . they're aboot people and
they're real."[37] Jane Turriff, another Scottish traveler singer,
has noted that "There's a story in every song," which James
Porter rightly interprets as referring to their "lived reality."[38]

34. Bertrand H. Bronson, ed., *The Traditional Tunes of the Child Ballads,* 4 vols. (Princeton, N.J.: Princeton University Press, 1959–1972), II,
p. 189.

35. Private tape recording, 1985. He has the same feeling about story-
telling; see *Tocher* 40 (1986): 177. See also Hodgart, *The Ballads,* p. 28,
where he offers a cinematic interpretation of the balladic narrative technique.

36. Private tape recording, 1981.

37. See Herschel Gower, "Jeannie Robertson: Portrait of a Traditional
Singer," *Scottish Studies* 12 (1968): 126, and Gower and Porter, "Jeannie
Robertson," p. 36.

38. James Porter, "The Turiff Family of Fetterangus: Society, Learning,
Creation, and Recreation of Traditional Song," *Folk Life* 16 (1978): 18;
Porter, "Ballad Explanations," p. 123.

This sense of reality in ballads is accentuated in the use of formulaic diction. The formulas' supra-narrative overtones— of foreboding of sexual attack, yearning for love, aggression, emotional submission, and so on—arise in connection with the narration of concrete events, challenging the characters to react to the basic conditions of human existence. The love-death dichotomy that is signaled by the formulas is presented as a reality of life.[39]

The interplay of the concepts of Love and Death gives ballads their peculiar strength and attraction as a popular art form. It is tempting to suggest that ballads tell stories of eternal truths, recounting perhaps a perceived universal battle between good and evil. Systematic formula analysis may at least point in that direction. I have not gone so far in my own studies of the formulaic diction of the English and Scottish popular ballads, however, and I certainly do not wish to claim that all stories ultimately express the same cultural meaning. Analyses of textual elements within a framework of universal application, seeking to establish "a coherent universe of meaning,"[40] would, as I see it, demand a level of abstraction which is far from the world of the ballads, or at any rate from that of the singers.

Because ballads are so concrete—in their use of imagery, in the 'moral' of the stories—the function of traditional ballads cannot be described in general, absolute terms, but must be seen in relation to the individual singer and his or her immediate context. For just as the form of a ballad will be modified in transmission, so the meaning may change over the years. We may, as J. Barre Toelken has pointed out, come across ballads in which a single text may have different meanings in different contexts.[41] And indeed, certain ballads may be used in contexts we would hardly have dreamed of: the tragic ballad of "Lord Lovat" was sung by Jeannie Robertson as a lullaby

39. See Andersen, *Commonplace and Creativity,* chap. 14. Christine Cartwright also singles out this dichotomy as essential to the ballad universe; "Barbara Allen," p. 243. Similar observations are made by Roger deV. Renwick in *English Folk Poetry.*

40. Renwick, *English Folk Poetry,* p. 110.

41. Toelken, "Context and Meaning," p. 47.

to her daughter Lizzie.[42] Given the generally high level of consciousness on the part of the singers, and the extremely complex picture of function and cultural meaning, I find it difficult
to subscribe to the view that a given singer should express only
one "meaning" in all his ballads. The situation becomes much
more complicated when we consider a family of singers, let
alone a whole community of singers.

The singers' concepts of their songs may be determined by
any number of influences, and in terms of impact on the singers' lives the traditional ballads do not seem to constitute a
distinct group. Thus Stanley Robertson, an active member of
the Mormon Church, observes that he has the same deep feelings about some of the religious songs in his repertoire. In his
case the difference between ballads and religious songs is not
one of cultural meaning. This strongly suggests that a purely
functional approach for outlining the generic features of the
traditional ballad would be insufficient.

If "function" is too elusive a term for a genre criterion, perhaps a formal characterization of the ballad will be feasible.
Here, too, we are in troubled water as we have to steer between the opposing forces of textual stability and variation.
Since Cecil Sharp formulated his catchphrase "The individual . . . invents; the community selects," which captures the
relationship between continuity and change in ballads, it has
been commonplace for scholars to note that ballads vary in the
process of transmission.[43] The bone of contention is not so
much whether variations occur as how to characterize the
amount of variation we witness. Are the variations extensive
enough to allow us to talk of improvisation, or, as I believe,
will we have to say that they are the by-products of a primarily
memorized process of oral transmission?

42. See Munro, "Lizzie Higgins," p. 160, and Stephanie Smith, "Lizzie
Higgins as a Transitional Figure in the Oral Tradition of Northeast Scotland" (diss., Edinburgh, 1975), p. 70.

43. In *English Folk Song: Some Conclusions* (1907; rpt. Wakefield: EP
Publishing Ltd., 1972), p. 40. Sharp's notion of continuity, variation, and
selection was taken over by the International Folk Song Council in their
definition of folk music in 1954; see *Journal of International Folk Music* 7
(1955): 23.

The singers themselves have differing views on what happens in transmission. Some singers claim that they never change a word in their ballads—they sing them as they were taught them. This accords with the claims made by some of the Serbo-Croatian *guslars* whom Parry and Lord recorded, and who could nevertheless be demonstrated to improvise their epics with a high degree of variation. Lizzie Higgins is one ballad singer who maintains that she does not vary her ballads, and yet in the same sentence acknowledges that ballads vary from singer to singer: "Ive never changed any words in any of my balladry. they are as I was teached them from my Parents, there is many different ways [of singing a ballad], they changed from Person to Person or from Family to Family or from Country to Country."[44]

Stanley Robertson recognizes the changes he introduces into the ballads that were handed down to him, such as his insertion of the line about the men "dressed in green" in "Lord Lovat's Lament."[45] This, however, is a one-time operation—once he has added this line he sticks to it at every rendition of the ballad—which could be taken to confirm the widely held view that singers develop their own versions of a given ballad and will reproduce it in identical shape from that point onward. Such a process is implied by the most recent exposition of this view, John Niles's theory of "recurrent thaw" in ballad transmission. Once learned the song is frozen, except for lapses of memory, the only real variation appears in the learning process, during which, in Niles's words, the "constituent elements of formulas, motifs, plot and tune become partially fluid" as the singer shapes the ballad into "his or her own di-

44. Private communication, 1983.

45. This line occurs in no other version of "Lord Lovel." It echoes, however, the formulation found in a number of versions of "Lord Thomas and Fair Annet" (Child 73), where it is used in connection with a wedding-cum-burial: "She dressed herself in gallant attire / Her merry men all in green / And every town that she passed through / She was taken to be some Queen" (Bronson 73.116, st. 8). See also Child 73D 11; Bronson 73.8, st. 1; 73.76, st. 2. The formulation is also present in a few versions of "Mary Hamilton" (Child 173), for example, 173G 8 and 173I 13.

alect, experience and aesthetic values."[46] This stable state does, however, leave room for minor variations. Even so conscious a singer as Stanley Robertson will change the odd word, even in so short a ballad as "Lord Lovat." Although Stanley at one stage claims that the travelers always sang "weeping for" as a corruption of "weeping sore" (st. 4, l. 4), he too occasionally sings the more intelligible "weeping sore"—presumably depending on his audience.

There is no doubt that the audience, the immediate context of the ballad performance, plays a significant role in shaping ballad material. Different situations naturally call for different types of ballads, but may also call for different versions of the same ballads. Thus Stanley Robertson carries in his mind two distinct versions of "Mill o' Tifty's Annie" (Child 233, "Andrew Lammie"). He has a very long version for private use, and a considerably shorter version to be used in public, at festivals and other events where he cannot expect to hold the audience for as long a time.[47] It has also been noted that singers will occasionally sing one version of a song in their own families and quite another to collectors.[48]

So in various senses for the singers there is no one version, no one ballad form. Singers do not conceive of ballads as fixed texts. Nevertheless we cannot generalize from Bertrand Bronson's observation about the famed Mrs. Brown of Falkland, Child's favorite singer, that for her "there was nothing sacred about the mere words of her ballads."[49] For Stanley Robertson there quite evidently is. Words matter. The "powerful imagery" has a very strong effect on him, and he is greatly influenced by the overtones of the formulaic phrases. Because

46. John D. Niles, "Context and Loss in Scottish Ballad Tradition," *Western Folklore* 45(1986): 92.

47. Private tape recording, 1985. Stanley Robertson is also aware of various interpretations of ballad texts. Thus he points out that his scenario for "Lord Lovat's Lament" is different from the one drawn up by the School of Scottish Studies (private tape recording, 1981).

48. This is the case of the two versions of "Earl Crawford" sung by mother and daughter; see Child 229Aa and 229Ab.

49. Bertrand H. Bronson, *The Ballad as Song* (Berkeley and Los Angeles: University of California Press, 1969), p. 69.

formulas of the same type or "family" serve the same supra-narrative task even if their wording differs, they are focal centers both of stability and of potential variation, and therefore vehicles for traditional re-creation.

Variation over a span of years is a hallmark of the traditional ballad. Parrotlike imitation is not the manner in which a tradition is kept alive, as the singers know full well. Stanley Robertson is capable of imitating the singing styles of his aunt Jeannie and his cousin Lizzie to perfection, but he will never sing like them in public. He points out that ballads are a living tradition precisely because new singers will sing the songs differently: "Mirror image is not what ballad singing is about."[50] Ballads, as Stanley observes, are a means of communication, communicating your own self rather than adopting other people's identities.

On the basis of the ethnic evidence presented here it is clear that our analytical concept of the traditional ballad needs to be somewhat revised. Following the hints from the singers themselves we must take into account their broad concept of the term "story," the narrative exposition in pure detail by means of powerful imagery, the true moral of the story, the slow and dignified manner of presentation. In particular we will have to consider the importance of the singers' own commitment to the ballads they sing—a commitment which, because of the variation of contexts and especially of singers themselves, allows many cultural meanings to emerge. Some singers, such as the Stewarts of Blair, use the term *connaich* to refer to this necessary emotional involvement in the big ballads, especially to the singer's ability to convey that involvement to the audience.[51]

It also follows that no single analytical element that I have been discussing in my paper can stand the test of being *the*

50. Private tape recording, 1981.
51. Sheila MacGregor, private tape recording, 1981. See also James Porter, "Parody and Satire as Mediators of Change in the Traditional Songs of Belle Stewart," in Edwards and Manley, *Narrative Folksong,* p. 327; Ewan MacColl and Peggy Seeger, *Till Doomsday in the Afternoon: The Folklore of a Family of Scots Travellers, the Stewarts of Blairgowrie* (Manchester: Manchester University Press, 1986), p. 163.

distinctive ballad characteristic. The elements become genre specific only in varying, scarcely exhaustible combinations. There is no doubt that traditional ballads are recognized by singers and scholars alike. We can each single out a group of songs as qualifying for ballad status. The problem is that no two groups are likely to be identical, as we have no steadfast formal criteria. Despite all our efforts at textual analysis, the constituent elements of the traditional ballad are still very much in the eyes of the beholder.

Viewed as a means of communication, on the other hand, ballads have to be defined in terms of encoded message as well as communication context. It has been customary for some time to say that ballads are a particular way of telling a story. But the medium itself is not the entire message. In light of the ethnic considerations presented here we need to specify this characterization: ballads are a particular way of telling particular stories—not only regarding subject matter, for example the love-death dichotomy, but also regarding their effect on singers and audiences alike.

In a communicative context the formulaic narrative mode is the vehicle through which the meaning of the ballads is encoded and subsequently decoded. Accordingly, the deep, powerful imagery, the formulas, the signifiers—or whatever term we use to characterize these linguistic, narrative signals—are of paramount importance for an understanding of how meanings are conveyed in this narrative form, and of how the texts are continually adapted to new contexts. Equally important, of course, are the specific paraphernalia of the ballad performance. We need contextual data concerning singers, audiences, and performance situations. Such information is just as necessary as but infinitely harder to obtain than the results derived from textual analyses of the formulaic techniques. So ballads are both relatively easy to spot, in terms of narrative technique, and extremely difficult to characterize, in terms of the varying ways in which this technique is employed to express distinct cultural meanings in different circumstances.

Even if we take narrative technique as the constant element in the changing world of ballad communication, as the mediator between text and context, we are still largely unable to characterize that technique more precisely in absolute terms. The analytical concept of formula will inevitably change over the years, and new cultural indicators will arise. Perhaps it is our good fortune that Child, the father of us all, did not leave a clear-cut definition of the English and Scottish popular ballads. As the matter stands now his scattered, often contradictory, observations are a much more stimulating guide for us, and provide a much better picture of the reality we have to cope with. Ballads are products of individual singers, and should be analyzed with close attention to idiosyncrasies of both texts and contexts. If this analysis does not produce a neat category of song with clear lines of demarcation, we must accept the contradictory and elusive character of the traditional ballad, and perhaps even embrace it—for after all variability is the prerequisite for the life, revival, and survival of the ballad tradition. The complex picture emerging from such considerations bears witness to the inherent problems of using the definitive article generically in forms such as "the ballad" or "the Child ballad"; the plural, with its suggestion of variety, would seem to provide a safer starting point for discussion.

HUGH SHIELDS

Popular Modes of Narration
and the Popular Ballad

The body of song which Child called the "true popular ballads" (*ESPB* I, p. vii) and never really defined except by editing is not easy to define by other means. The success of his edition reflects not only its merits as a processing of texts but also the unformulated stylistic criteria used in selecting them. This is not to say that the texts all display to the same extent the same stylistic criteria. But it is the question of poetic style which underlies the judiciousness of Child's selection, despite his description of the ballads—inscrutably astonishing to us today—as the "spontaneous products of nature" (p. vii). The conviction of some sort of generic unity in the English and Scottish ballads is enhanced by comparison with other European bodies of song which not only have similar stylistic features but also treat similar narratives. It is regrettable that comparative research between cultures has been pursued so much more on the narrative than on the stylistic level. It is true that quite a lot has been written on oral-formulaic techniques—those techniques which may or may not be perceived as the evidence of a wholly improvisatory method of performance-cum-composition. But the major emphasis of such research has not been cross-cultural, and the usefulness of some of the techniques to genre definition is limited by the fact that

40

they are shared by artforms as diverse as popular epics and advertising jingles. Those features which *are* of use to genre definition are ones which make (or do not make) ballad poetry what it is, which relate positively or negatively to the quality of its narrative method and to the lyric effects which give it ambiance and intensity.

This essay will deal with a few features which have to do with what might be summed up as narrative contingencies—features not notably Anglo-Scottish but of the neighbouring (but not Germanic) oral traditions, features which may seem unhelpful because they show more contrasts than parallels between cultures. Whether these features encourage a belief in the existence of an international ballad genre of medieval origin or simply raise new doubts about it depends, I imagine, on the temperament of the individual.

It is generally understood that the old, early, oral, or Child ballad, if it exists, is a song giving a report of fulfilled action—information about a series of intelligibly motivated events in the past. The report is formally detached in style, chronologically ordered, and sufficiently explicit to make clear, without apparent ambiguity, what the events were. But ballads are much more than a documentary report because these qualities of presentation generally tend strongly to a dramatic purpose. We may add that the events provide, in medieval terminology, an "argument," which medieval scholars might have disparaged as a fable: that is, they would have called it a lie, or in modern terminology, fiction. And it is as fiction that Child's texts strike the modern reader trying to form a picture of the genre in the days of its creation and vigorous promotion. It would, of course, be of the greatest interest to know how the factuality of ballad stories has been judged, down to the present, by their singers and listeners. But their judgments—in this as in other matters—are not abundant, explicit, or discriminatory enough, nor are they freely enough proferred, to allow us to defer as much as we would like to this potential primary source of taxonomic information. It is also of interest, and on the whole easier, to explore the fictional reality of the events as they are narrated in ballads and in songs likely to qualify as ballads. We may ask whether the text says that these events actually happened in the former time and place which it is intended to evoke. Is there doubt about what did happen or a lack of information to allow us to judge? Whose testimony is invoked? Are realized events juxtaposed with unrealized ones? In short, it is of interest to look for such kinds of stylistic polyvalence in the narrative as are inherent in lyric poetry in general.

Addressing these questions to the Anglo-Scottish repertory, though, may provoke an initial difficulty, summed up by another question: why should they be asked at all? Are not British ballads boldly consistent in their unambiguous presentation of fulfilled action? Are they not among the most consistent of European ballads in their use of the simple past tense of the indicative, even in many, though not all, of their formulaic incipits? "It fell about the Lammas time . . . There lived a lord all in this town . . ." (Child 84C; 100). French narrative songs, in contrast, are sometimes wholly in the historic present. One is tempted here into speculative asides. Is it possible to correlate the Anglo-Scottish adherence to past-tense narrative to the lack of *Bänkelsang* pictorial illustration in Britain?[1] Or to the success of ballad criticism in English, since past tenses contribute to the resolute demarcation of the ballad as a genre within lyric song? Not all European traditions of narrative lyric are so clearly marked. Nor are the Anglo-Scottish ballads so clearly marked in every aspect of their narrative.

A few examples will illustrate this. Realized narrative may be extended into the future by prediction. After the miracle of the bending cherry tree (Child 54) an angel prophesies the birth of Christ to St. Joseph, and the newborn child, on the request of the Virgin, himself prophesies his Passion and Resurrection. Were these prophecies fulfilled? And so do they figure here as something like dramatic irony? The intriguing text of "Judas" (Child 23) also ends on a prophecy and may be similarly interrogated. But in case it should seem that only explicitly reli-

1. On illustrated backdrops to the performance and marketing of street ballads on the Continent see Stefaan Top, *Komt vrienden, luistert naar mijn lied: Aspecten van de marktzanger in Vlaanderen (1750–1950)* (Tielt en Weesp: Lannoo, 1985).

gious narratives have such open conclusions, notice the future death and presumably subsequent penance that are predicted for the "Cruel Mother" by her murdered children in many versions of that ballad (Child 10). These are all dramatic passages, spoken in the fictional past, but extending narration into unrealized future time.

Almost entirely in dialogue are the songs which have been called "four black sheep among the 305": the chief of Child's riddle ballads Child 1–3 and 46. Under this title Tristram P. Coffin serves an exclusion order on the majority of the songs that David Buchan rejoices in renaming "wit-combat ballads."[2] Ballads they do seem to be, and come as near to any ballad ideal as they are allowed by their narrative structure, which has much in common with that of "Lord Randal" or the "Goodman" (Child 12, 274). In all these ballads an important, if not the principal, event lies outside the song, preceding or following the verbal narration; in the "wit combat" we might say that the event is made possible by a series of imperatives, wishes countermanding wishes, or other forms of intellectual superiority that are explicit as a mere verbal game.

Aspects of the realized action itself may show ambiguities or uncertainties. It is generally agreed that certain verbal formulas may carry meaning or narrative significance which is concealed, by convention, behind the lexical content. The phrase "pale and wan" may be such a case, being associated often, though not exclusively, in ballad texts with pregnancy.[3] "Willy of Winsbury" (Child 100) opens on a scene in which a

2. Coffin in James Porter, ed., *The Ballad Image: Essays Presented to Bertrand Harris Bronson* (Los Angeles: Center for the Study of Comparative Folklore and Mythology, 1983), pp. 30–38; Buchan, "The Wit-Combat Ballads," in Carol L. Edwards and Kathleen B. Manley, eds., *Narrative Folksong: New Directions; Essays in Appreciation of W. Edson Richmond* (Boulder, Colo.: Westview Press, 1985), pp. 380–400.

3. H. Shields, "Chanson de toile et ballade populaire: Problématique d'une comparaison," in Conrad Laforte, ed., *Ballades et chansons folkloriques: Proceedings of the 18th Conference of the "Kommission für Volksdichtung,"* (Quebec: CELAT, Université Laval, 1989), pp. 319–331; and "'The Grey Cock,' Dawn Song or Revenant Ballad?" in E. B. Lyle, ed., *Ballad Studies* (Cambridge, Eng.: Brewer, 1976), p. 87.

father asks his daughter why she looks so pale and wan, and
what ensues reveals that she is pregnant. Some versions omit
this revelation—or seem to—and refer only to her love; I recorded one of these in Ireland in 1969 and 1977:

> "What ails you, what ails you," her father did say,
>   "You look so pale and wan?
> Nor have you got some sore sickness," he says,
>   "Nor deceived by some young man, man,
>   Deceived by some young man?"

The difficulty is to know whether "pale and wan" signified
pregnancy in itself when speaking of a lovesick girl. Recently
I had the opportunity to ask the singer of that version this
question, and the answer he gave was firmly negative. But
there is no guarantee that he would not answer differently at
the next opportunity.[4]

In another case the identity of a speaker is in doubt, a fact
less interesting than the manner of referring to his identity.
Was it Christ the girl met at the well in the Irish version of
"The Maid and the Palmer" (Child 21), the only published version of the ballad with music, or was it simply the unidentified
"gentleman" indicated in the text? It was in a personal comment that the Irish singer made the identification with Christ.[5]
This interpretation is traditional and must be here construed
as proper exegetical lore, whether or not it has been "prosi-
fied" from a missing verse, but such lore has an important
place in Irish song tradition. This is not a minor phenomenon,
given the success of ballad singing in English in Ireland since
the eighteenth century, and the practice deserves attention in
relation to the narrative modes that seem most characteristic
of the medieval European ballad.

Unlike Britain, Gaelic Ireland did not participate fully in the
European ballad tradition, nor can it be said that any old bal-

4. For this version see H. Shields, "Old British Ballads in Ireland," *Folk
Life: Journal of the Society for Folk Life Studies* 10 (1972): 94–97.
5. "The Well below the Valley"; see Tom Munnelly, "The Man and his
Music . . . John Reilly," *Ceol: A Journal of Irish Music* 4:1 (1972): 3, 8; see
also 3:3 (1969): 66–67.

lads in English originated in Ireland. The Gaelic tradition of
the late medieval and early modern period had its heroic lays
and was perhaps content with them. But there was also a lyric
tradition which was probably more important than the lays, a
tradition to which the peculiar stylistic qualities of the ballad
seem to have been quite alien. Gaelic songs do not provide
sequential narratives in objective or explicit style, with fixed
temporal or spatial perspectives. Both motivation and identity
in them are often obscure. Consequently they are not dramatic
as ballads are, and are much more given to lingering than to
leaping. So much we learn from the inherited tradition, largely
postmedieval in origin as it is constituted today, though the
dating of material in so narrowly defined a cultural area is unusually frustrating. Nonetheless Irish Gaelic culture had a considerable degree of national unity—not reflected in political
unity as popularly understood today.

The openings of lyric songs in Irish often show intense concern with people and events:

> "Eirigh 's cuir ort do chuid éadaigh
>   mbearra mé féin do chúl,
> Go dté muid 'soir easpag na hÉirne
>   go gceangaltar mé 'gus tú . . ."

> "Rise up and put on your clothes
>   till I cut your hair,
> Till we go to the bishop of the Erne
>   and he joins me and you . . ."[6]

These four short lines give the following information: a woman
invites someone to rise, dress, get ready (by letting her cut his
hair) and go with her to a certain bishop who will marry them.
The ballad aficionado wonders who these two are and what will
happen next. Someone speaks again about a love relationship,
but it is a man and he is not speaking to the woman but about
a woman; it might be the following night. The song concludes
with his lament that he is not with the person he is thinking
about, in a remote place which he names and describes, where

6. Seán Ó Baoighill, *Cnuasacht de cheoltaí Uladh* (Comhaltas Uladh,
n.d. [ca. 1945]), pp. 28–29; orthography of text modernized.

he would cause the day to end by supernatural means. Now, despite the interest that supernatural effects in folksong tend to arouse, there is little we can say about this motif except that it would give trouble to a compiler of a thematic catalogue of narrative songs. It is hardly touched on, and in any case the day will inevitably end without any intervention. Action it is surely, but it could hardly be further from realization. The vast majority of songs in Irish are in similar ways so suggestive, without resolution, that the editor of an Ulster collection, Enrí Ó Muirgheasa, remarked of one of them: "It is a pity these songs are so little self-explanatory. How much more interesting many of them would be if we knew all the circumstances which are merely hinted at in the verses."[7] He was not wishing for verses that narrated facts plainly so much as mildly reproving the collector for not obtaining comment in the song in question. For Ó Muirgheasa knew better than most the importance to many Gaelic songs of commentary, or what we might call an unballad-like referential quality in them.

Unfortunately collectors much too often took for granted that everyone was familiar with "the circumstances that are merely hinted at in the verses" and so failed to record any comment on them. But critical interest in so prevalent a feature has been more apparent of late. Cathal Goan refers to the many songs which present simply "the denouement of a story which is known to the listeners or which the singer tells them at the time," and elsewhere edits an interesting example.[8] Angela Bourke envisages song and commentary as "two elements in a complex system of interlocking items available to the performer," whose taste "may be reflected in the combination of items."[9] D. K. Wilgus and Eleanor Long compare Irish songs to the so-called blues ballad and note in them an "emphasis

7. In his *Céad de cheoltaibh Uladh* (Dublin: M. H. MacGiolla, 1915), p. 255, note to the song "Is fada mo chosa gan bhróga."

8. In H. Shields, Cathal Goan, and Douglas Sealy, eds., *Scéalamhráin Cheilteacha* (Dublin: An Clóchomhar Tta., 1985), p. 10, my translation; Dhá amhráin ó Neilí Ní Dhónaill," *Ceol* 5:2 (1982): 38–42; 6:1 (1983): 2–4.

9. A summary of this unpublished paper is in H. Shields, ed., *Ballad Research: The Stranger in Ballad Narrative and Other Topics* (Dublin: Folk Music Society of Ireland, 1986), p. 73.

upon feeling and response to events" rather than on narration proper.[10] Writing in 1960 about songs in Irish which may derive from old ballads in English, Seán Ó Tuama drew attention to the absence of "any proper telling of the story" in them. "Sometimes it is in a prose story that goes with the song that one can recognize most plainly the substance of an international ballad."[11] And for the Irish treatment of certain international ballads I was unable to find a better term than *chantefable* to indicate "any combination of prose storytelling with sung verses."[12]

The term is certainly apt for many items of Irish oral literature, such as the long tale noted in a Folklore Commission MS under the title "King Connor's Daughter" (AT 851A).[13] A poor traveling woman's son succeeds in solving riddles put to him by a princess and provided mainly from the riddle ballad "Captain Wedderburn's Courtship" (Child 46), lines or verses of which punctuate the story in prose. Other similarly recorded items in prose and verse are too numerous to detail; some bring British ballads or ballad fragments into relation with Gaelic folktales, usually told in English, and others seem to extrapolate a tale or commentary from the ballad. Inevitably, all such records give an imperfect understanding of the traditional status of the prose-verse combination. Moreover, their existence in writing tends to give the misleading impression that the combination, once effected, has remained static and that its components are not separable. Even if the term *chantefable* is accepted as not giving this impression, it still hardly covers the complex modus vivendi of song and the complement of song which is native to Gaelic and is an acculturative feature of importance to British ballads in Ireland. But if it is in vain that we seek a native term to describe this inconstant combination, the notion of a basis for the making of the song is often explicit.

10. "The *Blues Ballad* and the Genesis of Style in Traditional Narrative Song," in Edwards and Manley, *Narrative Folksong,* pp. 435–482, esp. 466.

11. *An grá in amhráin na nDaoine* (Dublin: An Clóchomhar Tta., 1960), p. 325; my translation.

12. Shields, "Old British Ballads in Ireland," p. 71, n. 14.

13. University College, Dublin, Department of Irish Folklore, MS 670, pp. 185–198.

A listener may ask the singer for an "explanation" (Irish *míniú*), or what is the "force" or "meaning" of it (Irish *brí*); better still, the "authority" that was its prime mover (Irish *údar,* product of Latin *auctor*). When the song is next sung, of course, this listener will, or should, no longer need to ask.

I conclude this incursion into Irish song with two examples of the contingent character of the narrative element and its complex expression, which show that although uncertain or inexplicit this element may reflect an unambiguous reality. Lullabies frequently carry a message not at all proper for an infant. One of the best known in Irish, though apparently not sung traditionally today, was given by Petrie, its nineteenth-century editor, the undistinguished title "Seo hú leo" (lullaby vocables).[14] A woman speaks, calling to another woman by the side of a stream—they are presumably washing clothes—and tells her that a year earlier she had been abducted into a fairy fort, and describes the life there. She sends her husband word that he may disenchant her by traditional means while there is yet time. That the beliefs apparent in the song were meaningful around 1850 when it was collected is confirmed by a changeling murder and trial in the late 1880s, the subject of a broadside ballad in English in which similar procedures for disenchantment are said to have been tried.[15] The song in Irish is much older, and its theme agrees quite closely with that of the fragment "The Queen of Elfan's Nourice" (Child 40), though they do not seem textually related. Both omit the attempted recovery of the wife, which may be presumed to have been successful in the fragmentary ballad, and to have figured one way or the other in the "authority" of the Irish song which, as a song, is complete.[16] Unfortunately, no commentary seems to have been recorded; but several Irish prose accounts of such recov-

14. George Petrie, *Ancient Music of Ireland,* vol. I (Dublin: Society for the Preservation and Publication of the Melodies of Ireland, 1855), pp. 73–77.
15. A copy of the broadside is in Belfast Public Library, Bigger J2, p. 35; for fairy lore, see E. O'Curry in Petrie, *Ancient Music of Ireland.*
16. *ESPB,* I, pp. 358–359. Though no husband figures in the extant text, it is reasonable to suppose a denouement similar to that of "King Orfeo" (Child 19).

ery, studied by E. B. Lyle in connection with "Tam Lin" (Child 39), show that access to traditional methods of disenchantment did not guarantee success in the oral literature of such unearthly combats.[17]

The verses of this song are moderately explicit, leaving uncertain only this one important narrative feature. They are elliptical in a manner not unlike that of the ballad and outdo the ballad in making special demands on the listeners only by their expectation of a high standard of familiarity with fairy lore. But the verses also give information of relevance through their form, both musical and poetic: the abducted woman is nursing a child for the fairies (a requirement which was believed to occasion frequent abduction of nursing mothers) and the song is a lullaby.

> A bhean úd thíos ar bhruach an tsrutháin,
> *Seo hú leo, seo hú leo*
> An dtuigeann tusa fáth mo ghearáin?
> *Seo hú leo, seo hú leo*
> 'S gur bliain 's an lá 'niu 'fuadaíodh mé dho m' ghearrán
> *Seo hú leo, seo hú leo*
> 'S do rugadh isteach mé i lios an chnocáin.
> *Seo hú leo, seo hú leo*
> [four lines of lullaby vocables]
>
> "You woman at the edge of the stream,
> Have you understood why I lament?
> A year ago today I was taken off my horse
> And carried into the hill fort."

The apparent lullaby is, of course, a trick: a call for help disguised by its primary form, which the woman intends only to reassure her masters that she is properly employed. Hence the repetitive musical phrases and drawn-out lullaby vocables, as well as the monologue form. The lullaby, which is also a message, is furthermore for the adult listeners an evocation of events, like many other songs, only more tense and in this respect unusually dramatic. Yet all the time the primary function continues to dominate formally.

17. "The Ballad 'Tam Lin' and Traditional Tales of Recovery from the Fairy Troop," *Studies in Scottish Literature* 6 (1969): 175–185.

The other song is also a lullaby, also contains a message of
dramatic importance, and is of special interest to the ballad
genre since it seems to be a highly artistic adaptation of the
"Two Sisters" (Child 10).[18] This is one of the rare Scottish
Gaelic songs to have entered Irish oral tradition. This it did
bringing its narrative "authority" with it, for the practice is not
merely an Irish one. The words are enigmatic: a pregnant married woman is drowning and another woman refuses to give
her help; the victim laments her fate and gives information
about her circumstances in life. The explanation offered by a
singer from northwest Ireland was one of the briefest and may
be translated in full:

Two women were down at the shore gathering dulse or carrageen (edi-
ble seaweed) one time. And both of them were after the one man.
And she would have liked to get rid of the other woman, and she
didn't know the best thing to do. One of the women had three children
and the other had none, and she was after the woman's husband. And
she wanted to get rid of the woman. And she didn't know the best
thing to do. And when she got a chance—the woman's hair was long,
and she tied it to the seaweed that was floating on the rock and left
her there till she was drowned.[19]

We must turn to another singer for the end of the story as it is
usually told:

She got married to the husband after she had drowned his own wife.
And one day she was rocking her own child, and the man was outside
working and he heard her singing. And he listened, and he could tell
then that it was her that had drowned his wife. And he came in and
killed her.[20]

This denunciatory message is given inadvertently and unexpectedly; in a similar way in many versions of the "Two Sisters" a musical instrument made of part of the drowned wom-

18. Ethel Bassin, *The Old Songs of Skye: Frances Tolmie and Her Circle*,
ed. Derek Bowman (London: Routledge & Kegan Paul, 1977), pp. 193–196;
on the ballad and the Gaelic song see Shields, "Old British Ballads in Ireland," pp. 82–84.
    19. Shields, "Old British Ballads in Ireland," p. 83.
    20. Shields et al., *Scéalamhráin Cheilteacha*, p. 17.

an's body denounces the other unexpectedly. The Gaelic message is apparently given in the singing of the very song of which the story is an "authority." This technique suggests a term, originally of heraldry, which has been applied to literary and art criticism and used to describe the part functioning as a reflection of the whole: *mise en abîme*.[21] This song is both a commemoration of certain events and a motivating agent of one of them. There is irony in this technique which might be thought foreign to the ballad; nevertheless it could be of interest to examine ballads, and especially their refrains, for similarly ironic meaning.

This song is provided with a remarkable and artistic narrative as commentary. In others we may share O Muirgheasa's frustration from the conviction that certain events have occurred if only we knew what they were. The scope for creative talent filling such gaps is obvious. The traditional Gaelic practice of commentary on song arises from special regard for oral history (*seanchas*): it enhances the diachronic aspect of performance insofar as the song is a celebration of history. But it does not always seem plausible that missing comment could account satisfactorily for the obscurities of a song by exposing realized action underlying it. In numerous love songs, such as the first Gaelic song I referred to, identity and relationships are too confused, and the linguistic category of person seems almost irrelevant to the formulation of emotive thought: *I, you*, and *he* are just rather immaterial identities for one sentient being.

By now perhaps the reader has concluded that "these things are not ballads," I hope not adding "therefore not relevant." Comparative study of narrative method in traditional song is surely of value to our understanding of the European ballad movement. I now move into Continental, and specifically French, ballad territory, in order to ask how real, how unequivocal, or how dramatic is the action there.

Unlike Ireland, France had an important place in the traditional life of European ballads and has even been proposed as

21. Lucien Dällenbach, *Le récit spéculaire: Essai sur la mise en abyme* (Paris: Seuil, 1977).

the original focus of their composition. Lack of critical publication and research makes the repertory difficult to assess and the approximate date of items and their place in evolution difficult to establish. But the stylistic qualities which have been most prized in British and other ballads can be found in many French ones. I have remarked on the French liking for the present tense in narrative song. Yet many French ballads show the consistent adherence to past tense narrative remarked in the English ballads, and they may use it to great effect in contrast with the tense or mood of direct speech. Thus the grieving wife by her husband's tomb at the end of "Le Roi Renaud" (Laforte 2: A1 "Jean Renaud"):[22]

> "Terre, ouvre-toi, terre, fends-toi
> Que je rejoign' Renaud mon roi."
> Terre s'ouvrit et se fendit
> Et la belle rendit l'esprit [*variant:* fut engloutie].

> "Earth, open, earth, split apart
> That I may join Renaud my king."
> Earth opened, earth split apart
> And she gave up the ghost [was swallowed up].

If we consider rationality, evident in British ballads' tense usage, chronological perspective, and so on, as a basic attribute of genre, it could be said that French ballads, if all were like this one, are more "ballad-like" than those in English. For it is known that in addition they rarely use supernatural motifs, except in association with Christian belief and practice: Christ disguised as a beggar, or a miraculous harvest that saves the Holy Family (Laforte 2: B29 and 1: A2). Is the end of "Le Roi Renaud" then unusual? Perhaps the heroic quality of this song confers Christian piety on it, just as the Old French epic songs were songs of militant Christianity. However, one must also notice the terminal function of the motif as an emphatic hyper-

22. *Etnische muziek in België/Musique ethnique en Belgique*, LP, ed. Hendrik Daems (Brussels: Belgische Radio en Televisie, 1967). See Georges Doncieux, *Le romancéro populaire de la France* (Paris: E. Bouillon, 1904), p. 96. French songs are identified as far as possible in the following by references to Conrad Laforte, *Catalogue de la chanson folklorique française*, 2 vols. (Quebec: Presses de l'Université Laval, 1977, 1981).

bole and, perhaps, compare it with a hundred cases of similar but more extended lyric implausibility which conclude French narrative folk songs—songs which are generally less dramatic than "Renaud" because this feature contains no further development of the already realized action.

The slightest acquaintance with French traditional song must leave the impression of great use, if not of supernatural motifs, certainly of fantasy. The course of narration, in ballads, reaches moments at which the fictional reality seems to need embellishment, as in the interesting reaction of nature to a young man's drowning in "Le Plongeur noyé" (Laforte 1: B12): "There's not one fish, not one carp but sheds a tear, not one but the siren, the siren never stopped singing. Siren, sing on, sing on, you have good cause to sing: you have the sea to drink and my love to eat."[23] These lines are interpolated in this version, but the embellishment in a ballad of Mary Magdalen ("Les Atours de la Madeleine," Laforte 1: A4) is wholly integral. When her parents dress her in a rich costume before she goes to hear Christ preach, the effect is more hyperbolic than the costume: altars tremble and holy-water basins overturn.[24] Motifs like these produce drama, just as in "Halewijn" a series of questions and answers about the king's daughter's toilette prepares the drama of her abduction.[25] Terminal motifs, on the other hand, lead to no new action and rarely seem dramatic. Paul Bénichou used the term *rêverie* in referring to the conclusion of "La Pernette" (Laforte 1: B3); it can serve provisionally for this feature in general, which is usually in first-person discourse though not always easy to attribute, whether to a particular speaker or to the narrator.[26]

23. Jérome Bujeaud, *Chants et chansons populaires des provinces de l'Ouest: Poitou, Saintonge, Aunis et Angoumois, avec les airs originaux* (1895; rpt., Marseille: Laffitte, 1975), vol. 2, pp. 168–169.

24. Doncieux, *Romancéro populaire*, pp. 166–173.

25. Erich Seemann, Dag Strömbäck, and Bengt R. Jonsson, eds., *European Folk Ballad*, European Folklore Series 2 (Copenhagen: Rosenkilde and Bagger, 1967), pp. 36–43.

26. *Nerval et la chanson folklorique* (Paris: Corti, 1970), p. 162. This is the only comment on this feature which I have noticed.

"La Pernette" is an early ballad, better documented than
most. In the majority of modern versions, after a girl's fruitless
pleading with her mother to save the life of her lover, nothing
actually happens: the girl just tells her mother what her mother
must do and what will then ensue. But a daughter who wishes
for a double death and instructs her mother enquiring about
her welfare to hang her as well is not proposing a realizable
course of action:

"Se pendouratz moun Piarre   pendouratz-nous tous dous;
Pendetz-me iou à l'aubo,   et eou apres lou jour;
Au camin de Sant Jacque   entarratz-nous tous dous,
Curbetz lou eou de rosos,   tapetz-me iou de flours;
Tous les roumious que passoun   nen prendran quauque brout.
Diran 'Diou ague l'amo   des paures amourous
  Que nen souen mouerts tous dous.'"

"If you hang my Pierre   you must hang both of us;
Hang me at dawn   and him after day;
On the road to Compostela   bury us both,
Cover him with roses,   cover me with flowers;
All the pilgrims who pass   will take a bit of it.
They will say 'God save the souls   of the poor lovers
  That have both died of love.'"[27]

This is evident fantasy, though not at all supernatural. The *rêverie,* although explicitly addressed to her mother, might be better considered an internal monologue, in the style of the mono-
logues frequent in medieval novels. But that view of it does
not really explain its position at the end of the text.

The idea that this feature is an accretion naturally suggests
itself. And lo, the oldest text of "La Pernette," going back to
the fifteenth century, lacks the *rêverie.*[28] Yet it exists in the
song by 1614.[29] A similar and quite integral conclusion is to be

27. Damase Arbaud, *Chants populaires de la Provence,* 1 (Aix-en-Prov-
ence: Makaire, 1862), pp. 112–113.

28. Instead there is an obviously new narrative conclusion. See Henri
Davenson, *Le livre des chansons: ou, introduction à la connaissance de la
chanson populaire française* . . . (Neuchâtel: Baconnière, 1946), p. 174;
Doncieux, *Romancéro populaire,* pp. 23–24.

29. Eugène Rolland, *Recueil de chansons populaires* (1883–1890; rpt.,
Paris: Maisonneuve, 1967), vol. 4, pp. 21–22.

found in another lyrico-narrative song, which survives in a thirteenth-century manuscript. This image was apparently traditional in France, for it recurs in the nineteenth century: a bereaved lover proposes to build an abbey or similar pious retreat in commemoration of his or her love.[30] A fifteenth-century poem moreover indicates that retirement of a rejected lover to an abbey is a conventional ending in popular lyric.[31] In the oldest of these texts, a *chanson de toile,* a girl actually starts the building, so that a hypothesis partly becomes reality. But this is unimportant when the texts are viewed as a tradition: hypothesis may merge into realized action without loss of fantasy. In a similar way, one can say about the concluding *rêverie* in general that it follows straight upon an account of realized action without change of what we might call "narrative register"; and both French and Occitanian have an abundance of songs in which the *rêverie* seems thus organic. Perhaps the abrupt ending of a song or fragment is attenuated by a new appendix of the sort, but the patching up of faulty texts is only an incidental function of the *rêverie.* One collector noted a couplet which may be relevant, yelled at the top of their voices by drinkers who have filled their glasses:

> Toute chanson qui perd sa fin
> Mérit' toujours un coup de vin.
>
> A song that has lost its end
> Always deserves a drink.[32]

They seem to advocate leaving well enough alone.

If we look for narrative function in the speculative *rêverie* at the end of songs, we have to consider its affective value. As in "La Pernette" the *rêverie* is often attributable to one of the fictional characters and often has the tone of a lament. Similar in tone are unfulfilled, perhaps unfulfillable wishes. In an Occitanian song, obviously related to the well-known Spanish *romance* "El prisionero," instead of the abrupt and sad conclu-

---

30. Shields, "Chanson de toile."

31. Gaston Paris, *Chansons du quinzième siècle* . . . (Paris: Firmin-Didot, 1875), p. 106.

32. Bujeaud, *Chants et chansons populaires,* vol. 2, p. 364.

sion of the *romance*, the prisoner looks to the future in an extended *rêverie:* "I'll send word to my beloved to bake me a pie: not a hare pie or a swallow or fish pie but a hammer-and-file pie garnished by a blacksmith. So we shall file the fetters and hammer the tower and when the tower falls the prisoners will go free."[33] Improbable in a different fashion is the concluding stanza of "Le Marinier de Sainteville" (Laforte 2: C11), a song which scarcely narrates at all but does so on the theme of the "Grey Cock" (Child 248): "If only love grew like thyme in the garden I would plant it at the four corners, along and across; I would give some of it to lovers who had none."[34] The image lightens the tone by a touch of absurdity. In the case of the famous English general "Marlborough" and his nonreturn from war (Laforte 1: C7), absurdity extends to the more than slightly diverting spectacle of his funeral cortege, which was enshrined in pictorial imagery of the broadside press.[35]

Though many *rêveries* provide a quite serious conclusion expressing expectation, apprehension (at a prediction), or grief, there is more often a tendency in the feature to amuse. Here enters in the so-called *esprit gaulois,* as early as the fifteenth century, when a MS poem consisting almost entirely of hypotheses foretells to a lout (*lourdault*) what will happen if he marries a young wife and the priest sees her: a chain of circumstances will lead to bringing up "the child who will be nothing to you: though you'll be only too pleased to hear him call you daddy."[36] The tendency to amuse may well have serious implications; for it is possible that it should be considered alongside the fact that *rêveries* are commoner in songs, like the last one, which have the type of verse form called *laisses* by French Canadian writers—monorhyme assonance with rhythmic alternation of masculine and feminine stresses—and

33. Cécile Marie, *Anthologie de la chanson occitane* (Paris: Maisonneuve and Larose, 1975), pp. 260–261.

34. Shields, *Ballad Research,* p. 246.

35. Doncieux, *Romancéro populaire,* pp. 455–461; Davenson, *Livre des chansons,* pp. 419–424. The picture, with the words, is reproduced in André Gauthier, *Les chansons de notre histoire* (Paris: Pages-Club, 1967), pp. 82–83.

36. Paris, *Chansons du quinzième siècle,* pp. 69–70.

usually a refrain, songs suitable for dancing.[37] We may ask whether a mood of communal recreation has inspired so many appropriate concluding fantasies and, if so, whether the descent into irrationality or creative extravagance simply prepares the way for a musical conclusion or transition. To pursue this idea further would call for substantial historical and technical research. Interesting though it is we need to remind ourselves that there are also a certain number of songs in strophic form—that is, not in the monorhyme *laisses,* stichic in form—which conclude with a *rêverie.* Since they give no indication of being intended for the specific recreational function of dancing, these songs compel us to consider them as narrative fiction.

On this level it seems proper to give weight to the desire for simple emphasis. Makers of old ballads loved emphatic conclusions—sometimes if not always—and were ready to resort to gimmicks in achieving them. Thus were formulated the "impossibles" of English and other Germanic ballads, which do not overstep the bounds of nature but only envisage doing so to compare the supernatural with the desired but just as unattainable:

> "O, when will ye come back again,
>   My dear son, tell to me?"
> "When sun and moon gae three times round,
>   And this will never be." (Child 49F)[38]

The French speculative conclusions were formulated differently, less strictly confined and regulated; any narrative content in them may be diffuse, its motivation not always easy to understand. And they do not balk at declaring possible the supernatural or magical. The song sometimes entitled "La Magicienne" (Laforte 1: N4) tells of a jilted girl whose rival excels not in beauty but in power:

> Elle fait neiger, elle fait grêler,   elle fait le vent qui vente,
> Elle fait reluire le soleil   à minuit dans sa chambre,
> Elle fait pousser le romarin   sur le bord de la manche.

---

37. *Chansons en laisse* are the subject of vol. 1 of Laforte's *Catalogue.*
38. *ESPB,* I, pp. 442–443. See H. Shields, "Impossibles in Ballad Style," in Porter, *The Ballad Image,* pp. 192–214.

> She can make the snow fall, the hail fall,   the wind blow,
> She can make the sun shine   at midnight in her room,
> She can make rosemary grow   on the hem of her sleeve.[39]

Here the song ends though nothing previous has suggested that
the rival is a sorceress. May we conclude that this is not real
magic, but ironic play with the idea of it? It is possible of
course to seek erotic meaning in these particular images. But
the tone of the speculative conclusion in French songs generally is interesting in that it seems not only to emphasize traits
in the preceding realized narrative, but to encourage reflection
on the poetic fiction both as fiction and as poetry.

What contrasts and what parallels do these Irish and French
cases provide? Both might be said to lack drama in the ordinary sense of a well-conducted and concluded action. But
whereas the Irish habit is to string together apparently discon-
nected pieces of a single set of circumstances and to refer the
listener to another source for further information, the feature
of French songs which I have mostly called *rêverie* stands as
unfulfilled action, with comment, in place of a denouement of
realized action. The Irish inexplicit method finds parallels in
other countries. To the blues ballad might be added, in certain
respects, the local compositions of our day in many countries:
these often present an allusive narrative or sequence of events
in a field of action not clearly defined and with a certain
amount of ironic comment. French songs which narrate are
generally not inexplicit and proceed in a chronological perspective. The end of the perspective may not be in sight and
may be such as to remain unattainable; the events of Irish
songs are obscure but generally realized. One might tentatively
class the Irish tradition as history and the French tradition as
fiction.

Such categories have some validity but they lack finesse. It
is evident that these two cultures have simply taken to considerable lengths practices that are to be found to a smaller or

39. Ernest Gagnon, *Chansons populaires du Canada,* 2nd ed. (Quebec:
R. Morgan, 1880), pp. 303–305.

greater extent in oral traditions of song everywhere. From explorations of "contingency" in the narrative songs of European tradition therefore it could be hoped to obtain a more
subtle picture of the treatment of narrative in lyric than from
the principle of ballad canons too strictly applied. Child himself does not seem to uphold such application. As with many
popular genres of medieval elaboration the ballad has had a
focus rather than a canon, and characteristic practice has mat-
tered more than conformity.

In stylistic terms, Irish Gaelic song has scarcely felt the attraction of the ballad focus, resolutely maintaining an aesthetic
principle of apparent obscurity. The speculative *rêverie* of
French songs, on the other hand, does not necessarily represent an attempt to escape the attraction of the ballad focus or
to diminish its influence. It is a feature which would certainly
repay investigation in other ballad traditions. We have noticed
prophecies in English ballads. We notice also the string of
curses which terminates a Sephardic version of the *romance*
"Gaiferos jugador," and the wife's verses of lament at marital
estrangement in an extended monologue at the end of some
texts of "Jamie Douglas" (Child 204, esp. E and L).[40] These
Spanish and English ballads both evoke unrealized action in
the French manner. Such action is fully integral to the majority
of songs containing it, while Irish songs are depleted by the
lack of the "authority" which explains their meaning. Between
Irish obscurity and Gallic fantasy there is of course the important area of realized action in ballads. This essay has displayed
some of the obscurity and a little of the fantasy; but I hope that
it has a certain value as a reminder that the temporal perspective of narrative lyric song is not simple or uniform and also,
incidentally, that the ballad is a lyric song.

---

40. Samuel Armistead and J. H. Silverman, *The Judeo-Spanish Ballad
Chapbooks of Y. A. Yoná* (Berkeley and Los Angeles: University of California Press, 1971), p. 88.

DAVID BUCHAN

Talerole Analysis and Child's Supernatural Ballads

Francis James Child made manifold contributions to ballad study, not the least of which was his creation of a conceptual perspective whereby the popular ballad, as he termed it, was no longer lumped undiscriminatingly with that amorphous entity "Early Literature" but accorded a certain autonomy. In ballad studies B.C.—before Child—writers tended to follow the Grimms in equating folk literature with early literature; that which was "folk" was assumed to be "old" and therefore belonged to the heterogeneous mass of ancient poesy. The retention by some Nordic scholars of the adjective "medieval" to denote the genre Child called the popular ballad is one contemporary remnant of this attitude. There was, one should not forget, some warrant for it, in that folk literature and early literature often shared elements of both content and style. In his 1857 edition of *English and Scottish Ballads,* Child himself did not discriminate strenuously the traditional from the merely early, which may well have contributed to the dissatisfactions that drove him to construct the monumental later edition of *The English and Scottish Popular Ballads,* a title new characterized by the definite article and the defining adjective "popular." By 1882, Child had developed the perspective that demarcated this genre of folk literature from capital-E Early Literature, thereby in effect establishing folk literature as a separate constituency. Nowadays this separate constituency is recognized as possessing its own scholarly methodology and modes of critical analysis that apply across its various genres. When Child was constructing the later edition he frequently discussed in his letters to his friend and fellow editor, Svend Grundtvig, the problems inherent in ordering and classifying the ballads.[1] Today, more than one hundred years later, I would like to address a subgenre given early prominence by Child and one which exemplifies those problems—the supernatural ballads—by employing a means of analysis originally conceived for another genre of folk literature. Child contributed greatly to the recognition of the independence of folk literature and consequently of the critical interdependence of its genres; he provided the first serious exposition of ballad taxonomy; and of course by his scrupulous editorial labor he furnished us with an indispensable security in the texts. From all of these scholarly benefactions this essay benefits. There can be few scholars who exercise so profound an influence one hundred years on.

The analytic method to be employed on the supernatural ballads is that of talerole analysis. The concept of talerole was first enunciated by the Russian scholar Vladimir Propp in his *Morphology of the Folktale,* published in Russian in 1928 but not available in English until 1958.[2] In that work he constructed two morphological models for the genre he studied, the *Zaubermärchen* or wonder tale, one based on the action sequence and the other on the dramatic agents. The first model, much more fully developed, has generated much fruitful scholarly thinking. The second has been almost unregarded in anglophone scholarship, not just because it was less developed in Propp's writing but because it suffered from a deplorably inadequate English translation, as Heda Jason and Dmitri Segal have forcefully pointed out.[3] Propp's precept is in essence quite simple: he recommends that one distinguish be-

1. Sigurd B. Hustvedt, *Ballad Books and Ballad Men* (Cambridge, Mass.: Harvard University Press, 1930), pp. 268, 269, 270, 276–277.

2. *Morphology of the Folktale,* trans. L. Scott, 2nd rev. ed., ed. L. A. Wagner (Austin, Tex.: University of Texas Press, 1968).

3. *Patterns in Oral Literature* (The Hague: Mouton, 1977), pp. 313–320.

tween the concrete fact of character and the abstract concept
of talerole. This advocacy of bilevel analysis of the dramatic
agents accords with the habitual necessity in folk literature for
analysis on macro and micro levels simultaneously, as in such
familiar pairings as type and version, motifeme and motif, formulaic system and formula. The two Russian terms used by
Propp to denote talerole and character respectively were rendered indiscriminately in English by three terms, so that his
central distinction was lost in the translation. By this distinction he was able to offer as one of his two definitions of the
wonder tale that it is a tale subordinated to a seven-talerole
scheme—an exact but awkward formulation, he adds characteristically[4] (pp. 79–80, 100). In recent years I have used the
concept of talerole for analysis of the ballad: first in a study of
a repertoire to provide a generic cross-section and since then
in studies of subgenres and groupings within subgenres that I
have had to call minigenres, through lack of an established
term for an evident phenomenon. Talerole I have come to define, essentially, as the interactive function served by a character in a narrative.

My intention is to synthesize the talerole analysis of the
minigenres within the subgenre of supernatural balladry. This
subgenre I used to call, with an attempt at factual descriptive-

---

4. "The Wit-Combat Ballads," in Carol L. Edwards and Kathleen E. B.
Manley, eds., *Narrative Folksong: New Directions; Essays in Appreciation
of W. Edson Richmond* (Boulder, Colo.: Westview, 1985), pp. 380–400;
"Tale Roles and Revenants: A Morphology of Ghosts," *Western Folklore*
45 (1986): 143–160; "Taleroles and the Witch Ballads," in Zorica Rajković,
ed., *Ballads and Other Genres/Balladen und andere Gattungen* (Zagreb:
Zavod za istraživanje folklora, 1988), pp. 133–140; "Taleroles and the
Otherworld Ballads," in Walter Puchner, ed., *Tod und Jenseits im
europäischen Volkslied* (Ioannina: University of Ioannina, 1986 [1989]), pp.
247–261; "The Affinities of Revenant and Witcombat Ballads," in Conrad
Laforte, ed., *Ballades et chansons folkloriques* (Quebec: CELAT, Université Laval, 1989), pp. 333–339; "The Marvellous Creature Ballads," forth-
coming. See also "Propp's Tale Role and a Ballad Repertoire," *Journal of
American Folklore* 95 (1982): 159–172; "Traditional Patterns and the
Religious Ballads," in Rita Pedersen and Flemming G. Andersen, eds., *The
Concept of Tradition in Ballad Research* (Odense: Odense University Press,
1985), pp. 27–41, 49–52.

ness, the magical and marvelous ballads, because of the problems inherent in the term "supernatural," but I have given up
the ghost (or the revenant) and now employ the standard term
because of its widespread use. The generalizations that arise
from this analysis—perhaps appearing as mere assertions—are
substantiated in the relevant articles on the minigenres.[4]

Minigenre	Types
Otherworld Being	19, 37, 38, 39, 40, 41, 42/85, 113, 289
Witcombat	1, 2, 3, 46
Witch	6, 32, 34, 35, 36
Revenant	20, 47, 77, 78, 79
Revenant-Tragic	49B etc., 69A/77B etc., 72A/79B, 73E etc., 74A etc., 243A etc., 255, 272A etc., 265
Marvelous Creature	26, 43, 68, 82, 256

The subgenre comprises six minigenres, involving approximately 12 percent of ballad types in the British tradition. The
supernatural types are preponderantly Scottish rather than
English, which underlines the particular links of Scottish balladry with Nordic balladry, where supernatural ballads have
also flourished. In the subgenre appear such well-known types
as "Thomas Rymer" (Child 37), "The Twa Corbies" (Child
26), "The Fause Knicht Upon the Road" (Child 3), and "The
Wife of Usher's Well" (Child 79), and such relatively little-
known types as "The Laily Worm and the Machrel of the Sea"
(Child 36), "Willie's Fatal Visit" (Child 255), "Allison and Willie" (Child 256), and "The Queen of Elfan's Nourice" (Child
40).[5] The supernatural ballads may be defined for the moment
as those ballad-types where a being with supernatural powers
plays an integral and necessary part in the central ballad ac-

5. "Type" is a standard term and concept in ethnology and folkloristics
which may be defined for the general reader this way: A type constitutes,
on the theoretical level, the aggregate of all the versions (specific recordings) of a single story, song, play, etc., of folk literature, and on the practical
level of classification, the constants which inform the versions and identify
their genetic relationship.

tion; later it will be possible to define the subgenre in terms of the taleroles. It is not essential that the supernatural powers be exercised but it is essential that the potential be there; normally they are exercised, but in one minigenre, the witcombat ballads, the dramatic tension arises from the mortal's ability to frustrate the supernatural being's capacity to deploy his powers. The given definition, it should be noted, does not include the religious ballads, in which a divine being plays an integral and necessary part in the central ballad action.

The beings with supernatural powers fall into four classes: supernatural beings; supernatural ex-mortals; mortals with supernatural powers; and creatures with supernatural powers. In the first category, supernatural beings, appear fairies, giants, selchies, and mermaids; in the second, supernatural ex-mortals, are revenants; in the third, mortals with supernatural powers, are witches; and in the fourth, creatures with supernatural powers, are marvelous birds and beasts. Who, however, is not listed in this otherwise comprehensive gallery? A Scottish audience would respond rather promptly that missing is Auld Nick, the Devil, who bulks prominent in Scottish cultural thought—of whatever register—and who, unlike the others, comes not in the plural but in the singular, constituting theoretically a class of being on his own, although in practice on the folk-cultural register he and his powers and associated beliefs are frequently merged with other supernatural creatures and their attributes. To this singular class of supernatural being we shall return.

Talerole analysis reveals six minigenres within the subgenre: four major at its center and two hybrid at its periphery (see schema). The four main minigenres are the otherworld-being ballads, the witcombat ballads, the witch ballads, and the revenant ballads; the two hybrid minigenres are the revenant-tragic ballads and the marvelous-creature ballads. The four main minigenres share the same three taleroles, Bespeller, Bespelled, and Unspeller, while the hybrid minigenres have two related taleroles, a new one, and the three of another subgenre. The major taleroles define themselves in self-evident fashion: the Bespeller is a being with supernatural powers who lays a spell upon a mortal; the Bespelled is a mortal who

The Supernatural Ballads

Minigenres	Taleroles		
Otherworld Being	Bespeller	Bespelled	Unspeller
Witcombat	Bespeller neg.	Bespelled neg.	
Witch	Bespeller	Bespelled	Unspeller
Revenant		Bespelled/Visited	Unspeller/Revenant-Visitor
Hybrid Minigenres			
Revenant-Tragic		Visited	Revenant-Visitor + (Upholder × Opposer × Partner)
Marvelous Creature			Informer + (Upholder × Opposer × Opposer's Partner)

undergoes a spell; and the Unspeller is that character, mortal or otherwise, responsible for the lifting of a spell.

Two of the minigenres, the otherworld-being and witch groups, have all three taleroles; the other two main groups each have two of the three. The witcombat minigenre was originally accorded the talerole designations Poser and Matcher, which apply accurately at a very concrete level of analysis and which cover both the supernatural and the secular types and versions of the group. When, however, the supernatural types and versions are separated out and viewed in the perspective of the other supernatural ballads it becomes clear that they embody a Bespeller who fails to bespell and a mortal who resists being bespelled. The dissimilarity qualifying the essential similarity is shown on the schema by the Proppian contraction "neg.," for negative, indicating that the talerole character's failure to fulfill his or her purpose in fact constitutes his or her function.[6] The revenant minigenre also has its two talerole terms, Bespelled and Unspeller, qualified in this case by the concomitant terms Visited and Revenant-Visitor. Originally the latter set of terms was employed since they cover, at a fairly high level of generality, the types in both revenant and revenant-tragic minigenres, and they have been retained to indicate the relationship of the two groups. When, however, the core minigenre of revenant ballads is viewed in the perspective of the other supernatural ballads it becomes clear that we have another manifestation of the basic taleroles. To anticipate a future discussion somewhat: The central action in this minigenre concerns a mortal in an unhealthy emotional state who is released from that state by the revenant. The bespelling here is the condition of being in an unnatural state, one self-induced rather than externally brought about.

The two hybrid minigenres are so called because their taleroles incorporate the standard talerole pattern of the large romantic and tragic subgenre. The revenant-tragic minigenre contains both the Upholder $\times$ Opposer $\times$ Partner taleroles of the romantic and tragic subgenre and the two taleroles overlapping with the revenant group. The marvelous-creature mini-

6. Propp, *Morphology of the Folktale*, pp. 152, 154, 155.

genre has these three romantic and tragic taleroles and its own, defining, talerole, that of the marvelous Informer. In both hybrid minigenres the major focus is no longer exclusively on the interaction of mortal and being with supernatural powers, although such a being (for which I shall frequently use the term "unmortal") still plays a necessary and integral part in the central ballad action.

Establishment of the taleroles enables us to perceive the basic narrative patterns in the minigenres. In the otherworld-being minigenre, an otherworld being bespells a mortal and then the spell is terminated, either by its lifting or by its running a fatal course. This minigenre actually contains two subgroups, distinguished by whether the otherworld being is a land-based creature or a water-based creature: in the first, a land-based otherworld being abducts a mortal to the otherworld from where he or she is, after a period, liberated; in the second, a water-based otherworld being has contact with a mortal which ends with the death of one or the other. In the witch minigenre a witch bespells a man or woman who then has the spell climactically lifted. In the witcombat minigenre a mortal counters the tests of cleverness posed by an unmortal and thereby escapes being bespelled. In the revenant minigenre a person whose death has severed a relationship returns to rectify an emotional imbalance in the life of the survivor, thereby releasing him or her from a spell or unnatural state.

Clearly, the spell is crucial to the subgeneric action; one may define it as the condition of being in an unnatural state. The spell in the witch minigenre has the unmortal exercise her supernatural powers to transform her victim into an unnatural state both bodily and, not so obviously, emotional. The spell in the revenant minigenre has the mortal in an unnatural state of emotional transformation, from which the unmortal releases her. The spell in the otherworld-being minigenre has the mortal taken into the unmortal's power and translated bodily out of the natural world to the otherworld in the first subgroup, while in the second it has an unnatural contact between mortal and unmortal result in a death. In the witcombat minigenre, where the mortal avoids falling into the unmortal's power, the story's tension derives from the threat of the spell, which could involve transformation or translation or both. The spell subsumes three elements corresponding to the three taleroles, the bespelling, the state of being bespelled, and the unspelling, which are given different prominence in particular minigenres and particular types. The witcombat minigenre, for example, concentrates on the foiling of the bespelling whereas the revenant minigenre concentrates on the state of being bespelled and the unspelling; individual types within the other two minigenres also highlight differing elements of the spell.

The spell does not have such central importance in the basic narrative patterns of the hybrid minigenres. In the revenant-tragic group a man-woman relationship is severed by the death of one member through violence or the grief of disappointed love, the narratives dealing in varying proportions with the severance and its aftereffects and involving a revenant. In the marvelous-creature minigenre a marvelous bird or beast provides information which illuminates the fidelity or faithlessness within a man-woman relationship. In these minigenres a relatively greater narrative prominence is accorded the strictly mortal relationships. Before, however, we address the topic of relationships let us turn to the characters who fill the taleroles.

All the characters filling the Bespelled taleroles are mortals. In the otherworld-being and witch minigenres men are bespelled almost as often as women but in the witcombat and revenant minigenres those in the Bespelled role are all women, or in one instance a child. The Unspeller role is usually occupied by a mortal, often the hero, but sometimes by the otherworld figure of the Queen of Elfland, a character who can in the same story also act as the Bespeller. If we survey the characters in the Bespeller talerole minigenre by minigenre, some interesting points emerge. In the otherworld-being minigenre there are the Queen of Elfland (three times), the King of Elfland, an inhabitant of Elfland, a giant, a selchie, and a mermaid (twice). In the witch minigenre there are the hero's mother, the hero's stepmother, the heroine's stepmother (twice), and the heroine (the term is used denotatively not connotatively). And in the witcombat minigenre there is the Devil in three types and variously Devil, revenant, or Elphin character in a fourth. In the otherworld-being minigenre all the

Bespellers are in fact creatures from the otherworld, whereas in the witch minigenre the Bespellers are all mortals, though mortals with supernatural powers, who have familial or amatory links with the other main characters. This distinction would indicate that the two minigenres may concentrate on different kinds of relationships and that they may have different cultural concerns. That the predominant character in the witcombat Bespeller role should be the Devil requires some explanation.

The witcombat minigenre within the supernatural subgenre comprises four types: Child 1, 2, 3, and 46 ("Riddles Wisely Expounded," "The Elfin Knight," "The False Knight upon the Road," and "Captain Wedderburn's Courtship").[7] Two other types with witcombats as part of the narrative conform to the talerole and action patterns of the revenant minigenre—Child 47 and 78 ("Proud Lady Margaret" and "The Unquiet Grave")—and another, Child 45 ("King John and the Bishop"), is a secular type, likely of prose provenance. This minigenre raises a problem: it is the only minigenre not defined in title by a class of supernatural being. To that let me appose another problem. The relative absence of the Devil from Scottish balladry has always proved puzzling when he figures so prominently in Scottish tradition, especially legendary and proverbial lore; Scottish literature (for example, Burns's "Address to the Deil" or Hogg's *Memoirs and Confessions of a Justified Sinner*); and Scottish cultural thought generally. He does make appearances in the comic ballad "The Farmer's Curst Wife" (Child 278), and some versions of the revenant-tragic ballad "James Harris" (Child 243) and the historical ballad "The Laird of Wariston" (Child 194), but one would expect, a priori, the Devil to have his own distinct little class of

---

7. After a period of relative neglect the witcombat ballads have recently received some attention: Tristram Potter Coffin, "Four Black Sheep among the 305," in James Porter, ed., *The Ballad Image: Essays Presented to Bertrand Harris Bronson* (Los Angeles: Center for the Study of Comparative Folklore and Mythology, 1983), pp. 30–38; John Minton, "'The False Knight Upon the Road': A Reappraisal," *Journal of American Folklore* 98 (1985): 435–444; Susan Edmunds, "The Riddle Ballad and the Riddle," *Lore & Language* 5 (1986): 35–46.

story, especially since the other supernatural beings all have
one. The way the Bespeller talerole is occupied in the supernatural types and versions of the witcombat minigenre suggests that both problems may be solved by the same explanation.

First, let us examine more closely the types in which the
Devil appears. Child initially considered those versions of
"Riddles Wisely Expounded" containing the Devil as aberra-
tions from the type's secular norm, viewing the human being
as the original figure and the Devil as an intruder, but when by
Volume V the 1450 version, "Inter Diabolus et Virgo," turned
up he reversed his position (pp. 283–284). This now would be
the standard position, although one should note that a number
of secular versions exist, the Devil having been secularized in
some lines of transmission through the centuries. There is little
doubt of the Devil's status as "The False Knight upon the
Road" but it is worth remarking that many versions lack any
overt reference to his diabolic character. In "The Elfin
Knight" the Devil figures in some versions, but the role is also
occupied by an Elfin character, a revenant, and a mortal man.
The male interlocutor of " 'Captain Wedderburn's Courtship"
is in most versions an apparently mortal figure, though sixty
years ago Wimberly hazarded the prediction that a version
would turn up with a supernatural character involved.[8] Not
just one version but three, all recorded in Newfoundland and
Labrador, have since turned up, all three with the Devil and
one with the Virgin Mary as his opponent.[9] The question that
arises, of course, is whether the evidence indicates a regionally

8. Lowry C. Wimberly, *Folklore in the English and Scottish Popular
Ballads* (Chicago, 1928; rpt. New York: Dover, 1965), p. 309.

9. Maud Karpeles, ed., *Folk Songs from Newfoundland* (London: Faber
and Faber, 1971), pp. 40–41; MacEdward Leach, *Folk Ballads and Songs of
the Lower Labrador Coast* (Ottawa: National Museum of Canada, 1965),
pp. 26–29. See Roger deV. Renwick, in Tristram Potter Coffin, *The British
Traditional Ballad in North America,* rev. ed., supplement by Roger deV.
Renwick (Austin: University of Texas Press, 1977), p. 224, for the argument
that the Devil is the interlocutor in certain versions of type 46; for the close
relationships between types 1, 2, 3, and 46 see ibid., pp. 223–224 and 209–
211; Leach, *Folk Ballads and Songs,* pp. 27–28, and Coffin, "Four Black
Sheep."

created oikotype or a case of peripheral retention. The prediction of Wimberley would incline one to the latter explanation. The Devil, then, appears in all four types, with greater or lesser degrees of frequency and obviousness. Could it be that the Devil is the original interlocutor in the stories of "The Elfin Knight" and "Captain Wedderburn's Courtship" as, it is generally agreed, he is in "Riddles Wisely Expounded" and "The False Knight upon the Road"? Were that to be the case, then the Devil would have been changed into a mortal man in some transmissions of both stories and altered into another supernatural figure in some transmissions of "The Elfin Knight." The secularization need occasion no surprise, for this is what has happened in the other two types, fostered both by the traditional reticence in naming supernatural characters that produces euphemisms such as the "false knight" and by the Devil's presenting himself in the story as an ordinary mortal such as an "auld, auld man, / Wi his blue bonnet in his han" (Child 2I, st. 2). The alteration that would also have occurred in some transmissions of "The Elfin Knight" may be explicable as exemplifying the general phenomenon of the mingling of supernatural beliefs, visible also in the character of "James Harris," alternately demon and revenant.[10]

If, then, the Devil had at one time been the only and ubiquitous supernatural being in all four types, that would explain why the witcombat minigenre has a different configuration of the same taleroles from the other minigenres: because it deals, or has dealt, with a different class of being. The unsuccess of the Bespeller would derive from the cultural meaning intrinsic to this class of being; the Devil, whether official or traditional, can be repelled by the exercise of "wyssedom" (1A*, st. 3–4, 13–14), the right combination of intelligence and moral knowledge. All this gives rise to the hypothesis that the witcombat

---

10. On the phenomenon in general, see Wimberly, *Folklore;* Keith Thomas, *Religion and the Decline of Magic* (Harmondsworth: Penguin, 1971); Gillian Bennett, "Ghost and Witch in the Sixteenth and Seventeenth Centuries," *Folklore* 97 (1986): 3–14; and J. A. MacCulloch, "The Mingling of Fairy and Witch Beliefs in Sixteenth and Seventeenth Century Scotland," *Folklore* 32 (1921): 227–244.

minigenre within the supernatural subgenre owes its separate identity to having had its own class of supernatural being, namely the Devil, and that it could be more properly termed the Devil minigenre. Given the nature of tradition, this assertion cannot be proved in any demonstrably scientific way but it does stand as a hypothesis with a fair circumstantial likelihood.

The consideration of characters in taleroles also leads on to a discussion of relationships, that central concern of the classical ballad. The supernatural ballads, as one would imagine, deal with mortal-unmortal relationships, though not exclusively. In these ballads there are relationships between mortals and otherworld beings, witches, revenants, and the Devil. The stories show the dangers in these relationships, and how they can be evaded or mitigated. Along a spectrum of danger, one finds that the water-based otherworld beings are fatal, the witches are harmful, the land-based otherworld beings are potentially harmful but can be treated with, the Devil is repellable, and the revenants are helpful. The narratives demonstrate how to avoid such relationships, how to behave when you can't avoid them, how to end and how not to end them.

When one investigates the nature of the relationships through the taleroles of Bespeller and Bespelled, several features emerge. In the otherworld-being, witcombat, and revenant minigenres the interaction is mostly between male and female, the exceptions being, in the first minigenre, between female and female (Child 40), in the second, between boy and Devil (Child 3), and in the third, between female and genderless children (Child 20). In no case, interestingly, is there an interaction between a male unmortal and an adult male mortal. For a mortal, an encounter with an unmortal is most likely an encounter with a being of the opposite sex, a fact surely that would have inspired Freud to exploration. In two of the same three minigenres—the witcombat and the revenant—the Bespelled talerole is occupied only by mortal women or, in one instance, a child. It is the more vulnerable members of the community who are visited by the Devil or revenants, but the Devil can be repelled and the revenants can prove beneficial, if those visited have the right kind of moral knowledge or allow themselves to be led to self-knowledge. In the revenant mini-genre a central relationship has been severed by the death of one member, who returns to rectify an emotional imbalance in the life of the other caused in greater or lesser part by the dis-location of the death. The character filling the Bespelled tale-role, always a woman, suffers from an unhealthy or excessive reaction to the death or lack of the other person, and the revenant filling the Unspeller talerole serves to highlight the unhealthiness of the reaction and to supply its remedy. Through its dramatic action this kind of ballad both presents a psychological state brought about by the rupture of a relation-ship and proffers a way of coping with the dangers of that state.

The witch minigenre presents a different picture, for here all the Bespellers are women and the victims are both women and men. Evidently the supernatural subgenre has a particular con-cern with, and therefore relevance for, women. All but one of the Bespellers stand in close familial relationship to the Bespelled. One type deals with the tension of the mother-in-law relationship as it affects both daughter-in-law and son; an-other deals with the stepmother relationship as it affects step-son, stepdaughter, and husband; and another two with the stepmother-stepdaughter relationship. Two of these types, and the remaining one, also deal with man-woman relationships in which the woman has previously been injured and rejected. These familial and amatory relationships all have potential for tension, and the ballad stories show what can happen when the tension erupts and lives are severely disrupted. The spell crucial to these stories acts as a dramatic metaphor for the eruption of the tension. Witchcraft is a narrative mechanism for presenting certain problems of human interaction in ex-treme terms; the highly dramatic mode is consonant with the disruptive potential of the problems. Contemporary anthropol-ogists have shown that witchcraft accusations "provide us with a set of social strain-gauges for detecting where the ten-sions and role-conflicts in a particular society lie."[11] It would appear that these witch ballads, presenting a narrative explo-

11. "Introduction," in Max Marwick, ed., *Witchcraft and Sorcery* (Har-mondsworth: Penguin, 1970), p. 17.

ration of psychological tensions in small group interaction, may do likewise.

In the otherworld-being and witcombat minigenres the nature of the unmortal-mortal relationship is largely determined by the nature of the unmortal, whereas in the witch and revenant minigenres the unmortals and mortals also stand in familial or amatory relationship to one another. Some of the otherworld-being types (Child 41, 42, 113) also have unmortals and mortals in amatory relationships, while a number of the minigeneric types have in addition to the unmortal-mortal relationship a mortal relationship—amatory or, in one case, familial. Even versions of some witcombat types (Child 1, 2, 46) have a sexual or amatory undercurrent, although this element may have appeared with secularization. In short, the subgenre deals both with the relationships of unmortals and mortals and with the stuff of mortal relationships: the familial and amatory links that bind human beings together. The hybrid minigenres emphasize this duality. In the revenant-tragic group the emphasis falls primarily on the human relationship (depicted in talerole terms as Upholder × Opposer × Partner), with the Revenant-Visitor × Visited interaction underlining and extending it. Likewise, in the marvelous-creature minigenre the central focus is an amatory human relationship, one broken or spurned by one of its members. Here the marvelous creature is the means by which the nature of the relationship is explicated. Where, then, the otherworld and witcombat minigenres deal primarily with how to avoid and how to mitigate the dangers inherent in relationships with supernatural beings, the others are concerned primarily with human relationships, familial and amatory. The revenant and revenant-tragic minigenres deal with relationships severed by death; the witch minigenre with relationships fraught with tension and stress; and the marvelous-creature minigenre with amatory relationships broken by one of the members.

The distinguishing of the taleroles allows now an examination of the functions of the subgenre in culture. A major function is to convey useful cultural knowledge. Some supernatural types, for example, provide factual information that helps maintain a culture's belief system. They portray and thereby inform people about the otherworld, the nature, characteristics, and practices of its creatures, the otherworldly elements of the traditional cosmological picture, and the conceptual relationship of the otherworld to this world. On the basis of this information they furnish guidance for the behavior of mortals towards the otherworld folk in their mortal-unmortal interactions. One would learn to evade dealings with the water-creatures, and to avoid Elfin abduction through failure to observe certain taboos. One would learn, however, that when one is taken by the Elfin folk liberation is possible: if one dutifully performs the required service (as in Child 37 and 40); or if one exercises courage and initiative and at the same time uses the protection of the Church (as in Child 41), a special skill such as musicianship (as in Child 19), or a special knowledge such as that of the transformation ritual of "Tam Lin." In like fashion, the witcombat minigenre presents the knowledge and skills required by the more vulnerable members of the community to frustrate the attentions of the Devil. They too furnish models for behavior toward unchancy beings, and information to govern unmortal-mortal relationships.

The supernatural ballads also provide a related kind of cultural knowledge, knowledge about human relationships—a function shared with other ballad subgenres. In witch ballads, for example, the witchcraft spell works to show, through dramatic extremes, the possible results of stress affecting such relationships. Witchcraft in this context is, one could argue, a highly charged metaphor for human malice as it can operate within relationships, especially those by their nature fraught with some tension. The main cultural function of this minigenre is psychological: to explore, and through the vicarious understandings of art to inform people of, certain extremities of psychological behavior as they both derive from and affect close human relationships. The revenant ballads also serve a psychological function. They show people, and specifically women, how to cope with grieving and the dislocations of death. This minigenre explores the psychological states generated by death and the rupture of a relationship, and for the dangers of these states provides remedies which will help the individual toward adjustment and the restoration of balance.

The ballads, like other genres of folk literature, carry the lore of the tribe, which here concerns, rather arrestingly, the complex sensitivities of human emotion. They exemplify in this the methods by which a traditional community passes on its practical human wisdom, educates its members, and tries to maintain the mental balance of individuals and consequently the psychological equilibrium of the group.

The supernatural ballads transmit information about dangers in unmortal-mortal relations and dangers in human relations. The spell central to the ballad action is, in effect, a realized danger. In the otherworld-being and witcombat minigenres the spell represents the exercise of unchancy otherworld power, or the threat thereof; in the witch minigenre it portrays the effects of human malice; and in the revenant ballads it depicts the effects of death on mortal beings. In the first two the spell is magical and therefore a "real spell" by virtue of its unreality; in the second two it is a metaphorical spell, but no less real in the sense that it denotes emotional conditions that occur in real life. All four are concerned with providing strategies for survival, whether in the unpredictable interaction of the otherworld with this world or in the equally unpredictable vagaries of human interactions. The hybrid minigenres do not show their cultural functions quite so clearly but one can perceive their cultural concerns. The marvelous-creature ballads share a structural correspondence and a particular thematic, and therefore cultural, concern with fidelity and faithlessness in amatory relationships. In the revenant-tragic group the cultural concern of some of the types, as in the revenant group, lies with the disturbed emotional state of the mortal; but in others the concern lies with the perceived wrongdoing of the mortal, and in these the treatment of the revenant theme is either more sentimental or more sensational.

Delineation of the taleroles of the supernatural subgenre has made it possible to chart the pattern of action and of relationships, and to illuminate the cultural concerns and functions. As Propp did for the wonder tale one could now define the subgenre in terms of its taleroles, as a subgenre whose individual types contain two or more of the taleroles Bespeller, Bespelled, and Unspeller. This definition enables one to see clearly not only what belongs to the subgenre but also what does not. It enables one to distinguish between supernatural types and types or versions which have supernatural motifs but which conform essentially to the talerole patterning of other subgenres. It also enables one to distinguish, through the hybrid talerole patterns, what is shared by subgenres: at the level of minigenre, where the revenant-tragic and marvelous-creature groups have elements of both the supernatural and the romantic and tragic categories; at the level of type where, for example, "Clerk Colvill" (Child 42) has a tragic talerole along with two supernatural ones; and at the level of version where, for example, the C version of "The Wife of Usher's Well" (Child 79) contains taleroles from both the religious and the supernatural ballads.

As a taxonomic tool talerole analysis has considerable usefulness. In general, it demonstrates that the genre is essentially about relationships, expressed through the norm of a three-talerole interaction. It distinguishes the subgenres one from another. It distinguishes the minigenres, indicating their similarities and dissimilarities. It can show the affinities between individual types, and can distinguish between individual versions of the same type. Through the hybrids it can show the merging of patterns on various levels. Essentially the analytic method operates by distinguishing the constants from the variables, and these constants, when examined, disclose the cultural concerns and cultural statements that inform this long-lived genre.

Since Child's day context has become a major concern of ballad scholarship. Talerole analysis, this taxonomic tool that clarifies many of the classification problems which engaged Child, is also a tool of cultural analysis which allows for the elucidation of cultural concerns and functions and enables the correlation, diachronically as well as synchronically, of the ballads with their cultural context: an abstract way of saying it helps us to understand what the ballads meant to the people who sang them and, perhaps more important, those who heard them.

SIGRID RIEUWERTS

The Historical Moorings
of "The Gypsy Laddie":
Johnny Faa and Lady Cassillis

By far the most mysterious of Scottish traditionary tales is that referring to the abduction of a Countess of Cassilis by a certain John Faa,
or Faw. The story is generally believed to have had some foundation;
and yet, so far as I have been able to discover, there is no authentic
record or notice of any such event.[1]

The ballad Aytoun calls "the most mysterious" is generally
known as "The Gypsy Laddie" (Child 200). Its earliest texts
tell the story of a band of Gypsies singing in front of a castle
gate, attracting the attention of a lady, who comes down from
the castle. After the Gypsies have cast their glamor over her,
she is willing to follow Johnny Faa, their leader. When her
husband comes home and finds her gone, he sets out in pursuit
of the fugitives. The ballad ends abruptly with the hanging of
the Gypsies.

Popular tradition has it that the ballad is based on an actual
event which is supposed to have occurred at Lord Cassillis's
gate in Ayrshire, Scotland, in the first half of the seventeenth
century. Ballad editors in the early nineteenth century pro-
fessed to have established the historical truth of the ballad

1. William Edmondstoune Aytoun, ed., *The Ballads of Scotland* (Edinburgh: Blackwood, 1858), vol. 1, p. 182.

story, but to little avail. Their many differing accounts gave every reason for doubt; they turned it into a romantic story, and were more concerned with the moral issue of the high-born families said to have been involved than with pursuing a truthful investigation. The result was an even more mysterious tale.

When Francis James Child edited "The Gypsy Laddie" for the seventh part of his *English and Scottish Popular Ballads* in 1890, the mists of pseudohistoricity were dispelled. The generally accepted foundation of the story was overturned by Child's reversing the order of fact and fiction. It was not an actual event that gave rise to the popular tradition and to this ballad, Child argued; rather, the popular tradition grew out of the ballad. But if fiction precedes, it is fruitless to seek factual evidence of the ballad story. Child came to this conclusion by examining the earliest records referring to the main characters of the story. "The earliest edition of the ballad styles the gypsy John Faa, but gives no clew to the fair lady" (*ESPB* IV, p. 63), and her missing name is not recorded before the end of the eighteenth century.

Over the last hundred years Child's conclusion that the ballad has no historical foundation has been repeated time and again: it appears in ballad editions and on record jackets, and is even used by some singers to introduce the song. Other singers still believe the story to be true, despite the lack of fresh arguments to support this view. For ballad scholars Child seems to have settled the question once and for all, and none now treat "The Gypsy Laddie" as a historical or even semihistorical ballad.

Child himself, however, regarded the questions he raised in his prefaces as far from answered. Conceding that his "illustrations" or commentaries to the individual ballads were far from perfect, he tried to console himself with the observation that "the *texts* are the main thing for the world of scholars."[2] On several occasions he wrote to Grundtvig about his concern with the prefaces: "I am now becoming alarmed lest I should

2. See Child's correspondence with Svend Grundtvig in Sigurd Bernhard Hustvedt, *Ballad Books and Ballad Men* (Cambridge, Mass.: Harvard University Press, 1930), pp. 241–304, esp. 296–298, Child's letters to Grundtvig of Jan. 18, 1883, and Feb. 18, 1883.

never print the English Ballads, so many and so long have been
the interruptions to my progress. The one essential thing is for
me to give all our ballads in their best forms. Illustrations, the
best order, the literary history, are not so important, for somebody else can supply what I omit . . . My main object should
be to put the *English ballads* before the world as completely
as possibly. Elucidations and comparisons should be a secondary matter."[3]

Although these letters were written long before Child
worked on "The Gypsy Laddie," there can be no doubt that
he still regarded the illustration and elucidation of an individual
ballad as a secondary matter. On the January 10, 1890, Child
wrote to William Macmath, his informant for Part VII: "I have
nearly finished the Gypsy Laddie . . . Anything you have for
the G. L. had better come at once."[4] When Macmath not only
furnished him with valuable material for his historical sketch
of the ballad but also proposed "to give some intelligible explanation of how the Faws or Gypsies came to be associated,
in the popular mind, with a Countess of Cassillis," Child replied (February 21, 1890): "I would not bother over it."
Macmath took this as a rebuff, since it was "a very pertinent
enquiry" to him and the explanation of how a Countess of Cassillis came into the ballad was "the only point to be made in
the story."[5]

It is well attested that Child saw less importance in the prefaces than in a definitive presentation of the texts; yet these
notes of his have hardly ever been questioned. It would be useful, then, to subject Child's work on "The Gypsy Laddie" to a
thorough investigation; in this essay, however, I will confine
myself chiefly to the relationship Child proposes between fact
and fiction. His arguments against the historicity of the ballad
will be weighed and his generalizations tested. To shed new
light on the historicity of Child 200, however, will involve not
only historical research but also textual criticism.

3. Ibid., pp. 279 and 292, letters of Jan. 30, 1882, and Oct. 13, 1877.
4. I would like to thank James D. Reppert for kindly making available to
me his transcriptions of the Child-Macmath correspondence on "The Gypsy
Laddie."
5. Macmath's letters to Child of Jan. 25, March 4, and April 4, 1890,
Child Manuscripts, Houghton Library, XXVII, 830–832.

This reinvestigation of the historicity of "The Gypsy Laddie" was suggested by a close reading of Child's specific findings on this ballad: "Toward the end of the last century we begin to hear that the people in Ayrshire make the wife of the Earl of Cassilis the heroine of the ballad. This name, under the instruction of Burns, was adopted into the copy in Johnson's Museum (which, as to the rest, is Ramsay's)" (*ESPB*, IV, p. 64). This statement must come as a surprise to those familiar with Child's earlier ballad collection, *English and Scottish Ballads* (1857–1859). In his notes to "The Gypsy Laddie" there (vol. 4, pp. 114–115) he refers to William Dauney's *Ancient Scotish Melodies* (1838).[6] Dauney gives a tune, set in tablature for five-course mandore, from the Skene Manuscript (1630–1640), which he quite rightly associates with a variant of Child 200.[7] The title of that tune in the old manuscript is "lady Cassilles Lilt"—the oldest known allusion, it seems, to the ballad. The name Cassillis was thus associated with the ballad "Johnny Faa, the Gypsy Laddie" long before "the end of the last century."

Child's second point is that the name Cassillis was adopted into the copy in Johnson's *Museum* (1788) under the instruction of Burns.[8] Indeed, apart from the name Cassillis the text is a reprint of an earlier version of the "Gypsy Laddie" from Ramsay (Child 200A). Burns had a special interest in this ballad, the only one he could trace to his native Ayrshire, which, perhaps explains Child's assertion.[9] Furthermore, when Burns joined Johnson in editing the Scottish ballads, he welcomed the undertaking as "exactly to my taste. I have collected, begged, borrowed and stolen, all the songs I could meet with."[10] So why should Child not assume that Burns adopted the name Cassillis into the ballad in 1788?

6. Edinburgh: Edinburgh Printing and Publishing Company, 1838.

7. Skene Manuscript, National Library of Scotland, no. 30.

8. James Johnson, ed., *The Scots Musical Museum;* rpt. ed. William Stenhouse, 2 vols. (Hatboro, Pa.: Folklore Associates, 1962).

9. See James C. Dick, *Notes on Scottish Song by Robert Burns* (London: Frowde, 1908), p. 31.

10. *The Letters of Robert Burns,* ed. J. De Lancey Ferguson (Oxford: Clarendon, 1931), vol. 1, p. 179, Burns's letter to James Candlish of February 1788(?).

The point seemed well supported. Yet an old manuscript was recovered after Child's death that shows that Burns cannot be held responsible for filling in the name Cassillis. The Mansfield Manuscript has the name of the lady in the first and last line of its text (which is also basically Ramsay's): "The Gypseys came to Lord Cassillis's gate . . . And we were a' put down fair ane / The Earle o Cassillis Lady."[11] The manuscript dates from 1770–1780: thus the wife of the Earl of Cassillis had been made the heroine of the ballad at least one decade, if not two, before Robert Burns worked on Johnson's *Museum*.

Since Child's argumentation on these two points cannot hold, the question about the factual basis of the ballad "Johnny Faa, the Gypsy Laddie" must be asked anew. Burns leaves no doubt about the authenticity of the ballad. In an interleaved copy of the *Scots Musical Museum* which he presented to Robert Riddle, he refers to a popular tradition in Ayrshire:

The people in Ayrshire begin this song—
    The gypsies cam to my Lord Cassilis' yett.
They have a great many more stanzas in this song than I ever yet saw in any printed copy.—
The castle is still remaining at Maybole, where his lordship shut up his wayward spouse, and kept her for life.[12]

Can we reasonably assume, then, that Johnny Faa and Lady Cassillis have always been associated with the ballad? If so, is there any historical basis for the ballad story? Burns points to a popular tradition, but are there any references to such an incident in a more reliable (that is, official) document? To find an answer we should take the earliest extant examples of the ballad as a starting point. The crucial question is, after all: how old is the association of the names Cassillis and Faa with the ballad or its story?

The textual record for the ballad does not extend back beyond 1720. In fact, the first text we can date accurately is

---

11. Quoted in Frank Miller, *The Mansfield Manuscript: An Old Edinburgh Collection of Songs and Ballads* (Dumfries: Hunter, Watson & Co., 1935), p. 29.

12. Dick, *Notes on Scottish Song*, p. 35.

Ramsay's in the fourth volume of *The Tea-Table Miscellany*.
Child had to take this text, his A-text, from the 1763 edition
although he knew it had first been printed in 1740—"but no
copy of that edition has been recovered" (*ESPB* IV, p. 61). A
complete four-volume set of the 1740 edition, has, however,
since been found and placed in the British Library; and we also
now know of an even earlier edition of the fourth volume,
which was printed separately as early as 1737.[13] The text of
"The Gypsy Laddie" from this edition differs only slightly
from the text that Child used.

Ramsay's *Tea-Table Miscellany* met a specific need in cater-
ing to a female, upper-class audience; the songs consequently
became immensely popular on both sides of the Tweed. The
first volume appeared in 1723 and the second in 1726, the third
following a year later. However, it took Ramsay ten years to
get the fourth and final volume into print. The numerous re-
prints (fifteen during his lifetime and about thirty by the turn
of the century) amply justify Friedman's remark that "*The Tea-
Table Miscellany* was perhaps the most widely read book of
poetry in the eighteenth century."[14]

A number of questions concern us: Where did Ramsay obtain his text of "Johnny Faa, the Gypsy Laddie"—from a
broadside copy, from other songbooks, or, indeed, from an oral
source? What, if anything, did he change while editing the ballad? Is there any indication that the name of the lady was more
definite than "wanton lady"? Or can the authorship of the ballad even be ascribed to him or one of his friends? These questions need to be considered in order to form an opinion about
the historicity of the ballad.

It is of some significance that the earliest known version of
"The Gypsy Laddie" in *The Tea-Table Miscellany* can now be

13. Allan Ramsay, *The Tea-Table Miscellany: or, a Collection of Choice
Songs Scots and English. In Four Volumes. The Tenth Edition* . . . Printed
for A. Millar . . . And sold by him, and by J. Hodges . . . (1740), pp. 427–
428. The earlier edition of vol. 4 (Edinburgh, 1737) exists in a unique copy
in the Henry E. Huntington Library.

14. Albert B. Friedman, *The Ballad Revival: Studies in the Influence of
Popular on Sophisticated Poetry* (Chicago: University of Chicago Press), p.
144, n. 63.

dated 1737. Because the 1740 edition did not mention Ramsay as publisher or even as bookseller, his role as an editor of the fourth volume has been doubted.[15] This doubt was strengthened by several of Ramsay's letters that show he retired from active business in 1740. Since the recovery of the 1737 edition, however, there can be no doubt, for Ramsay is listed there as publisher and bookseller of the fourth volume.

Even if we can assume that Ramsay was the general editor of the fourth volume, his exact responsibility for the ballad remains problematic. Some have gone further than arguing that Ramsay edited "The Gypsy Laddie" to claim that he wrote the song himself or used the composition of a friend. Davidson Cook, for example, refers to a manuscript which was written by the "unknown" poet "Patrick Chamers of the ancient Aberdeenshire family of Balnacraig" in 1719. It contains a long poem which—according to Cook—recounts the story of "The Gypsy Laddie":

> The Earle of Duglass Daughter Bessy by name
> A Lady of Honour and great Fame
> Was bewitched by magick art as I heard say
> And by one Francy Fa an Egyptian stoln away
> From her fathers Castle and defiled.[16]

These lines, he continues, establish the true identity of the hero and the heroine. "It is not unlikely that Allan Ramsay may have derived some of his knowledge, if not the *Tea-Table Miscellany* version, of the ballad from his fellow poet" (p. 106). Although Cook tries to prove the historicity of the ballad by recourse to the peerage of the Douglas family, he fails to provide any firm evidence. Furthermore, there are no convincing echoes from Chamers's poem in Ramsay's text, so there is little that reasonably supports a connection between these two texts.

---

15. Oliphant Smeaton, *Allan Ramsay* (Edinburgh: Anderson and Ferrier, 1896; rpt., New York: AMS Press, 1979), p. 79; see also Burns Martin, *Allan Ramsay* (Cambridge, Mass.: Harvard University Press, 1931; rpt. Westport, Conn.: Greenwood, 1973), p. 99.

16. Davidson Cook, "The Gypsy Laddie and the Fair Lady of the Ballad," *Journal of the Gypsy Lore Society*, 3rd ser., 15 (1936): 102.

Neither the text and style of "The Gypsy Laddie" in *The Tea-Table Miscellany* nor what we know of Ramsay's mental and economic situation in 1737 suggest that the editor was also the author. In fact, Ramsay's poetry shows a significant decline in quantity and quality during the 1730s. Ramsay himself must have been aware of this, since he writes in a letter of May 10, 1736, to John Smibert (1688–1751) in colonial Boston: "These six or seven years past I have not wrote a line of poetry; I e'en gave o'er in good time, before the coolness of fancy that attends advanced years should make me risk the reputation I had acquired."[17] But even if Ramsay felt the "coolness of fancy" after 1730, he was still a clever businessman. To compensate for the losses incurred by his playhouse, he urgently needed a successful publication. As the three volumes of *The Tea-Table Miscellany* had proved such an enormous success, why should he not offer a fourth? The fourth volume is edited in general accord with its predecessors. Among many songs of English and Scottish origin, the fourth volume contains a number of "classical" ballads and a selection of songs from John Gay's *Beggar's Opera*. Many of the songs Ramsay chose seem to have been well known at the time; in fact, their popularity appears to have been the criterion for including them.

Although Ramsay gives only the words, the popularity of some of his songs evidently rested on the tune. The ballad "Johnny Faa, the Gypsy Laddie" can definitely be counted among those with a very popular tune. It appears in contemporary collections such as Barsanti's *Old Scots Tunes* and McGibbon's *Collection of Scots Tunes*.[18] William McGibbon and Francesco Barsanti belonged to a small group of composers in Edinburgh who wanted to develop a new musical style, known as the "Scots drawing-room style," by refining old

17. *The Works of Allan Ramsay,* ed. Alexander M. Kinghorn and Alexander Law (Edinburgh: Blackwood, 1970), vol. 4, p. 206.

18. Francesco Barsanti, *A Collection of Old Scots Tunes, with the Bass for Violincello or Harpsichord* (Edinburgh: Baillie, 1742); William McGibbon, *A Collection of Scots Tunes: for the Violin or German Flute, and a Bass for the Violincello or Harpsichord* . . . (London: Preston, 1742–1745).

Scottish melodies with European harmonies: "'Refinement' would be achieved by mixing the Scots tunes with elements of Italian music, just as Ramsay's *Tea-Table Miscellany* was mixing traditional Scots lyrics with elements of London fashionable verse."[19]

The old Scottish tunes these composers wanted to refine for the drawing room were most probably derived from an oral tradition. This seems to have been the case with the tune "Johnny Faa." McGibbon's version of this air, for example, resembles "Ladie Cassilles' Lilt" from the Skene Manuscript (1630–1640); this is indeed remarkable, since the Skene Manuscript could not have been known to the composers of the Scots drawing-room style nor later to Robert Burns who set Ramsay's version of the ballad to an almost identical tune.[20] Only an oral source can account for the similarities between the tune from the Skene Manuscript and the tunes given by Barsanti, McGibbon, Burns, and others in the eighteenth century. Therefore, we may reasonably assume that "The Gypsy Laddie" was in oral circulation for some time before its appearance in *The Tea-Table Miscellany*. Yet is highly improbable that Ramsay himself collected the text of the ballad "Johnny Faa" from oral tradition, since it is well known that he had no antiquarian interests. Nor was he part of the Scottish folk tradition, although he must have had at least some knowledge of it.

Since one of the other classical ballads in the fourth volume of *The Tea-Table Miscellany*, "Bonny Barbara Allan" (Child 84), is known to have been printed as a broadside in the seventeenth century, "The Gypsy Laddie" might also have been available to Ramsay in a broadside copy. And one text of this ballad (G) does appear to have circulated as a broadside by 1720 if not earlier. The British Library tentatively dates a broadside version of the ballad in the Roxburghe Collection as

---

19. David Johnson, *Scottish Fiddle Music in the Eighteenth Century: A Musical Collection and Historical Study* (Edinburgh: John Donald, 1984), p. 35.

20. See Francis Collinson, *The Traditional and National Music of Scotland* (London: Routledge & Kegan Paul, 1966), p. 123.

"Newcastle-upon-Tyne 1720" (III, 685). Since this broadside (a white-letter slip ballad) has neither a woodcut nor the name of a printer, its date is necessarily uncertain. Yet it can hardly be doubted that it is older than Ramsay's.

The text from *The Tea-Table Miscellany* (A) and the English broadside (G) are similar in story, structure, and motif. But they have different dialogue scenes: the first concentrates on the dialogue between the lady and Johnny Faa, while the second devotes more stanzas to the conflict between husband and wife at the end of the story so that the hanging scene does not follow immediately upon the saddle-formula. "It is extremely likely that this version [A] has lost several stanzas," Child notes (*ESPB*, IV, p. 62); and the English broadside indeed supports his argument.

Ramsay's variant bears too many resemblances to the Roxburghe broadside for it to be argued that they belong to independent versions, yet they differ too greatly for one to be derived from the other. The English broadside undoubtedly goes back to a Scottish oral tradition, since it contains many instances of misunderstood Scottish words. The most striking blunder is probably the rendering of what should be "They coost the Glamer o'er her" as "They called their grandmother over" (G).

The similarities and differences between these two texts can be accounted for if we assume an oral source for both. Each has taken up different elements and stanzas from an oral Scottish tradition. The reason for this might have simply been the limited format of a slip ballad: it could not take up more than forty to forty-eight lines, or ten to twelve stanzas of four lines each. This, however, accounts only for the Roxburghe broadside since *The Tea-Table Miscellany* had no format limitations. A likely explanation for the truncation of Ramsay's text (by comparison to the putative oral source) is that it made its way from an oral tradition in Scotland to a broadside copy and from there into *The Tea-Table Miscellany*.

Since we have no broadside copy of this ballad which might have furnished Ramsay with his text, it is difficult to say how much in the text we owe to Ramsay's editorial practice and how much to his broadside source. It is well known that

Ramsay felt no compunction about altering or even rewriting
an old song; this may well have led him to disfigure many of
them. This, of course, we find regrettable today; at the same
time, it cannot be denied that his song collections reflect the
mood of his time. As a commercial publisher, why should he
not, in the interest of broader dissemination and in hope of
greater profit, alter an old song? Ramsay adjusted what he offered to the taste of his female audience by selecting already
popular songs and by guaranteeing their moral quality.[21] Yet
the text he gives of "The Gypsy Laddie" in *The Tea-Table Miscellany* does not seem to have been subjected to much alteration, since it does not at all points accord with his own textual
and moral standards.

It is, however, rather odd to encounter the name Cassillis
mentioned by Burns and also as the title of an early tune
("Lady Cassillis Lilt") to which Ramsay's text was undoubtedly sung, and *not* to find it in Ramsay's version of the ballad.
Did Ramsay simply substitute "a wanton lady" for "Cassillis
lady"? The English broadside from about 1720 suggests as
much, for here a similar name, "The Earl of Castle's lady,"
occurs several times. If a Scottish oral tradition lies behind this
broadside ballad, the derivation of the awkward "Earl of
Castle's lady" may be explained as an acoustical error: because the Scottish pronunciation of "Cassillis" can hardly be
distinguished from the English pronunciation of "Castle's," it
is very likely that "Cassillis" was anglicized by some southern
printer. When even the English broadside gives the name of
the lady as Cassillis/Castle's, why would the Scottish publisher
Ramsay not follow suit? True, the name might have been missing in the broadside version he used, yet it seems more likely
that he replaced the name "Cassillis." He had ample reason to
refrain from associating this family with any shameful elopement with a tinker or Gypsy. First, he had dedicated an earlier

21. "In my Compositions and Collections, I have kept out all Smut and
Ribaldry, that the modest Voice and Ear of the fair Singer might meet with
no Affront; the chief Bent of all my Studies being, to gain their good Graces:
And it shall always be my Care, to ward off these Frowns that would prove
mortal to my Muse" (Ramsay, *Works,* vol. 4, pp. 239–240).

work, *The Gentle Shepherd,* to Susanna Countess of Eglintoun, who was of the House of Culzean and would have been
a direct descendant of Lady Cassillis. Second, "The R.H. Earl
of Cassils" is mentioned in Ramsay's lists as a subscriber to
his works (*Works,* vol. 2, p. xvi). As a good businessman, he
would not be interested in losing subscribers, particularly if
they had money or influence. Third, Ramsay was aiming at a
widely dispersed audience, and his English and Irish readers
might have misunderstood, or even been irritated by, the name
of this Scottish earl. Both Cassillis and Faa were well-known
names in the South of Scotland when the ballad was first
printed in the early eighteenth century. Their removal, therefore, would have generalized the appeal of the text.

Gypsies, or Romany, are generally supposed not to have entered England and Scotland much earlier than 1500. This date
must serve as a *terminus post quem* and the first recordings of
the ballad as a *terminus ad quem.* Thus, our investigation must
be limited to the sixteenth and seventeenth centuries. Child
finds the name "Johnny Faa" on record in 1540, 1541, 1611,
1615, 1616, and 1624; yet it is not clear from his account that
these are references to only four different persons.[22]

The first person Child mentions by the name of Johnny Faa
is probably the most famous. In 1540 a Rom or tinker called
Johnne Faw was recognized by James V of Scotland as "lord
and erle of Litill Egipt" and the local authorities are instructed
"to assist him [Faa] in executioune of justice vpoun his cumpany and folkis, conforme to the lawis of EGIPT, and in punis-
sing of all thaim that rebellis aganis him." Furthermore the
King allowed none of his subjects to "molest, vex, inquiet, or
trouble the said JOHNNE FAW and his cumpany in doing of thair
lefull besynes" (Pitcairn, vol. 3, app. 592–593). Whatever King
James's reasons for recognizing Johnny Faa as the Earl of
Little Egypt and granting him these remarkable privileges—

22. *ESPB* IV, pp. 63–64, citing Robert Pitcairn, *Ancient Criminal Trials
in Scotland: Compiled from the Original Records and Mss., with Historical
Illustrations,* 3 vols. (Edinburgh: Bannatyne, 1833). See also *The Register
of the Privy Council of Scotland,* ed. David Masson, 14 vols. (Edinburgh:
General Register House, 1877–1898). Subsequent references to the *Register*
in the text give only volume and page number.

whether this was truly a gesture of favor or whether James wanted to manipulate the Earl of Little Egypt in order to gather the whole tribe and for "furing of thame furth of oure realme to the partis bezond sey" (as the letter says)—it enabled Johnny Faa and his company to prolong their stay in Scotland.

It is not surprising that a number of tinkers claimed to be "Johnny Faa"; the name became very popular as the news of the royal privileges spread. In 1540 a traveler in trouble with the sheriffs in Aberdeen laid claim to the privileges of the Lord and Earl of Little Egypt, and instead of being sentenced to death this Johnny Faa and his brother George (who was really the captain of the tribe) were merely banished from the city.[23] A few months later a man called "Johannis Wanne" appealed to the Privy Council to be recognized as son and heir of "Johannis Fall." Although he was successful, the original privileges were withdrawn by an Act of the Lords of Council in June 1541 and "Jhone Faw" (not Wanne) and his company were ordered under pain of death to leave Scotland within thirty days (Pitcairn, vol. 3, app. 594). The Johnny Faa from Aberdeen must have obeyed this injunction, for in 1549 Johnny Faa's brother George and his friends were arrested in England on the grounds that "they had counterfeited the King's Majesty's great seal."[24]

A number of laws discriminating against Gypsies were issued in the second half of the sixteenth century, but it was not until 1609 that full-scale anti-Romany legislation was launched. By an Act of Parliament in that year all travelers were expelled from Scotland under pain of death. Moses Faw appealed in 1609 to the Privy Council and claimed an exemption from this act (8: 372). Because he produced "surety in relief," he was allowed to stay in Scotland. Only two years later, however, the judges and magistrates of Selkirkshire were accused by the Privy Councillors of neglecting their duty and of pretending

23. *Extracts from the Council Register of the Burgh of Aberdeen, 1398–1570* (Aberdeen: Spalding Club, 1844), pp. 168–169.

24. Edmund Lodge, *Illustrations of British History, Biography, and Manners*, 2nd rev. ed. (London: Chidley, 1838), vol. 1, p. 165.

"want of warrant in excuse for not apprehending" Moyses Fa, Dauid Fa, Robert Fa, and Johnne, alias Willie Fa. The local authorities were ordered to bring these men to trial without further delay in Edinburgh, where they were sentenced to be hanged on July 31, 1611. It is of considerable interest to us that one of those Privy Councillors responsible for the death of the Faas was the fifth Earl of Cassillis (9: 171, 205).

Many Faas were hanged under the Act of Parliament of 1609: Captain Harie Faa was hanged with his family and friends on September 27, 1611, for remaining in Scotland and for "abusing the simple ones with telling of dreames and fortounis, and utheris foleyis nawyws sufferable in a Christeane commounwele" (11: 256). The same fate was suffered by Johnny Faa *père et fils* in Scalloway, Shetland, on August 22, 1612.[25] It was a crime not only to be a traveler or to be known as one, but also to give them support. Despite this regulation, "gritc nomberis of his Majesties subjectis, of whome some outwardlie pretendis to be famous and unspotted gentilmen, hes gevin and gevis oppin and avowed protectioun, ressett, supplie, and mantenance upoun thair ground and landis to the saidis vagaboundis" (10: 656). First to be accused of protecting Johnny Faa, in January 1615, was a certain William Auchterlony of Cairny; there followed, in July 1616, the Sheriff of Forfar. This was the Johnny Faa whom Child mentions twice. He was condemned to be hanged on July 24, 1616. What is remarkable about this case is that the death sentence was not carried out immediately, which would have been the usual procedure. Instead, we hear of him and his friends again in a Privy Council Minute of August 28, 1616, announcing a stay of execution: "*The Counsell,* according to HIS MA[TIES] direction, hes gevin Warrand for staying the pronouncing of Dome, till HIS MA[TIES] farder pleasure be knawin" (*Denmylne MSS,* quoted in Pitcairn, vol. 3, p. 397). The royal pardon extended to Johnny Faa and his friends and family was eventually issued on November 12 under the condition of perpetual banishment (10:

---

25. David MacRitchie, *Scottish Gypsies under the Stewarts* (Edinburgh: Douglas, 1894), p. 53.

655). Thus, Child's reference to Johnny Faa's death sentence in 1616 is misleading and must be corrected.

Another major blow was struck on January 24, 1624, when the Faas' Captain, Johnne, and seven others were condemned to be hanged; but execution was stayed yet again:

> thay wer in the executionaris handis and at the verie poynt to haif undergone thair punishement, thair come a warrand frome his Majesteis Counsell to the saidis baillies to superseid thair executioun for some dayis and to tak thame bak agane to thair warde; at the presenting of the quhilk warrand thair araise suche a shouting and cryeing amangs the confused multitude who come to be beholdaris of the executioun, and the confusioun and disorder wes so grite amangs thame, that one of the lymmaris, callit Gawin Trotter, wes cunninglie and craftelie convoyed away and the cordis whairwith he wes bundin wer cuttit, and the rest of the lymmaris with verie grite difficultie wer preserved frome the confused multitude, who preast lykewayes to haif cutt thair cordis and to haif sett thame free yf the cair and foirsight of the saidis baillies had not prevented the same (13: 410).

In the end, the majority of the Privy Councillors favored the execution, which was carried out on January 27, 1624 (13: 406–408).[26] Although the wives and children of these outlaws were sentenced on January 29 to be drowned, their lives were eventually spared by the King on March 13 (Pitcairn, vol. 3, pp. 559–562).

These are not the only accounts of the Faas in official Scottish documents: they were hanged, drowned, banished, and later even deported to the new plantations. The instances are far too numerous to mention, and since none of the many Johnny Faas is accused of abducting a lady, the present account may suffice. It is impossible to isolate an individual event or a single Johnny Faa that would prove the historicity of "The Gypsy Laddie" beyond doubt. Travelers bearing the name Faa are recorded all over the British Isles, in the south

26. "It wes thairfoir resolvit in Counsell, as the best expedient to gif a terrour to the whole companyis of thir lawles lymmaris, that examplair punishement sould be inflictit upoun thir that wer in handis and of aige" (13: 415).

of England as well as on the Shetland Islands and in Ireland.[27] The name Faa was especially popular along the English and Scottish border, where it was almost universally applied to travelers: "the non-Gypsy population, recognizing that Faw, or Fall, was one of the most famous names among the Gypsies, had applied it loosely to the whole people."[28] It is hard to establish the identity of the "true" Johnny Faa if all travelers and tinkers could have been called Faa at one time or other.

There can, however, be no doubt about the heroine of "The Gypsy Laddie." Although the ballad gives only the title "Lady Cassillis," the popular tradition is unanimous in identifying her as Lady Jean Hamilton (1607–1642). She married the sixth Earl of Cassillis in 1621 and had four children by him. The "grave and solemn Earl," as he was called, was a member of the Privy Council and Lord Justice General; he is described as "a person of great virtue, and zealously attached to the Presbyterian form of worship."[29]

Yet nothing seems to point to the incident referred to in the ballad. "I finde it so hard to digest the want of a deare friend, suche as my beloved yoke-fellow was," writes Lord Cassillis in a letter immediately after the death of his wife.[30] There is no

27. See MacRitchie, *Scottish Gypsies;* Walter Simson, *A History of the Gipsies* (London: Sampson, Low, Son and Marston, 1865); H. T. Crofton, "Early Annals of the Gypsies in England," *Journal of the Gypsy Lore Society* 1 (1888): 5–24; Eric Otto Winstedt, "Early British Gypsies," ibid., new ser., 7 (1913–14): 5–37; T. Pringle, "Notices Concerning the Scottish Gypsies," *Blackwood's Edinburgh Magazine* 1 (1817): 43–58, 65–66, 154–161, 167, 615–620.

28. MacRitchie, *Scottish Gypsies,* p. 15; see also Stephen Oliver, *Rambles in Northumberland, and on the Scottish Border* (London: Chapman and Hall, 1835), p. 271.

29. James Paterson, *History of the County of Ayr: With a Genealogical Account of the Families of Ayrshire,* 2 vols. (Ayr: Dick and Stevenson, 1847–1852), vol. 2, p. 286. See also Robert Douglas and John Philips Wood, *The Peerage of Scotland: Historical and Genealogical Account of the Nobility of That Kingdom from Their Origin to the Present Generation,* 2nd rev. ed., 2 vols. (Edinburgh: Ramsay, 1813).

30. Wodrow Collection of MSS., quoted in Johnson, *The Scots Musical Museum,* vol. 2, pp. 218–219*. His letter of December 14, 1642, to a min-

reason to doubt the earl's affection for his wife, for in another letter on the same subject he also speaks of his "deir bedfellow."[31] There is, however, an incident which deserves mention. The sixth Earl of Cassillis—the very earl whose wife is said to have been abducted by Johnny Faa—appealed to the Privy Council on April 21, 1630, for advice about certain Romany and tinkers he had arrested on his domain. The response was in full accordance with the law of the day: execute them.[32]

Once again we find an Earl of Cassillis responsible for the hanging of Gypsies. The Ayrshire historian Robertson thinks it not unlikely that there is a connection between the hanging and the ballad: "it may have been that [John, sixth Earl of Cassillis's] association with the tradition of Johnny Faa and the Earl of Cassillis's Lady may have arisen from this incident, and from his subsequent dealing with the wanderers."[33] It should not be overlooked, however, that none of the "Egyptians" was charged with any crime, not even with abducting a

---

ister at Edinburgh concludes: "My losse is great, bot to the judgement of us q[a] beheld the comfortible close of her dayes, shee hes made a glorious and happie change, manifesting in her speeches bothe a full submission to the onelie absolute Soveraine, and a sweet sense of his presence in mercie, applying to her selfe manie comfortable passages of God's worde, and closing with those last words, when I asked q[t] she was doing; her answer was, shee was longing to goe home."

31. William Fraser, *Memorials of the Montgomeries Earls of Eglington* (Edinburgh, 1889), vol. 1, pp. 259–260, "John, sixth Earl of Cassillis, to Alexander, sixth Earl of Eglintoun, 15th December 1642."

32. "Supplication by John, Earl of Cassillis, bailie principal of Carrick, and [blank], his bailie depute, as follows:—The latter has apprehended and imprisoned a number of 'vagabound theeves callit Egyptians going athort the countrie,' but as 'they ar not tane with ane fang and none challenges thame for anie crymes,' they crave direction as to their disposal. The Lords ordain them 'to putt the Act of Parliament made aganis thir counterfoote theeves and lymmars callit Egyptians to dew and full executioun aganis so manie of thir persouns as ar men and weomen conforme to the tennour thairof in all points, or ellis to exhibite thame before his Majesteis Justice to underly thair deserved punishment.'" *The Register of the Privy Council of Scotland,* ed. David Masson, 2nd ser. (Edinburgh: General Register House, 1899–1901), vol. 3, p. 533, April 21, 1630.

33. William Robertson, *Ayrshire: Its History and Historic Families* (Kilmarnock: Dunlop and Drennan, 1908), vol. 2, p. 25.

high-born lady; nor were any names given, least of all the one name we are looking for, Johnny Faa.

There are thus at least two instances on record where Earls of Cassillis exert their power over the traveling people. It is tempting to speculate that the narrative has evolved from local accounts of these events. But to put forward a hypothesis concerning the connection between Lady Cassillis and Johnny Faa is to add yet another version to the many possible and even more numerous impossible explanations.

So far, we have discussed only the documentary evidence for the historicity of the ballad. The next step would be to evaluate the legendary material. There can be no doubt that "local legend is potential historical data" despite the "untrustworthy" form it takes.[34] A ballad story that is not well attested in an official document may still be based on an actual event. A singer's personal rendering is, however, more likely to be shaped by popular versions of the story than by any official account of the event; his or her interest cannot be called historical. To seek to determine the historical accuracy of any particular singer's ballad story would seem to be a scholarly misconception. A historical incident may simply have served as a source of inspiration to the singer, as a starting point for telling what is true and what is relevant to the performer about a particular story. Without reference to written accounts, which were scarce, there is nothing to keep a story within certain limits. It takes just a little imagination to cast a local event into a good story and to keep it going. In the process of transmission "how it could have been" will be reinterpreted as "how it was." It is easy to ascribe a certain locality to a ballad story or to give names to the protagonists. It is less easy to disprove such events or identifications.

Even Child could not disprove the relevance of the Cassillis-Faa connection by arguing that "The Gypsy Laddie" is itself the origin of the popular tradition. The names Cassillis and Faa have been associated with the earliest recorded versions of this ballad; the legend is indeed of long standing. There is also suf-

34. Roderick J. Roberts, "Legend and Local History," *New York Folklore Quarterly* 26 (1970): 83.

ficient evidence that the ballad was in oral circulation in Scotland before it was picked up by the broadside press and eventually by Ramsay. The official records dealing with the Johnny Faas in Scotland and with the Cassillis family show that the ballad story is anchored in an actual state of affairs. We still do not know whether the popular tradition associated with the ballad faithfully encompasses a specific local event; such considerations, however, can no longer be thrown out of court. How the Countess of Cassillis came to be associated with Johnny Faa is still a mystery, but the popular tradition has gained measurably in probability and credibility.

WILLIAM B. MCCARTHY

The Americanization of Scottish Ballads: Counterevidence from the Southwest of Scotland

In the years after the publication of *The English and Scottish Popular Ballads* American scholars exulted in the wealth of Child ballads they discovered on this side of the Atlantic, especially in the southern mountains and on the northern coast. Subsequent ballad anthologies and handbooks frequently list distinctive ways these American variants of the classic ballads differ from the Child texts.[1] The list varies from handbook to handbook, critic to critic. But on almost every list pride of place goes to rationalization, or suppression of supernatural

1. See Roger D. Abrahams and George Foss, *Anglo-American Folksong Style* (Englewood Cliffs, N.J.: Prentice-Hall, 1968); Jan Harold Brunvand, *The Study of American Folklore,* 3rd ed. (New York: W. W. Norton, 1986); Tristram Potter Coffin, *The British Traditional Ballad in North America,* rev. ed. with supplement by Roger deV. Renwick (Austin: University of Texas Press, 1977); Albert B. Friedman, *The Penguin Book of Folk Ballads of the English-Speaking World* (1956; rpt., New York: Penguin, 1977); Gordon Hall Gerould, *The Ballad of Tradition* (1932; rpt., New York: Oxford University Press, 1957); Stanley Edgar Hyman, "The Child Ballad in America," *Journal of American Folklore* 70 (1957): 235–239; MacEdward Leach, *The Ballad Book* New York: Harper, 1955). Coffin in the introduction to his "syllabus" includes many of the differences hereinafter cited, but goes far beyond this list to provide a broad discussion of ballad change in general, though with particular reference to the American experience.

97

elements. A second trait frequently cited is compression or "skeletonizing" (Leach's word). Other traits frequently included are changes of tone that make the text more pious, more sentimental, or less impersonal; suppression of sexual details, especially incest; dropping of the trappings of chivalry; forgetting of the ending of the story; moralizing; and deterioration of lyric quality. The lists go on, and in some cases, according to Coffin, the transformations even make a new ballad out of an old.

A particularly negative example of this sort of listmaking was Stanley Edgar Hyman's article in the *Journal of American Folklore* in 1957. In his final paragraph Hyman wrote:

What has happened to the Child ballad in America, in sum, is that it has become inadequate narrative, aborted drama, happy-ending tragedy, corrupt and meaningless verbiage, and bad poetry in general. Some of this may be the effect of transmission in time, which seems to degenerate and deteriorate folk literature wherever we can observe its effects. Some of it, however, is certainly the effect of the American ethos, with its denial of death, its resistance to the tragic experience, its deep repression of sexuality, its overriding pieties, and its frantic emphasis on the rationalistic, the inconsequential, and the optimistic. It almost seems that these ballad texts are bad precisely to the degree that they have become successfully American . . . (p. 239).

D. K. Wilgus was quick to respond to Hyman's catalog of errors of American balladry.[2] He pointed out that the ballads which Hyman accuses Americans of forgetting have also been forgotten in Great Britain, and that the examples of suppression and trivialization which Hyman alleges have their parallels and in some cases their foundations in English and Scottish tradition. Leach, whose *Ballad Book* occasioned the Hyman article, had attributed these phenomena to modernization, not Americanization, pointing out that they occurred in recent British tradition as well as in American tradition. But Wilgus went further, showing that these changes were already apparent in seventeenth-century British broadsides and in classic texts collected by the likes of Kinloch and Scott. Indeed, as

2. D. K. Wilgus, "Shooting Fish in a Barrel: The Child Ballad in America," *Journal of American Folklore* 71 (1958): 161–164.

Wilgus observed, "Riddles Wisely Expounded" (Child 1A), the text that leads off *The English and Scottish Popular Ballads,* already shows compression and loss of narrative, to which might be added suppression of sexuality and of supernatural elements.

Despite Wilgus's hard-hitting rebuttal of Hyman, distinctions between British and American ballad styles based on lists of American traits are still the received doctrine.[3] Perhaps this is because, inaccurate though such distinctions are, they embody a perception which is not inaccurate. The lists seem to be created by comparing twentieth-century American texts to impressionistic memories of texts from Percy or from the Scottish Northeast, texts that are frequently anthologized because of their poetic qualities, the very texts that in all likelihood first attracted those critics (and this critic as well) to balladry. Indeed there is a difference in style between those American ballads, southern mountain ballads in particular, and the much esteemed and much discussed items from Percy and Mrs. Brown of Falkland. But the difference is not exclusively one between British and American traditions, but one found as well within British balladry itself, particularly within the Scottish tradition.

The Child compendium documents two great branches in Scottish balladry of the classical period (late seventeenth to early nineteenth century). The first is the Northeastern tradition, drawn upon by Percy, represented by Mrs. Brown of Falkland, imitated by Scott, still vital in the collection of Gavin Greig, and analyzed by David Buchan in *The Ballad and the Folk.*[4] For many people this is balladry par excellence, the finest that the folk muse has to offer.

The second tradition is that of the Southwest, well represented by the ballads William Motherwell of Paisley collected in Renfrewshire and neighboring counties between 1824 and

3. See, for example, Jan Harold Brunvand's treatment of the ballad in his popular textbook *The Study of American Folklore,* which went into its third edition in 1986. The Hyman article is cited with approval in the not-yet-superseded *Anglo-American Folksong Style* by Abrahams and Foss (p. 25).

4. London: Routledge and Kegan Paul, 1972.

1826. Motherwell's careful fieldwork and subsequent editorial integrity have attracted favorable attention over the years, and approximately ten percent of the texts in Child come from his manuscripts. But what is significant for our purposes is that all of the distinctively American (or modern) traits cited above are to be found firmly entrenched in this Paisley collection from the 1820s. These tendencies, then, were already dominant in the tradition when Scots from the Southwest region immigrated into North America, bringing that tradition with them. A brief look at immigrant patterns in the seventeenth and eighteenth centuries will explain why these ballad traits came to dominate in the American tradition as well.

William Brock and Roger Cunningham are agreed that Southwest Scotland is where the vast majority of early Scottish immigrants to the present United States had their roots.[5] These immigrants were either Lowlanders from Scotland proper, or Ulster Scots (Scotch-Irish) from Northern Ireland.[6] The main ports of debarkation were in the Strathclyde district of the Southwest, and Lowlander immigrants from Scotland proper came largely from that region, though Brock adds that Aberdeen did send out a few "humble emigrants, younger sons of lairds in search of prosperity, tutors, schoolmasters, and episcopal clergy" (not very likely ballad singers). The Scotch-Irish, though coming out from Ireland, also had their roots in Presbyterian Lowland Scotland. They had come to Ireland from all parts of Lowland Scotland, "but especially from the Southwest, from Strathclyde and Galloway."[7] The vast majority of seventeenth- and eighteenth-century Scottish immigrants, then, came from the Southwest either directly or at one remove. The direct immigrants, the Lowland Scots, ended up in Tidewater Virginia and Maryland. The indirect immigrants, the Scotch-Irish, ended up in the Appalachian region. Few

5. William R. Brock, *Scotus Americanus* (Edinburgh: Edinburgh University Press, 1982), pp. 1–3; Roger Cunningham, *Apples on the Flood: The Southern Mountain Experience* (Knoxville: University of Tennessee Press, 1987), pp. 8–9.

6. A third group of Scottish immigrants from this period, the Highlanders, as Gaelic speakers are not pertinent to this discussion.

7. Cunningham, *Apples,* p. 8.

Scots in the seventeenth and eighteenth centuries went any further north in the United States.[8]

These immigrants from the Southwest are the ones who brought Scottish ballads to the southern mountains and adjacent Tidewater region. No one was collecting ballads in America in those formative days. But Motherwell collected at the mother lode very shortly afterward. We can, then, arrive at a fair idea of what this strand of early American balladry was like by examining the Motherwell ballads from the Scottish Southwest. And what we find is that the "distinctly American" traits and tendencies are already evident in these Scottish texts. I will confine myself to three examples from the Motherwell collection. Two, "Young Hunting" (Child 68D) and "The Sweet Trinity" (Child 286Cf), are versions of ballads still extremely popular in the United States, especially in the southern Appalachians, though "Young Hunting" has since died out in Scottish tradition. The third, "Sheath and Knife" (Child 15B and 16F), is a rarer item never collected on this side of the Atlantic. But all three, the two that made it over and the one that did not, exhibit these "modern" or "American" traits.

Some critics have attributed the changes in tradition to lapses of memory. Such an explanation does not seem to apply generally to these three texts. All come from Agnes Lyle of Kilbarchan, a singer who, as I have tried to show elsewhere, was an orally recreative singer, not a simple memorizer.[9] And yet the single biggest change in any of these three texts does seem to be due to forgetting—not words but plot details. Early versions of "Young Hunting" build to an elaborate ending. In the Herd Manuscript, for example, the hero's father suspects that the rejected lover has murdered his son. He sends divers or "duckers" to the river to look for the body. The divers give

---

8. Philadelphia seems to have attracted folk from Edinburgh (Brock, *Scotus,* p. 169). The Highlanders ended up in Georgia and Piedmont North Carolina (and in Canada).

9. William B. McCarthy, "Creativity, Tradition, and History: The Ballads of Agnes Lyle of Kilbarchan," (diss., Indiana University, 1978); *The Ballad Matrix* (Bloomington: Indiana University Press, forthcoming).

up, but a bird tells them to try again by night, floating candles
on the water. Guided by the brightness of the flame, the divers
retrieve the hero's body. When the murderess is confronted
with the corpse its wounds bleed afresh, but she manages to
convince the authorities that her maid, not she, is the guilty
one. When the maid comes to the stake, the fire refuses to be
a party to such an injustice, and does not burn her. But when
the lady herself comes to the stake, the fire consumes her ut-
terly. This long, involved denouement did not survive the
Atlantic crossing. In fact, it is hard to see how such a complex
denouement ever made it into balladry at all, though easy to
see how it disappeared: singers like Agnes Lyle forgot it. In
the case of the Lyle text Motherwell noted in his manuscript,
"The catastrophe wanting, but the lady's treachery was discovered, and she was burned."[10]

The Child E, F, G, and I texts, like the Lyle text, lack the
catastrophe. Of these, only the G text contains any hint that
the story goes on. From these truncated texts it is but a short
step to the quite satisfying American treatment that ends the
story with the murderess confronted not by the corpse but by
the bird (see especially Child F). This new ending gives the
story an unsettling ambiguity. The lady has disposed of the
body, but "a little bird" knows all and can not be cajoled into
a cage. The lady, consequently, will never be able to enjoy an
easy night's sleep. The bird becomes not the transmigrated
soul of the murdered lover, nor an instrument of revenge, but
a projection of the conscience of the murderess. The parrot
characteristic of many American versions seems a typical New
World rationalization of the supernatural, until we realize that
it is also a parrot in the Kinloch and Harris Manuscript versions from Lowland Scotland while in the Lyle text it is a mag-
pie, another bird with a reputation for talkativeness.

"Young Hunting" is a ballad that achieved extraordinary
popularity in the southern mountains, but died out in Scottish
tradition. My second example is from a distinctly Scottish tradition that apparently never crossed to North America. Child

10. Motherwell MS. as quoted in *ESPB* II, p. 155.

15 and 16 form an odd pair of ballads with distinctive motifs.
In "Leesome Brand," a wife in labor sends her husband hunting because it is not proper for him to be present, but warns
him not to shoot the white hind. When he spots a white hind,
it reminds him of his wife, and he returns to find her and the
baby dead. Apparently in older versions he actually shoots the
hind, who is in some way his wife. At the end of the ballad his
mother pities his grief and tells him how he can restore his wife
and child to life. "Sheath and Knife" tells of a girl who becomes pregnant by her brother and dies in childbirth, leaving
him desolate. Agnes Lyle sang for Motherwell a ballad related
to these two. The text of that ballad apparently crossed Child's
desk twice. The copy in the Motherwell manuscript he printed
under number 15, though remarking in the notes that it might
almost as well be put with the following ballad. Years later he
found another copy in a Motherwell letter and, not remembering that he had already printed the piece, assigned it to number
16 in the additions and corrections to Volume V. Though the
Lyle version does seem related to both ballads, it lacks both
the white-hind wife and resurrection motifs of "Leesome
Brand" and the incest motif of "Sheath and Knife."

Read as a variation of either ballad, the Lyle text makes little
sense. But read on its own terms it tells a fairly coherent story:
A couple is living away from the man's parents. There has been
a rift between father and son, and apparently the father does
not know that the son is married. The father gives a great feast
and asks his son to return home. The son's wife, though far
advanced in her pregnancy, insists that they should go; it is an
ideal opportunity for reconciliation. On the journey she goes
into labor. Because it is improper for a man to observe this
woman's mystery, she urges her husband to busy himself with
hunting until her agony is past. When she finally lies still he
comes running, only to find that she has died in childbirth. The
child is stillborn, or perhaps is killed by its father. After bury-
ing child and mother the young man goes on his way to be
reunited with his father. When his father asks why he seems
so sad, he is unable to express his feelings directly. Like the
bereaved heroes of both "Leesome Brand" and "Sheath and

Knife" he resorts to metaphor, calling his son a knife and the mother who bore him in her womb a sheath:

"Oh," said he, "Father, I've lost my knife
I loved as dear almost as my own life.

"But I have lost a far better thing,
I lost the sheath that the knife was in . . .

"A' the ships eer sailed the sea
Neer'll bring such a sheath and knife to me.

"A' the smiths that lives on land
Will neer bring such a sheath and knife to my hand." (Child 15B)

Three textual difficulties present themselves in connection with this interpretation. First of all, stanza 3 reads: "He's tane his lady on his back, / And his auld son in his coat lap." This stanza makes little sense in the present position, especially if the ballad concerns the woman's first pregnancy. But the stanza, as given, is probably a slip of the tongue. I would suggest that the singer habitually sang a more appropriate stanza at this point in the ballad, for instance describing how the hero takes his lady and lays her down on the ground. The preserved stanza 3 would then come after stanza 8, where it makes very good sense. If the two stanzas had similar phrasing, or even identical first lines, it would be easy for the singer to slip up and sing the wrong stanza at this point. Such an error would probably cause her to omit the stanza later.[11]

The second point concerns the word *auld*. In this context it is probably a term of endearment, not an age designation. A similar usage occurs in Agnes Lyle's "Johnie Scot" (Child 99G), where the princess is called the king's "old dochter dear" (st. 2; compare st. 15). Even more to the point is this

---

11. The confused rhyme schemes of stanzas 2 and 4 of Agnes Lyle's "The Baffled Knight" (Child 112E) and of stanzas 15 and 16 of her "Sir Patrick Spens" (Child 58E) suggest that this singer made similar transpositions in these ballads. In these cases, however, the four-line stanza left room for the singer to correct herself with appropriate third and fourth lines even though similarity of phrasing had caused her to begin a stanza out of order.

singer's "Fair Janet" (Child 64B), in which Janet's mother
gives Willie Janet's newborn baby and says:

> "Come take your auld son in your arms,
>   He is both large and lang;
> Come take your auld son in your arms,
>   And for a nourice gang."   (st. 7)

Like the "auld son" in this stanza from "Fair Janet," the boy
in "Sheath and Knife" has just been born.

The third difficulty is with the word *shot* in stanza 8: "It was
nae wonder his heart was sad / When he shot his auld son at
her head." The Child glossary, in connection with Child 81K,
suggests "looked at" as a meaning of *shot*. Accordingly, the
singer may here be saying that the hero looked at his (stillborn)
son. But it is not impossible that she is saying that he himself
killed the infant because it could not survive without its mother
or to accompany its mother in death. The latter interpretation
makes the ballad more poignant and horrific, but does not otherwise affect the overall plot line.

This interesting Scottish text exhibits a quintet of traits usually associated with North American texts. The text is sentimental in some of the stanzas already quoted, and especially
in the following stanza: "It was nae wonder his heart was
sair / When he shooled the moles on her yellow hair." Though
the text seems clearly to belong to the tradition of Child 15–
16, there are no supernatural elements. Likewise, there is no
incest motif. The narrative is extremely compressed or skele-
tal. And a new ballad seems to have been formed from one, or
perhaps two old ones.

Other common so-called American traits occur abundantly
in the Motherwell collection and in the Lyle repertoire in particular. Figures such as Sir Patrick Spens or Lord William lose
their chivalric status and become simply Young Patrick or
Sweet William. The localizations caused Motherwell himself
trouble, as he confesses, when he questioned singers about
them.[12] In length, too, the texts are like American texts; Agnes

12. William Motherwell: *Minstrelsy: Ancient and Modern, with an Historical Introduction and Notes* (Glasgow: John Wylie, 1827), p. xxvii.

Lyle's range from seven stanzas for "The Sweet Trinity" to twenty-five for "Little Musgrave and Lady Barnard." The alleged deterioration of lyric quality is less easy to document (and the judgment may reflect application of inappropriate criteria in the first place); still, one might point out that these are not the texts usually anthologized in poetry collections and translated into foreign languages.

Let me close with one final example, perhaps the most like an American text among the Lyle ballads (Child 286Cf):

> I spied a ship and a ship was she,
>   Sing, Oh, the low and the Lowlands low,
> And she was called the Turkish Galley,
>   She was sailing in the Lowlands, low, low, low,
>   She was sailing in the Lowlands low.
>
> "Master, master, what wud ye gie me
> Gin I wud sink yon Turkish galley?
>   She's sailing," etc.
>
> "I'll gie you gold, I'll gie you fee,
> Gin ye wud sink yon Turkish galley,
>   That is sailing," etc.
>
> He bent his breast, and awa swam he,
> Till he cam to yon Turkish galley,
>   That's sailing, etc.
>
> He had an instrument, made for the use,
> He bored nine holes in her water-sluice,
>   Left her sinking, etc.
>
> Some took their hats, and some took their caps,
> All for to stop her watery leaks.
>   She was sinking, etc.
>
> They took him up by their ship-side,
> They sewed him in an auld cow's hide,
>   Left him sinking, etc.

In general feel this text is much like many American versions of traditional ballads. But beyond that, it exhibits particular features found in southern mountain versions of this ballad but not generally found in later British or Scottish versions. For instance, Bronson's texts with the complex of "an instrument made for the use," nine holes, and hats and caps—a complex found in this early Lowland Scots version—are all from Kentucky, Tennessee, North Carolina, or Arkansas (a state largely settled by emigrants from Appalachia).[13] The Bronson text (no. 103) closest to the Lyle text is from Allie Long Parker of Hog Scald Holler, Arkansas, collected in 1958. The Parker version includes the tool for use, nine holes, and hats and caps, calls the ship the "Turkish Ugarlee" (compare "galley"), and even interjects the "Lowlands low" refrain after the first line in a rather unusual pattern also characteristic of the Lyle version.

Besides resembling Appalachian and Ozark versions of the ballad, but not English and Scottish versions, the Lyle text exhibits certain undesirable qualities frequently associated with American balladry. At seven stanzas the text is skimpy. Furthermore, the story is remembered badly and makes little sense. For instance, the refusal of the captain to take the boy back on board is lost, and the boy's death must be attributed to simple exhaustion. The final transition from the sinking of the enemy ship to the strange shipboard funeral in which the cabin boy is sewn in an old cow's hide is abrupt even by ballad standards.

The dialect and the diction of this text, of course, are not American. Nor do I dispute the linguistic differences, both accidental and substantial, between Southwest Scots and North American ballad texts—though, as Herschel Gower points out, these differences are often more superficial than might at first appear, masking a strong verbal dependence of the American tradition on the Scottish.[14] But linguistic differences aside, this text, like many of the other texts from the Lyle repertoire and the Motherwell collection, has more in common with North American texts than with Northeast Scottish texts.

The Southwest tradition is dominant in the Scotch-Irish–

13. Bertrand H. Bronson, *The Traditional Tunes of the Child Ballads,* 4 vols. (Princeton: Princeton University Press, 1959–1972).

14. Herschel Gower, "The Scottish Element in Traditional Ballads Collected in America," in E. B. Lyle, ed., *Ballad Studies* (London: D. S. Brewer and Rowan and Littlefield, 1976), pp. 117–151. I go beyond Gower, however, in claiming that southern mountain balladry has its principal roots not in Scotland as a whole but in Southwest Scotland in particular.

settled southern mountain region and the Lowland-Scottish–
settled Tidewater region, but not all American versions of
ballads, even of these regions, came there from Southwest
Scotland. The traditions of England and Ireland and even the
Scottish Northeast also made their contributions, as did print
sources. My point is simply that many traits often listed as
distinctive of modern and American texts are in fact found in
the classic period on the other side of the Atlantic, especially
in the Scottish Southwest. This suggests that at least one strain
of American balladry has its principal roots in the region from
which non-Gaelic Scots came to America in the seventeenth
and eighteenth century, namely the Southwest. We have become accustomed to speaking of an English tradition, a Scots
tradition, and an American tradition. It may be that in the future we will speak of an English tradition, a Northeast Scots
tradition, and a Southwest Scots–American tradition.

Indeed, it may be time to step back and reexamine the
whole spectrum of balladry within the English-Scottish-Irish-
American tradition, time to ask again what the separate traditions are and what distinguishes each. A beginning has already
been made in identifying the distinctively Scottish and Irish
repertoires, in describing the narrative technique of Northeast
Scotland, in distinguishing English from other uses of
commonplaces, and in separating northern coast and southern
mountain subtypes of some ballad types. Furthering this enterprise will be especially helpful for those of us interested in
the relevance of post-Parry oral studies to the traditional ballad. The more accurately we can identify and understand these
separate branches of the ballad tradition, the better we will be
able to articulate the place of the ballad within the larger world
of oral culture.

EMILY LYLE

Parity of Ignorance: Child's Judgment on "Sir Colin" and the Scottish Verdict "Not Proven"

Although I have chosen to focus on the judgment that Francis James Child made on a ballad, I have a theoretical point to make about proof which I hope may be found useful in the study of oral traditional material generally. The definition and naming of a cognitive condition—"parity of ignorance"— should enable us to identify, and refute, instances of a recurrent fallacy, just as, for example, we can identify and expose a false premise in a logical argument. My discussion falls into three parts, the first dealing with the Scottish verdict "not proven," the second with the ballad "Sir Colin," and the last with the identification of the fallacy.

Let me begin with a definition given in the *Oxford English Dictionary* at *Prove* B.II.5: "To establish (a thing) as true; to make certain; to demonstrate the truth of by evidence or argument . . . In this sense the Sc. pa. pple. *proven* is often used, esp. in the verdict 'Not proven', which is admitted, besides 'Guilty' and 'Not guilty', in criminal trials in Sc. law." The past participle "proven," from "preve," follows the strong verbs, for example "weave," and, accordingly, the word as used in Scots law is pronounced to rhyme with "woven."

My attention was called forcibly to the idea of "not proven" by two songs in *The Greig-Duncan Folk Song Collection* that

deal with deaths by swallowing arsenic which took place in
Scotland in 1826 and 1827 in rather similar circumstances.[1]
One tells how Mrs. Smith, "the wife o' Denside" near Ar-
broath, "poisoned her maid to keep up her pride" when she
suspected that the maid was with child by her son. The jury
returned a verdict of "not proven," but popular opinion held
that Mrs. Smith was guilty and the song blames what was felt
to be a false verdict on the eloquence of Francis Jeffery, the
counsel for the defense:

> O, Jaffray! oh, Jaffray! ye hinna dune fair;
> Ye've robbit the gallows o' its born heir.
> Had it no been for her gold and grandeur sae free,
> She'd ha'e hung like a troot at the Cross o' Dundee.[2]

In the other case, a young farmer called John Lovie got his
servant maid with child, and arsenic was found in her body
after her sudden death. Again, the song has no doubt concerning the guilt of the accused, but when Lovie was "brought to
the jile" and "the day o' his trial" arrived "the indictment,
though guilty, was provèd by none," and the final verse states:

> The guilt it's nae proven and the verdict it's passed,
> And we'll leave him to Heaven's just judgement at last,
> Although present banishment his wyte canna reach,
> He must stand at the bar o' an impartial judge.[3]

I merely give the songs as instances. For present purposes I
am concerned with the notion of the verdict itself. As has been
remarked in connection with the trials dealt with in these
songs, there are cases "which by their very nature preclude
the possibility of direct proof."[4] Whatever is thought of the
virtue of bringing in a verdict of "not proven" in a court of

1. Patrick Shuldham-Shaw and Emily B. Lyle, eds., *The Greig-Duncan
Folk Song Collection* (Aberdeen: Aberdeen University Press, 1981–),
vol. 2, pp. 56–57.
    2. David Grewar, "Popular Rhymes of Forfarshire," *"Aberdeen Jour-
nal" Notes and Queries* 5 (1912): 148.
    3. Shuldham-Shaw and Lyle, *Folk Song Collection,* vol. 2, p. 57.
    4. William Roughead, *Twelve Scots Trials* (Edinburgh and London: Wil-
liam Green and Sons, 1913), p. 161.

law, the verdict can have some scholarly value as I hope to show. For the purpose of discussion in the context of scholarship, of course, the moral aspect of the matter has to be dropped, allowing "guilt" to relate simply to a deed done, an act or fact—an entity whose existence can be questioned with a positive or negative result.

To turn now to "Sir Colin." Child gives only one text, "Sir Cawline" (Child 61), from an English source, the seventeenth-century Percy Folio. He has an appendix, however, with two Scottish versions, the one I have used for my title, "Sir Colin," which is from the Harris manuscript, and "King Malcolm and Sir Colvin," from Peter Buchan. We do not know Peter Buchan's source, but there is a general consensus now, based on our growing understanding of the song culture of Northeast Scotland, that his texts are basically drawn from tradition. But Child saw red whenever Peter Buchan's texts came up, and his judgment here was probably affected by his having had to rely partly on a Buchan text. However, the Harris version is fully authenticated and could have served as a guarantee. The manuscript known to Child, which includes both the words and music of "Sir Colin," was written specifically for him in 1872 by Amelia Harris, aged fifty-seven, and her sister Jane Harris, who was eight years her junior.[5] An earlier manuscript, written in 1859 and unavailable at the time Child was making his enquiries, also includes a text of "Sir Colin" in Amelia Harris's hand. The Harris sisters had learned "Sir Colin" from their mother, whose maiden name was Grace Dow and who had died in 1845 before either of the manuscripts was prepared.[6] In addition to the tune in the 1872 Harris manuscript, there is a different tune from Northeast Scotland which was published by William Christie in 1881.[7]

Although the ballad was not widely known, there seems every ground for seeing it as embedded in Scottish tradition,

5. Houghton Library MS 25241.17*; Hew Scott, *Fasti Ecclesiae Scoticanae* (Edinburgh: Oliver and Boyd, 1915–1928), vol. 5, p. 397.

6. On the two Harris manuscripts, see Emily B. Lyle, "Child's Scottish Harvest," *Harvard Library Bulletin* 25 (1977): 127.

7. W. Christie, *Traditional Ballad Airs* (Edinburgh: David Douglas, 1876–1881), vol. 2, p. 18.

and Bertrand H. Bronson brought this out strongly in his discussion of it in *The Traditional Tunes of the Child Ballads*. Oddly, Child had not seen it this way. He claimed that the two Scottish versions he printed were "simple rifacimenti" of the ballad in Percy's *Reliques* which had the Percy Folio text as source (*ESPB* II, p. 56). That is, considering the matter graphically, he drew a straight line of descent from the version published by Percy in the eighteenth century to the nineteenth-century Scottish versions. Bronson, in his headnote to "Sir Cawline," showed how improbable this was, and suggested that the two Scottish versions were "descendants of an older and more deeply-rooted tradition" and should be promoted from the appendix.[8]

This was in 1962; ten years later there was the completely unexpected discovery in the Scottish Record Office in Edinburgh of a Scottish version of "Sir Colin" in a dilapidated sixteenth-century manuscript which includes the date 1583 at the end of the ballad. The discovery was made by Marion Stewart, who published the ballad in 1972 in *Scottish Studies,* and again the next year in a separate booklet.[9] The same manuscript also contains a most intriguing item that we would never have anticipated finding—a Scottish composition called "King Orphius" corresponding to the well-known English short romance "Sir Orfeo."[10]

Here in the recently discovered manuscript is a sixteenth-century Scottish form of the ballad which offers proof that the nineteenth-century Scottish versions could have been descendants of a deeply rooted Scottish tradition just as Bronson supposed. By the way, it should be said that, so far as this discussion is concerned, any degree of memorization or of recreation could have been involved in the transmission; I regard it as the

8. Bertrand H. Bronson, ed., *The Traditional Tunes of the Child Ballads* (Princeton, N.J.: Princeton University Press, 1959–1972), vol. 2, p. 37.

9. Marion Stewart, "A Recently-Discovered Manuscript: 'ane taill of Sir colling ye kny¹,'" *Scottish Studies* 16 (1972): 23–39; Marion Stewart and Helena M. Shire, eds., *King Orphius, Sir Colling, The brother's lament, Litel Musgray* (Cambridge: Ninth of May, 1973), pp. 11–17.

10. Stewart and Shire, *King Orphius,* pp. 7–10, and Marion Stewart, "King Orphius," *Scottish Studies* 17 (1973): 1–16.

same ballad when the unusual ballad name of the hero is the same and when it tells or includes a specific story of a knight, a princess, his supernatural adversary, and the adversary's lady. As regards the name of the hero, it may be of some interest to note here that Hamish Henderson has recently suggested relating it to the "Schyr Colyne Cambell" in Barbour's *Bruce* who accompanied Edward Bruce to Ireland, as the hero of the ballad is said to have done.[11]

Child would have reversed his judgment if he had known the Scottish sixteenth-century version, just as he reversed his judgment on the matter of whether the questioner in "Riddles Wisely Expounded" was originally a supernatural figure when he learned of the fifteenth-century dialogue "Inter diabolus et virgo."[12] That is to say that Child would necessarily have yielded ground in the face of the indisputable evidence of a surviving early text. My point here, however, is that it is not sufficient to admit, when an early Scottish form of "Sir Colin" comes to light, that a mistake was made in this single instance. It is necessary to see that the mistake belongs to a class of mistakes resulting from an underlying, insidious error in methodology that needs to be strenuously rebutted.

As events turned out, we know that it would have been wiser of Child to conclude that it was "not proven" whether or not there had been an early Scottish form of "Sir Colin." We are now in a position to say definitely that there was an early Scottish ballad because we have a physical object, a manuscript text. But if that text had been destroyed before we learned of it, it would no less have existed in the sixteenth century. I propose to introduce a technical expression which may make it easier to speak accurately of the hinterland behind datable elements.

11. Hamish Henderson, "The Ballad and Popular Tradition to 1660," in *The History of Scottish Literature*, vol. 1., *Origins to 1660 (Mediaeval and Renaissance)*, ed. R. D. S. Jack (Aberdeen: Aberdeen University Press, 1988). pp. 264–265.

12. *ESPB* I, p. 3, and V, pp. 283–284. See also David Buchan, "The Wit-Combat Ballads," in Carol L. Edwards and Kathleen E. B. Manley, eds., *Narrative Folksong: New Directions; Essays in Appreciation of W. Edson Richmond* (Boulder, Colo.: Westview Press, 1985), p. 393.

If we consider the case of texts of "Sir Colin" as known to Child, the Percy Folio can be marked on a diachronic scale as existing in England in the seventeenth century and two other versions as existing in Scotland in the nineteenth century. As we look back in time beyond the date of the Percy Folio in the mid-seventeenth century, there is an impenetrable barrier to knowledge, a veil through which we cannot see. We just do not know. We do not know positively and we do not know negatively. I have found the expression "parity of ignorance" used by Max Black very helpful in conveying this position and in exposing the fallacy one sometimes finds when it is said or implied that it is somehow safer to say that there is nothing behind the veil than that there is something.[13] As we just do not know, we cannot say either way, and a case for the probability of the existence or nonexistence of an instance prior to the known instance must be built up on other grounds. The lack of known precedent for an item is not evidence in itself for the absence of that item earlier on the diachronic scale. There is nothing safe or objective about taking first known occurrence as directly indicative of first occurrence. Diachronic ordering by first known occurrence can, of course, quite reasonably be used as a convenient method of sorting material into a sequence, but each instance may be erroneous, the cumulative error may be enormous, and scholarly accuracy demands that we constantly keep in mind the tentative nature of the structure.

Awareness of the state of parity of ignorance can be valuable in other contexts also. It should serve, for example, to prevent the hasty assumption that a later traditional form which has some similarity to an early text necessarily derives from that text. The early text that we have could have been the only instance, or it could have been surrounded by other early instances lost to us. When we are in a state of equal ignorance

13. Max Black, *Margins of Precision: Essays in Logic and Language* (Ithaca, N.Y., and London: Cornell University Press, 1970), p. 123, included in a chapter on "Probability" (pp. 91–136) which was reprinted from *The Encyclopedia of Philosophy,* ed. Paul Edwards (New York and London: Macmillan, 1967), vol. 6, pp. 464–479.

about whether or not other early texts existed, a presumption that a known early instance is a more likely source than an unknown one is unjustifiable. As Child argued rather forcefully in a comparable situation in his discussion of "Hind Horn," a case has to be made out for taking one position or the other (*ESPB* I, p. 193). There may well be valid arguments that will tip the balance, but what has to be avoided is the facile but false assumption that it is "safer" to draw a straight line of descent from the only known early instance when we have no certainty as to whether or not other early instances existed. When the state of our knowledge in an area of enquiry can be defined as one of parity of ignorance, we may be well advised to invoke the verdict "not proven."

VÉSTEINN ÓLASON

Literary Backgrounds of the Scandinavian Ballad

Ballads have been recorded from oral tradition up to the present time, and there has never been any doubt that orality is a basic criterion in the definition of this type of song. It is, of course, not always verifiable that ballad manuscripts contain records of ballads as sung or recited; among the poems in early manuscripts that have balladic or balladesque characteristics there are some that have been changed from the way they were sung and others which without doubt are in fact literary imitations of the oral ballad.[1] But while the orality of the majority of ballads is indisputable, scholars have not agreed whether they are composed and transmitted in a way similar to the South Slavic epic poetry collected and analyzed by Parry and Lord and their disciples and defined as oral-formulaic. The controversy about memorization of ballads versus improvisa-

1. The word "balladesque" is used here to refer to certain characteristics of ballad style as defined by Otto Holzapfel in his book *Det balladeske: Fortællemåden i den ældre episke folkevise* (Odense: Odense Universitetsforlag, 1980). The term is further defined in Flemming G. Andersen, Otto Holzapfel, and Thomas Pettit, *The Ballad as Narrative* (Odense: Odense University Press, 1983). See also Flemming G. Andersen, *Commonplace and Creativity: The Role of Formulaic Diction in Anglo-Scottish Traditional Balladry* (Odense: Odense University Press, 1985).

116

tion—or rather composition-in-performance—with the help of formulaic diction had already begun in the early 1960s, and since then important contributions to the debate have been made, although the issue is by no means decided.[2] It seems self-evident, for example, that relatively short stanzaic songs are composed and transmitted in ways quite different from what appears to be the case with long epics in a stichic meter. Nevertheless the oral theory has radically altered our understanding of the differences between written and oral poetry, and it must be taken into account in all studies of the ballad. As a matter of fact one can find definitions of "formulaic" that apply well to traditional ballad style, such as this one by Donald Fry:

> What do we mean by formulaic? I think we mean the typical traditionally expressed. We mean that traditional poets sound like the poets of their past, like their contemporaries, and like their own previous performances. They tell stories familiar to their audiences, organized in narrative and imagistic patterns familiar to their audiences, and expressed in diction familiar to their audiences.[3]

I do not intend to enter directly into the debate about memorization versus improvisation—neither word is actually well chosen to describe the alternatives, and other terms have been used by many of the scholars involved. However, I should like to take a look at the relationship between oral and written literature in Scandinavia with special reference to Norway, the Faroes, and Iceland.

Generalizations about oral as opposed to written literature would be safer and easier if we were always dealing with either a totally oral or a totally literate society, but in most cases the

2. See, for example, James H. Jones, "Commonplace and Memorization in the Oral Tradition of the English and Scottish Popular Ballads," and Albert B. Friedman, "The Formulaic Improvisation Theory of Ballad Tradition—A Counterstatement," *Journal of American Folklore* 74 (1961): 97–112, 113–115; David Buchan, *The Ballad and the Folk* (London: Routledge & Kegan Paul, 1972); Wolfhart Anders, *Balladensänger und mündliche Tradition* (Munich: Fink, 1974).

3. "The Memory of Caedmon," in John Miles Foley, ed., *Oral Traditional Literature: A Festschrift for Albert Bates Lord* (Columbus, Ohio: Slavica Publishers, 1981), pp. 282–293.

oral poetry we have on record is collected in societies with some, or even widespread, literacy. As far as the ballads are concerned, this is certainly the case; the highly literate Mrs. Brown of Falkland—one of the best singers represented in the Child edition—is a good example. It has been suggested that Mrs. Brown partook of two traditions, which she kept apart in her mind: the literate culture and standard English of her day, and a lower-class culture transmitted in the local dialect.[4] A much clearer example of cultural division was found both in the Norwegian countryside and in the Faroes in the last century. The official language, used by church and officials, was Danish, and everything that was written was written in Danish. In their daily lives people spoke dialects so different from Danish that they are best described as different languages. As a matter of fact the creation of New-Norwegian and Faroese as literary languages was carried through by the same wave of national romanticism that inspired ballad collectors in the mid-nineteenth century. In the Faroes it was even the same man: V. U. Hammershaimb, who was the greatest collector and editor of ballads, created a Faroese orthography and gave the language the form it still has in print.

In Iceland the situation was different because Iceland had a literary language of its own with a rich literature from the twelfth century onward and practically no dialects. In the Middle Ages, this was the language of the Norwegians and their descendants in the colonies in the Atlantic: the Orkney Islands, the Shetland Islands, the Faroe Islands, Iceland, and Greenland. Down to the end of the Middle Ages, literature in this language was understood, read, or listened to by people in this whole area. The Faroese have always understood the written language, although the differences between spoken Icelandic and spoken Faroese have increased during the last centuries. The influence of Old Icelandic or Norse literature on later Norwegian and especially Faroese literature appears most clearly in the ballads of these countries. I should like to discuss a few unequivocal examples of ballads that are based on Norse literary works, and the kind of orality they show. Thereafter, I shall discuss the different types of the Scandinavian ballads in

4. Buchan, *The Ballad and the Folk*, pp. 62–73.

more general terms, maintaining that their orality, which is undeniable, is deeply conditioned by reference to a literate culture to such an extent that one is justified in talking about a symbiosis between oral poetry and written literature.

First, a look at my own country, Iceland. Literacy seems to have been more widespread there in the Middle Ages and in the following centuries than in the rest of Scandinavia. From the fourteenth century on many sagas—narrative prose genres composed or written down chiefly beginning in the thirteenth century—were retold in the uniquely Icelandic rhymed metrical form known as *rímur*. *Rímur*, which are clearly to be distinguished from ballads of the international type, were no doubt composed and preserved with the aid of writing, but they have also been memorized, and in previous centuries they were probably often sung or chanted by illiterate people. Essentially they are popular poetry, intended to be sung or chanted for an audience, and this inevitably influences the form. Both in form and diction the *rímur* are much more complicated and difficult to comprehend than ballads, but nevertheless they show clear indications of an anticipation of the performance situation of ballads. Once an audience is familiar with the conventions underlying their ways of expression, it can easily follow the story. Iceland has only a few true ballads based on sagas, probably because *rímur* were considered more appropriate for the subject matter. However, there are three Icelandic ballads that take their matter from existing sagas and even occasionally show in their phrasing direct influence from their sources. These three ballads are quite different in the extent to which they conform to the balladesque way of telling a story. It is tempting to see them as a result of a struggle, by ballad language, in the widest sense, to break the fetters of the written text.

One of these ballads, probably the youngest, composed in the early seventeenth century, "Gunnars kvæði," is based on the well-known, and in Iceland immensely popular, *Njáls saga*.[5] It is composed in ballad couplet meter, but the meter is

5. Vésteinn Ólason, ed., *Sagnadansar* (Reykjavík: Menningarsjóður, 1979), pp. 278–279.

clumsily handled. The poet's, or should I say rhymer's, knowledge of ballad conventions seems to be limited, but an awareness of the basic demands of a ballad plot appears in the choice of topic. Two scenes from the book are chosen, one where the hero slaps his wife in the face because he feels she has dishonored him, and another when she reminds him of this and denies him a favor that could have saved his life when against heavy odds he is fighting his final battle. The two scenes are opposed to each other in a genuine balladesque manner, and the ballad's usual emphasis on the emotional aspect of the action is present. However, the ballad as such is obviously in an embryonic stage. The poem we have has not been received and recreated by a ballad community. There are no repeated phrases or formulaic stanzas and one misses the stylistic grace of a real ballad. Perhaps it was carved out from the saga too late, when the creative force of the ballad community was disappearing; perhaps the presence of this popular and well-known saga, the presence of the fixed text, was too overwhelming and did not allow scope for artistic innovation in the treatment of the material.

Another example is a ballad based on the part of Snorri Sturluson's *Heimskringla* that deals with the most popular and famous of the kings of Norway, Óláfr Haraldsson, Saint Olaf.[6] The ballad, "Ólafs vísur," tells the story of the king's romance with one of the queen's maids, resulting in the birth of a boy who was later to be King Magnús the Good. The names and the main events in the story are taken directly from the saga, but some scenes and details are added that are quite balladesque and also strengthen the composition. The ballad is in quatrains without refrain and it does not contain any commonplace stanzas, but repeated phrases demonstrating the poet's or singer's thrift occur; the ballad meter is expertly handled and the poem sounds like a true ballad, apart from a couple of singer's intrusions in the first person and a final prayer. Certain traits, however, show that the ballad is to some extent still dominated by the written text.[7] Perhaps one could say that

6. Ibid., pp. 298–301.
7. See Vésteinn Ólason, "Saint Olaf in Medieval Icelandic Poetry," in

some of the ideas are not quite the essential, that is to say traditional, ideas conveyed by ballad language. This and a few other features of the text, such as the 'authorial' intrusions, show that although "Ólafs vísur" is a much more successful ballad than "Gunnars kvæði," it does not in all respects live a life of its own as a ballad: the written source looms in the background.

The third example is "Tristrams kvæði," based on the Norse version of the French *roman* by Thomas.[8] The taleroles in this poem fit a typical ballad pattern. The lovers, of course, dominate the scene, while their respective spouses play smaller but important roles. Tristan's wife is here called "Ísodd the Black" (*Ísodd svarta*) while the heroine has the name "Ísodd the Bright" (*Ísodd bjarta*). The dark Ísodd is here a pure villain, in contrast to the saga where her fatal lie causing Tristan's death is seen in connection with the fact that she has been greatly wronged through no fault of her own. King Mark is a shadowy person in the ballad, and he is soon convinced that his wife must go and heal his kinsman. The narrative technique is typically balladesque. Repetition of stanzas with variations in rhyme, the so-called incremental repetition, is frequent. In the oldest variant (late seventeenth century), eight stanzas out of thirty include a variation on the preceding stanza. However, only two add no new information; the other six are partly repetition and partly new information, and are thus truly incremental. The variations are used with taste to dwell on important moments in the narrative and to slow down the action before the climax. One of the later variants (eighteenth century) uses even more variation, with similar effects. The content of this ballad is rather specific, but when occasion arises to treat the material in a conventional way, it is used: in the descriptions of the journey by sea, the landing on the white sand and going ashore, and the formal appearance before queen and king.

Carol L. Edwards and Kathleen E. B. Manley, eds. *Narrative Folksong: New Directions; Essays in Appreciation of W. Edson Richmond* (Boulder, Colo.: Westview Press, 1985), pp. 6–17.
    8. Ólason, *Sagnadansar,* pp. 141–151.

When "Tristrams kvæði" was composed by someone who had either read the saga or heard it read or faithfully retold, what might be called ballad competence must have been alive in the Icelandic community; either the original composer had mastered it, or it was sufficiently alive in the audience to result in the adaptation of the song to ballad norms. The result must in fact be due to both, although the audience, the transmitters, are the more important link. The stylistic differences among these three ballads could be the result of differences in age. "Tristrams kvæði" would be the oldest, composed while the ballad community was still creative; "Ólafs vísur" would have originated somewhat later, when ballad composition was faltering, and "Gunnars kvæði" after it was practically only repetitive and no longer creative or recreative.[9] It is an interesting coincidence, however, that the quality of these poems as ballads stands in an inverse relation to the popularity of the sagas in question among Icelandic audiences: from the number of manuscripts and references in other texts it can be concluded that *Njáls saga* was by far the most popular; *Heimskringla* or *Óláfs saga helga* was less popular, but well known and respected; *Tristrams saga* was the least known, and thus the singers' consciousness of the written text and its authority would have been more limited.

From these ballads, which without doubt are Icelandic and quite close to the sagas in the details of the story, we move eastward to the Faroes and Norway, to find yet another famous hero treated by ballad singers, namely Roland. In the thirteenth century a number of *chansons de geste* of the Charlemagne cycle were translated into Norse, and with some addition of material from other sources these translations were used to form a long saga of Charlemagne and his peers, *Karlamagnús saga*. The text of this saga is preserved in four Icelandic manuscripts and five fragments, one of which is Norwegian and dates from the thirteenth century. This conglomerate saga soon became well known in the other Scandinavian countries, and there still exist an abridged Danish ver-

---

9. See Vésteinn Ólason, *The Traditional Ballads of Iceland* (Reykjavík: Stofnun Árna Magnússonar, 1982), pp. 28–29.

sion and a Swedish translation of two branches, one of them based on the translation of the *Chanson de Roland, Runzivals stríð* (Battle of Roncevaux). The Danish version is known in a manuscript from 1480, and it was printed several times in the sixteenth century.[10]

The popularity of this saga is witnessed by the fact that in Iceland four cycles of *rímur* were based on it, the one about the battle at Roncevaux having been composed in the late sixteenth century. In the Faroes twelve ballads are more or less directly based on *Karlamagnús saga,* sometimes also influenced by the Danish chapbook.[11] The most popular of these ballads is "Runsivals stríð." In the standard edition of the Faroese ballads there are eight variants of this ballad, collected in the late eighteenth and nineteenth centuries.[12] The length varies but the longest is about 150 stanzas. In Norway a ballad from the same matter was recorded twice in the nineteenth century: "Roland og Magnus kongjen." In Denmark and Sweden this matter is represented in a ballad about Holger Danske (Ogier le Danois), which in its original form seems to have been based on the story of Oddgeir danski as told in the saga.[13] This ballad was recorded in the sixteenth and seventeenth centuries, but there is evidence that it was known in Sweden in the fifteenth century. It has been argued that it was originally Norwegian.[14]

I want to take a closer look at the Faroese and Norwegian ballads about Roland. Two of the Faroese variants of "Runsivals stríð" (A and F) begin with a discussion about who should

10. See E. F. Halvorsen, *The Norse Version of the Chanson de Roland:* Bibliotheca Arnamagnæana 19 (Copenhagen: Munksgaard, 1959), pp. 32–38.

11. See Povl Skårup, "Kilderne til de færøske viser om Karl den store," *Fróðskaparrit: Annales societatis scientiarium Færoensis* 15 (1966): 31–69.

12. *Føroya kvæði: Corpus carminum færoensium a Sv. Grundtvig et J. Bloch comparatum,* vol. 5, ed. N. Djurhuus (Copenhagen: Akademisk forlag, 1968), pp. 68–113.

13. See Halvorsen, *The Norse Version,* pp. 49–52.

14. See Sverker Ek, *Norsk kämpavisa i östnordisk tradition: Et försök till tudelning av det nordiska folkvisematerialet,* Göteborgs Högskolas Årsskrift (Göteborg, 1921), pp. 69–83.

be sent to the heathen king; Rólant suggests "Gýðin jall
[earl]"—Gvinelun (Ganelon) in the saga. Gýðin reacts with an-
ger and threats, but goes nevertheless. He then conspires with
the heathen king that this Angelund shall gather three armies
to meet the emperor. There is some confusion, however, because when Gýðin jall comes home, he simply tells Karlamag-
nus that the heathen king is coming to fight him. The emperor
sends his twelve peers, and when they come to Runzival they
realize that they are greatly outnumbered. Rólant at first refuses to blow the horn when Óluvur jall (the form of Oliver's
name varies) encourages him to do so: "God let it not be told
about me at home that I was afraid of the heathens fighting
against us today"—words which are actually quite similar to
his answers in the saga. He fights valiantly, and the first
heathen army is annihilated; but King Angelund sends the second army. Now Rólant does blow the horn, but Gýðin jall con-
vinces the emperor that he is just entertaining his men. However, the French succeed in slaughtering this army too. Now
the heathen king himself comes with the third army, and Rólant
blows his horn again. Here, as in the saga, Óluvur inadvertently wounds Rólant during the fight. In the end all the peers
are killed. Rólant is the one who lives longest and gathers the
bodies in one place. A boy tries to take the horn or the sword
from his hand but does not succeed. When Rólant is dead, Kar-
lamagnus arrives with his army and kills the remaining heathens. The body of the traitor, Gýðin jall, is torn apart by horses.

The Faroese ballad is rich in detail. Many names are mentioned, both of people taking part in the fight on each side, and
of things such as the sword Dýrindal and the horn Óluvant
(name forms that vary among the variants). It is much more
detailed and filled with material than is usual in Scandinavian
ballads, apart from the Faroese ballads about champions. In
the battle descriptions, for instance, Rólant is not the only hero
we hear of; there is a long description of Óluvur's fighting with
one of the heathens. Such shifts of narrative focus are unusual
in the average European ballad and reveal the influence of the
literary source. However, there is much more simplification of
content and more stylization here than in the *rímur*. The battle
is described through strong images of streams of blood flowing

like ocean tides and bodies covering the earth and filling valleys. There is considerable variation among the recordings, in both names and details of the action, but in general the ballad follows the saga faithfully, although the narrative is of course much simpler and the episodes are often only briefly linked. The influence of the balladesque way of telling a story appears in conventional descriptions of blows and other feats in the battle, but above all in the repetitions. Some of the variants from the mid-nineteenth century are considerably longer than the eighteenth-century variant (A), although they include less information from the story itself. The expansion is almost exclusively achieved with incremental repetition and other ways of repeating the same idea with variations in its expression. Scholars studying the Faroese ballads have pointed out that such repetitions are not quite comparable with the formulas of epic, but I think they would agree that this use of repetitions and commonplaces reveals the traditional, oral nature of these ballads, as does the variation among the recordings.[15] It does not necessarily follow that they were composed in performance.

The Norwegian ballad "Roland og Magnus kongjen" exists in two recordings, of twenty-six and twenty-seven stanzas respectively. The variants were collected in Telemark within a period of thirty years in the mid-nineteenth century and are quite close to each other in their wording.[16] This ballad is considerably more simplified than the Faroese one and farther removed from the saga, but the most significant features are nevertheless preserved. The story, which proceeds abruptly and not without confusions, is as follows:

King Magnus divides his men: six of them are to stay at home and take care of his gold, six are to try the cold iron (i.e., weapons) in the land of the heathens. Then it is told, with com-

15. See Wayne O'Neil, "The Oral-Formulaic Structure of the Faroese *kvæði*," *Fróðskaparrit* 18 (1970): 59–68; Patricia Conroy, "Ballad Composition in Faroese Heroic Tradition: The Case of 'Hernilds kvæði,'" *Fróðskaparrit* 27 (1979): 75–101, and "Oral Composition in Faroese Ballads," *Jahrbuch für Volksliedforschung* 25 (1980): 34–50.

16. Ådel Gjøstein Blom and Olav Bø, eds., *Norske balladar i oppskrifter frå 1800–talet* (Oslo: Det norske samlaget, 1973), pp. 213–219, 366–367.

monplace stanzas, that they sail to the heathen land, and that
Magnus is the first to go ashore. Next we find Roland fighting
the heathens far away from the king. When the army has arrived in the heathen country, Roland seems to be asking the
king of the heathens to pay tax; but when he refuses, Roland
says he is going to fight him at Runsarvollen. (This motif, refusal to pay tax or tribute as an occasion for fighting, is well
known from both romances like *Tristan* and Norse sagas, but
it is obviously an addition here, a step in adapting the story to
a fixed pattern.) The fighting starts, and they fight for days; the
heathens fall before Roland's sword like grass before the sickle
or as the snow falls in the mountains, and the sun cannot shine
through the steam rising from human blood. (In the saga there
is darkness at noon, and the sun cannot be seen in France.)
Now there appear so many black men that they cast a shadow
upon the sun, and the peers become afraid and ask Roland to
blow the horn. Roland refuses angrily and fights until his
sword, Dvelgedolgen (enemy of the dwarfs) is broken. The
heathen king tells his men to take the sword from Roland's
hand, but they cannot do it. Now Roland blows the horn so
hard that walls and stones are broken and the sound is carried
across the land; he blows so hard that the sound can be heard
as far as one travels in nine days, and he blows so hard that
the eyes fall out of his head. King Magnus hears this and arrives
on the scene to find Roland dead on the battlefield. There is a
new battle, and again the heathens fall like grass, etc. When Magnus and his men come back home, the queen asks why they are
so sad; and the king tells her that it is no wonder since Roland,
the king's kinsman, and other good men are dead.

Little is left here of the details of the saga, and yet the most
important events of the story are there: the separation of
Roland from the king and the main army, the fighting against
odds, refusal to blow the horn—and the bursting of his head
when he does blow it, although death does not follow at once—
finally, the arrival of the king too late, and his revenge on the
heathens. Only in connection with the blowing of the horn does
the ballad echo the wording of the saga. The saga text goes:

Nú setti Rollant horn á munn sér og lét í rödd sina og blés harðliga,
svo at fimmtán frakkneskar mílur mátti heyra . . . Rollant blæs í

hornið í annað sinn svo ákaflega, að blóð flaut af munni honum og
heili brast út af þunnvanga honum . . . Nú setur Rollant hornið á
munn sér blóðgan hið þriðja sinn . . .

Now Roland put the horn to his mouth and gave it voice and blew so
hard that it could be heard fifteen Frankish miles away . . . Roland
blew the horn a second time so violently that blood streamed from his
mouth and his brain burst out through his temples . . . Now Roland
put the horn to *his bloody mouth* for the third time. . . .[17]

In the Faroese ballad he blows the horn for the first time so
hard that it is heard thirty miles (in the oldest variant, A; the
others have up to one hundred); the second time he blows so
hard that the doors of the castle fly open and the drinks on the
emperor's table are spilled; some variants mention a third time
when Rólant's brain was blown through his skull. But the Norwegian ballad echoes the "bloody mouth" of the saga:

> Han sette luren for *blogga munne*
> han blæso i mæ avle
> de rivna jor å jarerikje
> å ljoi ber av gari.

> Han sette luren for *blogga munne*
> blæs han i mæ vreie
> då rivna jor å marmorstein
> i nie døgrir av leie

> De va Roland kungensfrænden
> han bles sine augor or haus
> so hart hånom hedningann trengde
> at Magnus kungjen de hørde.

He put the horn to his *bloody mouth;* he blew into it with such force
that land and world were riven and the sound carried afar. He put the
horn to his *bloody mouth;* he blew into it with wrath; then land and
marble stone were riven for the distance of a nine-days' journey. It
was Roland, the king's kinsman; he blew his eyes out of his skull—so
hard did the heathen press him—so that King Magnus heard it.[18]

17. *Karlamagnús saga og kappa hans,* ed. Bjarni Vilhjálmsson, vol. 3,
(Reykjavík: Íslendingasagnaútgáfan, 1954), pp. 829–830.
    18. Blom and Bø, *Norske balladar,* pp. 218–219 (Bugge variant, st. 17–
19).

In the Norwegian version it is obvious that the understanding of the story is limited. It has been isolated from its context, simplified to the extent that both the friend Oliver and the traitor Ganelon have disappeared. The king and Roland remain, and the peers as a nameless group of *jevningar* (the same word as in the saga) with a very limited role. The heathens are all nameless. The horn no longer has a name, but Roland's sword retains a name still vaguely reminiscent of Dýrumdal.

The differences between the Faroese ballad and the Norwegian one are so great that it is not justifiable to talk of them as versions of the same ballad. The Norwegian ballad shows signs of a long life in oral tradition, but the two variants are not so different from each other that there is any reason to assume composition-in-performance in the period between the recordings. The Faroese tradition shows many more signs of a free treatment of the material within certain limits, in spite of its proximity to the saga text. The differences between the ballads are typical of the general difference between Faroese and Norwegian ballads with subject matter taken from the sagas: the Faroese ballads are long and detailed with a great many names and minor details of the saga plots preserved, while the Norwegian ballads are much shorter with few characters and a plot which often shows confusion in important details.

One explanation for this difference is no doubt that at the time of the recordings the Faroese tradition was more alive than the Norwegian one and that it was kept alive by its function in the dance, where ballads with heroic subject matter were particularly popular and where it was a matter of great prestige in the community to be a good ballad singer able to entertain in the dance with many and long "heroic ballads."[19] (This term is regularly used for the large group of West Scandinavian, mainly Norwegian and Faroese, ballads with plots concerning heroic battles and fantastic adventures.)[20] How-

19. See Hjalmar Thuren, *Folkesangen paa Færøerne* (Copenhagen: A. F. Høst & søns forlag, 1908), p. 8.
20. See Bengt R. Jonsson, Svale R. Solheim, and Eva Danielsson, eds., *Types of the Scandinavian Medieval Ballad: A Descriptive Catalogue* [hereafter *TSB*] (Oslo: Universitetsforlaget, 1978), p. 17 (Group E) for further definition.

ever, this explanation implies that such *kämpavisor* sung in
Norway, and probably all over Scandinavia, may at one time
have been as long or in any case as detailed as the Faroese
ballads. This is of course not impossible. Quite long and detailed ballads have been recorded in Denmark, some of them
parallel to Faroese ballad versions. However, very long Danish
ballads are sentimental rather than heroic, and it is most likely
that they arose later and were either originally broadside ballads or have been expanded as such. The length of the Faroese
ballads with Norse material can not be accounted for by lost
broadsides as can sometimes be done where Danish ballads are
concerned.

We cannot know how ballads sounded in Scandinavia during
the Middle Ages. It is possible that long ballad-like poems
based on sagas were made in Norway and that these poems
developed into the ballad versions we find in Norway and in
the Faroes, and even elsewhere. On the other hand it is likely
that the general ballad paradigm, or the set of conventions governing the composition of ballads in the Middle Ages, was simpler and more concentrated on emotional conflicts than are the
surviving Faroese heroic ballads. My suggestion is then that
the heroic ballad has from its inception existed in a gray zone
between the literary texts or pre-texts and the informing influence of the oral ballad model. A ballad made on the basis of a
saga must either center on one or two crucial scenes—like the
Icelandic "Gunnars kvæði" and "Tristrams kvæði"—or attempt to present a whole story, like the Faroese "Runsivals
stríð." In the first case the ballad might be short and rely on
knowledge of the source for full understanding. In the second
case we get a long and detailed poem, an oral parallel to the
literary *rímur.*

Both kinds have as precondition some knowledge or consciousness of the literary text, and this is exactly what is lost
in the Norwegian ballad. A ballad which has lost its context,
so to speak, is not necessarily a bad poem. "Roland og Magnus
kongjen" is in a state of dissolution, obviously, but it is easy
to imagine a somewhat older version that would have functioned better as an artistic whole without being any closer to
the Norse saga. The resistance to simplification and to the general ballad model in the Faroes seems to me to be best ex-

plained by the persistence of the knowledge of sagas, of the pre-text, in the Faroes into the time of collection. Manuscripts with Icelandic or Norwegian prose works, such as *Karlamagnús saga,* have no doubt been known in the Faroes, although no Norse manuscript has actually been found there. Many Faroese ballads begin with a commonplace stanza: "Frøðið er komið úr Íslandi / skrivað í bók so breiða" (The story has come from Iceland, written in a large book). The Faroese have always been able to understand texts in the Norse language, and soon after printed sagas were available, ballads in the old style were made, based on them.

It is well known that down to the end of the Middle Ages a great number of Norse manuscripts was found in Norway, but the language changed much in the late Middle Ages, and in the sixteenth century Norwegians no longer understood the Old Norse language, with the exception of a few people who had preserved enough knowledge to be able to read old law books. This means that from around 1500 or even earlier the consciousness of a literary text underlying a ballad no longer was strong enough to affect the singers with regard to details. The ballad was now on its own and would gradually be adapted to the mainstream of balladry. However, this development did not take place overnight. The older Danish and Swedish recordings of ballads with saga material often preserve many traits of the champion or heroic mode, and the same applies even to the much younger Norwegian recordings of the same kind of ballad.

These remarks on the literary backgrounds of the Scandinavian heroic ballads will not come as news to scholars in the field. My point is that such ballads seem to thrive in oral tradition with many oral characteristics of style and presentation, although they may be different from the characteristics of long epic poems. The consciousness of the written source of course binds the singers to some extent, but it also gives them strength to resist pressure toward uniformity of themes and details. Loss of contact with the written source cannot be seen to have any positive effect on the creativity of the singers, but simply furthers uniformity and sometimes weakens the plot-structure.

*   *   *

Heroic ballads or *kämpavisor* are not the only Scandinavian ballads with literary antecedents. What first comes to mind are the legendary ballads, ballads about saints, miracles, or visions of the other world.[21] Many such ballads are based directly on lives of saints or apostles or other medieval religious works. For some strange reason, ballad scholars have tended to think that these ballads are a relatively late phenomenon in the history of Scandinavian balladry. Such ideas probably began with Grundtvig and his contemporaries, who thought the ballad genre had its roots as far back as heathen times. Few Scandinavian ballads, however, have a stronger claim to being really medieval than these ballads that are based on literature and ideas of the time before the Reformation when all of Scandinavia was Roman Catholic. Ballads of this kind are generally not found in the ballad books of the sixteenth-century aristocracy in Denmark and Sweden because such poetry could not be regarded as proper for well-educated people to read or hear while the Protestant agitation against everything that had to do with Catholicism was at its height. The common people on the other hand continued to cherish these old songs regardless of the critical attitude of the church.

As an example of a legendary ballad based on written sources one could pick the ballad about St. James, "St. Jakob" (*TSB* B7). The story is as follows: Jakob goes or is sent by Christ to a pagan country. He sails there on a stone. Jakob then goes to the pagan king who says he will believe in Christ if Jakob can bring back to life his drowned son. Jakob reads and sings from a book until the dead young man rises from the sea. The son tells of the happiness in heaven and gives a detailed account of the punishments in hell. The king and his people are christened.

The ballad as a whole cannot be traced back to a single written source and consequently is probably an oral composition, but the details are all found in legends of saints and apostles. It is common in the legends of the apostles that the Lord himself orders the apostle to go to a heathen land as a missionary.

---

21. In *TSB* the legendary ballads are registered under the letter B.

The journey itself is miraculous in one way or another. In the heathen land, the apostle comes into contact with a king or another influential person, and through some kind of miracle this important person is convinced of the power of the new religion. Often these legends include a martyrdom. All the motifs in the ballad are found in Old Norse translations of legends of the apostles and in such popular medieval collections as the *Legenda aurea*.[22] The ballad is closest to the legend of St. James the Elder: after the Ascension of Christ he went to Spain, where he had little success as a missionary and so went back to Judea. There he showed the power of his faith in a competition with a magician, and made a convert of one of his main opponents. After his death by martyrdom, Christians brought his body on board a ship. Immediately they fell asleep, and an angel of God steered them to Galicia (in a Faroese version of the ballad St. Jakob goes to Garsialand). The queen there took the body and laid it on a stone, and the stone yielded like wax and formed a sarcophagus around the body. The motif of resurrection does not occur, though it does appear in the Norse legends about St. Peter.

It is most likely that this ballad and other legendary ballads in Scandinavia are based on oral legends, but ultimately they go back to books, whether it be the Old Norse translations, *Legenda aurea* itself, or other works.[23]

One of the most studied and discussed of the Scandinavian ballads is the Norwegian "Draumkvædet," found in numerous variants, often fragmentary, collected almost exclusively in Telemark in southern Norway in the nineteenth century. It is a visionary poem telling the tale of one Olav Åkneson or Åsteson, who slept through the thirteen days of Christmas and was led through the otherworld and allowed to see both pun-

---

22. The Old Norse legends of the apostles, mainly preserved in Icelandic manuscripts, are published in C. R. Unger, ed., *Postola sögur: Legendariske fortællinger om apostlernes liv, deres kamp for kristendommens udbredelse, samt deres martyrdöd* (Christiania: Bentzen, 1874).

23. The sources of this ballad are studied in Ådel Gjøstein Blom, *Ballader og legender: Fra norsk middelalderdiktning* (Oslo: Universitetsforlaget, 1971), pp. 55–69.

ishment and reward. Scholars have spared no effort to connect the poem with specific medieval visions. Knut Liestøl argued that there must be direct influence from three British visions from the twelfth and thirteenth centuries: the *Visio Tundali*, translated into Norse as *Duggals leizla*, the *Vision of Gundelin*, translated into Old Norse and printed in *Maríu saga*, and the *Vision of Thurkill*, which is not known to have been translated into Norse.[24] The vision motifs found in "Draumkvædet," however, are in most cases also found in many other visions, and scholars have lately been more inclined to think that the ballad is built on a conglomerate of oral tales about visions which ultimately must go back to written texts or be inspired by them.[25]

Neither "St. Jakob" nor "Draumkvædet" show signs of being improvised poetry, but the text has not been fixed or rigidly memorized either.[26] Many of the stanzas of "Draumkvædet" are peculiar and exclusively found in this ballad while others have been recorded as single stanzas, *gamlestev*. A few stanzas are found in Faroese and Norwegian ballads reminiscent of "Draumkvædet," but it seems to have been kept pretty much apart from other ballads in the minds of the singers. There are repeated phrases in the recordings, especially repetitions of stanzas beginning with the same phrases and adding new material in the latter half, but the poem cannot be considered oral-formulaic in any narrow sense. On the other hand, the order of the stanzas has been quite free when the ballad

24. *Duggals leizla,* ed. Peter Cahill (Reykjavík: Stofnun Árna Magnússonar, 1984); *Maríu saga: Legender om jomfru Maria og hendes jertegn,* ed. C. R. Unger (Christiania: Brögger & Christie, [1868–]71). See Knut Liestøl, *Draumkvæde: A Norwegian Visionary Poem from the Middle Ages* (Oslo: Aschehoug, 1946).

25. See, for instance, Blom, *Ballader og legender;* Brynjulf Alver, *Draumkvedet: Folkevise eller lærd kopidikting* (Oslo: Universitetsforlaget, 1971); and Michael Barnes, *Draumkvæde: An Edition and Study* (Oslo: Universitetsforlaget, 1974).

26. See Ådel Gjøstein Blom, *Norsk legendevisemateriale—en muntlig overlevert diktning: Studie over formler og litterær innvirkning* (Oslo: Solum, 1985).

was recorded, and only exceptionally is there a coherent plot
or a logical order to the stanzas.[27]

The distribution of legendary material is a striking example
of how the written word entered into and affected the life of
the illiterate as well as the literate in the Middle Ages. *Legenda,* words that are meant to be read out loud, were one of
the most effective implements of instruction through entertainment. People have always marveled at things rare and astonishing, be it the miracle of St. James sailing on a ship steered
by an angel or a stone being formed into a sarcophagus by
itself—two miracles united in the ballad into a stone serving as
a boat—or the terrible and wonderful visions of Tundal and
other medieval visionaries. Having been read aloud or told to
a congregation, such tales were no doubt spread further
through word of mouth, and the poets or singers of popular
songs found in them good material. The result could be a very
free treatment of the matter at hand, but hardly ever without
consciousness of the existence of written texts about the same
or similar matters.

People in the ballad communities of Norway and the Faroes
no doubt had a strong sense of the authority of the book as
such, or rather of the written text—a sense probably strengthened by the fact that the written word was not in their everyday language but in the language used by the church and the
representatives of king and crown. This is actually testified to
by ballad singers themselves. I have previously mentioned the
Faroese commonplace found at the beginning of a number of
ballads to the effect that the story has come from Iceland written in a large book. This is obviously a statement intended to
increase respect for the story, a way of saying that it is true.
Books and reading appear elsewhere in the ballads. In his competition with the heathen king in the Norwegian ballad, St.
Jakob reads in a book to resurrect the king's son from the
dead—an obvious tribute to the power and authority of the
written word. The same commonplace also appears elsewhere

27. The fullest editions of "Draumkvædet" are Ådel Gjøstein Blom, ed.,
Norske mellomalderballadar, vol. 1, *Legendeviser* (Oslo: Universitetsforlaget, 1982), pp. 110–136; see also pp. 140–144 and Barnes, *Draumkvæde.*

in both Norwegian and Faroese ballads and always has the same significance.

The cases of a literary background I have discussed so far are indisputable, but it must be admitted that neither the heroic ballads nor the legendary ballads are typical Scandinavian ballads. It is natural to ask: What about the central groups, ballads of the supernatural and the ballads of chivalry (groups A and D in *TSB*)—are they not pure oral poetry? I should like to ask in return: Was there any such thing as pure oral poetry in the late Middle Ages, let alone after the Reformation, and down to the time the ballads were collected? Is it not possible that all oral poetry, or in any case all ballads, were in one way or another influenced and conditioned by the existence of written literature on similar themes? My own answer to the last question is yes. Although the stories told in ballads of the supernatural and ballads of chivalry in Scandinavia seldom are based directly on written sources, they refer to the world of knights and ladies delineated in chivalric romances and the Breton *lais,* in German and English literary works derived from or closely related to this poetry, as well as in the Norse translations of such literature. Studies in the origin of the Scandinavian ballad usually end up finding the most likely models for the first Scandinavian ballads among French songs preserved as parts of courtly romances.[28]

The ladies embroidering in their bowers and the knights wooing them, figures which frequent such ballads, are not likely to be modeled on real-life persons: they are literary clichés. And even in the ballads of the supernatural there are obvious parallels to chivalric romances. Herr Olof riding through the greenwood and meeting an elf-maiden could as well be a character in a romance as Liden Kirsten, who sews pictures of hunting scenes on the shirt she is sending to Herr Asbjørn (*TSB* A63 and D16). Of course the ballads have also in many cases been colored by the surroundings where they

28. See, for instance, J. H. C. R. Steenstrup, "De danske Folkevisers ældste Tid og Visernes Herkomst," *Historisk Tidsskrift* (1919), and David Colbert, "The Medieval Origin of the Scandinavian Knightly Ballad" (diss., University of Washington, 1982).

were composed and sung—or one may at least assume this about the ballads preserved among the Danish and Swedish aristocracy—but it is difficult to point to individual traits that could not have their roots in literature as well as in real life.

I have pointed out several instances of individual Scandinavian ballads or even whole groups of ballads whose stories obviously originate in written texts. I have, moreover, suggested that not only these types of ballads, but also major subgenres, such as the ballads of chivalry, refer in the final analysis to a world that is at least partly a literary world, a world defined in written texts. What is the significance of these literary backgrounds?

First of all I want to emphasize that my intention is not to advocate any idea of an absolute primacy of the literary over the oral in the late Middle Ages. As a matter of fact, the literary texts I have pointed out as ballad sources are themselves in most or all cases heavily dependent on oral tales. The case of Charlemagne and Roland, for instance, is quite complicated. The emperor was a historical person, as everyone knows, and there are contemporary written sources about his life, but the story told about him and his peers in the *Chanson de Roland* or in the *Runzivals þáttr* in *Karlamagnús saga* is certainly not history, and it has been argued, although this view is probably still controversial, that the *Chanson de Roland* is a recording based on oral songs.[29] The courtly romances, as is well known, whether *Tristan* or others, drew heavily on oral tales, especially Celtic ones. In legends of apostles and saints it is probably impossible to trace the origin of individual motifs, but no doubt they are often oral.

In a recent book the anthropologist Jack Goody describes, with reference to a vast amount of material, the radical influence on the human mind of literacy and the possibilities of communication it brings about. Both his work and other recent ones, such as Brian Stock's very thorough study of the implications of literacy in eleventh- and twelfth-century culture, should remind students of oral—and of written—literature to

---

29. J. J. Duggan, *The Song of Roland: Formulaic Style and Poetic Craft* (Berkeley: University of California Press, 1973).

ask questions not only of orality *or* literacy, but of stages in the development brought about by the interaction of the two.[30]

The Middle Ages, the period in which the Child ballads or the Grundtvig ballads undeniably have their roots, was characterized by rich literature and in general by a gradual increase in the importance of the written word in several spheres of life. At the same time this was a period when literacy was a privilege of the few.[31] Books were expensive and their production time-consuming. However, this does not mean that the influence of the written word was confined to a narrow group of the learned and wealthy. This was a time when reading out loud was the rule, and books were frequently read to groups of illiterate people. Thus respect for the authority of the written word as well as the content of books was spread among the illiterate majority. Not only the voices of other singers resounded in the mind of the ballad singer, but also the voice of the reader from books, the voice of the written text. Its strength has varied, and it sometimes may have been no more than a scarcely noticeable bass in the background, but it nonetheless changed the total effect. It may be confusing to use the term "intertextuality" in this context, but it may also help us understand the importance of the written word, even for an illiterate ballad singer. At the moment of performance, his or her song activated in the audience chains of references in many directions, references which defined the song and gave it meaning. Somewhere in the web of references behind each ballad is the written word, sometimes close as in the case of the Icelan-

30. Jack Goody, *The Interface between the Written and the Oral* (Cambridge, Eng.: Cambridge University Press, 1987); Brian Stock, *The Implications of Literacy: Written Language and Models of Interpretation in the Eleventh and Twelfth Centuries* (Princeton, N.J.: Princeton University Press, 1983). See also Franz H. Bäuml, "Varieties and Consequences of Medieval Literacy and Illiteracy," *Speculum* 55 (1980): 237–265.

31. Stock says of this: "the evidence, such as it is, suggests that at no point in the subsequent three centuries [after the millennium] was a significant percentage of laymen able to read and to write . . . Down to the age of print and in many regions long afterwards, literacy remained the exception rather than the rule. Despite primary schools, cheap paper, spectacles, and the growing body of legal and administrative material, the masses of both town and countryside as late as the Reformation remained relatively indifferent to writing" (p. 13).

dic or Faroese ballads based on sagas or in some legendary
ballads, sometimes distant as in the case of the Norwegian ballad about Roland or ballads of chivalry with no specifiable literary source.

Looking back upon cultures where oral narrative is known
or assumed to have been thriving before the advent of writing,
one is tempted to see history as divided into two eras, before
and after the Fall, before and after the advent of literacy. Like
all myths or even more than other myths, the myth of life in
Paradise before the Fall has its strong appeal and its own
beauty. It expresses our deep longing for an innocent, creative
past before we were subdued by the reality principle, to put it
in Freudian terms. As a historical interpretation, however, this
myth is usually highly misleading. Our culture cannot be studied, unfortunately, in its preliterate, purely oral past, although
anthropologists have studied other cultures that come close to
this state. It seems evident not only that the advent of literacy
has enhanced the possibilities for the development of society
and culture in many respects which are commonly recognized,
but also that we should seriously consider the possibility that
oral literature has been enriched by its interaction with written
literature. I imagine, although this is something that cannot be
proved or disproved, that the specific cultural values of an era
with limited literacy and much reading out loud, like the Middle Ages in Europe, are based on exactly the dialectic between
the oral and the written.

The examples of Scandinavian ballads that take their material from written texts can by no means be used to argue
against theories about the creative art of singers of tales, nor
against the theory that close dependence on a written model
may thwart the creative ability of a singer. On the contrary, I
feel that there is a tangible state of conflict between oral creativity, in our case the generative force of ballad competence,
and the stabilizing force of the written text. In a society with
limited literacy and strong poetic traditions, the singers of tales
do not have to be losers. The illiterate community eagerly
grabs the delicacies from the rich table of the literate, turns
them to its own advantage, and devises a feast which may be
different but can be gorgeous.

BENGT R. JONSSON

Oral Literature, Written Literature:
The Ballad and Old Norse Genres

If the Scandinavian ballad is to be explained—
not its external technique alone but also its
inner essence—it is necessary to resort to
literature outside the North, especially to
French poetry, for it is clear at first glance that
the Nordic ballad has much more in common
with it, in inner as well as in outer
construction, than with the ancient
Scandinavian mythic and heroic lay.

Hans E. Kinck, 1892

Scholarship in the fields of Scandinavian balladry and Old
Norse literature, respectively, has more or less drifted apart
since the days of Svend Grundtvig and Sophus Bugge. It is true
that in this century scholars like Heusler, Neckel, de Boor, de
Vries, and Hempel have studied ballads, primarily Faroese
Nibelungen ballads, but their results have not been very much
discussed in Scandinavia. More astonishing, however, is the
almost total silence from ballad specialists about the really
important theory concerning Danish ballads set forward by
Wolfgang Mohr in 1938–1940 and since then referred to in a
number of works on eddic poetry.[1] It seems that the opinions
of Mohr have simply been more or less unknown to most peo-

---

1. Wolfgang Mohr, "Entstehungsgeschichte und Heimat der jüngeren
Eddalieder südgermanischen Stoffes," *Zeitschrift für deutsches Altertum*
75 (1938–39): 217–280; "Wortschatz und Motive der jüngeren Eddalieder
mit südgermanischem Stoff," *Zeitschrift für deutsches Altertum* 76 (1939–
40): 149–217.

ple in the ballad field.[2] On the other hand, Mohr himself, like some of his predecessors and followers, seems to be not overly well acquainted with certain results of ballad research proper. These circumstances illustrate the assertion in my opening sentence. I certainly do not imagine that the present sketch—short, selective, and necessarily somewhat superficial—will in itself do much to amend the deplorable situation, nor do I pretend to have bridged the gap in a more substantial way. But I dare to think that some of the ideas put forward in this essay might be of interest not only to my colleagues in the ballad area but also, and perhaps primarily, to students of Old Norse.

The Scandinavian medieval ballad is an unusually well-defined genre (with a restricted number of stanzaic forms and an easily recognizable style), consisting of some 830 types.[3] Borderline cases are strikingly few, and although there are clear subgenres or categories within the genre, I particularly want to stress that we are dealing with what is fundamentally one single genre. In this respect the Scandinavian ballad—like many of the English and Scottish Child ballads—differs from songs labeled as ballads elsewhere, for example, in Germany, where narrative songs appeared in many different forms and do not constitute one special genre.

The ballad is a folksong (*folkvisa*) in the sense that it is an anonymous song, for which the authorized archetype is unknown. What we have is a greater or smaller number of versions or variants, mainly produced in oral tradition. Thus the ballad is only one among many folksong genres.[4] It should be

2. Mohr's papers are not mentioned in Erik Dal, *Nordisk folkevise-forskning siden 1800: Omrids af text- og melodistudiets historie og proble-mer især i Danmark* (Copenhagen: Schultz, 1956), or David Colbert, *The Birth of the Ballad: The Scandinavian Medieval Genre* (Stockholm: Svenskt visarkiv, 1989). An exception is Otto Holzapfel, in "Studien zur Formel-haftigkeit der mittelalterlichen dänischen Volksballade" (diss., Frankfurt am Main, 1969), p. 7, and elsewhere.

3. Bengt R. Jonsson, Svale Solheim, and Eva Danielson, *The Types of the Scandinavian Medieval Ballad* (Oslo and Stockholm: Universitetsfor-laget, 1978); hereafter *TSB*.

4. My terminology, which seems to have become generally accepted in Scandinavia, is presented in my *Svenska balladtradition* I (Stockholm:

observed that this definition has no sociological implications whatsoever.

The ballad is conceived, performed, and transmitted orally. This statement must of course be amplified owing to the fact that ballads were printed in broadsides from, let us say, the middle of the sixteenth century onward in Denmark, and somewhat later in Sweden. In 1591 the Danish historian Anders Sørensen Vedel published his famous collection of 100 songs, almost exclusively ballads. His book was reprinted at least ten times during the following century (once in Norway) before it was augmented with another 100 songs by Peder Syv in 1695 (this edition was issued several times, for the last time in 1787). The Vedel-Syv collection was, accordingly, widely available in Denmark and Norway, Iceland and the Faroe Islands, and not unknown in Sweden either. It furthermore served as a source for the publishers of broadsides.

The broadside texts of the ballads had either an introductory or a normative function—that is, they introduced ballad types into areas where they were hitherto unknown (alternatively, presented ballads which had not appeared in oral tradition at all), or they influenced an already existing tradition of the types in question. The latter is most easily observed in Norway and the Faroes, resulting in a mixed language form between the native language and the Danish of the printed texts, which were often regarded with special awe—printing errors and all—and had besides the obvious advantage of being fixed in written form. This led the early collectors to regard these texts as originally Danish but "destroyed" by the singers; a closer analysis is necessary to decide the truth in each case.

Important as it is to be aware of the influence from printed sources, not least the Danish texts in Norway, we must above all study the ballad as the oral genre it principally is. An interest in variation, and in the use of set phrases and stanzas, appeared in ballad research long before the Parry-Lord wave reached this field (for example, Ernst von der Recke's register

---

Svenskt visarkiv, 1967), p. 3, and in my "Visa och folkvisa," in *Visa och visforskning,* ed. Ann-Mari Häggman (Helsinki: Svenska litteratursällskapet, 1974), pp. 37–41.

from ca. 1890 to 1910 of what he called "parallels"). There is, of course, a fundamental difference between the stichic verse in the Yugoslavian epics and Homer on one hand, and the ballad on the other. In the ballad the unit is the stanza, with its couplet of end rhymes (and tune), and to a lesser extent the single line. But formulaic variations have without any doubt taken place. As an example I shall quote the beginning of two Swedish texts of the same ballad, both collected in the nineteenth century.[5]

B   Det bodde en Herre i Widingestad
           Han fästade sig fru Silfverla.
           —Så ädela mig en skjön jungfru.

           Han fästade henne och förde henne hem
           Med rödan gullkrona och blekblomman kind.

           De voro ej ihop mer än årena sju
           De fingo ej mer än småbarnen tu:

           Förrn döden han kom i Widingestad
           Så tog han bort fru Silfverla.

           Den Herren han gick sig att vandra
           Så fäste han sig den andra.

           Han fästade henne han förde henne hem
           Med rödan gullkronan och rödblomman kind.

Ia   Och konungen red sig söder under ö,
           så fäste han fru Silfva dervid.
           —du ädela min den skönaste.

           Han reste med henne öfver vatten och land,
           tills han kom hem till sitt eget land.

           De lefde tillsammans i årena sju,
           hon födde honom de tre barnen nu.

           Men sedan kom döden uti deras gård
           fru Silfva blef lagd uppå svartan bår.

5. *Sveriges Medeltida Ballader* (Stockholm: Almqvist & Wiksell, 1983–); hereafter *SMB*. Vols. 1 (1983) and 2 (1986) have appeared, while vol. 3 is scheduled for 1990; editors are Bengt R. Jonsson, Sven-Bertil Jansson, and Margareta Jersild. The quotations here are from vol. 1 (nos. 33B and 33Ia, respectively).

Och Konungen reste söder under ö,
så fäste han fru Frödenborg dervid.

Han reste med henne öfver vatten och land,
tills han kom hem i sitt eget land.

B   There dwelt a lord in Widingestad,
He wooed and won Lady Silfverla.
—So noble a beautiful maiden.

He wed her and led her home
With red-gold crown and pale blooming cheeks.

They were not together more than seven years,
They got no more than two babies:

Before Death came into Widingestad
And he took away Lady Silfverla.

The Lord began to wander,
And so he wooed and won another.

He wed her and led her home
With red-gold crown and red blooming cheeks.

Ia   And the king rode south through the isle,
and there he wooed and won Lady Silfva.
—my noble one, you most beautiful.

He traveled with her over sea and land
till he came home to his own land.

They lived together for seven years,
she gave birth to three children.

But then came Death into their yard,
lady Silfva was laid upon a black bier.

And the king traveled south through the isle,
and there he wooed and won Lady
         Frödenborg.

He traveled with her over sea and land
till he came home to his own land.

The refrain and one of the proper names are basically identical.
The story told is the same; it progresses from stanza to stanza
in the same sequence. But not one stanza in B is identical with

the corresponding one in Ia. When the same situation is depicted twice in the story, each text twice uses its special stanza for that description (B, st. 2, 6; Ia, st. 2, 6; compare Ia, st. 1, 5). Different sets of standard stanzas have evidently been used.[6] In a few cases we are able to study this process at work. The foremost Swedish ballad singer we know is Ingierd Gunnarsdotter (1601/02–1686).[7] She was a farmer's widow in Lyrestad, Västergötland, when parts of her repertoire were recorded in the 1670s. She was said to have known more than three hundred ballads. This is doubtless an exaggeration, but forty-seven ballads are actually recorded from her; of these, five are recorded twice, one three times, and one no less than four times. We can accordingly compare how Ingierd performed the same ballad on different occasions. The differences are, as a rule, slight. In the ballad about Thor and his stolen hammer ("Synes wara af Edda Island," "seems to be from the Edda of Iceland," is written over one of these texts), one stanza in one text is substituted by a synonymous one in the other.[8] Trolletram (þrymr) speaks:

> Tårkars hammer haar Jagh tagit,
> Jagh dölljern icke et tahl
> Fembtan Fambner och fyratijo
> ligger han vthj graaff
> —Thorer tämmier Fåhlan sin i tömme.

> Torkars hammar haar Jag tagit
> Jagh döljer honom eij et ord
> Femtan fambnar och fyratijo
> ligger han vnder Jord.
> —Thorir tämjer Fåhlan sin i tömme.

---

6. We can see that some of the standard stanzas for set situations and descriptions are frequent in certain regions, while others are preferred in the traditions of other areas. Differences among the Nordic countries, partly explainable by the linguistic differences, are numerous.

7. See Jonsson, *Svensk balladtradition* I, pp. 272–281.

8. *1500- och 1600-talens visböcker,* VIII: K. Bibliotekets visbok i 4:0, ed. Adolf Noreen and J. A. Lundell (Uppsala: Svenska litteratursällskapet, 1913–1915), pp. 351, 392.

Old Thor's hammer I have taken,
I do not hide (from him) a word
    (speech).
Fifteen fathoms and forty
does it lie buried (under earth).
Refrain: Thorir tames his horse to the
    reins.

Ingierd's ballads were recorded for patriotic historical-antiquarian reasons with the support of the highest authorities in Sweden; she had the reputation of knowing a song about the battle of Lena (in 1208, when "the Danes" were defeated). Otherwise her repertoire might not have been recorded. Why, indeed, should oral poetry be written down at all?

This is a well-known question (also concerning "Edda Island") that I do not need to discuss in general terms here. What is astonishing is that one sometimes must emphasize that *the natural state for oral poetry is to remain oral* and also stress the fact that such poetry is rarely written down without a real incitement and—what scholars have tended to ignore—a proper vehicle, that is, a suitable form of written language.[9] Norway and the Faroes were radically different from Denmark, Iceland, and Sweden in both these respects in the sixteenth, seventeenth, and eighteenth centuries in so far as the official language there was not the indigenous spoken language; Norwegian as a written language had already deteriorated by the second half of the fourteenth century. The officials, civil servants, and clergy were to a great extent born or educated in Denmark. Whereas translations of the Bible were printed soon after the Reformation in Sweden, Denmark, and Iceland, such was not the case in Norway and the Faroes, where the Danish Bible was instead made obligatory, certainly a most decisive circumstance. Danish political and cultural imperialism rendered written recording of oral poetry in Norway and the Faroes very difficult.[10] This must always be taken into

9. The great and fascinating change from an aural to a visual conception of language and poetry cannot be commented upon in this paper. The notation of music—including ballad tunes—presents parallel problems.

10. A few efforts were made to overcome these difficulties, most remark-

consideration when one speaks of the lack of early ballad recordings in these countries.

As a matter of fact, the shaping of the national written languages in Norway and especially in the Faroes around the middle of the nineteenth century was strongly connected with the collecting of ballads in these countries. It should be added that the situation in the Faroes, where the linguistic differences from Danish were more important, was not wholly the same as in Norway.[11] The few Norwegian ballads recorded before the 1840s exemplify, all of them, this dilemma of language.[12] An open question is whether the oldest true ballad text in Danish, "Ridderen i Hjorteham" (DgF 67A, there printed in a particularly pompous typography by Grundtvig) is such an example. At the same time it is an illustrative example of prejudice in scholarship. Let us have a look at it.

A man named Mattis Nielsson in "Byörnetweth" gave to the parish church of Solum, Telemark, a *postilla* in Swedish but copied in Norway as is shown by a great number of Norwegianisms. The MS may be dated ca. 1480–1490.[13] On the page where the information about the donation is inserted (in Latin), Mattis has himself written his name ("Jek Mattis") and there is also the ballad text, in all probability in his own handwriting. Svend Grundtvig regarded the text as Danish, and, convinced of Danish hegemony where ballads are concerned, H. Grüner Nielsen (DgF X:1, 1933, p. 76) rather naively suggested that "Byörnetweth" was identical with a certain "Bjer-

---

ably J. C. Svabo's recording of Færoese ballads in the 1780s by using a kind of phonetic writing.

11. V. U. Hammershaimb was, as is well known, the one to grasp the full consequences of this dilemma.

12. These texts are listed in Ådel Gjøstein Blom, *Norske mellomalderballadar* 1 (Oslo: Universitetsforlaget, 1982), pp. 179–186; hereafter *NMB*. Some of them are printed in Ådel Gjøstein Blom and Olav Bø, eds., *Norske balladar i oppskrifter frå 1800–talet* (Oslo: Samlaget, 1973); one is treated in Brynjulf Alver, "Friarferda til Gjøtland," *Tradisjon* 11 (1981): 61–78.

13. Bertil Ejder, ed., *Svenska medeltidspostillor*, 6–7 (Uppsala: Almqvist & Wiksell, 1974), pp. 8–9. Ejder seems completely unaware of his role as an editor of this famous ballad text. The best edition is by Lindegård Hjorth; see note 15.

nedegaard" in the Danish Zealand. But there is a farm Björn-tvet in the parish of Solum, and a Mattis Nielsson is mentioned in official sources as *lagrettisman* (lawman) in this very district (Skien) 1481–1516, clearly a man in the position to act as a donor to the local church. The name of his predecessor as *lagrettisman* was Nyklis (Niels) Mattisson (who served 1446–1481); evidently Mattis inherited the office from his father and was born in the area.

The Danish lexicographer Kaj Bom pointed out a number of possible Norwegianisms in the ballad text in a paper with the startling title "Danmarks norske folkeviser" (Denmark's Norwegian ballads).[14] The majority of Bom's conclusions were refuted by Poul Lindegård Hjorth, who nevertheless made some concessions to Bom's main idea.[15] After a perfectly thorough examination of the MS and a close analysis of the ballad text, Lindegård Hjorth concludes that the language form of the ballad "as a whole" is Danish but also that a few details are "possibly not Danish."[16] Used to working primarily with literary texts, neither Bom nor Lindegård Hjorth discusses what I regard as the central problem: how to fix a piece of oral poetry in script, given the linguistic conditions of the place and the time. To me, the text (seemingly a copy) is just about what one would expect under the circumstances: behind the Danish dress we sense a Norwegian singer.

From one point of view it might be primarily symbolic that the oldest "Danish" ballad text may represent a Norwegian original. From another, however, the Solum text is not merely a symbol. It also illustrates the fact that a new and different interest in ballads appeared at just this time in Denmark and that the Danes then looked to Norway for ballads and ballad themes. Skien, Mattis Nielsson's town, was the center for

14. *Danske Studier* (1973): 185–190, M44–M74, M159–M160, esp. M52–M57. Also published as *Meddelanden från Svenskt visarkiv* 32 (Stockholm: Svenskt visarkiv, n.d.).

15. Poul Lindegård Hjorth, "Linköping-handskriftet og 'Ridderen i Hjorteham,'" *Danske Studier* (1976): 5–35. Also published as *Meddelanden från Svenskt visarkiv* 35 (Stockholm: Svenskt visarkiv, n.d.).

16. Ibid., p. 33.

commercial and cultural contacts between Denmark and
Telemark, probably already the foremost ballad region of Norway. And Norway was the country where—in my opinion, but
contrary to the accepted view—the Scandinavian ballad originated.

That the formal models for the Scandinavian ballad are
French has long been acknowledged. We find them above all
in the *chansons d'histoire/chansons de toile,* songs that we
primarily know from the quotations and insertions in Jean
Renart's verse romance *Guillaume de Dôle* (ca. 1228).[17] The
Norwegian folklorist Moltke Moe seems to have been one of
the first to recognize this fact (in general, that is), as witnessed
by his pupil Hans E. Kinck in a paper from 1892 (printed posthumously forty years later) from which I have taken the final
sentence as a motto for my present sketch.[18] Independent of
each other (and maybe also of Moe), Jan de Vries and, especially, the Danish historian J. C. H. R. Steenstrup a few decades later arrived at the same result.[19] Their findings have

17. The dating of the work (preserved, obviously in a copy, in a MS from
the second part of the thirteenth century) is based on the identification of
contemporary persons appearing in the poem. The first editor, G. Servois
(1893), dated it on these grounds to 1199–1201, while Rita Lejeune, in her
important treatise *L'oeuvre de Jean Renart* (Liège: Faculté de philosophie
et lettres, 1935), pp. 104–105, as well as in her edition of *Le roman de la
rose ou de Guillaume de Dôle* (Paris: E. Droz, 1936), is of the opinion that
it should be placed within the years 1212–1213. Felix Lecoy, in "Sur la date
du Guillaume de Dôle," *Romania* 82 (1961): 379–402, very convincingly argues for the date 1227–1228. Lecoy gives the same date in his edition *Le
roman de la rose ou de Guillaume de Dôle* (Paris: Champion, 1979), pp. vi–
viii: "On doit donc être près de la vérité en plaçant le *Guillaume de Dôle*
en 1228, date moyenne."

18. Hans E. Kinck, "Forholdet mellem middelalderens balladedigtning
og oldtidens mythisk-heroiske digtning i Norden," *Edda* 32 (1932): 113–272.
See Knut Liestøl and Moltke Moe, *Norske folkeviser fra middelalderen*
(Kristiania: Dybwad, 1912), pp. 8–9, and Bengt R. Jonsson, "Richard
Steffen, Norge och enstrofingen," *Norveg* 21 (1978); 246–248.

19. Jan de Vries, "Quelques particularités de la poésie populaire," *Edda*
10 (1918, pr. 1919): 165–187, a rather vague exposition; Johannes C. H. R.
Steenstrup, "De danske Folkevisers ældste Tid og Visernes Herkomst,"
Historisk Tidsskrift (Copenhagen) 9 (1919): 232–254, 355–397 (also published separately).

been confirmed by other scholars, most recently by David Colbert, who, painting on a somewhat broader canvas, has come to similar conclusions.[20] This theory of French models for the Scandinavian ballad was strongly challenged by the Danish Romance philologist Knud Togeby in 1963.[21] The *chansons d'histoire*, he says, have been regarded as a very old and popular genre, one of the prerequisites for the Danish *folkeviser;* this cannot be true as the *chansons d'histoire* constitute but a short-lived, artificial genre from the early thirteenth century; only twenty specimens are preserved.[22] Togeby is right in his implicit criticism of some unwarranted conclusions drawn by the early propounders of the French theory. But he misjudged both the *chanson d'histoire* and especially (according to my theory) the origin, social and geographic, of the Scandinavian ballad. Consequently, Togeby came to misinterpret completely the issue at stake.

The *chansons d'histoire* were evidently à la mode when Jean Renart wrote *Guillaume de Dôle* and might have been a rather new genre at that time. In any case Renart made the innova-

20. Colbert, *Birth of the Ballad*, chap. 4.

21. P. Krarup, H. Holmboe, and Kr. Gierow, eds., *Vor Kulturarv* (Copenhagen, Oslo, and Hälsingborg: Forlaget for faglitterature, 1961–1970), vol. 2 (1963), pp. 267–269. Togeby also holds the same position in F. J. Billeskov Jansen, H. Stangerup, and P. H. Traustedt, eds., *Verdens litteraturhistorie*, vol. 2 (Copenhagen: Gyldendal, 1971), pp. 360–361 (pp. 354–356 in the Norwegian edition [Oslo, 1971]), the only difference being that in 1971 he accepts Lecoy's dating of *Guillaume de Dôle* to 1227–1228. According to Togeby (*Vor Kulturarv*, 2:300; *Verdens litteraturhistorie* 2:558) the ballad genre came to Scandinavia from England in 1406, an impossible idea which I have criticized for a long time.

22. The standard editions of these songs are by Karl Bartsch, *Altfranzösische Romanzen und Pastourellen* (Leipzig, 1870; rpt. Geneva: Slatkine, 1973, and Darmstadt: Wissenschaftliche Buchgesellschaft, 1975), and by Guido Saba, *Le "chansons de toile" o "chansons d'histoire": Edizione critica* (Modena: Società tipografica modenese, 1955). The genre is discussed in Edmond Faral, "Les chansons de toile ou chansons d'histoire," *Romania* 69 (1947): 433–462, and Raymond Joly, "Les chansons d'histoire," *Romanistisches Jahrbuch* 12 (1961): 51–66. I would like to point out that the dating of *Guillaume de Dôle* to 1227–1228 instead of to the end of the twelfth century is of essential importance not only for Scandinavian ballad scholarship but also for the understanding of the *chanson d'histoire* itself.

tion, as he himself tells us, of including such songs in his romance. His example was soon followed by Gerbert de Montreuil in his *Roman de la Violette* and then by others. In these romances the songs are usually performed in an aristocratic milieu, something that doubtless depicts their true *Sitz im Leben*. This does not, however, mean that the *chansons d'histoire* and related genres were not oral genres.[23] The role of Jean Renart and Gerbert de Montreuil is, as far as these songs are concerned, that of a recorder: without their quotations and excerpts we would have known much less about the very existence of the *chanson d'histoire/chanson de toile* as a genre, the extent of which we cannot estimate. Once again we may observe how oral poetry is preserved only owing to especially lucky circumstances; it should be repeated that *Guillaume de Dôle* exists in but one single MS.[24]

23. They may also generally be regarded as dance songs, in the sense that they could be and certainly often were used as such. We should, however, avoid the noun *carole* as a literary term, for example for the *chanson d'histoire,* as it refers to the dance and says nothing about the song text (except that it, as a rule, has a refrain).

24. In Scandinavian ballad research the *Guillaume de Dôle* is often mentioned. Normally the source has been Steenstrup's treatise from 1919, and as Jean Renart's authorship (in spite of a suggestion by P. Meyer in 1894) was not established by then, the work is presented as anonymous (for example, in Dal, *Nordisk folkeviseforskning,* and by Oluf Friis, Karl-Ivar Hildeman, et al., in standard textbooks) and is also given too early a date. Ballad scholars have not commented upon the fact that the only preserved text of *Guillaume* is a copy in the Vatican MS Reg. 1725 that once belonged to Queen Christina of Sweden; it would have been fascinating if this MS (like others in her library) had been in Scandinavia in the Middle Ages. Christina, however, bought it in Paris in 1659 (five years after her abdication). To my knowledge, Paul Verrier alone touches on the subject, in "Bele Aiglentine et Petite Christine," *Romania* 63 (1937): 359–360, but from another angle. Verrier discusses and rejects the possibility that the Danish ballad editor Peder Syv saw the MS in Sweden and used it for his book of 1695. There is another neglected side of the matter. The MS (which is from the last third of the thirteenth century) contains not only the *Guillaume* but also one verse romance by Raoul de Hondenc and two by Chrétien de Troyes: the *Chevalier de la Charette* and the *Chevalier au Lion* (*Yvain*). The *Yvain* and the *Guillaume* are actually next to each other in the MS. As has been demonstrated by Wendelin Foerster and Eugen Kölbing, it is not the textual branch of *Yvain* represented in Vat. Reg. 1725 (α) that was used for

The *chanson d'histoire* was an oral genre but it was associated with the *courtoisie* of the aristocratic circles. It may have had some influence on later French folksongs, but the genre as such did not become an element of French and European folk culture. In this limited sense Togeby was right: the *chanson d'histoire* was not a "folksong" by the conventional definition of the term, to which he adhered.[25] Nor was the Scandinavian ballad at the initial stage. The picture, envisaged by so many scholars, of the French genres "wandering" through Germany up to Scandinavia, especially Denmark of course, or alternatively brought to Denmark by students from the university of Paris, must be suspected to be a false one. The *chanson de toile*, oral or recorded in writing, was part of the French *courtois* literature. All other forms of that literature came, as far as we know, to Scandinavia from Anglo-Norman England; consequently, it is natural to think that the same goes for the ballad. And Scandinavia in this connection means, first and above all, Norway. In other words: the ballad should be placed together with the romantic literature so much appreciated at the

the *Ívents saga*, even if there are some puzzling similarities. The author of the Swedish *Ivan Lejonriddaren* may have had access to a text of *Yvain* belonging to branch α, but the indications are few and inconclusive. We cannot, accordingly, confirm that Jean Renart's *Guillaume* was known in Scandinavia. Nevertheless, it is important to establish that the *Guillaume de Dôle*, with its *chansons d'histoire*, was distributed together with works like those of Chrétien and thus for the same public.

25. Many other scholars—in Scandinavia and not least in France—have muddled the question unnecessarily. Dance songs, many of them doubtless with refrains, were part of the folk culture in France (and elsewhere on the European continent) and duly condemned by Church councils. What happened in thirteenth-century France was that out of popular songs was created an aristocratic, *courtois* genre (attested by Jean Renart and his followers and further developed by Audefroy le Bâtard), consciously including some poetical archaisms and linked to forms of folk dances. (Almost all fashionable dances are stylized folk dances.) It was this *courtois* genre that was taken via Anglo-Norman England as a pattern in Scandinavia. In Scandinavia the ballad genre became popular, as did in France some songs and traits of the *courtois* song genres, but the genre itself at its initial and formative stage was not brought from the common people in France to their fellows in Scandinavia. These remarks are also relevant, *mutatis mutandis*, to the so-called Kölbigk stanza, "Equitabat Bovo."

court of king Håkon Håkonsson (1217–1263) and his descendants.

The sheer bulk of Danish ballad MSS from the sixteenth and seventeenth centuries has without doubt hindered the sight of this, the most natural explanation, and has led ballad scholarship astray. Nobody seems to have taken into consideration that Denmark was the very last country in Scandinavia to be reached by the literary current of French *courtoisie*. Here is neither the space nor the need for a detailed picture of the impressive work done by Brother Robert and his Norwegian and Icelandic successors (and possible predecessors) as translators and editors in the thirteenth century of this mostly French literature. It is important in our context, however, to note that they transformed French verse into Norse prose: the romances of Chrétien de Troyes, the lais of Marie de France, and so on.

The center of these literary activities, expressed in a simplified way, was the hall of the Bergen castle (Håkonshallen); that's where, we may imagine, the works were read aloud during the reigns of Håkon Håkonsson, his son Magnus Lawmender (1263–1280), and his grandson Eirik Magnusson (1280–1299). Eirik's younger brother Håkon was the duke of the southeastern part of Norway, Viken, where he made the city of Oslo his capital of a sort. When Eirik died in 1299, he was succeeded as king by Håkon (1299–1319) who preferred to keep Oslo as his main residence and had a new castle, Akershus, built there. Although Bergen was still of the utmost importance, not only as the leading seaport but also in cultural and literary matters as the excavations at Bryggen have demonstrated, the political center shifted to Oslo.

A number of political events toward the end of the thirteenth century in Denmark (the murder of Erik Klipping in 1286, the struggle between king and archbishop) and Sweden (Folke Algotsson's abduction of Ingrid Svantepolksdotter in 1288) drove magnates and their followers into exile in Norway. Thus was created an unusually pan-Scandinavian cultural setting in southeastern Norway during the decades around the year 1300; the dramatic events of the preceding years, by the way, furnished subject for ballads, some of which became essential to the further development of the genre. The political pattern

in Scandinavia at the time made it possible for the rather un-
scrupulous Swedish duke Erik Magnusson (d. 1318) to play a
game of his own, endeavoring to create a state made up of
adjacent parts of Denmark, western Sweden, and Norway. A
move in this game which opened even wider perspectives to
him was his betrothal in 1301 and, after periods of em-
broilment, eventual marriage in 1312 to the heiress to the
Norwegian throne, king Håkon's daughter Ingebjörg.

Duke Erik is depicted as a veritable flower of *courtoisie* in
the Swedish rhymed chronicle *Erikskrönikan* (ca. 1330), of
which he is the hero. According to this chronicle Erik was regarded as a true Prince Charming by the ladies at the royal
court in Oslo. However that may be—*Erikskrönikan* is an extremely biased source—he certainly seems to have made an
impression upon the most important woman in the scheme,
namely Ingebjörg's mother. Queen Eufemia was of North
German princely stock, with a family tradition of literary interests and abilities. To honor her would-be son-in-law she ordered three literary works to be composed in Swedish: *Herr
Ivan Lejonriddaren* (1301), *Hertig Fredrik av Normandie*
(1308), *Flores och Blanzeflor* (1312). These romances, called
Eufemiavisorna after their patroness, were written in rhymed
verse couplets (*knittel*), a highly significant fact.

The earliest and for that reason most interesting of these
verse romances, *Herr Ivan,* illustrates the point I want to
make. Whereas earlier in the thirteenth century Chrétien's
Yvain was transformed from French verse into Norse prose
(*Ívents saga*), at the turn of the century the tide of literary
form in high society turned: now prose was transformed into
end-rhymed verse, out of *Ívents saga* came *Herr Ivan
Lejonriddaren*. German literary models, such as *Reimchro-
niken,* may have been of influence, perhaps mediated by
Queen Eufemia herself. Some lyrical expressions and formulas, presumably of German origin, seem to have been in existence already and could now be put to a new use. But it was
doubtless the ballad genre that made the writing of *Herr Ivan*
possible, or at least much easier. The existence of a poetic language for narrative verse, with a set of formulas and stock
phrases in rhymed couplet constellations was of the greatest

importance to the author. It is not farfetched to think that ballads gave the impetus for a work of this kind.[26] It is now almost unanimously agreed that the author (a more appropriate term than "editor" or "translator") of *Herr Ivan* used not only *Ívents saga* but Chrétien's *Yvain* as well. This makes it highly probable that the Swedish author (maybe exiled since 1288) wrote his work at, or in the vicinity of, the Norwegian court in Oslo. As a center for this royally supported *courtoisie* in chivalric poetry, *Bergenhus* was evidently superseded by *Akershus*.

Comparisons between on the one hand *Herr Ivan*, on the other *Ívents saga* and *Yvain*, make it completely clear that *Herr Ivan* borrowed from an existing ballad genre.[27] Later, the

---

26. Marianne A. Kalinke, among others, sees in the strong tradition of the sagas the main reason that in Norway works like those of Chrétien were transmitted into prose; see *King Arthur North-by-Northwest* (Copenhagen: Bibliotheca Arnamagnaeana, 1981), p. 133. She does not reflect on whether, as early as during the reign of Håkon Håkonsson, there was a poetic tradition at hand adequate for the purpose. Andreas Heusler, in "Über die Balladendichtung des Spätmittelalters namentlich im skandinavischen Norden," *Germanisch-Romanische Monatsschrift* 10 (1922): 16–31, while supporting the conventional Danish theory, also discusses a possible Norwegian origin of the Scandinavian ballad genre (partly on assumptions that now must be regarded as false or dubious): "Anders würde sich die deutsche Einwirkung stellen, wenn man den Ursprung der Folkevise in Norwegen suchte: in dem Norwegen unter Hakon IV., dem einzigen nordischen Lande, das damals ein ritterliches Schrifttum pflegte. Wir wissen, dass um 1250 in Norwegen deutsche Heldengedichte vorgetragen und in der Thidrekssaga nacherzählt wurden; ferner, dass einige dieser Gedichte zu Balladen geformt wurden—norwegischen Balladen, wie die neuere Forschung gesehen hat. Dass aber hier die *Anfänge* der nordischen Folkevise liegen, hätte doch einiges gegen sich" (p. 26). But Heusler also presents a real argument for his own rejection of Norwegian origin: "Beachtung verdient, dass die eingehende Schilderung der höfischen Sitte im norwegischen Königsspiegel, um 1250, keinen Tanz kennt" (p. 31, n. 44). This is true, but the argument is of value only if the ballad genre existed at that time. It may, instead, be used in support of my view regarding the age of that genre. For the time some fifty years later, Heusler could have found "höfischer Tanz" mentioned in the *Eufemiavisor* and the *Erikskrönikan*, not to mention that a high official in Norway was nicknamed "Krökedans."

27. See Ernst Frandsen, *Folkevisen: Studier i middelalderens poetiske litteratur* (Aarhus and Copenhagen: Universitetsforlaget, 1935); Stanislaw

Eufemia romances in their turn seem to have been utilized by ballad makers. We are thus able to observe an interchange between ballads and romances. They belong to the same environment and are but different expressions of the same ideals, the same tastes. I think we could with reasonable safety place the ballad genre in the 1290s but not earlier. For several reasons it is clear that the ballad had its first heyday in or around the highest aristocratic circles from about 1300 up to, let us say, 1320.

It has long been acknowledged that Norse written sagas like *Karlamagnús saga* and *þiðriks saga af Bern* are the sources for Scandinavian ballads of the heroic kind (*kämpavisor*), and that *fornaldarsögur* (oral or written mythic-heroic sagas) have provided themes for a number of the somewhat drastic *trollvisor*. Grundtvig was of the opinion that the *kämpavisor* constituted the oldest stratum in the ballad genre, in some cases going back to the eleventh or even the tenth century; this was in agreement with his well-known ideas about eddic poetry as a common Scandinavian heritage. Since the connection between the heroic ballads and Norse literature was recognized, the *kämpavisor* have been looked upon as the most recent category within the ballad genre. Behind this view lies the supposition that the ballad genre originated in the twelfth century or, the current view, in the first half of the thirteenth century, whereas the *kämpavisor* should be dated to the late fourteenth century or the fifteenth; the arguments are mainly based on the stylistic differences between the *kämpavisor* and the knightly ballads (the ballads of chivalry). I regard this view as the rather primitive relic of a simplified evolutionism, a tendency to construct a linear scheme at any price. Differences in mood and style must not necessarily be interpreted in chronological terms. The Norse sagas from the thirteenth century (of Karlamagnús, þiðrik, Tristram, and the other *riddarasö-*

Sawicki, *Die Eufemiavisor: Stilstudien zur nordischen Reimliteratur des Mittelalters* (Lund: Gleerup, 1939); Colbert, *Birth of the Ballad*. Erik Noreen made a capital error when he declared that the ballads were of no importance for the *Eufemiavisor*, in *Samlaren* (1930), p. 58, and elsewhere.

gur) are themselves the best proof to the contrary. And most of them are used by the ballad poets.

A detailed study gives the result that these sagas have furnished the ballads with stories, plots, personal names, place names, and pregnant expressions.[28] Most evidence points to the solution that the ballad poets had not had access to the written sagas but had heard them, listened to them being read aloud, and, following the advice of Kalebrant in *Ívents saga*, listened carefully. The ballads, an oral genre, were then used not only by the author of the *Eufemiavisor* but also by others, authors and translators. The Swede who translated *Þiðriks saga* in the middle of the 15th century knew and used the ballads based upon his Norse original; the author of the Icelandic *Saga af Tristram ok Ísoddu* seems to have known the Tristan ballad based upon the older (Brother Robert's) *Tristrams saga*.

But the ballads did not rely on prose sagas alone. It is well known that some ballads are based upon eddic poems; *Þrymskviða* is just one example. It was with the evidence of a ballad that Sophus Bugge could prove that *Grógaldr* and *Fjölsvinnsmál* are but two parts of one lay, *Svipdagsmál*. This connection between eddic poetry and ballads ought to show that some of the eddic lays were known in Norway around 1300 (a fact in harmony with the runic inscriptions found in Bergen) and also, naturally strengthens my theory about ballad origins.

---

28. Space permits a single example to show the borrowing of a detail. In *Karlamagnús saga* the king "reið heim til Frakklands með her sínum há fjöll ok myrkva dali ok furðuliga þröngva, svá at *15 mílur valskar* mátti heyra vápnagný af liði þeirra" (ed. Unger, p. 501; my italics). As pointed out by Cederschiöld in *Fornsögur Suðrlanda* (Lund, 1884), p. xxxv, this is a straightforward translation of the corresponding line in the *Chanson de Roland*, v. 817 "De .XV. liues en ot hom la rimur." Now, in the oldest Swedish text of the ballad about Folke Algotsson's bridal abduction "home to Norway" (*SMB* 60A, from ca. 1570), a messenger rides to tell the deprived fiancé about the event, and he rides "femton välske milar" (st. 12). One Danish text of the ballad also has "femten valske mill" (*DgF* 180 B:5). The preserved Norwegian texts of this ballad, all printed in Blom and Bø, *Norske ballader*, pp. 120–127, have nothing equivalent but are the only ones to have remembered the historical name (only slightly changed) of Folke's rival. "Femton välske milar" in the ballad—one of those I regard as "Akershus" ballads—must go back to *Karlamagnús saga*.

It is, on the other hand, not very plausible that eddic poetry gave rise to ballads as late as the fifteenth century, which has been suggested even in very recent times. As eddic poetry also was an oral genre, the transformation from eddic lay to ballad represents an encounter between two genres of oral poetry, one older and one younger, two different systems of making verse with some formal elements in common. A third genre, with similarities to the other two, may sometimes have come into the picture: the *rímur*. It is not entirely out of the question that the Icelandic *rímur* called *þrymlur* is based not only on the eddic *þrymskviða* but also on its ballad derivative *Torsvisan*.[29]

29. The oral character of the *þrymlur* is vindicated by Jón Helgason in "Noter til þrymlur," *Opuscula* V (Bibliotheca Arnamagnæana XXXI, 1975), p. 246. Sophus Bugge gave an extremely complicated version of the connections between *þrymskviða, þrymlur,* and *Torsvisen* in his and Moltke Moe's *Torsvisen i sin norske form* (Christiana, 1897), pp. 111–118: the ballad in its original form was Norwegian, and was then transformed into a Danish one in the style of the knightly ballads. So far Bugge was certainly right, and his theory actually contained the nucleus of the view, systematized by Sverker Ek in 1921, that Norwegian (mostly heroic) ballads were taken over by Danes and reworked in a late chivalric direction. But as Bugge discovered some similarities between on the one hand the Norwegian ballad and the *þrymlur,* on the other between another *rímur* cycle (*Lokrur*) and the Danish ballad version, he elaborated his theory further. He suggested that the Norwegian *Thor* ballad was created in Iceland, and the Danish adaptation as well; both poets had been in Iceland at the same time or almost the same time, the first of them learning from the *þrymlur,* the other one from the *Lokrur.* In 1898 Axel Olrik declared his skepticism about the Icelandic origin of the ballad when he discussed Bugge's and Moe's book in his survey article "Nordisk folkeviseliteratur i de sidste år," *Dania* VI: 92–110. Olrik accepted Bugge's view of the *Thor* ballad's having originated in Norwegian and of the Swedish version as a secondary mixture of the Norwegian and Danish ones (p. 106). In other respects he was rather vague: "den nöjere betegnelse af alder og hjemsted står for mig som en ganske uvis sag" (p. 108). But there is every reason to believe that the ballad was created in Norway early in the fourteenth century (when *þrymskviða* might still have been known there) and from Norway came to Sweden and Denmark. While the Swedish version keeps the style and spirit of the Norwegian original, the Danish version A in MSS from the sixteenth century bears all the hallmarks of *la seconde chevalerie* (the Danish C, recorded from oral tradition in the nineteenth century, is closer to the Norwegian and Swedish forms). There is not one single trait in the texts to support Bugge's (and Olrik's) idea that the Swedish version was dependent on the Danish one. As for

Summing up: the Scandinavian ballad originated in circles close to the Norwegian court and the literature appreciated there. The idea that only the category of heroic ballads had this origin should be abandoned. True, a few other ballads have generally been regarded as Norwegian, such as the romantic *Tristan* ballad (*TSB* D383, preserved in Icelandic), the related *Bendik og Årolilja* (*TSB* D434, mainly an offshoot of the Hagbard story), and one of the legendary ballads: the mighty visionary poem *Draumkvædet* (*TSB* B31, *NMB* 54), found exclusively in Norway (but whose age is much in dispute).[30] The presupposition of Danish priority has, however, hampered efforts to appreciate the Norwegian role in the making of the Scandinavian ballad.[31] On the other hand, a fact already men-

---

Bugge's dating of the ballad to the fifteenth century, this was based on the supposed borrowing from the *rímur* in question. Other scholars have pointed to the jocular, exaggerated style, which they regard as characteristic of the fifteenth and sixteenth centuries; they seem to have neglected the style of the *þrymskviða* itself, the source of the ballad. According to Olrik, the similarities between the *rímur* and the ballad are more or less accidental (pp. 107ff). He may be right, but if some details should be explained as signs of a direct connection between the *þrymlur* and the ballad, it is more natural to think that the author of the *þrymlur* (ca. 1400) knew the Norwegian ballad. Instead of discussing these details (all made easily available by Bugge and Moe) I would like to point out that there are some traces of a possible influence from ballad style in the *þrymlur* (especially in the first *ríma*):

Gengo þeir fagra	Upp í fagran Freyju garð
Freyio túna	Fyst nam þór að ganga,
ok hann þat orða	segir hann hvað að sorgum marð
allz fyrst um kvað:	og sína mæði stránga:
(*þrymskviða*, 3)	(*þrymlur*, I:14)

The "balladesque" character of the *þrymskviða* is mentioned by many scholars, most often in a rather general way. For chronological reasons I regard an influence from ballads on the eddic lay (even if it could be dated so late as the first half of the thirteenth century) as impossible, but the *þrymskviða* may, on the other hand, belong to the stuff out of which ballads (not only *Torsvisen*) and the ballad style were made.

30. See Appendix.

31. The strong belief in Danish priority has been held completely independent of the widely differing views concerning the age of the genre and

tioned must be kept in mind: the mixed Scandinavian (including Icelandic) nature of the circles around the Norwegian court. Poetry of an older and somewhat different kind existing also in Sweden and Denmark, as well as prose traditions from these countries, may have contributed at this initial stage. Almost at once the ballad may have developed into a truly joint Scandinavian genre, carried by the sort of dance that still prevails in the Faroes. The choreographic element probably best explains the wide distribution of the ballad not only geographically (the linguistic barriers were relatively negligible) but, not very long after its birth, also socially.

The dance, a cultural sphere in which the interchange between the folk—usually the more influential partner in this field—and the à la mode culture of the upper classes has always been very strong, rather soon made the ballad a "folksong" in the sociological sense of the term. We may observe this also in the contents and tendencies of some ballads; thus we cannot cling to a simple *Rezeptionstheorie*. An anti-aristocratic tendency is evident, for instance, in "Bønderne dræber herr Tidemand" (*TSB* D315: "Man demands taxes from peasants who kill him"; DgF 317), a favorite of Friedrich Engels, who knew it from the German translation in Wilhelm Grimm's *Altdänische Heldenlieder* (1811).

A very odd conception indeed sometimes arises, especially in Denmark: that the ballad genre was taken up or "taken over" by the common people only late, in the seventeenth century or thereabouts, when it was growing out of fashion with the nobility and the gentry.[32] Why and how the upper classes should give away the ballad, like old clothes, to the needy poor

---

of individual ballads. Gustav Storm, for one, strongly challenged Grundtvig's opinion about the age of the Didrik ballads but, like Grundtvig, took their Danish origin for granted. As a strange corollary, ballads of recognized Norwegian origin have as a rule been given a late dating, often based on the fact that Norwegian ballads differ stylistically from the "older" Danish ones. A circle.

32. See Inger M. Boberg, *Dansk folketradition i tro og digtning og deraf afhængig skik* (Copenhagen: Munksgaard, 1962), p. 89: "Først senere, da de højere kredse havde tabt interessen for dem, gik viserne efterhånden over i folketraditionen, hvor mange af dem har levet videre lige til vor tid."

is not explained. In reality, of course, the upper social stratum with its "mobile" culture (to use Sigurd Erixon's term) was more open to novelties, while the peasantry kept to the older but still viable heritage. Investigations into the Norwegian ballad tradition have taught me that a similar change took place as late as in the nineteenth century: M. B. Landstad in the 1840s recorded ballads from many peasant proprietors, while Sophus Bugge some twenty years later found them almost exclusively among crofters. The taste, though, was the same—although small but significant differences according to the sex of the singer are noticeable—within this rural society (Telemark): there was an unparalleled dominance of the heroic categories *kämpavisor* and *trollvisor,* with whose heroes the rustic singers could identify themselves.[33] The early disappearance of a national Norwegian nobility diminished the market for knightly ballads.

Some ballad motifs may have been introduced together with the French formal models. Other international motifs arrived later, in the fourteenth and fifteenth centuries. A great number of these are met with in folksongs from many parts of Europe.[34] The Hungarian ballad scholar Lajos Vargyas remarked that the Danish (Scandinavian) forms of these "international" ballads differed from the Continental ones; they were influenced by "other literary genres."[35] As David Colbert recently has pointed out, these "other literary genres" are none other than the Scandinavian medieval ballad itself.[36] The genre was strong enough to recast foreign models in its own stylistic mold. This phenomenon may also be observed in later times.[37]

33. Compare the similar conditions in the Færoes.
34. See E. Seemann, D. Strömbäck, and B. R. Jonsson, eds., *European Folk Ballads* (Copenhagen: Rosenkilde & Bagger, 1967).
35. Lajos Vargyas, *Hungarian Ballads and the European Ballad Tradition,* tr. Imre Gombos, 2 vols. (Budapest: Akadémiai Kiadó, 1983), vol. 1, p. 132.
36. Colbert, *Birth of the Ballad,* p. 21.
37. See Bengt R. Jonsson, "Ältere deutsche Lieder in schwedischer Überlieferung," *Jahrbuch für Volksliedforschung* 9, Festschrift Erich Seemann (1964): 45–51; Jonsson, "Visan om Stångebro slag 1598," *Om visor och låtar: Studier tillägnade Sven Salén* (Stockholm: Svenskt visarkiv, 1960), pp. 73–95.

Now to Denmark. As mentioned, the ballad had certainly arrived there by ca. 1300 and flourished in oral tradition during the fourteenth and fifteenth centuries. Then, about 1480, during the reign of King Hans (1481–1513), there appeared what I like to describe as *une seconde chevalerie*. If not literally true in all details, the anecdote told by the Danish chronicler Arild Huitfeldt about King Hans's personal interest in Arthurian literature contains a symbolic truth.[38] Only now were the three *Eufemiavisor* translated from Swedish into Danish verse (and at least three other verse romances were created: *Persenober, Dværgekongen Laurin,* and *Den kyske dronning*). Now the *Karlamagnús saga* was also translated into Danish. And, somewhat apart from these genres, the Danish *Rimkrønike* was written in the latter part of the 1470s, about 150 years later than the Swedish *Erikskrönikan* (and in most respects different from it).

It is only logical that a new interest in the ballad genre should arise in the literary climate among the nobility around the royal court.[39] The ballads, living in the oral tradition of the common people and perhaps the gentry, were discovered and recorded. But they were also edited, worked over, changed. As so often happens in renaissances the characteristics of the idealized object were used in an exaggerated way. The ballads of chivalry, naturally the most favored category, were made more chivalric than ever. With real zeal the Danes made up for the lost two centuries.

---

38. See Jürg Glauser, "Höfisch-ritterliche Epik in Dänemark zwischen Spätmittelalter und Frühneuzeit," *Beiträge zur nordischen Philologie* 15, Festschrift Oskar Bandle (1986): 191–207.

39. This renaissance phenomenon was mistaken by the Dane Erik Sønderholm for the very birth of the Scandinavian ballad genre; see his paper "The Importance of the Oldest Ballad Manuscripts for the Dating of the Ballad Genre," *Ballads and Ballad Research: Selected Papers of the International Conference on Nordic and Anglo-American Ballad Research,* ed. Patricia Conroy (Seattle: University of Washington Press, 1978), pp. 231–237, and his last contribution, "Randebemærkninger til en disputats," *Gripla* 6 (1984): 165–186 (with a rejoinder by Vésteinn Ólason, pp. 191–201). Inadvertently, Sønderholm gave passive support to my theory concerning the Danish role in Scandinavian balladry.

It was, however, not only a question of energetic editorial work: a great number of new ballads were written. I consciously use the term "written," because the ballad now became a literary genre in the true sense of the word. Small ballad collections circulated in manuscript among the nobility; some of them may be easily reconstructed from the copied texts in the existing voluminous manuscripts from the middle of the sixteenth century onward. In their search for ballads the Danish nobility turned not only to the oral tradition in Denmark itself but also to that of Norway. Even if these Norwegian ballads obviously belonged to different categories, the cases easiest observed are the heroic ballads and those built upon *fornaldarsögur;* owing to the preferences in the ballad reservation of upper Telemark, it is mainly among these ballads that we are able to compare the more "chevaleresque" or "balladesque" Danish forms with their Norwegian originals.

That a great number of the ballads in the MSS of the Danish nobility were late and literary was pointed out by Ernst von der Recke, for example.[40] But a clearer distinction between this literary tradition and the older, oral tradition was made only a few years ago by Iørn Piø.[41] He demonstrated that Anders Vedel had been aware of this difference but collected from both source groups. Some ballad types appear, as one could expect, in only one of these groups, and when they appear in both there is a more or less marked divergence between the respective texts. Printed versions (Vedel, Syv, broadsides) were instrumental in getting these newer types or texts into oral tradition in Denmark and also in the other Nordic countries.

Denmark's place in the history of the Scandinavian ballad can now be defined. One may very well call it a leading role,

---

40. *Danmarks Fornviser* I (Copenhagen, 1927), p. xvii: "Der findes Viser i Mængde, som kun haves danske og i Adelsopskrifter; ved adskillige af dem kan der være a 1 Grund til at spørge, om de nogensinde have existeret undenfor de Blade, hvorpaa de findes optegnede . . ."

41. *Nye veje til folkevisen* (Copenhagen: Gyldendal, 1985). See my review in *Sumlen* (1986): 166–170.

but that role is not the one that earlier and more romantic generations of scholars imagined. The quantity of preserved texts in relatively old manuscripts, the early printed editions by Vedel and Syv, the admirable editorial work by Svend Grundtvig (DgF) and his well-deserved authority as a truly great scholar—all this has combined to create a picture of the origin and earliest history of the genre that, alas, cannot stand up to critical scrutiny.

Connected with the question of locality is the chronological problem. Scholars, even long after Grundtvig's day, regarded it as a matter of course that the ballad should be linked to what is called the great period of the Valdemars ("Valdemarernes storhedstid"). During most of this period (1157–1241) Denmark exercised a strong political power eastward along the coast of the Baltic, and this period also produced a writer like Saxo Grammaticus. But Saxo wrote in Latin, and practically all historiographic literature was written in that language. Of even greater importance is that Denmark, at least since the time of the duke Knud Lavard (d. 1131), was under exceedingly strong cultural influence from Germany, something about which Saxo complained. It may be added that this cultural connection, some would say dominance, was of long duration: later on, German *Minnesänger* were rather frequent guests— as were, by the way, Icelandic skalds (up to the middle of the thirteenth century)—at the Danish court. No less a personage than Tannhäuser wrote poems to the young King Erik Klipping in 1263 and 1268; when Erik was murdered in 1286, this event, which we have encountered as a ballad theme, became in Denmark the subject for a German poem by Meister Rûmelant.

An early example of a German singer in Denmark, often discussed in the literature because of its bearing on the *Poetic Edda,* dates from 1131. Jan de Vries writes:

The Danish ballad [*folkevise*] is probably finally traceable to the French narrative-lyric poems which have been sparsely transmitted to us under the name of "chansons de toile." This influence from France operated on Scandinavia through Germany, and so we must insert narrative-lyric poems in Lower Saxony. The proof of them is offered by the often-cited passage in the thirteenth book of Saxo Grammaticus's *History of the Danes,* where he tells how a Saxon minstrel gave the Danish king Knud Lavard warning about a planned ambush. "So he purposely began to relate in a noble song the treachery of Grimilda towards her brothers, attempting through this notorious example of betrayal to inspire him with apprehensions of a similar fate." That happened in the year 1131. Saxo speaks of a "singer" and of a "song"; from that I conclude that we should not imagine a minstrel epic but rather a sung poetic form which could best be compared with the Danish ballad. For a warning, especially in the delicate situation of the Saxon singer, should be brief and penetrating; a short epic of a thousand or more lines is probably very ill-suited to that. The younger Hildebrand poem should give us an impression of this genre.[42]

The key sentence here is the second one: the French form and style reached Scandinavia by way of Germany, and so "we must insert" Low Saxon epic-lyrical songs (in this case, at least, with a Nibelungen theme) as intermediaries between the French *chansons de toile* and the Danish *folkevise* (the Scandinavian ballad). This is an altogether unwarranted conclusion, based upon purely axiomatic presumptions about a completely unknown entity. We must remember that not one single ballad of the French and Scandinavian kind is to be found in German.[43] Jan de Vries was of the opinion concerning narrative folksongs that "solche Liedchen unbemerkt über die Grenzen geschlüpft sind."[44] But he fails to make the distinction

42. "Das zweite Gudrunlied," *Zeitschrift für deutsche Philologie* 77 (1958): 176–199; rpt. in de Vries, *Kleine Schriften* (Berlin: de Gruyter, 1965), pp. 263–284; quotation, p. 280. Latin translation from Saxo Grammaticus, *Danorum Regum Heroumque Historia, Books X–XVI*, tr. Eric Chritiansen (Oxford: British Archeological Reports, 1980), p. 128.
43. The only apparent exceptions, "Herr Hinrich und sine Bröder" (*Deutsche Volkslieder mit ihren Melodien*, no. 43; from Ditmarsken) and the Frisian "Bai Rädder" (ibid., no. 71) are both modeled on Danish patterns. See Otto Holzapfel, *Folkevise und Volksballade: Die Nachbarschaft deutscher und skandinavischer Texte*, (Munich: Fink, 1976), pp. 58, 71.
44. *Altnordische Literaturgeschichte*, 2 vols. (Berlin: W. de Gruyter, 1942), vol. 2, p. 501; 2d. ed. (Berlin: W. de Gruyter, 1964–1967), vol. 2, p. 544. The next sentence runs: "Aber wenn eine norwegische 'Folkevise' den letzten Zug von Håkon Håkonarsson behandelt, dann muss im 13. Jahrhundert diese Dichtgattung schon früh [1965: muss schon früh im 13. Jahrhundert dieser Gattung] bekannt gewesen sein." Why a ballad about an event of 1263 dates the genre to the earliest part of the thirteenth century

between content and form and neglects the ever-important question of genre. The most striking fact is that the singer was a German, performing the German version of the story.[45]

Jan de Vries relies upon results and theories presented by Wolfgang Mohr. My criticism thus applies to Mohr as well. His two extensive investigations offer much of indisputable value to both eddic and ballad research. The weak point is his general conception of the age and origin of the Scandinavian ballad. Mohr cannot be blamed, of course, for accepting the conventional view of Denmark as the earliest center of the genre. But he should have been more critical toward ideas like those held by Svend Grundtvig in DgF, vol. 1, concerning a direct German origin of many heroic ballads, however, appealing such views must be to a scholar making serious efforts to reconstruct a lost Low German genre. It must also be said that Mohr is too indiscriminate in his choice of ballad parallels; he lacks a method.

Nobody can be surprised if I, in light of the theory set forward in the present sketch, have come to conclusions other than Mohr's, often exactly opposite ones. Take the relationship between *Guðrúnarhvöt* and DgF 285, "Grevens Datter af Vendel" (or 285/286). There are some striking similarities, as observed also by others. Mohr describes these traits and gives several quotations. He mentions that Hugo Gering also lists these *Gemeinsamkeiten* but "does not say how he accounts for them." Mohr himself feels somewhat uncertain: "I must confess I cannot get a clear picture of the relationship of the ballad to the eddic poem. It would be simplest to assume again that a 'novelistic song'—this time one from the cycle of stepmother ballads—had been made over into a heroic elegy in Denmark or Lower Germany . . . The agreements between *Guðrúnarhvöt* and the ballad cannot be dismissed as accidental. No one would want to conceive the influence as running

---

remains a riddle, even if the ballad in question (*DgF* 142; *TSB* C11) was contemporary with the event, which is certainly not the case.

45. In this context it deserves to be mentioned that Denmark, as distinguished from Norway and Sweden, lacks pictorial representations of the Nibelungen material.

from the eddic poem to the ballad since DgF 285 is not a 'heroic ballad' [*Kæmpevise*]."[46]

The last phrase, "keine Kæmpevise," reveals Mohr's rather awkward dilemma. He cannot accept what he really sees as the best solution, that the ballad has borrowed from the eddic lay. The motif has probably been part of a Norwegian ballad but, as so often, is preserved only in later Danish texts (and their Icelandic and Swedish derivatives).[47] Mohr's investigations certainly deserve close scrutiny from ballad scholars. I regret that I have the occasion here only to stress the negative side. But I might as well finish my criticism by saying that he—like de Vries—mixes genres, different in age, style, and function, in a very free way into a kind of literary hodgepodge.

I am not denying that Denmark received much from German tradition. On the contrary, I think that Denmark was strongly influenced by German culture. This may, indeed, be the main reason for Denmark's late drinking from the French *courtois* well and for the more humble role of the Danes in the early history of the Scandinavian ballad. German motifs came early into the ballads, but through the *þiðriks saga*. I think we should accept the view that the saga was translated from a *written* German original (as suggested by E. F. Halvorsen and, more recently, Theodore Andersson).[48] Many ballads took their subjects from this saga, not only the Didrik ballads proper.[49]

46. *Zeitschrift für deutsches Altertum* 75 (1938–39); 250–251.

47. See Vésteinn Ólason, *The Traditional Ballads of Iceland: Historical Studies* (Reykjavík: Stofnun Árna Magnússonar, 1982), pp. 194–198.

48. Halvorsen in *Kulturhistorisk leksikon for nordisk middelalder* 3 (1958): cols. 75–76; Andersson, "An Interpretation of *þiðreks saga*," in John Lindow, Lars Lönnroth and Gerd Wolfgang Weber, eds., *Structure and Meaning in Old Norse Literature* (Odense: Odense University Press, 1986), pp. 347–377.

49. Colbert, *Birth of the Ballad,* pp. 93–95, suggests that *þiðriks saga* has borrowed from Scandinavian ballads. To take this view he is forced to antedate the ballad genre or—as he evidently prefers—to date the *þiðriks saga* very late (p. 182, n. 175), in contrast to the current tendency in saga research. Colbert's very valuable treatise is based upon the conventional belief in Danish priority where ballads are concerned. I, on the contrary, regard the elopement tales in the *þiðriks saga* as the main sources for a number of Scandinavian ballads, including the controversial "Ribold" (*TSB* A41; *DgF* 82; *SMB* 15).

Of greatest importance for our understanding of the literary climate in medieval Sweden and Denmark is the strong influence of oral ballads on written literature, a matter I have already touched upon. Oskar Klockhoff denied the now generally accepted fact that the Didrik ballads, based upon the Norse saga, in their turn influenced the Swedish translator of the saga. One of his arguments was that it implied that the translator had ballads ringing in his ears all the time.[50] Klockhoff did not believe in this. He was totally wrong, however. We are able to observe this phenomenon everywhere (*Konung Alexander, Schacktavelslek, Den danske rimkrønike,* and so on), not only in the cases I have already mentioned, such as the Swedish and Danish translations of the *Karlamagnús saga,* even if in those cases we may observe a specially rewarding example of the repeated interchange between written literature and oral poetry in ballad form.

Appendix: The Date of *Draumkvæde*

Moltke Moe dated the *Draumkvæde* to the end of the twelfth century and thought that the translator of *Duggals leizla* (Tundal's vision) in the middle of the thirteenth century had borrowed details from the ballad; in reality it is certainly the other way around. Knut Liestøl dated the ballad in 1925 to the end of the thirteenth century or to ca. 1300, but in 1946 changed his mind: the poem belonged to "roughly, the central sixty years of the thirteenth century" and "cannot be much older than from the middle of the thirteenth century." *Draumkvæde: A Norwegian Visionary Poem from the Middle Ages* (Oslo, 1946), p. 130. For many reasons I regard Liestøl's earlier view preferable to his last one, which is unacceptable. Starting in the very same year, 1946, a general tendency among scholars has been to make the *Draumkvæde* much younger; for a survey see Michael Barnes, *Draumkvæde: An Edition and Study* (Oslo, 1974), pp. 3–68. I must confess that I do not feel

---

50. O. Klockhoff, "Folkvisan om konung Didrik och hans kämpar," *Arkiv för nordisk filologi* 16 (1900): 126: "Den som skrifvit de nu befintliga handskrifterna af sv. öfvers., har alltså enligt hans [Grundtvigs] mening haft sitt hufvud så fullt af folksviseuttryck, att han ej kunnat bibehålla originalets lika goda uttryck, utan måst ditsätta visans."

fully convinced by the arguments presented. Here I can only, and in brief, express my doubts concerning some ideas held by three of my friends.

Brynjulf Alver, in *Draumkvedet: Folkevise eller lærd kopidiktning* (Oslo, 1971), suggests that the ballad was composed in the eighteenth century by somebody who had listened to sermons in church. My work with the ballad tradition in Telemark has given me the impression that clergymen then were more interested in propagandizing for an increased planting of potatoes than in teaching a "papistic" topography of the otherworld and condemning marriage between cousins in such a remarkable manner.

Karl-Ivar Hildeman, "I marginalen till Draumkvædet," in *Medeltid på vers* (Stockholm: Svenskt visarkiv, 1958), dates the ballad to "the closing period of the Middle Ages" (p. 258), perhaps ca. 1500; one reason is the division of the ballad into several sections (marked by different refrains), another is the presence of an opening "minstrel's" stanza in which the singer addresses his audience and presents the subject. But a division into "fyttes" appears not only in, for example, "A Gest of Robyn Hode" (Child 117) but also in Faroese ballads (some of which certainly are of Norwegian origin from the fourteenth century) and in the Norwegian ballad or ballad cycle about Didrik of Bern. A trait like a ministrel's introduction is very difficult to use for dating; it is a more or less ageless style in performance. Hildeman ought perhaps to have mentioned that a similar opening is found in "Robin and Gandeleyn" (Child 115, in a MS from ca. 1450), actually the only Child quatrain ballad that, like the Scandinavian four-lined ballads, has a refrain ("Robyn lyth in grene wode bowndyn"); see also the introductory lines of *Herr Ivan Lejonriddaren* (without equivalents in *Yvain* or *Ívents saga*).

Dag Strömbäck, "Om Draumkvædet och dess källor," *Arv* 2 (1946): 35–70, rpt. in *Folklore och filologi* (Uppsala: Kungl. Gustav Adolfs akademien, 1970): 1–33, writes particularly— and very well at that—about the conception of the *Gjallarbrú*, known from Norse mythology (see *Gylfaginning,* chap. 48), referred to in Sturla Þorðarsson's *Hákonarkviða* (from ca. 1264), and playing an important part in the *Draumkvæde*. He

independently finds the same parallels as Liestøl in his book
from 1946 (pp. 64–70)—for instance the Scottish "Lyke-Wake
Dirge" ("This æ night," printed in Walter Scott's *Minstrelsy;*
it has never become the anthology item it deserves to be), in
which the bridge is called "Brig o' Dread." Both Liestøl and
Strömbäck discuss the presence of a *Gillebro* in Danish (and
Norwegian) ballads as well as in Swedish lay preaching toward
the end of the sixteenth century. While Liestøl does not draw
any conclusions at all from these facts regarding the age of the
Draumkvæde, Strömbäck comes to the view that the occurrence of the *Gillebro* in Denmark and especially in the Swedish
sources demonstrates that the conception was widely distributed and also productive after the Reformation; accordingly,
the *Draumkvæde* may be of a rather late origin but, owing to
its Catholic spirit, probably not later than the late Middle
Ages. Strömbäck's arguments have never been challenged
(only used, as we have seen, to propound an even later dating).

I venture to suggest another explanation. When *Gillebro* appears in other ballads the expression may very well be borrowed from the *Draumkvæde,* especially as some of these
other ballads are of Norwegian origin. In the case of the ballad
Aslag Tordsøn og skøn Valborg (DgF 475; TSB D87; SMB 85)
we encounter a very interesting phenomenon. This is a late
Danish ballad, belonging to *la seconde chevalerie* and perhaps
from no earlier than the middle of the sixteenth century; it has
a Norwegian setting almost extreme in its "Norwegianness."
It is only logical that the *Gillebro* (symptomatically combined
with the mention of St. Olav) is one of these Norwegian ingre-
dients. Axel Olrik registered this Norwegianism but regarded
it as "hardly an intended one" (*DgF,* vol. 8, p. 143n); Strömbäck quotes Olrik, in whom he always had a great faith. To
me, this detail is included just to give an added *couleur locale,*
and its appearance in this function proves exactly the opposite
of what Strömbäck was apt to believe. As for the occurrence
of *Gillebro* in Swedish lay preaching, it is remarkable that both
known examples come from the 1580s, the period of what
might be called the Swedish Counter-Reformation under King
Johan III. *Spiritus rector* of this movement was none other
than the Norwegian Jesuit father Lavrens Nilssøn (Laurentius

Nicolai, nicknamed "Kloster-Lasse"), and one of the sources in which *gillebro* appears (together with a number of other traits known from the *Draumkvæde*) is a poetic pamphlet against him and his teaching. The other source, a report of Jöns Andersson's preachings, also has some details we recognize from the *Draumkvæde;* it should be added that, according to Jöns, the *gillebro* was "15 milar långh" (see n. 28 above). I think we may, with reasonable safety, assume that the Norwegian "Kloster-Lasse" directly or indirectly knew the *Draumkvæde* and that the Swedish sources from his time are the oldest summaries of an important part of its contents. Thus they do not prove a real existence in Sweden of the *Gjallarbrú* motif; what they illustrate is the tradition of the Norwegian ballad but they cannot be used for dating its origin. I would place it in the fourteenth century, and I have a feeling that my old teacher Dag Strömbäck would have gladly accepted critical views that led to this result.

As for the "Lyke-Wake Dirge" we cannot entirely dismiss the possibility that we have to do with one out of many examples of Norwegian influence on Scottish tradition.

NATASCHA WÜRZBACH

Tradition and Innovation: The Influence of Child Ballads on the Anglo-American Literary Ballad

The English and Scottish Popular Ballads was Francis James Child's life work. In it he collected, ordered, and preserved an immense treasure of ballads and made them accessible to the public. His text corpus has become not only the basis but also the classificatory and aesthetic yardstick for ballad research. The apparently closed, complete, and authoritative status of Child's canon, however, has often been accused of fostering mistaken understandings of the spectrum of folksong and ballad-like poetry and even of hindering ballad research. Child's collection contained a number of ballads which had not only been popular in oral tradition but had also been in print before his original edition appeared in 1857–1858. During the eighteenth century a new interest in the ballad manifested itself in the publication of numerous miscellanies containing traditional ballads, street ballads, and songs of all sorts, in the ballad criticism of Addison and others, and in some ballad editions proper. Ballads in general and in particular those which were later to be called Child ballads became a stimulus and model for the emergence of the literary ballad in the course of the eighteenth century and the basis of its establishment as a

171

genre toward the end of the eighteenth and the beginning of the nineteenth century.[1]

By literary ballads I mean those whose writers can be historically and biographically authenticated and which were published and read in poetry volumes and anthologies. Literary ballads are characterized by a relatively high degree of individuality reflecting an author's personal style and communicative intentions as well as the period style of a literary era. At the same time, however, they remain in many different ways indebted to the model of the traditional ballad. In a fuller account of the intertextuality of the literary ballad other models and occasional influences would also have to be accounted for, prominent among them the street ballad tradition and the tradition of the literary ballad itself. But the intertextual matrix can never be exhaustively mapped; I will confine myself to the relationship between the Child corpus and a few significant literary ballads, with the larger hope of glimpsing a typology of such relationships.[2]

Literary ballads can take from particular traditional ballads quotations, motifs, scenes, sequences of events, certain character constellations, or dialogue structures. They may also use

1. Albert B. Friedman, *The Ballad Revival: Studies in the Influence of the Popular on Sophisticated Literature* (Chicago: University of Chicago Press, 1961) gives a detailed survey of the ballad tradition in print. G. Malcolm Laws, Jr., *The British Literary Ballad: A Study in Poetic Imitation* (Carbondale and Edwardsville: Southern Illinois University Press, 1972) is the only extended study on the English literary ballad available. See also Anne Henry Ehrenpreis, ed., *The Literary Ballad* (London: Camelot Press, 1966) pp. 9–19; Gisela Hoffman, ed., *Englische und amerikanische Balladen: Zweisprachig* (Stuttgart: Reclam, 1982), pp. 15–46; Tristram P. Coffin, "The Folk Ballad and the Literary Ballad: An Essay in Classification," *Midwest Folklore* 9 (1959):5–18; J. S. Bratton, *The Victorian Popular Ballad* (London and Basingstroke: Macmillan, 1975), chaps. 1, 3, and 7.

2. For the theory of intertextuality see Ulrich Broich and Manfred Pfister, eds., *Intertextualität: Formen, Funktionen und anglistische Fallstudien* (Tübingen: Niemeyer, 1985); Renate Lachmann, "Intertextualität als Sinnkonstitution," *Poetica* 15 (1983): 66–107; Wolf Schmid and Wolf-Dieter Stempel, eds., *Dialog der Texte: Hamburger Kolloquium zur Intertextualität* (Vienna: Wiener slawistischer Almanach, 1983). My criteria, classification, and investigation are based on these works, although I hope to offer a clearer and more easily applicable system.

such genre-typical procedures as the ballad stanza, incremental repetition, leaping and lingering, predominance of dialogue and related scenes along with virtual absence of description, emotional suggestiveness, and smaller features of linguistic style. Thus in a literary ballad allusions may be found to a particular traditional ballad (single-text reference) or to the whole genre (system reference). These intertextual references can be classified according to the following criteria:[3] *quantity,* the number, extent, and distribution of the textual components taken over;[4] *recognizability,* on a scale ranging from clear to subtle; *function,* the arising of additional meaning potential from the tension between correspondence and divergence. This extension of meaning, achieved through orientation toward the traditional ballad, I shall call *intertextual relevance.*

The Anglo-American literary ballads chosen for this study can be related in various ways to some of the best-known or "classical" Child ballads according to these criteria. At the same time they are oriented toward the genre features of the traditional ballad in general. I have arranged the textual examples not by date but according to decreasing similarity and increasing originality in relation to their model. The intertextual typology may suggest literary-historical evolution, but theoretically the type of relationship explored here can be realized at any time.

A historical preliminary stage to the literary ballad can be seen in the collation and stylistic changes of traditional ballads by editors in the second half of the eighteenth century and the beginning of the nineteenth. Though Percy, Buchan, Scott,

3. The description of intertextual relations assumes a familiarity with the models (individual text, genre) and therefore depends on the perception of the reader in his or her capacity as interpreter. It is neither possible nor necessary for the reader's conclusions to coincide completely with the knowledge, intentions, or creative consciousness of the author, regarding whose creative process we can of course know nothing.

4. By textual components I mean both the content and the structural constituents of a text. It is clear that content and structure are always interwoven in varying ratios of predominance. Thus for example the motif has the structural aspect of the specific figure constellation and the content aspect of a plot potential.

Herder, and others have to be criticized from the point of view of editorial fidelity to the text, correspondence to the original in a broad sense remained predominant. From the point of view of genre history, however, their efforts to modernize the style and ensure completeness of content signal the beginning of an independent analysis of the genre model. The emergence of the literary ballad in England and Germany in the eighteenth century should be seen in the context of an awakening interest in the ballad among educated men of letters, an interest motivated by antiquarian, historical-intellectual, nationalistic, and literary considerations. The numerous collectors and editors of the period created the necessary conditions, and their efforts culminated in Child's publications, the first truly scholarly editions in the English-speaking world.

The close relationship between ballad editor and ballad author is particularly evident in Swinburne. The poet was inspired by Scott's *Minstrelsy of the Scottish Border* (1802–1803), W.E. Aytoun's *Ballads of Scotland* (1861) and Child's first ballad edition to edit, collate, and write ballads himself between 1861 and 1863.[5] His ballad "The Bloody Son" is an excellent example of an adaptation which adheres closely to its original model, "Edward" (Child 13). He takes over the question-and-answer between mother and son with its repetition, variation, and schematization, augmenting it with three inner refrains. He extends the legacy stanzas from three to five heirs. As in many of his other ballads, Swinburne is here trying to be more "ballad-like" than the traditional ballad.

> "And where gat ye thae sleeves of red,
> My merry son, come tell me hither?
> And where gat ye thae sleeves of red?
> And I wot I hae not anither."
> "I have slain my brither by the weary waterhead,
> O dear mither."

---

5. Some of these appeared in *Poems and Ballads* (1866), others posthumously. William A. MacInnes published a complete edition arranged in three groups ("imitations," "ballads in which the poet has treated a favourite Border theme in his own way," and "modern ballads"): *Ballads of the English Border by Algernon Charles Swinburne* (London: Heinemann, 1925); see p. xi.

> "And where will ye gang to mak your mend,
> My merry son, come tell me hither?
> And where will ye gang to mak your mend,
> An' I wot I hae not anither."
> "The warldis way, to the warldis end,
> O dear mither."   (st. 4–5)

The hypertrophy of incremental repetition combines with the (not always accurate) use of Scottish dialect and conscious archaisms of style to produce a labored and somewhat artificial imitation of the traditional ballad. Swinburne omits the curse upon the mother, which suggested her complicity in the murder. The mother-son relationship is thereby relieved of the guilt element, and is portrayed through the refrains as particularly close. This slight change of emphasis, where the two texts are otherwise markedly similar, is of minor intertextual relevance. "The Bloody Son" is more a tour de force in ballad imitation. In one or two other ballads such as "The Bride's Tragedy" or "The King's Daughter" Swinburne clearly adhered to the genre and to the motifs of certain traditional ballads but achieved more originality through changes in content, the use of incremental repetition for acoustic effects, and the decorative, vivid style of Pre-Raphaelite poetry.[6]

Longfellow's famous ballad "The Wreck of the Hesperus" is an example of greater "originality" than Swinburne's "The Bloody Son." The connection with "Sir Patrick Spens" (Child 58) would not be immediately obvious if the warning stanza had not been taken over complete with the reference to the change in the moon's appearance (though with certain modifications):[7]

> Late late yestreen I saw the new moone,
> Wi the auld moone in hir arme,

6. For Swinburne's treatment of Child ballads, see C. Rummons, "The Ballad Imitations of Swinburne," *Poet Lore* 33 (1922): 54–84; Clyde K. Hyder, "Swinburne and the Popular Ballad," *PMLA* 49 (1934): 295–309; Anne Henry Ehrenpreis, "Swinburne's Edition of Popular Ballads," *PMLA* 78 (1963): 559–571.

7. *The Complete Poetical Works of Longfellow* (Boston: Houghton Mifflin, 1922), pp. 14–15. "Sir Patrick Spens" is only sparsely represented in the American ballad tradition. It is possible that Longfellow came across

And I feir, I feir, my deir master,
That we will cum to harme. (Child 58A7)

'Last night the moon had a golden ring,
And to-night no moon we see!'
The skipper he blew a whiff from his pipe,
And a scornful laugh laughed he. ("Hesperus," st. 5)

Longfellow also took over some characteristic formulae.[8] The
shipwreck motif is greatly modified in both choice of characters and content.[9] Whereas Sir Patrick undertakes the voyage
on stormy seas out of allegiance to the king, Longfellow's skipper carelessly dismisses the warning and perishes along with
his daughter. The tragic death of a hero is replaced by a disaster at sea caused by foolhardy hubris. This change in the
basic theme of the ballad is reinforced by Longfellow through
an appropriate change in the role of the shipwreck's witnesses.
In the traditional ballad these are the women waiting on the
shore, the bereaved whose heartfelt mourning is indicated. In
"The Wreck of the Hesperus," however, a fisherman who has
taken no part in the action sees the frozen, ice-encrusted
corpse of the skipper's daughter floating on the mast of the
wrecked ship, and his reaction conveys sheer horror.

In Longfellow's ballad the change in figure constellation renders the relationship between father and daughter central. This
time the clearly recognizable borrowing is from within the tradition of the literary ballad, from Goethe's "Erlkönig": during
a stormy journey the father in Longfellow's poem takes on the
role of protector of his daughter, echoing the situation and

---

the ballad by way of Herder's translation, since he took an interest in
German classical and romantic literature.

8. "A loud laugh laughed he" (58A, st. 4, l. 2, and in most other variants)—"a scornful laugh laughed he" ("Hesperus," st. 5, l. 4). "Up and
spak an eldern knight" (58A, st. 2, l. 1, and in other variants)—"Then up
and spak an old Sailor" ("Hesperus," st. 4, l. 1). "Come down, come
down" (58C, st. 14, l. 1, and st. 15, l. 1)—"Come hither! Come hither!"
("Hesperus," st. 8, l. 1).

9. The description of the shipwreck is of course missing in 58A;
Longfellow, however, like any other reader could deduce this part of the
action from the context, if he was not familiar with other variants.

roles of father and son in Goethe's famous poem; of course both fathers fail.[10] The core of both texts is the dialogue between the frightened child, who senses the approach of danger, and the father, who is trying to give reassurance. By combining the motif of shipwreck after previous warning from "Sir Patrick Spens" with the role relationships from "Erlkönig," Longfellow rationalized and naturalized the element of mortal danger, purging in his borrowing any hint of the (homo?)erotic horror of "Erlkönig." The child's perspective contributes to the terror of both poems, but Longfellow's fisherman adds a dramatic, nonauthorial confirmation. Descriptions of the raging storm (Goethe's blustery night is evoked in a few words) and the wrecking of the ship in the breakers (st. 6–7, 15–19), together with the girl's beauty and its destruction in death (st. 2 and 21), flesh out Longfellow's conception well beyond Goethe's hints:

> The breakers were right beneath her bows,
> She drifted a weary wreck,
> And a whooping billow swept the crew
> Like icicles from her deck.
>
> She struck where the white and fleecy waves
> Looked soft like carded wool,
> But the cruel rocks, they gored her side
> Like the horns of an angry bull.   (st. 17–18)

The detail and imagery of the description are modernization of traditional ballad style, which Longfellow however conforms to in his predominant use of parataxis, with its avoidance of conjunctions and relative pronouns.[11] His orientation toward

10. Longfellow's intense interest in Goethe's work makes it seem certain that he was familiar with what is probably Goethe's most famous ballad. "Erlkönig," in turn, is oriented toward the Danish traditional ballad "The Elfshot." See Erik Dal, ed., *Danish Ballads and Folk Songs* (Copenhagen and New York: Rosenkilde & Bagger, 1967), no. 2. Goethe was familiar with Herder's translation "Erlkönigs Tochter"; see Johann Gottfried Herder, *"Stimmen der Völker in Liedern": Volkslieder; Zwei Teile 1778/79*, ed. Heinz Rölleke (Stuttgart: Reclam, 1975), pp. 281–282 and 450nn. 86–88.

11. See Wolfgang G. Müller, "Syntactic Features of the Folk Ballad," *Arbeiten aus Anglistik und Amerikanistik* 6 (1981): 227–240.

the traditional ballad as a genre is also apparent in his balancing of question and answer between daughter and father in identically constructed stanzas using incremental repetition (st. 10–12). He also takes over the ballad stanza, with its semantic rhythm of rise and fall in density of information through the use of weak lines.

Altogether "The Wreck of the Hesperus," through its dual reference—on the one hand to an individual text and on the other to a generic rhetoric combined with stylistic tendencies to modernization—proves a reasonably successful revival of the traditional ballad. Some additional meaning is achieved by the convincing depiction of mortal danger. The reader can, however, appreciate this without any knowledge of "Sir Patrick Spens" and "Erlkönig" and the intertextual relevance is therefore only slight since the level of tension between the original texts and the new text cannot be described as high.

John Greenleaf Whittier's ballad "The Sisters" shows, by contrast, a definite increase in meaning against the background of "The Twa Sisters" (Child 10).[12] Whittier takes the triangle of characters from the Child ballad, but changes the course of the action by replacing the elder sister's murder of the younger by the death of the suitor who drowns at sea on his way to the sisters (the Hero-Leander motif). Whittier's aim in effecting this alteration is the psychological portrayal of the rivalry between the sisters which in the Child ballad is only indicated by the course of the action. He succeeds using only means typical of the ballad: he brings the sisters face-to-face in dialogue. The difference in their experience is shown in their words. The younger sister Annie demonstrates her true love in her fear for the man out at sea, hears his cries for help, and finally reacts to his death with a mixture of pain and joy since he now belongs to her absolutely in a spiritual union. The love of the

---

12. *The Complete Poetical Works of John Greenleaf Whittier* (Boston: Houghton Mifflin, 1894), pp. 100–101. The occurrence of Child 10 in American tradition is widespread over various regions (New England, Missouri, North Carolina, and Virginia). The differences in the variants are only slight and pertain for the most part to the second part (the robbery of the corpse), which has no relevance for Whittier's ballad.

elder sister Rhoda, on the other hand, is seen in this nocturnal conversation to be pitiless and possessive; she is determined not to hear the shouts of the drowning man, preferring his death to the possibility that his cries might be for Annie. The dramatic nature of the confrontation between the sisters is underlined by the ballad-like terseness of formulation and the rapid alternation of ripostes, and further reinforced by the adoption of the two-line stanza from the Child original:

> "Hush and harken!" she cried in fear,
> "Hearest thou nothing, sister dear?"
>
> "I hear the sea, and the plash of rain,
> And roar of the northeast hurricane." (st. 4–5)

In linguistic style also Whittier evokes the old genre, less through literal copying than through the imitation of set dual phrases such as "ramp and roar" and "loud and long" and the use of rhetorical contrast ("Thou in heaven and I on earth!"; "Thine the living, and mine the dead!"), parataxis, and simple, if modern, vocabulary. In this, one of his few successful ballads, Whittier on the whole adheres closely to the original text and to the genre of the traditional ballad, without exaggerating its features as Swinburne does.[13] By diverging significantly from "The Twa Sisters" he is also able to make the time-honored story plausible, thereby making it more accessible to the nineteenth-century reader than its archaically condensed presentation in the Child ballad.

The three literary ballads discussed so far show, in their treatment of motifs, story patterns, and (in the case of Swinburne and Longfellow) almost literal borrowings, clear links with certain Child ballads. Over and above this they are in differing ways fairly closely oriented toward genre-typical procedures of the traditional ballad. The group of literary ballads to be taken up next use only the motifs of well-known Child ballads, distancing themselves in linguistic style and presentation from the genre features of the traditional ballad. Such

13. Other successful ballads include "The New Wife and the Old" (*Poetical Works*, pp. 21–23), "Kathleen" (pp. 37–39), "Maud Muller" (pp. 47–48), "King Volmer and Elsie" (pp. 112–115), and a few others.

a mode of composition concentrates in the motif alone the tension relevant to meaning between the original text and the new text. It arises primarily through the author's adopting certain partial aspects of motif while diverging from others. Correspondence and divergence are here to some extent plainly distinguishable and form a clear contrast.[14] The greater this contrast is, the more obvious becomes the effect of the tension between the texts and the intertextual relevance of correspondence and divergence.

A number of literary ballads take up the motif in certain Child ballads of the appearance of a dead lover as a revenant or ghost. The appearance of the revenant Margaret in "Fair Margaret and Sweet William" (Child 74) is founded on the rivalry between two women over a man and the latter's infidelity to his first lover. In "Sweet William's Ghost" (Child 77) and "The Unquiet Grave" (Child 78), however, the triangle constellation is absent. The restlessness of the dead lover (in this case a man) derives from the fact that the emotional ties between the couple are unresolved, which finds expression in the dead man's plea for release from his vows and an end to her mourning.

The eighteenth-century text "William and Margaret" is held to be one of the earliest literary ballads. In fact, however, it is a street-ballad version of Child 74 known from the Roxburghe Collection, which a certain David Mallet (1705–1765), with a few changes in wording, gave out as a literary product of his own.[15] The question of guilt, implicit in the traditional ballad, is here made clear in the detailed reproaches of Margaret's ghost (st. 8–14) in line with the unambiguous moral ideas of the street ballad. The tragic element of William's insuperable conflict of choice in Child 74 is thus reduced to a straightforward matter of guilt and expiation. Furthermore, the appearance of the dead woman is not taken for granted as is the custom in the traditional ballad but is transformed, in a manner more typ-

14. Whittier's ballad "The Sisters," on the other hand, only brings out more clearly aspects of the core motif which are inherent in Child 10.
15. Roxburghe Coll. f. 1, folio 107. See also William Chappell, ed., *The Roxburghe Ballads,* vol. 3 (1880), pp. 667–673.

ical of the street ballad, into an uncanny and sensational spectral manifestation:

> Awake! she cry'd, thy True Love calls,
> Come from her midnight grave;
> Now let thy Pity hear the maid,
> Thy Love refus'd to save.
>
> This is the dumb and dreary hour,
> When injur'd ghosts complain;
> When yauning graves give up their dead
> To haunt the faithless swain.   (st. 6–7)

The treatment of the central motif in the Roxburghe-Mallet text deviates significantly from Child 77 and 78. That is, the intertextual relationship diverges distinctly from the corresponding old texts, and the original ballad motif undergoes simplification and trivialization.

Whittier changes the ghost motif in his ballad "The New Wife and the Old" in a different way.[16] He reduces the triangle constellation and the question of implicit guilt to a remarriage of the hero, now an older man, after the death of his wife. The appearance of the ghost does contain elements of terror, but it is reduced to the sensation of a cold hand removing jewelry from the young and happy bride after the wedding night:

> Ring and bracelet all are gone,
> And that ice-cold hand withdrawn;
> But she hears a murmur low,
> Full of sweetness, full of woe,
> Half a sigh and half a moan:
> "Fear not! give the dead her own!"   (st. 12)

The demarcation of the rights of the dead and the living wife contains an element almost of reconciliation. This mood continues in the terrified bride's turning for comfort to her awakening husband, the absence of unfaithfulness (the ballad only vaguely suggests difficulties in the husband's first marriage), and the lack of appropriate atonement through the husband's

16. *Poetical Works*, p. 21. American variants of Child 74 are very widespread, whereas Child 77 and 78 are only sparsely represented.

death. At the end we have the narrator's exhortation to the
reader not to forget the influence of the dead on the living (st.
20–21). Between the treatment of this motif in Child 74 and in
Whittier's ballad there is a noticeable weakening of the potential for conflict, which relates to the desire for harmonization
in the bourgeois concepts of the fireside poets and their readers.

Thus the Roxburghe-Mallet text and Whittier's ballad offer
us two contrasting literary realizations of the story of Fair
Margaret's return to Sweet William. Both alter the story formula, establishing a new meaning in relation to the original;
one simplifies and trivializes, the other weakens the potential
conflicts of the oppositions of the original, reducing tragedy to
unhappiness as life goes on. In the two literary ballads from
the end of the nineteenth century which I shall now discuss,
there is a radical reversal of the central meaning of the ghost
motif in Child 77 and 78: the restlessness of the dead is motivated no longer by the desire for release from emotional ties
but by the hope of their continuation beyond death. This hope
is in both cases bitterly dashed. In A. E. Housman's ballad "Is
my team ploughing, / That I was used to drive" the dead youth
asks after his carthorses, his football mates, the girl he loved,
and finally his best friend; the questions are directed to the
friend himself.[17] The dead youth is made to realize that life
goes on without him, and the bitter twist at the end is the information that his girl and his friend are now a couple:

> "Is my friend hearty,
> Now I am thin and pine,
> And has he found to sleep in
> A better bed than mine?"

---

17. *The Collected Poems of A. E. Housman* (London: Jonathan Cape,
1972), pp. 31–32. The ballad forms part of the collection *A Shropshire Lad,*
published in 1887. The thematic and stylistic influence of the Child ballads
on Housman's poetry has frequently been described, although the identification of echoes, usually with regard to single stanzas, is not always convincing. See Tom Burns Haber, "The Influence of the Ballads in Housman's
Poetry," *Studies in Philology* 39 (1942): 118–129, and *A. E. Housman* (New
York: Twayne, 1967), pp. 123–134; Norman Marlow, *A. E. Housman:
Scholar and Poet* (London: Routledge & Kegan Paul, 1958), pp. 70–103.

> "Yes, lad, I lie easy,
> I lie as lads would choose;
> I cheer a dead man's sweetheart,
> Never ask me whose."   (st. 7–8)

In a famous ballad of Hardy's similar questions regarding the living are asked in the context of someone disturbing the grave of a dead young woman: "Ah, are you digging on my grave . . .?"[18] The answers similarly show the indifference of those left behind, especially that of the lover in marrying another. The disappointment is further pointed up by the revelation at the end that it is the dead girl's dog that digs at her grave, not out of affection but in order to bury a bone:

> "Mistress, I dug upon your grave
> To bury a bone, in case
> I should be hungry near this spot
> When passing on my daily trot.
> I am sorry, but I quite forgot
> It was your resting-place."   (st. 6)

The failure to keep the memory of the dead and to love beyond the grave in the ballads by Housman and Hardy is emphasized even more when contrasted with the relevant Child ballads. There the living wish to uphold the relationship with the dead against the latter's will. The drastic alterations of the narrative idea by Housman and Hardy establish a tension with the traditional ballad that inspired them, an intertextual relevance which intensifies the pessimistic but also realistic textual message of the two literary ballads.

The treatment of the relationship between the living and the dead using the ghost motif of Child 74, 77, and 78 acquires a comic and even macabre twist in two further literary ballads which make use of the presentation methods of the street ballad. In George Colman's ballad "Miss Bailey's Ghost" a girl

18. *Collected Poems of Thomas Hardy* (London: Macmillan, 1923), pp. 310–311. The first line contains very strong echoes of Child 78: "Oh who sits weeping on my grave, / And will not let me sleep?" (Child 78A, st. 3). Hardy's lyrical oeuvre includes a considerable number of ballads more or less obviously oriented toward the traditional ballad.

who was seduced and then committed suicide appears before her seducer as a ghost.[19] Colman gives the basic situation of the ghost motif a grotesque twist: the former lover placates the dead girl with a financial arrangement to bribe the grave-digger to bury the suicide:

> "Dear Corpse," said he, "since you and I accounts must once
>   for all close,
> I've really got a one pound note in my regimental small
>   clothes;
> 'Twill bribe the sexton for your grave."—The ghost then
>   vanish'd gaily,
> Crying, "Bless you wicked Captain Smith, remember poor
>   Miss Bailey."
>   *Oh, Miss Bailey! unfortunate Miss Bailey.*   (st. 4)

Roughly contemporary is Thomas Hood's ballad "Mary's Ghost," in which the restlessness of the dead girl is founded on the mutilation of her corpse by medical grave-robbers ("resurrectionists").[20] The pointlessness of mourning follows logically—the grave is empty:

> You thought that I was buried deep,
> Quite decent like and chary,
> But from her grave in Mary-bone
> They've come and bon'd your Mary . . .
>
> Don't go to weep upon my grave,
> And think that there I be,
> They haven't left an atom there,
> Of my anatomie.   (st. 5 and 12)

The tension between correspondence and divergence in the use of motif, with its intensification of meaning, lies in the ma-

19. Hoffmann, *Englische und amerikanische Balladen,* pp. 224–227. Colman (1762–1836) wrote ballads and songs in ballad style for the music hall at the beginning of the nineteenth century. The appearance of the ghost at the sleeping lover's bedside and the question of guilt link Colman's ballad more closely with the Roxburghe-Mallet text than with the Child ballads.

20. *Selected Poems of Thomas Hood,* ed. John Clubbe (Cambridge, Mass.: Harvard University Press, 1970), pp. 84–86. Hood wrote a number of narrative poems and ballads with a comic or socially critical content, which should be assigned to the street-ballad tradition rather than to the traditional ballads.

cabre and grotesque portrayal of the theft of the corpse and its exploitation for purposes of anatomical research.[21] Black humor results in a distancing from the pain of parting and grief, whereas the traditional ballad depicts the problem of parting with the aid of magical or mythical concepts.

In the six versions of the ghost motif described above some textual content components were taken over as is and others altered, thereby constituting new textual meanings. Such a poetic result can also be achieved when a structure is borrowed at the same time the content is changed. Kipling's ballad "Soldier, Soldier" uses the structure of the question-and-answer dialogue in "Edward" (Child 13), but the figure constellation and the content are changed.[22] With the same urgency as the mother in the traditional ballad, a girl questions a soldier returned from the wars as to the whereabouts of her lover. At first, like the mother in "Edward," she receives evasive answers, until finally she learns that her lover has fallen in battle and is buried in a communal grave:

> "Soldier, soldier come from the wars,
> Why don't you march with my true love?"
> "We're fresh from off the ship an' 'e's maybe give the slip,
> An' you'd best go look for a new love."
>
> "Soldier, soldier come from the wars,
> I'll up an' tend to my true love!"
> "'E's lying on the dead with a bullet through 's 'ead,
> An' you'd best go look for a new love."   (st. 1 and 5)

If the structure of the dialogue in the Edward ballad, with its schematization through incremental repetition in question and answer, is recognized as the basis of this ballad, there arises in the reader the expectation of the revelation of a murder. But the result of the interrogation of a surviving witness is the brutally simple message of the soldier's death, so that the death and war itself are seen in a satirical-critical light against the background of the original murder story. In the tension be-

---

21. This motif echoes the construction of a musical instrument from parts of a body in "The Twa Sisters" (Child 10).

22. *The Complete Barrack-Room Ballads of Rudyard Kipling*, ed. Charles Carrington (London: Methuen, 1974), pp. 62–64.

tween similarity of structure and divergence of content, a soldier's death and murder become equivalent.[23] Kipling makes
similar use of intertextual relevance as an artistic device in
"The Widow's Party."[24] This ballad takes over the structure
and basic content of the dialogue in "Lord Randal" (Child 12):
"Where have you been this while away, Johnnie, Johnnie?"—
"What did you get to eat and drink . . .?" In place of the poisoning in a private drama we have the serving of unwholesome
and harmful food to a number of young men at a party. In the
fantastic and ambiguous, even allegorical, narrative of the man
who is being questioned this party proves to be a military en-
gagement; the widow—Queen Victoria—bears the responsibility, as hostess, for the destructive outcome and ultimate pointlessness.

In all the literary ballads so far discussed, some relation to
one or several Child ballads has been recognizable. The man-
ifest nature of the intertextual relation is based on either fairly extensive correspondences and similarities (Swinburne,
Longfellow, Whittier) or on alteration of a significant borrowing of narrative motif; Kipling's structural borrowings with divergence of content are also quite discernible. Three further
ballads demonstrate that orientation toward particular Child
ballads can be much subtler while being no less effective. On
the contrary, the intertextual relevance, that extra dimension
of meaning that depends on tension between correspondence
and divergence, may be increased even further if the original
text is not clearly recognizable in the new text.

Housman's ballad "Farewell to barn and stack and tree" is
just about recognizable in its connection with the Edward ballad.[25] It takes over as content fratricide, the mother's suffering,
atonement, and parting but does not use the characteristic
structures of the question-and-answer dialogue or the legacy
stanzas. Here no confession is wrung from a murderer; instead

23. The fate of the girl left behind is altered from traditional ballads such
as "Edward" to fit the stark modern context: the returning soldier simply
advises the girl to find a new lover.

24. *Barrack-Room Ballads*, pp. 44–46.

25. *Collected Poems*, pp. 16–17.

the protagonist communicates certain information to his close
friend in which imminent departure from the homeland becomes the prevalent theme:

> Farewell to barn and stack and tree,
> Farewell to Severn shore,
> Terence, look your last at me,
> For I come home no more.
>
> The sun burns on the half-mown hill,
> By now the blood is dried;
> And Maurice amongst the hay lies still,
> And my knife is in his side.
>
> . . . . .
> Long for me the rick will wait,
> And long will wait the fold,
> And long will stand the empty plate,
> And dinner will be cold.[26]   (st. 1, 2, 6)

In the Edward ballad past and future events are dramatically
compressed in the mother-son dialogue. Housman transforms
this dialogue into a predominantly lyrical personal statement
in which murder, the mother's suffering (st. 3), guilt (st. 4–5),
and atonement through self-imposed exile are subordinated
to the pain of parting, constituting merely its background.
Housman's poem, with its reminiscent content, simple linguistic style relying on suggestion, and use of the metrical and content structure of the ballad stanza, seems not so far removed
from the Edward ballad. Yet it is precisely when contrasted
with its background in the traditional ballad that this literary
ballad exhibits its originality as a moving poem of parting. In
place of brutal tragedy there is pain and affliction, reflected in
the studied simplicity of Housman's language.

This combination of subtle similarity to and subtle divergence from the original text I will call functional transformation. It produces a high degree of intertextual tension and relevance. A comparable, if rather different, process can be seen

26. This stanza echoes the waiting stanzas in "Sir Patrick Spens": "O
lang, lang may their ladies sit"—"O lang, lang may the ladies stand . . ."
(58A, st. 9 and 10; also in other versions).

in Tennyson's ballad "The Sisters."[27] The figure constellation
is borrowed from "The Twa Sisters" (Child 10). The rivalry
between the two sisters over a lover, however, is largely
passed over in favor of one sister's revenge on the seducer of
the other sister, who has meanwhile died (of guilt?).[28] This is
an echo of the motif of "revenge on an intruder into the family"
as in "Earl Brand" (Child 7) and "Clerk Saunders" (Child 69),
though no plot details have been lifted.[29] Tennyson complicates
the figure constellation in a way not characteristic of the ballad—the dead sister's seducer becomes the lover of the other
sister, who then kills him after the night of consummation. The
comparable murder of a lover takes place in "Young Hunting"
(Child 68), motivated by jealousy, a passion absent from
Tennyson's ballad. The actions of the elder sister are rather
characterized by contradictory desires for love and revenge:

> I made a feast; I bade him come:
> I won his love, I brought him home.
> The wind is roaring in turret and tree.
> And after supper, on a bed,
> Upon my lap he laid his head:
> O the Earl was fair to see!
>
> I kiss'd his eyelids into rest:
> His ruddy cheek upon my breast,
> The wind is raging in turret and tree.
> I hated him with the hate of hell,
> But I loved his beauty passing well.
> O the Earl was fair to see!   (st. 3–4)

There is also something of this emotional ambivalence in
"Lady Isabel and the Elf-Knight" (Child 4), though it becomes
understandable through chronological sequence: Lady Isabel
is at first fascinated by the strange knight; it is only when he

27. *In Memoriam, Maud and Other Poems,* ed. John Davis Jump
(London: Dent, 1974), p. 21.
28. "She died; she went to burning flame: / She mix'd her ancient blood
with shame" (st. 2).
29. Earl Brand elopes with the woman who loves him; her father and
seven brothers pursue the couple and kill him. In "Clerk Saunders" the
brothers kill their sister's lover on the love-couch.

threatens her with death that she kills him, using several variants of love declaration as a trick (4A, st. 10–11; 4B, st. 11–12). The combination of caresses and murder reappears in Tennyson's ballad with startling similarity of detail, although with a significant difference in the motivation for the compound of love and hate.

The various echoes in Tennyson's ballad "The Sisters" of course do not preserve the full meaning of the original ballad motifs. It is impossible to know to what degree Tennyson consciously incorporated his knowledge of ballads into his creative process. The reader atuned to ballads, however, perceives several associations. The shifting pattern of intertextual references that emerges captures the complexity and ambivalence of the protagonist's action and experience. The functional transformation from ballad materials is so subtle that a clear definition of the dividing line between borrowing and divergence is not possible; such subtlety does, however, accentuate the modern psychological nature of the theme.

In Housman's "Farewell to barn and stack and tree" and Tennyson's "The Sisters" the functional transformations involve components of content. In conclusion I would like to analyze a modern ballad in which procedures typical of the traditional ballad are transformed with comparable subtlety. Bob Dylan's well-known song "A Hard Rain's A Gonna Fall" is related to "Lord Randal" by its use of the question-and-answer dialogue.[30] However, as with the ballads by Kipling discussed above, the tension produced by expectation is guided in another direction: instead of revealing a murder by poisoning, the son who is being questioned tells in apocalyptic images of a spiritual and physical poisoning of the world and humanity, of the destruction of nature, danger, violence and cruelty,

---

30. *Bob Dylan: Writings and Drawings; Texte und Zeichnungen,* trans. Carl Weissner (Frankfurt: Zweitausendeins, 1975), pp. 114–117. The song was written in 1963 in response to the Cuban missile crisis. See also Aidan Day, *Jokerman: Reading the Lyrics of Bob Dylan* (Oxford: Blackwell, 1988); Michael Gray, *Song & Dance Man: The Art of Bob Dylan* (London: Hart-Davis, Mac Gibbon, 1972); Mathis R. Schmidt, *Bob Dylan's "message songs" der Sechziger Jahre* (Frankfurt am Main: Peter Lang, 1982).

and loneliness and suffering. Against the background of the
private tragedy in "Lord Randal" the expansion to embrace a
tragedy of the whole human race is all the more effective. Nor
is it possible to apportion personal guilt; no one feels responsible for the collective wretchedness of the human race:

> Oh, where have you been, my blue-eyed son?
> Oh, where have you been, my darling young one?
> I've stumbled on the side of twelve misty mountains;
> I've walked and I've crawled on six crooked highways;
> I've stepped in the middle of seven sad forests,
> I been out in front of a dozen dead oceans,
> I been ten thousand miles in the mouth of a graveyard,
> And it's a hard, hard, hard, hard,
> It's a hard rain's a gonna fall.
>
> What have you seen, my blue-eyed son?
> What have you seen, my darling young one?
> I saw a newborn babe with wild wolves around it;
> I saw a highway of gold with nobody on it;
> I saw a black branch with blood that kept dripping;
> I saw a room full of men with their hammers a-bleeding;
> I saw a white ladder all covered with water;
> I saw ten thousand talkers whose tongues were all broken;
> I saw guns and sharp swords in the hands of young children.
> And it's a hard, hard, hard, hard,
> It's a hard rain's a gonna fall.   (st. 1–2)

The mother's (or father's) questions determine the type of actions and perceptions in the son's answers, and each type is
underscored by anaphora.[31] The archaic schematic form of
identically constructed stanzas in "Lord Randal" is, however,
transformed into a more modern form of incremental repetition. The repetitions of the traditional ballad are here reduced
in favor of significant new information. In combination with
the horrific series of images, the repetitions at the beginning of
the lines produce the cumulative effect of intensifying the overwhelming profusion of images of cruelty and destruction. Each
image has at the same time a very much wider range of mean-

---

31. "What did you hear . . .?" (st. 3); "Who did you meet . . .?" (st. 4);
"Well, what'll you do now . . .?" (st. 5).

ing than any similar visual allusion in a traditional ballad. The suggestivity endemic to the traditional genre is thus magnified in Bob Dylan's text to the level of the ambiguity of modern lyric poetry.[32]

The unconnected string of different images, rapidly succeeding each other, has an effect on the imagination similar to that of the traditional ballad's abrupt changes of scene and omission of steps in the action, though in Dylan's ballad the process is more rapid.[33] The heterogeneity of the images is, however, counteracted by subtextual coherences: connotations of adversity, affliction, and death link the lines of the first stanza. Danger and cruelty are suggested in various images in the second stanza. The alternation between heterogeneity on the perceptual level of images and homogeneity on the emotional level of meaning of the images can in my view be read and experienced as a transformation of the leaping and lingering of the traditional ballad. Whereas in the traditional ballad there is an alternation of heterogeneity and homogeneity, in Dylan's text heterogeneity in the imagery of the text and homogeneity in the subtext become united in a single effect. In this protest song from the beginning of the sixties Bob Dylan remains indebted to the ballad tradition, which he subtly transforms into a vehicle for the communication of new messages of immediate topicality.

A fairly large number of English and American literary ballads are oriented toward Child ballads either as individual texts or as parts of a generic system. Through the examples selected here I have attempted to demonstrate how, in various ways, additional meaning potential arises from the tension between the original ballad and the new text. This intertextual rele-

32. An interpretation of the images, some of which are highly cryptic, is not possible here. I can merely point out the wealth of meaning implied by "a hard rain": environmental pollution, napalm, nuclear fallout, possibly also a general upheaval in the sense of "hard times."

33. Regarding the poetic images in this song, Betsy Bowden remarks: "A listener . . . makes a visual and emotional leap from one line to the next . . . The line-by-line shifts in 'Hard Rain' make it resemble a Child ballad being run through a projector too fast." *Performed Literature: Words and Music by Bob Dylan* (Bloomington: Indiana University Press, 1982), pp. 16 and 18.

vance seems to increase with the independence of the literary ballad from the Child ballad and from traditional ballad procedures, as long as the original remains recognizable. When there is no connection with an individual text, however, and a literary ballad is oriented only toward genre-typical content and traditional ballad procedures, intertextual relevance seems to contribute less to the literary effect. In my sample direct influences from traditional ballads mainly involve the best-known and most popular Child texts. At the same time we should not overlook the fact that the new literary ballads for their part illuminate the immanent meaning potential of the older texts. During the course of literary history the popular ballad has entered into a fertile dialogue with the literary ballad.[34]

34. The notion of the "dialogue nature" of the texts is an essential component of the discussion of intertextuality; see also note 2.

I should like to thank Gayna Walls for the assistance she gave me with the English version of this paper.

JAN ZIOLKOWSKI

Cultural Diglossia and the Nature
of Medieval Latin Literature

For Albert B. Lord

How did oral vernacular cultures contribute to medieval Latin literature? In this preliminary sounding of a bottomless topic, my goal is to survey promising avenues of research rather than to present findings regarding any specific text or group of texts. Because the Latin Middle Ages encompass much both chronologically and geographically, few generalizations will apply to all places at all times.

A prerequisite to understanding the relationship between orality and literacy in the so-called Latin Middle Ages is to grasp the linguistic situation. Because of our own cultural experience, juxtaposing the words "orality" and "medieval Latin literature" may seem oxymoronic. We tend to separate languages into two rigid compartments: dead languages such as ancient Greek and Latin, and living languages such as English and Spanish. According to this inadequate taxonomy Latin remained alive through late antiquity, but has been dead since then.

Such a division does not do justice to all linguistic milieus, especially to cases of cultural diglossia.[1] For instance, in the

1. I derive the expression "cultural diglossia" from Walter J. Ong, "Orality, Literacy, and Medieval Textualization," *New Literary History* 16

modern Arab world much of daily life is transacted in a spoken language existing alongside an ancient scriptural language that remains essential in religion, education, and various sorts of formal communication. Colloquial Arabic is a living but not fully literary language, whereas classical Arabic is literary but not entirely living.

The linguistic arrangement during the Latin Middle Ages was quite similar. All people had a mother tongue, such as the languages we know as Old English, Old Norse, and Old French. After the sixth or seventh century Latin ceased to be a mother tongue, because it was spoken by no one from the cradle.[2] Nonetheless, Latin did not become a dead language until after the Middle Ages. During the Middle Ages it hovered in a limbo of the unliving and undead. Whereas the mother tongues of the Middle Ages varied from place to place and time to time, Latin was a comparatively constant prestige language. As Dante put it: "Latin is perpetual and incorruptible, and the vulgar language is unstable and corruptible."[3] Latin was a *lingua paterna*—a father tongue.[4] This designation is particularly

---

(1984) 1–12. The word "diglossia" has been current among medievalists in North America thanks to Brian Stock, *The Implications of Literacy: Written Language and Models of Interpretation in the Eleventh and Twelfth Centuries* (Princeton: Princeton University Press, 1983), p. 24.

2. See Roger Wright, *Late Latin and Early Romance in Spain and Carolingian France* (Liverpool: Francis Cairns, 1982).

3. *Convivio* 1.5.7: "lo latino è perpetuo e non corruttibile, e lo volgare è non stabile e corruttibile."

4. The expressions *lingua patria* and *sermo patrius* mean "mother tongue." For a use of *lingua paterna* that may anticipate the modern "father tongue," see Nigel of Canterbury (de Longchamp, Wireker), *Tractatus contra curiales et officiales clericos,* ed. André Boutemy (Paris: Presses universitaires de France, 1959). In the verse composition that accompanies the *Tractatus* Nigel tells his book to behave properly—and to speak properly to its dedicatee, the Norman William Longchamp: "Lingua tamen caveas ne sit materna, sed illa / Quam dedit et docuit lingua paterna tibi" (p. 148, ll. 165–166). This couplet could be interpreted in two ways: either the "mother tongue" is English and the "father tongue" French (with the implication that Nigel's father spoke French, his mother English), or else the "mother tongue" is a vernacular language (French or English) and the "ancestral tongue" Latin (pp. 13, 31).

appropriate since medieval Latin was used predominantly by males to uphold a male-dominated or patriarchal society.[5] It was a tongue that boys were forced to learn en route to positions in the Church, university, and state.

In appraising the consequences of cultural diglossia for Latin literature in the Middle Ages we must avoid drawing hasty correspondences between vernacular, oral, and unlearned, or between Latin, literate, and learned; for there were no absolutes. The vernacular was not always oral, the Latin not always literate. Even the most unlettered peasant was aware of the textuality of the culture around him; even the most literate Latin-writing cleric was steeped in both spoken Latin and spoken vernacular traditions.[6] In the mother tongue we should look for varying degrees of orality, but because of the nature of the records we should not expect to encounter what is sometimes called "primary orality" ("the pristine orality of cultures with no knowledge of writing").[7] We should be equally prepared to find that the Latin used in the church, schools, universities, and courts was as much an oral as a written language.

Indeed, there was in Latin what can be styled "academic orality."[8] Latin was a learned language, but none of the ancient or medieval cultures in which it was used were fully literate. Rather, the Latin-using cultures were in transitional phases between fully oral traditional cultures and the largely literate cultures that are typical of modern Western Europe. To be taught effectively to children who came from these transitional cultures, Latin had to be taught as both an oral and a literate/textual phenomenon. As is well known, the act of reading was

5. Walter J. Ong, *Orality and Literacy: The Technologizing of the Word* (London and New York: Methuen, 1982), p. 113.

6. On the differences between literacy and textuality, see Stock, *Implications of Literacy*, p. 7. Although Franz H. Bäuml did not use the term "textuality," he wrote of "the use of literacy by individuals who were themselves illiterate or only partly literate in Latin." "Varieties and Consequences of Medieval Literacy and Illiteracy," *Speculum* 55 (1980): 237–265; quotation from p. 239.

7. Ong, "Orality," p. 1.

8. Ibid., p. 3.

itself both intensely oral and visual: a text was read not simply
through being scanned with the eyes, but also through being
mouthed or sounded aloud. Thus although Latin was closely
bound to set scriptures, liturgies, and laws, much of the information contained in these texts was communicated orally in
schools (commentaries, colloquies, dialogues, and debates)
and churches (homilies and sermons).[9]

The native language was sometimes employed in the basic
instruction of pupils who had not yet achieved a command of
elementary Latin, but it was not usually used in the teaching
of reading and writing. King Alfred, although arguably repre-
sentative of England in his times, was exceptional for the Middle Ages as a whole in having learned to read from a book of
English poetry:[10] most little pupils memorized the entire Latin
psalter either before or while learning to read.[11] So strong was
the oral and oratorical component in medieval education that

9. On colloquies, dialogues, and debates, see Lloyd William Daly, "The
Altercatio Hadriani Augusti et Epicteti Philosophi and the Question-and-
Answer Dialogue," *Illinois Studies in Language and Literature*, vol. 24, no.
1 (1939): 5–94; G. N. Garmonsway, "The Development of the Colloquy,"
in Peter Clemoes, ed., *The Anglo-Saxons: Studies in Some Aspects of Their
History and Culture Presented to Bruce Dickins* (London: Bowes & Bowes,
1959), pp. 248–261; Peter L. Schmidt, "Zur Typologie und Literarisierung
des frühchristlichen lateinischen Dialogs," in Manfred Fuhrmann, ed.,
*Christianisme et formes littéraires de l'antiquité tardive en occident: Van-
doeuvres—Genève 23–28 août 1976* (Geneva: Fondation Hart; Berne: Dé-
positaire pour la Suisse, Franke, 1977), pp. 101–180; Hans Walther, *Das
Streitgedicht in der lateinischen Literatur des Mittelalters* (Munich: Beck,
1920); and Michael Winterbottom, "On the *Hisperica Famina*," *Celtica* 8
(1967): 126–139.

10. See Asser, *Life of King Alfred (De rebus gestis Ælfredi)*, 23.2–3
("quendam Saxonicum poematicae artis librum"), ed. William Henry
Stevenson (Oxford: Clarendon, 1959), p. 20, and D. A. Bullough, "The Education Tradition in England from Alfred to Aelfric: Teaching *utriusque linguae*," in *La Scuola nell' Occidente Latino del' Alto Medioevo* (Spoleto:
Centro italiano di studi sull' Alto Medioevo, 1972), pp. 453–495.

11. See Franz Falk, *Bibelstudien: Bibelhandschriften und Bibeldrucke in
Mainz vom achten Jahrhundert bis zur Gegenwart* (Mainz: Franz
Kirchheim, 1901), pp. 28–29, and Pierre Riché, *Education and Culture in
the Barbarian West from the Sixth through the Eighth Century*, trans. John
J. Contreni (Columbia: University of South Carolina Press, 1976), pp. 282
and 463–465.

a person could be educated and proficient in speaking Latin without being able to write it comfortably. In other words, schooling and literacy were not identical. Walter Map was only stating the obvious when he pointed out that scribes sometimes copied texts that they could not understand.[12] The converse was that well-educated people sometimes were unable to handle quill and parchment. Furthermore, they sometimes learned their Latin as a nontextual language or in a nontextual way. Einhard reports that Charlemagne "was not content with his own mother tongue, but took the trouble to learn foreign languages. He learnt Latin so well that he spoke it as fluently as his own tongue . . . He also tried to learn to write . . . but, although he tried very hard, he had begun too late in life and he made little progress."[13]

No matter how much Latin was used by a given speaker or writer, it remained a foreign tongue. Around 865 Otfrid of Weissenburg explained in a letter that he had composed vernacular poems about the Gospels so that people who were daunted by Latin might come to terms with the Scriptures *propria lingua* (in one's own language).[14] In the early eleventh century Notker III of St. Gall, as he explained his reasons for translating Latin works into Old High German, used the negative of this phrase to characterize Latin: it was *lingua non propria* (a language not one's own).[15] Although a person con-

---

12. Walter Map, *De nugis curialium: Courtiers' Trifles,* Distinctio 4, Chapter 1, Prologue, ed. and trans. M. R. James, rev. C. N. L. Brooke and R. A. B. Mynors (Oxford: Clarendon, 1983), pp. 278–279; discussed by M. T. Clanchy, *From Memory to Written Record: England, 1066–1307* (Cambridge, Mass.: Harvard University Press, 1979), pp. 181 and 218.

13. *Vita Karoli Magni Imperatoris,* Chapter 25, ed. Louis Halphen (Paris: "Les Belles Lettres," 1938), pp. 74–76; translation from *Einhard and Notker the Stammerer: Two Lives of Charlemagne,* trans. Lewis Thorpe (Baltimore: Penguin Books, 1969), p. 79.

14. For the passage and bibliography, see Michael Richter, "Kommunikationsprobleme im lateinischen Mittelalter," *Historische Zeitschrift* 222 (1976): 43–80; quotation from p. 61, n. 49.

15. "Scio tamen quia primum abhorrebitis quasi ab insuetis. Sed paulatim forte incipient se commendare uobis et preualebitis ad legendum et ad dinoscendum quam cito capiuntur per patriam linguam que aut uix aut non

versant only with the mother tongue could be called an "idiot"
(*idiotae* sometimes meant "monoglot")[16] and although the
mother tongue was considered the handmaiden (as the word
"vernacular" implies) of the father tongue, the mother tongue
was not forgotten by anyone or despised by everyone who
committed himself to the learned world.

The interaction of oral and written, vernacular and Latin,
and improvised and fixed was much more complicated than
any congeries of simple polarities will describe. Take by way
of evidence the last days of the Latin historian and exegete
Bede in 735, as described in an eyewitness account written by
his pupil Cuthbert: Bede gave daily lessons to students, sang
psalms, ruminated upon scriptural passages, recited a one-
sentence Old English poem ("Bede's Death Song") on the
theme of death,[17] and dictated a translation from Latin into Old
English of the Gospel of John and extracts from the writings
of Isidore of Seville.[18] To move to a less elaborate death scene

---

integre capienda forent in lingua non propria." "I know nevertheless that
at first you will shrink as if from unfamiliar things; but perhaps little by little
they will begin to commend themselves to your attention, and you will man-
age to read and to recognize how quickly things can be understood in the
mother tongue which could barely or not fully be understood in a language
not one's own." *Die Schriften Notkers und seiner Schule,* ed. Paul Piper,
vol. 1 (Freiburg and Tübingen: J. C. B. Mohr, 1882), pp. 859–861. For discussion see Richter, "Kommunikationsprobleme," pp. 70, 73–75.

16. Bede defines the medieval sense of the word bluntly in the "Epistola
Bede ad Ecgbertum Episcopum," in *Historia ecclesiastica gentis anglorum; Historia abbatum; Epistola ad Ecgberctum; una cum Historia abbatum auctore anonymo,* ed. Carolus Plummer, 2 vols. (Oxford: Clarendon,
1896), vol. 1, pp. 405–423: "idiotas, hoc est, eos qui propriae tantum linguae
notitiam habent"—"*idiotae,* that is, those who know only their own language" (p. 409). On the shift to the modern meaning, see Herbert Grundmann,
"*Litteratus-Illiteratus:* Der Wandel einer Bildungsnorm vom Altertum zum
Mittelalter," *Archiv für Kulturgeschichte* 40 (1958): 1–65, esp. p. 2, n. 4.

17. Cuthbert leaves unclear whether the poem was composed by Bede
himself, recited by memory from a poem that Bede had heard, or recited by
memory from a text that he had read.

18. *Bede's Ecclesiastical History of the English People,* ed. and trans.
Bertram Colgrave and R. A. B. Mynors (Oxford: Clarendon Press, 1969),
pp. 579–587. The most readily available translation is in Bede, *A History of
the English Church and People,* trans. Leo Sherley-Price, rev. R. E.
Latham (Baltimore: Penguin Books, 1968), pp. 18–21.

in the twelfth century, recall the last words of Aelred of Rievaulx: "Festinate, for crist luue" (Hasten, for the love of
Christ). Aelred's hagiographer explains that the saint spoke the
Lord's name in English because it was "a word of one syllable
in this tongue and easier to utter, and in some ways sweeter to
hear."[19]

My proposal is a straightforward one: that, like Bede and
Aelred, no medieval Latin author would have forgotten altogether the tone and literature of his *lingua propria*. Many authors who wrote in Latin would have continued to live part of
their lives in the local spoken language or languages. Even a
person who took a solemn vow to communicate solely in Latin
would not have been free from the vernacular: his thoughts and
his means of framing them would have been shaped partly by
his vernacular.[20]

The most explicit occasions on which a Latin speaker or
writer had to come to grips with the spoken language was when
translating verbatim. Historians often purported to record actual speeches or conversations, but it is notoriously difficult to
determine how much faith they show to oral vernacular or
Latin rhetoric and how much they accommodate it to the conventions of written Latin rhetoric.

More promising are cases in which writers transformed vernacular verse into Latin. Usually too little of the native verse
tradition is known for the extant Latin to be more than tanta-
lizing evidence of all that has been lost. For instance, when
Bishop Julian of Toledo (680–691) encourages a correspondent
to eschew "cantica vulgarium poetarum" (songs of vernacular
poets), he cites as an example a Latin recasting of one verse
from a popular song of a wolf and an ass: "Lupus dum ambu-
laret viam, incontravit asinum" (as the wolf was walking down
the road, it met an ass).[21] Since next to nothing is known of

19. See Walter Daniel, *The Life of Ailred of Rievaulx,* Chapter 54, ed.
and trans. F. M. Powicke (London: Thomas Nelson, 1950), p. 60.

20. On pacts to speak only Latin, see Michael Winterbottom, "On the
Hisperica famina," *Celtica* 8 (1967): 126–139, esp. 129, 131–132.

21. Bernhard Bischoff, "Ein Brief Julians von Toledo über Rythmen, me-
trische Dichtung und Prosa," *Hermes* 87 (1959): 247–256, rpt. *Mittelalter-
liche Studien,* vol. 1 (Stuttgart: Hiersemann, 1966), pp. 288–298, quotation,

seventh-century Visigothic literature, there is no basis for re-
constructing either the form or the content of the song that
Julian had heard. But sometimes scraps can be pieced together, as when the twelfth-century English historian Henry of
Huntingdon quotes a few Latin lines that imitate (as italics will
show) the alliterative pattern of Old English verse: "unde dicitur; '*Amn*is Idle *Ang*lorum *s*anguine *s*orduit'" (whence it is
said: 'The river Idle was soiled with the blood of Englishmen');
"unde dicitur, 'In *Win*wed *amne vin*dicata est caedes *Annae*'"
(whence it is said: 'Anna's slaughter was avenged at the river
Winwæd'); "unde dicitur, '*Cam*pus Masefeld sanctorum *can*-
duit ossibus'" (whence it is said: 'The field of Maserfield
gleamed white with the bones of saints'); and "unde dicitur:
'Ellendune *rivu*s cruore *ru*buit, *rui*na *r*estitit, fætore tabuit'"
(whence it is said: 'The river Ellendune was ruddy with blood,
came to a standstill because of the debris, rotted away with the
stench').[22]

In rare instances good fortune permits comparison between
vernacular originals and Latin *contrafacta*. In the *Historia ecclesiastica* Bede paraphrased "Caedmon's Hymn" in Latin,
acknowledging perspicaciously: "This is the general sense, but
not the actual words that Caedmon sang in his dream; for
verses, however masterly, cannot be translated literally from
one language into another without losing much of their beauty
and dignity."[23] To remedy the insufficiency of Bede's Latin in
conveying the flavor of Old English, scribes frequently in-

---

p. 296. See Dronke in the discussion following Ferruccio Bertini, "Gli ani-
mali nella favolistica medievale dal *Romulus* al secolo XII," in *L'Uomo di
fronte al mondo animale nell'alto medioevo, 7–13 aprile 1983* (Spoleto:
Centro italiano di studi sull'alto medioevo, 1985), vol. 2, pp. 1031–51 and
1053–56 (discussion).

22. Henry of Huntingdon, *Historia Anglorum: The History of the
English*, 2.30, 2.34, 3.39, and 4.29, ed. Thomas Arnold, Rolls Series 74
(London: Longman, 1879), pp. 56, 60, 95, and 132. R. M. Wilson, *The Lost
Literature of Medieval England*, 2nd ed. (London: Methuen, 1970), pp.
28–29, notes that many of these lines, "when turned into Old English, seem
to fall naturally into alliterative verse," but he does not remark that the
Latin is alliterative.

23. *Ecclesiastical History* 4.24, trans. Sherley-Price and Latham, p. 251.

cluded what appear to be the original verses either in the margin, at the end of the manuscript, or in the text.[24]

Less widely known than the Latin and Old English of "Caedmon's Hymn" are the two versions of the poem "Munkat ec nefna," composed in Old Norse by an Icelander named Stefnir þorgilsson about 1000. The lost Latin original of the *Saga of Óláfr Tryggvason* by Oddr Snorrason (around 1190) included a translation of the poem. When an anonymous author translated the Latin saga into Old Norse (around 1200), either he or a copyist retained the first stanza of the Latin translation of Stefnir's poem and inserted after it the Old Norse original.

Nec nominabo	Munkat ec nefna
pene monstrabo	nær mun ec stefna.
curuus est de orsum	niðr biugt er nef
nasus in apostata	a niþingi;
qui sueion regem	þann er suein konung
de terra seduxit	sueik or landi
et filium tryggva	oc tryggua son
traxit in dolo.	a talar dro.

His name I say not, but his mark I'll tell;
A crooked nose the craven has,
Who lured King Swein forth from his land,
And Tryggwi's son enticed
Into the toils.[25]

Here the Latin poet replicates both the texture of the Old Norse poetic syntax, by weaving into the main sentence other threads of thought ("pene monstrabo: curuus est deorsum nasus in apostata"), and the alliterative pattern of the

24. See Elliott Van Kirk Dobbie, ed., *The Anglo-Saxon Minor Poems* (New York: Columbia University Press, 1942), pp. c–cvii and 105–106.

25. The texts are quoted and discussed in Karsten Friis-Jensen, *Saxo Grammaticus as Latin Poet: Studies of the Verse Passages of the Gesta Danorum* (Rome: L'Erma di Bretschneider, 1987), p. 40. The standard edition is *Saga Óláfs Tryggvasonar: Af Oddr Snorrason, munk*, ed. Finnur Jónsson (Copenhagen 1932). The English is from *The Saga of King Olaf Tryggwason*, trans. J. Sephton (London: David Nutt, 1895), p. 441.

fornyrðislag meter ("*s*ueion . . . *s*eduxit . . . *t*ryggva *t*raxit").[26] The closing verse of the Latin seems to cap the imitation by rearranging the vowels and consonants of the Old Norse.[27]

Direct translation was not the only circumstance in which the vernacular entered into the composition of Latin literature. The special brands of bilingualism and multilingualism in the Latin Middle Ages brought with them a heightened sensitivity to what a linguist might call code-switching. In written literature such code-switching is readily detected when an author interjects words or phrases from one language into a text written in another language.[28]

The starkest form of code-switching occurs in macaronic poetry. Although the term was coined to describe Renaissance poetry in which words of a vernacular language were inflected with Latin endings, it has been transferred to medieval literature to designate poems in one language or dialect that systematically incorporate words or phrases from at least one other language or dialect.[29] Such macaronic poems may have tail-rhyme stanzas in one language with varying *caudae* in another, stanzas in one language with a regular refrain in another, or lines which are half vernacular and half Latin.[30]

---

26. These are Friis-Jensen's observations (p. 40).

27. *Pace* Friis-Jensen, to whom the Latin is "a clumsy direct rendering" of the Norse.

28. See August Grünewald, *Die lateinischen Einschiebsel in den deutschen Gedichten von der Mitte des 11. bis gegen Ende des 12. Jahrhunderts* (Göttingen: E. A. Huth, 1908); Otto Müller, *Die lateinischen Einschiebsel in den französischen Literatur des Mittelalters* (Zurich: Leemann, 1919); and Siegfried Wenzel, "The English Verses in the *Fasciculus Morum*," in Beryl Rowland, ed., *Chaucer and Middle English Studies in Honor of Rossell Hope Robbins* (Kent, Ohio: Kent State University Press, 1974), pp. 230–248.

29. Other terms that have not been widely accepted are *barbarolexis*, proposed by Emil Henrici, *Sprachmischung in älterer Dichtung Deutschlands* (Berlin: Julius Klönne Nachfolger, 1913–1914), 2 vols.; and *poésie bilingue*, put forth by Paul Zumthor, "Un problème d'esthétique médiévale: l'utilisation poétique du bilinguisme," *Le Moyen Age* 66 (1960): 301–336.

30. The fullest typology is in William O. Wehrle, "The Macaronic Hymn Tradition in Medieval English Literature" (diss., Catholic University, Washington, D.C., 1933).

More needs to be determined about the meters in which medieval macaronic verses were composed. In the early period macaronic poems seem to have been written most often in meters usually employed in the native language, with vernacular and Latin half-lines alternating regularly (as in the case of the closing lines of the Old English *Phoenix,* the Old English *Summons to Prayer,* and the Old High German *De Heinrico*).[31] But later in the Middle Ages the meters of macaronic poems were not so likely to have been dictated by the vernacular; the *Carmina burana* contain Latin poems with refrains in German or Romance as well as Latin poems with final strophes in German in the same metrical form.[32]

In one sense, a macaronic poem that combines Latin and another language can be fully meaningful only to a very narrow circle: the few people to comprehend the whole poem will be those who command both Latin and the local language. Yet a carefully conceived macaronic poem could have appealed to the tastes and aptitudes of two audiences. For instance, both the Latin and vernacular bits of the macaronic lyrics in the *Carmina burana* would have been intelligible to the people who knew Latin (mainly men), while the German or Old French sections alone would have been appreciated by those who had no Latin (including most women).[33] Besides involving

31. See *The Exeter Book,* ed. George Philip Krapp and Elliott Van Kirk Dobbie (New York: Columbia University Press, 1936), pp. 94–113, esp. 112–113, ll. 667–677; Dobbie, *The Minor Poems,* pp. 69–70; and Karl Strecker, ed. *Die Cambridger Lieder,* Monumenta Germaniae Historica 40, 2nd ed. (Berlin, 1955), pp. 57–60, no. 19. On the meter of the *De Heinrico,* see Paul Habermann, *Die Metrik der kleineren althochdeutschen Reimgedichte* (Halle: Max Niemeyer, 1909), pp. 65–77.

32. See Bruce A. Beatie, "Macaronic Poetry in the *Carmina Burana,*" *Vivarium* 5 (1967): 16–24.

33. What I hypothesize for the *Carmina burana* could also be true of Arabic and Hebrew *muwashshaḥa-s,* which conclude with final stanzas that feature words in a colloquial idiom (usually Arabic, but sometimes Romance). For texts, see Klaus Heger, *Die bisher veröffentlichten Harǧas und ihre Deutungen,* Zeitschrift für romanische Philologie, Beiheft 101 (Tübingen: Niemeyer, 1960); J. M. Sola-Solé, *Corpus de poesía mozárabe (las ḫarǧa-s andalusíes)* (Barcelona: Ediciones Hispam, 1973); and Samuel M. Stern, *Hispano-Arabic Strophic Poetry: Studies by Samuel Miklos*

two audiences, the macaronic poems could have provided a
forum for antiphonal singing by two sorts of performers: clerics could have sung in the learned language, while laymen or
laywomen could have delivered the vernacular stanzas.

But the effect of macaronic poetry may not always have
been to involve two different groups of listeners or performers.
In the case of macaronic English-Latin carols another explanation is possible. More than a third of English carols include
Latin lines or phrases, most of which derive ultimately from a
small corpus of liturgical hymns well known even to Latin-less
congregations.[34] Even if the bilingualism of the carols was not
designed to bring together laymen and clerics, it would still
have added the luster and special authority of Latin's prestige.

To turn to another genre, the Old French play known as
Sponsus is a drama about the coming of the bridegroom (Matthew 25:1–13) that includes refrains in French as well as
speeches both partly and wholly in French.[35] The linguistic arrangement of the *Sponsus* quite possibly reflects a desire to
make the Latin service more engaging and meaningful to laymen through incorporating the vernacular. If so, the *Sponsus*
would be comparable to two paraliturgical macaronic compositions extant from the first half of the twelfth century: a Latin
play about St. Nicholas written by Hilary the Englishman in
which the refrains are French[36] and an interpolated epistle
(*épître farcie*) used on the feast of St. Stephen in which each
Latin verse is followed by one or more French strophes.[37]

The stimulation of living in a diglossic culture could have
partly inspired other classes of macaronic poetry, such as

Stern, sel. and ed. L. P. Harvey (Oxford: Clarendon Press, 1974). For a
guide to scholarship, see Richard Hitchcock, *The Kharjas: A Critical Bibliography* (London: Grant and Cutler, 1977).

34. See Richard Leighton Greene, *The Early English Carols* (Oxford:
Clarendon Press, 1935), pp. lx–xcii.

35. For information see Grace Frank, *The Medieval French Drama* (Oxford: Clarendon Press, 1954), pp. 58–64.

36. See "Die Gedichte und Mysterienspiele des Hilarius von Orléans,"
ed. Nikolaus M. Häring, *Studi Medievali* 17 (1976): 915–968, esp. 950–953.

37. See Urban Tigner Homes, Jr., *A History of Old French Literature
from the Origins to 1300* (New York: F. S. Crofts, 1948), pp. 55 and 58.

Latin poems in which Greek words were included,[38] vernacular poems with admixtures of both Latin and Greek,[39] and poems with blends of two vernaculars and Latin.[40] As these diverse examples suggest, "macaronic poetry" has been used to describe poems that differ sharply from each other in form, content, and presumed audiences. Before a more serviceable terminology can be developed, macaronic poems in a range of different vernaculars must be examined together. The poems should also be compared and contrasted with mixed Latin-vernacular prose, to determine whether or not macaronic verse and prose are interrelated.

In the case of the macaronic poems the inspiration of diglossia is self-evident. The same inspiration could underlie compositions such as the Old English rune poem and three similar Germanic, Icelandic, and Norwegian rune poems, in which two types of script are implied or even explicitly employed.[41] Such poems could even be dubbed "script macaronic poems."

Yet the interaction between Latin and the vernacular languages was not confined to macaronic poetry, which, no matter how broadly defined, was only a narrow byway in medieval literature. The vernaculars exerted a constant linguistic pressure upon Latin. For instance, people have always tended to pronounce Latin "in some consonance with . . . native non-Latin speech."[42] Accordingly, an arrangement of Latin words that would produce a pun in one region might have no such effect in another. The native languages probably also colored spelling, intonation, and syntax, although these are questions

---

38. For a rudimentary and outdated consideration see Henrici, *Sprachmischung,* pp. 8–15.

39. For example, see the Old English *Aldhelm,* in Van Kirk Dobbie, ed., *The Anglo-Saxon Minor Poems,* pp. 97–98.

40. See the two love letters entitled *De Amico ad Amicam* and *Responcio* in E. K. Chambers and F. Sidgwick, *Early English Lyrics: Amorous, Divine, Moral and Trivial* (London: Sidgwick & Jackson, 1921), pp. 15–19, nos. 8 and 9.

41. See Maureen Halsall, ed., *The Old English Rune Poem: A Critical Edition* (Toronto: University of Toronto Press, 1981).

42. G. Herbert Fowler, "Notes on the Pronunciation of Medieval Latin in England," *History* 22 (1938): 97–109; quotation from p. 97.

that demand further research.[43] Least disputable is that the vernacular languages contributed to medieval Latin many words for objects or concepts which could not have been expressed in pure classical Latin.

Thus far I have focused mainly upon direct verbal or linguistic contributions from the mother tongues into medieval Latin. Before turning to the literary influences of the vernaculars upon medieval Latin, a further caveat is in order. Because many medieval Latinists begin their careers as classical philologists, the study of medieval Latin literature has tended to emphasize the continuity of the classical tradition and the unifying force of Latin, and to pay less heed to the presence of popular tradition in medieval Latin literature. The governing conception is of *European Literature and the Latin Middle Ages* (no matter how coolly medieval Latinists have tended to regard Curtius's book), rather than "Latin literature in the European Middle Ages." This emphasis sometimes brings with it a kind of cultural colonialism: we suppose that medieval Latin authors at most took raw materials from the *Volk* and adapted them to classical conventions and Christian contexts, but remained otherwise unsullied by popular culture. This supposition has some truth to it, since no one can deny the non-popular and nonvernacular dimensions of poems such as the *Waltharius, Unibos,* and medieval Latin beast epics, or *prosimetra* such as Saxo Grammaticus's *Danorum Regum Heroumque Historia;* but it is not the whole picture.

With some notable exceptions, medievalists have been inclined to believe that the relationship between Latin and oral culture was mainly one-way, with most influence running from

---

43. P. B. Corbett, "Local Variation of Spelling in Latin MSS," *Studia Patristica* 1 (1957): 188–193; Norbert Fickermann, "Schreibfehler oder Sprachtatsache? Stichproben aus der mittellateinischen Formenlehre," in Bernhard Bischoff and Suse Brechter, eds., *Liber Floridus: Mittellateinische Studien Paul Lehmann gewidmet* (St. Ottilien: Eos Verlag der Erzabtei, 1950), pp. 19–26; Einar Löfstedt, "Regionale Unterschiede im Lateinischen," in *Late Latin* (Oslo: Universitetforlaget, 1959), pp. 39–58; K. Sittl, *Die lokalen Verschiedenheiten der lateinischen Sprache* (Erlangen: A. Deichert, 1882); and E. Vandvik, "National Admixture in Medieval Latin," *Symbolae Osloenses* 23 (1944): 81–101.

the former to the latter.[44] Scholars of vernacular literatures have done little to dissuade us. For all the fine studies that trace the debt of vernacular literature to Latin syntax, prose-rhythm and *cursus,* and rhetoric,[45] there are relatively few systematically to document the effect of vernacular languages and oral literatures upon either the style or content of medieval Latin writings.[46]

In some cases no one is to blame: the necessary data for a clear appreciation are often not available, since so little vernacular literature is extant from many areas of Europe at many times in the Middle Ages.[47] For every Charlemagne whose goodwill caused "age-old narrative poems" to be collected, there was a Louis the Pious whose disapproval would have consigned such collections to oblivion.[48] To make matters worse, what little vernacular literature survives was often chosen and shaped by clerics, who in many periods controlled the

44. See Peter Dronke, "Curtius as Medievalist and Modernist," *Times Literary Supplement,* October 3, 1980, pp. 1103–1106.

45. On Old English, see Joshua H. Bonner, "Toward a Unified Critical Approach to Old English Poetic Composition," *Modern Philology* 73 (1976): 219–228, and three articles by Jackson J. Campbell, "Learned Rhetoric in Old English Poetry," *Modern Philology* 63 (1966): 189–201; "Knowledge of Rhetorical Figures in Anglo-Saxon England," *Journal of English and Germanic Philology* 66 (1967): 1–20; and "Adaptation of Classical Rhetoric in Old English Literature," in James J. Murphy, ed., *Medieval Eloquence: Studies in the Theory and Practice of Medieval Rhetoric* (Berkeley: University of California Press, 1978), pp. 173–197. On Old Norse, see Frederick Amory, "Saga Style in Some Kings' Sagas, and Early Medieval Latin Narrative," *Acta Philologica Scandinavica* 32 (1978): 67–86, and Peter Foote, "Latin Rhetoric and Icelandic Poetry: Some Contacts," *Saga och sed: Kungl. Gustav Adolfs Akademiens Årsbok* (1982): 107–127.

46. Two exceptions are Alexandra Hennessey Olsen, "Old English Poetry and Latin Prose: The Reverse Context," *Classica et Mediaevalia* 34 (1983): 273–282, and Colin C. Smith, "Latin Histories and Vernacular Epic in Twelfth-Century Spain: Similarities of Spririt and Style," *Bulletin of Hispanic Studies* 48 (1971): 1–19.

47. R. M. Wilson's *The Lost Literature of Medieval England* takes stock of what has perished.

48. See Einhard, *Vita Karoli,* Chapter 29, ed. Halphen, p. 82, trans. Thorpe, p. 82; and Thegan, *Vita Ludowici imperatoris,* ed. G. H. Pertz, Monumenta Germaniae Historica, Scriptores 2 (1829): pp. 590–603.

technology of writing. When considering early appearances of
vernacular languages and literatures as mere insertions (*Einschiebsel*) in Latin texts, we should bear in mind that Latin
itself was no more than an insertion in the whole scheme of
medieval life.

To round out our understanding of the Middle Ages we are
duty-bound to reconstruct what we can of the lost literature
and to look for ways in which it could have infiltrated Latin
literature. It is evident that the school training of those literate
in Latin emphasized admiration and imitation of canonical authors, whose writings were filled with the authoritative observations known as *auctoritates*. But it is equally true that their
schooling inculcated an esteem for *consuetudo*, for customary
practice.[49] To put Gregory's letter to Mellitus into literary
terms, or to follow Augustine's Egyptian-gold and Jerome's
slave-girl images to their logical conclusions, school training
could have allowed an author to take what was profitable and
attractive from native culture so long as it was applied to a
proper end.[50]

What could medieval Latin authors have gained from oral
literature in their native languages? Although in all cases we
must take into account special qualities of the vernacular in
which the poet lived, a few general categories that suggest

49. For example, Maximus Victorinus, *Ars grammatica,* in Heinrich
Keil, ed. *Grammatici Latini,* 8 vols. (Leipzig: B. G. Teubner, 1857–1880),
vol. 6, pp. 187–205: "Quot modis constat latinitas? Tribus. Quibus? Ra-
tione, auctoritate, consuetudine . . . Quid consuetudine? Eorum verborum,
quae e medio loquendi usu placita adsumptaque sunt" (p. 189). This passage
is also in Augustine, *Ars pro fratrum mediocritate breuiata,* ed. Keil, vol.
5, p. 494.

50. For Gregory's letter, see Bede, *Ecclesiastical History,* 1.30. For the
Egyptian gold, see Augustine, *De doctrina christiana,* 2. 40. 60–61 (on
Exodus 3:22 and 12:35–36), in *Sancti Aurelii Augustini Opera Pars* 4, 1, ed.
I. Martin and K. -D. Daur, Corpus Christianorum Series Latina 32 (Turn-
hout: Brepols, 1961), pp. 73–75. For the slave girl (from Deuteronomy
21:11–12), see Jerome, *Epistle* 21:13, "Ad Damasum," in *Sancti Eusebii
Hieronymi epistulae,* 1, ed. Isidorus Hilberg, Corpus Scriptorum Ecclesias-
ticorum Latinorum 54 (Vienna: F. Tempsky, 1910), p. 122, l. 12–p. 123, l. 7;
and *Epistle* 70. 2 ("ad Magnum, oratorem urbis Romae"), in ibid., p. 702,
ll. 6–14.

themselves are content, meter, genre, methods of organization, and even methods of inspiration. In the remainder of this essay I will glance at the ways in which the style of oral native literature could have conditioned the style of Latin authors.

One aspect of style that makes an interesting test case is alliteration. Of course, any given instance of this phenomenon in medieval Latin could be explained as a learned touch. Medieval Latin readers could have noticed alliteration in classical poetry (since alliteration appears there occasionally, as it does in all literature) and adopted it as an embellishment in their own compositions.[51] Yet whereas alliteration was only casual in classical Latin, it was an essential constituent of early Germanic verse forms. One early medieval Latin poet whose alliteration has been interpreted variously as oral/native and as written/learned is Aldhelm, the seventh-century scholar and poet.[52] My own inclination would be to suspect the influence of native poetic practice, since Aldhelm came from a Germanic culture and since he is reputed to have been a vernacular poet: William of Malmesbury related that Aldhelm lured lukewarm congregations into church by singing heroic lays in the native language.[53]

Another stylistic trait that vernacular literature could have instilled in medieval Latin writers is an appetite for neologisms. In the tenth and eleventh centuries there evolved a characteristically obscure medieval Latin style, "whose most strik-

51. On alliteration in classical Latin, see J. Marouzeau, *Traité de stylistique latine* (Paris: "Les Belles Lettres," 1946), pp. 45–50, and J. B. Hofmann and Anton Szantyr, *Lateinische Syntax und Stilistik* (Munich: Beck, 1965), pp. 700–702.

52. In favor of Old English influence, see Whitney F. Bolton, *A History of Anglo-Latin Literature 597–1066,* vol. 1 (Princeton: Princeton University Press, 1967), p. 75; Michael Lapidge, "Aldhelm's Latin Poetry and Old English Verse," *Comparative Literature* 31 (1979): 209–230; and Olsen, "Old English Poetry and Latin Prose," p. 276. In favor of classical inspiration, see Michael Winterbottom, "Aldhelm's Prose Style and Its Origins," *Anglo-Saxon England* 6 (1977): 39–76. On a similar difficulty with alliteration in Old Norse, see Amory, "Saga Style," p. 68.

53. William of Malmesbury, *De gestis pontificum Anglorum,* Book 5, chap. 190, ed. N. E. S. A. Hamilton, Rolls Series 52 (London: Her Majesty's Stationery Office, 1870), p. 336.

ing feature is the ostentatious parade of unusual, often very arcane and apparently learned vocabulary."[54] For this style the designation *glossematic* seems especially apt, since it draws attention to the glosses from which the extraordinary vocabulary was drawn.[55] Yet although the vocabulary was thoroughly learned, could the taste for new words in some texts not be an attempt to recreate in Latin the ease of coining compound words and the consequent abundance of hapax legomena that characterize the poetic thesaurus in Germanic and Celtic languages?

A third stylistic feature common in medieval Latin writings is the repetition of the same thought in different words. Here the style can be traced in learned Latin literature to Isidore's *Synonyma* and similar thesauruses of Latin synonyms, sometimes accompanied by vernacular translations; but not all manifestations of this style are necessarily learned and Isidorean in inspiration.[56] Another explanation for the ubiquity of this device in early medieval Latin literature is that authors needed to be sure their audiences, whose Latin was sometimes shaky, had understood them. To this end they would use both a pure Latin word and a Romance equivalent.[57] A further explanation would be that the principle of variation is common to the po-

---

54. See Michael Lapidge, "The Hermeneutic Style in Tenth-Century Anglo-Latin Literature," *Anglo-Saxon England* 4 (1975): 67–111; quotation from p. 67.

55. Georg Goetz derived the term *glossematisch* from Diomedes, *Ars grammatica* 2, ed. Keil, *Grammatici latini*, vol. 1 (1857), pp. 299–529, esp. 440; see Georg Goetz, "Über Dunkel- und Geheim-sprachen im späten und mittelalterlichen Latein," *Berichte über die Verhandlungen der Königlich Sächsischen Gessellschaft der Wissenschaften zu Leipzig, philologisch-historische Classe* 48 (1896): 62–92.

56. For the text, see Isidore, *Synonyma de lamentatione animae peccatricis,* in *Patrologiae cursus completus,* Series latina, 221 vols., ed. J.-P. Migne (Paris, 1841–1864), vol. 83, col. 827–868. For interpretation, see J. Fontaine, "Théorie et pratique du style chez Isidore de Seville," *Vigiliae Christianae* 14 (1960): 65–101.

57. See Robert L. Politzer, "Synonymic Repetition in Late Latin and Romance," *Language* 37 (1961): 484–487, and Smith, "Latin Histories and Vernacular Epic in Twelfth-Century Spain," pp. 10–11.

etics of many oral traditions, including such Germanic oral traditions as Old English.

Even more widespread in medieval Latin literature than alliteration, neologisms, and variation is a fourth stylistic habit, that of reusing the same patterns of words. To see the tolerance or even fondness of medieval Latin authors for such reuse both within a poem and between one poem and another, one need only look at the *Lateinisches Hexameter-Lexikon,* a compendium of phrases that recur in hexameter poetry between Ennius and the Archpoet.[58] These five plump volumes, essentially one man's gleaning of commonplace phrases from his readings in hexameter poetry, could be expanded exponentially.

How should we regard this stock of phrases used in composing medieval Latin hexameter poetry? According to the canons of style that govern twentieth-century English writing, many forms of repetition indicate a writer's ineptitude or lack of versatility. Yet in the past repetition was often tolerated, expected, and even enjoyed, because writers and audiences were raised to honor different canons. Indeed, much of ancient and medieval Latin rhetoric was retained from oral practices that required vast memory and permitted repetition: only with the allowance of repetition was an oral-formulaic poet or a public speaker able to compose without hesitating or stopping.[59]

It is worth considering that medieval Latin poets may have retained poetic techniques from their native cultures as they composed Latin writings. In particular, we should be open to the possibility that medieval Latin poets could have exploited their *koine* of well-known phrases much as oral-formulaic singers used their knowledge of formulas. No doubt such Latin phrases are not generally equivalent to formulas in oral-traditional formulaic poetry, any more than the words "for-

58. Otto Schumann, *Lateinisches Hexameter-Lexikon: Dichterisches Formelgut von Ennius bis zum Archipoeta,* Monumenta Germaniae Historica: Hilfsmittel, 4, 1–6 (Munich: Monumenta Germaniae Historica, 1979–1983).

59. Ong, *Orality,* pp. 40–41.

mula" and "repetition" are synonymous.[60] On the contrary, most of the Latin phrases are tags that facilitated the composition of written poetry, and they were acquired through reading and writing poetry in a learned language, rather than through hearing and composing oral poetry in a mother tongue. But sometimes the Latin phrases could be attempts to recreate or imitate within Latin the formulaic style of oral poetry in the poet's mother tongue. A skillful poet could have used *repetitions* in Latin to convey the flavor of *formulas* in the poetic system of the vernacular. Finally, under rare conditions the Latin phrases could have served some of the same functions as formulas in oral-traditional formulaic composition,[61] especially if the poems in which the Latin phrases appear are likely to have been composed during intramural and interscholastic competitions in debate and versification.[62]

60. The fundamental definition of formula is "a group of words which is regularly employed under the same metrical conditions to express a given essential idea": Milman Parry, "Studies in the Epic Technique of Oral Verse-Making, I: Homer and Homeric Style," *Harvard Studies in Classical Philology* 41 (1930): 73–147, rpt. in Adam Parry, ed., *The Making of Homeric Verse: The Collected Papers of Milman Parry* (Oxford: Clarendon Press, 1971), pp. 266–324; quotation from p. 272. This definition was amplified and supplemented by Albert B. Lord, *The Singer of Tales* (Cambridge, Mass.: Harvard University Press, 1960), esp. pp. 30–67.

61. For a recent history of the research that has arisen from the work of Milman Parry and Albert B. Lord, see John Miles Foley, *The Theory of Oral Composition: History and Methodology* (Bloomington and Indianapolis: Indiana University Press, 1988).

62. Consider the description of twelfth-century school debates in William FitzStephen, "Descriptio nobilissimæ civitatis Londoniæ," in *Vita Sancti Thomæ, Cantuariensis archiepiscopi et martyris,* ed. James Craigie Robertson, *Materials for the History of Thomas Becket, Archbishop of Canterbury,* vol. 3, Rolls Series (London: Longman, 1877), pp. 2–13: "Disputant scholares, quidam demonstrative, dialectice alii; hi rotant enthymemata, hi perfectis melius utuntur syllogismis. . . . Pueri diversarum scholarum versibus inter se conrixantur; aut de principiis artis grammaticæ, vel regulis præteritorum vel supinorum, contendunt. Sunt alii qui in epigrammatibus, rhythmis et metris, utuntur vetere illa triviali dicacitate . . ." "The scholars dispute, some in demonstrative rhetoric, others in dialectic. Some reel off enthymemes, others make better use of full syllogisms . . . Boys of different schools compete against one another in verse; or they contend about the principles of grammar, or the rules of the past and future tenses. There are

My aim in this short voyage through medieval Latin has not been to blot out necessary and indisputable distinctions between oral and literate, vernacular and Latin, or popular and learned, but to issue the reminder that these distinctions should not be drawn hastily and prejudicially. Just as it would be misguided to disregard the classical and Christian in appraising Old English literature, so it would be folly to forget the style and content of oral vernacular compositions in coming to grips with medieval Latin literature. The Latin texts that we read may be in one language, but we should never study the Latin texts in isolation from vernacular oral and literary traditions insofar as they can be reconstructed. In other words, we should always be alert to the possibility that a person who wrote in Latin could have borrowed either deliberately or unconsciously from a native language and literature. The Latin Middle Ages were neither Latin to the exclusion of the vernaculars, nor literate to the exclusion of the oral.

---

others who employ the old crude wit of the crossroads in epigrams, rhythmic poems, and metrical poems . . ." (pp. 4–5). But little information about "the old crude wit of the crossroads" earlier in the Middle Ages has been gathered.

GREGORY NAGY

Song and Dance: Reflections on a Comparison of Faroese Ballad with Greek Choral Lyric

In Faroese tradition, dance functions as an optional element in the performance of ballads—a point of considerable interest to ethnomusicologists (Nettl, 1965, p. 56). In ancient Greek tradition, dance is a key element of what is normally called choral lyric poetry. I propose to compare these two traditions in an effort to discover what such comparisons may tell us about the very nature of song and dance.

Let us begin with the Faroese evidence. The details about dance as an aspect of ballad performance in Faroese society have been outlined in a recent book on Faroese culture (Wylie and Margolin 1981, pp. 99, 115, 117). I note in particular the following description:

At the village dancehall—or, before villages had dancehalls, in a house rented for the occasion—men and women link arms to form a long, twisting circle. Anyone may join the circle at any point. They dance with a rhythmically shuffling, kicking step to the singing of the ballads. There is no instrumental accompaniment. A *skipari* (leader) sings the verses of a ballad, while the rest of the singers join in on the verses (if they know them) and on the refrain. When one ballad ends, the ring keeps moving round for a few moments until a new *skipari* starts up a new one. (p. 99)

214

For the Greek evidence, an admirable point of departure is the discussion in Plato *Laws* 653e–654a (also *Laws* 665a), where the combination of rhythmic and melodic idiom is synthetically visualized as *khoreiā* (choral song and dance). It is a historical given that the ancient Greek *khoros* (chorus) is an ensemble that sings *and* dances; the term *khorōidiā* (choral song) designates a performance by a nonprofessional *khoros,* a singing and dancing ensemble of selected men, boys, or girls.[1] A given chorus in a given *polis* (city-state) may perform a wide variety of compositions related to various local or civic rituals. The range of this variety is apparent from the book titles in the Alexandrian editions of Pindar's choral compositions or "odes." There are, for example, his maiden-songs or *parthenia,* related ultimately to local or civic rituals of coming of age (Calame 1977, vol. 1, pp. 18–20, 117, 249). There are also choral odes connected directly with cults of the gods, such as the *paiānes* (pacans) in honor of Apollo. The list could be extended at length, but it will suffice here to summarize the essence of performance by a *khoros*: Greek choral lyric performance is public, a thing of the community or *polis.* The Spartans, for example, actually referred to the interior of their civic space as the *Khoros* (Pausanias 3.11.9; see Calame 1977, vol. 1, p. 277).

For typological parallels, I cite Marius Schneider's useful cross-cultural survey of collective performance (Scheider 1957). Although this work is in some respects outdated, many of its formulations have a lasting value, such as the following: "But the participation of a [chorus] not only helps the regularity of the rhythmic movement: it also contributes materially to the unification of the melodic line" (p. 4). As an example, he cites the following observation about collective performance in African pygmy society, which normally begins "with a wild cry for all the singers out of which a comparative union gradually emerges. The melodic line and the various rhythms of the opening gradually adjust themselves to one another and in

---

1. The element of dancing is made explicit in this context—*orkhēsesi* (dances). *Laws* 764e.

the end there emerges a completely regular community chant."
As Schneider notes further on, "the powerful influence of collective performance on the development of primitive music
can be seen from the fact that even funeral music and love-
songs are also very largely choral" (p. 4).

Such typological parallels, however, raise the fundamental
question: how are we to define song itself? In traditional societies, not only the smaller-scale but the more complex as well,
there is a pattern of opposition between song and speech. By
speech I mean everyday or unmarked language, and by song I
mean special or marked language that is set off from speech on
the formal level of phonology, morphology, syntax, or any
combination of these three.[2] From a functional point of view,
song would be any speech-act that is *considered* to be set apart
from plain or everyday speech by a given society.[3]

The perception of plain or everyday speech is a variable abstraction that depends on the concrete realization of whatever
special speech, or song, is set apart for a special context. In
small-scale societies, the setting apart would normally happen
through myth and ritual. I use the word "ritual" here not in
terms of our own cultural preconceptions but in terms of the
broadest possible anthropological perspective (see Leach
1982, esp. pp. 4–5). For the moment, I invoke the working definition of ritual offered by Walter Burkert: "Ritual, in its out-
ward aspect, is a programme of demonstrative acts to be
performed in set sequence and often at a set place and time—
sacred insofar as every omission or deviation arouses deep

2. The terms "marked" and "unmarked" have been defined as follows
by Roman Jakobson: "The general meaning of a marked category states the
presence of a certain (whether positive or negative) property A; the general
meaning of the corresponding unmarked category states nothing about the
presence of A" (Jakobson 1984, p. 47). I omit the final segment of Jakobson's definition, "the general meaning of the corresponding unmarked category states nothing about the presence of A, *and is used chiefly, but not
exclusively, to indicate the absence of A,*" in light of the discussion by Comrie (1976, p. 122 and n2). For further updating on the semantic applications
of the terms "marked and "unmarked," with bibliography, see Waugh 1982.

3. On the notion of speech-act as applied to traditional poetic forms from
the standpoint of social anthropology, see Martin 1989.

anxiety and calls forth sanctions. As communication and social imprinting, ritual establishes and secures the solidarity of the closed group" (Burkert 1958, p. 8). The insistence of ritual on a set order of things should not be misunderstood to mean that all rituals are static and that all aspects of rituals are rigid. Even in cases where a given society deems a given ritual to be static and never-changing, it may in fact be dynamic and ever-changing, responding to the ever-changing structure of the society that it articulates. Also, even within the strict framework of a given ritual, the various rigid patterns that conform to an ideology of unchangeability may be combined with various flexible patterns that conform to the needs of the here-and-now. As for myth, it can be defined for the moment as "a traditional narrative that is used as a designation of reality. Myth is applied narrative. Myth describes a meaningful and important reality that applies to the aggregate, going beyond the individual."[4]

It is in small-scale rather than complex societies that we can observe most clearly the symbiosis of ritual and myth, how neither is to be derived from the other, and how the language of ritual and myth is marked—let us continue to call it "song"—while everyday language, speech, is unmarked. To repeat, the perception of plain or everyday speech is a variable abstraction that depends on the concrete realization of the special speech that is set apart for a special context, or occasion. In small-scale societies, the setting apart is normally a matter of ritual and myth, and the ritual may include such diverse occasions as hunting, gathering, farming, building, traveling, meeting, eating and drinking, courtship, and the like (see Leach 1982, pp. 5–6). The marked speech-acts associated with the special occasions of ritual and myth are what we are calling song. Internal criteria for marked speech acts can be expected to vary from society to society: what may be marked in one may be unmarked or "everyday" in another. A striking example is the Bahutu convention of singing one kind of song

----

4. My translation, with slight modifications, of Burkert 1979b, p. 29. For an illuminating discussion of myth, especially useful to those who are unfamiliar with the perspectives of social anthropology, see Leach 1982.

while paddling upstream, another while paddling downstream (Nettl 1965, p. 120). I should add that there are potential differentiations of marked and unmarked categories within everyday language as well.

In complex societies, and the ancient Greek as well as the latter-day Faroese contexts can be described as such, the pervasiveness of myth and ritual, as well as their connectedness with each other, may be considerably weakened. Still, the marking of speech—that is, the turning of unmarked speech into marked song—may persist as the basic way to convey meaning in the context of ritual and myth. Let us for the moment take it as a given, then, that the function of marked speech or song is to convey meaning in the context of ritual and myth.

From the standpoint of our own cultural preconceptions, song in the sense of "singing a song" is a patterning of both melody (stylized tone or intonation) and rhythm (stylized duration and/or intensity).[5] From a cross-cultural survey of a variety of societies, however, it is evident that "singing" may also be equated with many other types of stylized phonological patterning, such as isosyllabism, rhyme, assonance, and alliteration, and that the patterning of song extends to the levels of morphology and syntax as well.[6] Moreover, there is a potential reinforcement of song with motor activity, as minimal as muscular tension or as maximal as corresponding movement of the body in the form of dance.[7]

5. On duration and intensity as aspects of "stress," see Devine and Stephens 1985, p. 152.

6. See Guillén 1985, pp. 93–121, esp. 103–104; also Bright 1963, p. 29. One feature of the fusion of experience in ritual, as Stanley Tambiah suggests, is "the hyper-regular surface structure of ritual language: the poetic devices such as rhyme, meter, assonance, and alliteration generate an overall quality of union and a blurring of grammatical boundaries" (Tambiah 1985, p. 165). See also Jakobson 1960, p. 358.

7. Note the following remark of Alan Merriam: "some connection is made between pitch and muscle tension; the musician becomes accustomed to the muscle tension which he knows to be correct. One Basongye musician expressed this by saying that he chooses a pitch 'which does not make me sweat,' and the same musician very logically noted that he comes to

The concept of dance should not be defined narrowly on the basis of our own cultural preconceptions. The categories of stylized bodily movement corresponding to our notion of dance vary from society to society (see Royce 1977). With this caution duly recorded, let us consider further the two examples of traditions where dance is indeed an aspect of song, the Faroese and the ancient Greek.

In the case of the Faroese evidence, as outlined in the description quoted above, I stress that people are described as dancing *to* the song. From this point onward, I shall be arguing that the activity of dancing *to* the words of song is primary, whereas dancing without the subtext, as it were, of song is secondary.[8] The positing of this hierarchy leads us to the subject of yet another type of markedness, yet another level of reinforcement for song—that is, instrumental music: I shall also be arguing that instrumental accompaniment of the words of song is primary, whereas instrumental solo is secondary.[9] In the case of instrumental music, there can even come about a transition from *marking speech as special* to *imitating special speech*.[10] In making these arguments, my central point remains

---

know the voices of the people with whom he sings and thus chooses a starting pitch 'in the middle' which he knows will suit all the voices" (Merriam 1964, p. 119). See also Allen 1973, p. 100.

8. See the ethnographic testimony discussed briefly in Merriam 1964, p. 275.

9. See Herzog 1934; Schneider 1957, pp. 32–33. Note too Bake (1957, pp. 196–197) on the Indic traditional teaching that vocal music is "pure" sound while instrumental music is a "manifestation" of sound. As Nettl (1965, p. 51) points out, the limitations of the human voice (not to mention the limitations of the human ear), as contrasted with the relatively greater freedom of sound-range in musical instruments, lead to differences in the patterns of evolution for vocal and instrumental music. In this connection, it is useful to ponder the discussion of Bright (1963, p. 27). See in general the survey of the relationships between language and "music" in Nettl 1964, pp. 281–292. On the tendency of specialization and even professionalization in the social position of those who perform song with instrumental accompaniment and, by extension, of those who perform on musical instruments, see Nettl 1965, p. 50.

10. Hence the notion of "talking instruments," as discussed in Stern 1957; see also Ong 1977b. On instrumental music as imitation of the "special

that the essential characteristic of song is the simple fact of its actual markedness or distinctness from everyday speech.

Here we turn to the evidence of ancient Greek. Let us pursue the question of song and speech with a tentative formulation on the level of phonology, considering the elements of rhythm and melody, prime constituents of our notion of singing. From the standpoint of the Greek language, what potentially sets song apart from speech is a differentiation in patterns of duration/intensity (eventually rhythm) and pitch (eventually melody).[11]

In ancient Greek traditions, we can see clearly a further stage of differentiation: just as song is set apart from speech, so also poetry is set apart from song. The differentiation takes place on the level of pitch (melody), in that song is "plus melody" while poetry is "minus melody" or "reduced melody." The notion of "plus melody" is in line with such terms as "lyric poetry" or "melic poetry," applicable to the medium of choral lyric.

---

speech" of birdsong, see Merriam 1964, p. 75. Conversely, at one step further removed, unusual vocal techniques like Alpine yodeling can be traced back to the imitation of instruments; see Nettl 1956, p. 58.

11. On "stress" in ancient Greek, which includes the phonological features of duration and intensity but not pitch, see the fundamental work of W. S. Allen (1973); for an updated defense of Allen's formulation, see Devine and Stephens 1985. From the standpoint of general phonetics, stress may be a matter of duration, intensity, *and* pitch. From a survey of typological evidence, Devine and Stephens point to "instances of languages in which intensity is independent of both pitch and duration (Japanese), languages in which intensity is independent of duration and combines with pitch as an exponent of stress (Estonian, Komi), and languages in which intensity combines with both pitch and duration as an exponent of stress (English)" (p. 152). When differences in pitch have a lexical function, as in ancient Greek, it is a matter of tone; when they have a syntactical function, as in English, it is a matter of intonation. In ancient Greek, pitch is thus a matter of morphology as well as phonology. That is what is being taught today as the sum total of Greek accentuation. Allen's discovery, that ancient Greek also had a system of duration and intensity that was independent of its system of pitch, suggests that the two systems merged in modern Greek, where the inherited patterns of pitch are correlated with both duration and intensity (Devine and Stephens 1985, p. 146, n. 83).

This view of poetry as something derived from song and differentiated from song runs counter to the view of metricians for whom song is poetry set to music. According to this second of two possible lines of thought, music would be something that is extrinsic to language. Such a view, however, contradicts the experience of fieldwork in ethnomusicology, a discipline that has over the years built a strong case against the fallacy of treating music as a "universal language" (see Merriam 1964, pp. 10–11). Our own cultural prejudices in favor of such a concept can be traced back to medieval European traditions, where the eventual dissociation of language and music is already under way (see Zumthor 1972, p. 100). Toward the end of the fourteenth century, Eustache Deschamps is already making a distinction between the "natural music" of language and the "artificial music" of traditional melodies (ibid.). But it is clear in this case that the association of language and music is primary. For example, a study of attested traditions of Provençal singing has shown how it is only with the eventual divorce of melody from text that melody can take on the characteristics that we, from the standpoint of our own cultural preconceptions, can recognize as music.[12] With the advent of polyphony, the motet can triumph over its libretto; but before that, in the twelfth and thirteenth centuries, the melodic traditions are still bound to phraseological traditions of song (Zink 1972, pp. 17–24, esp. 23, n. 2). To be recognized, from the standpoint of medieval poetics, as one who is good at melodies was merely to possess a good vocal register; a singer could be good at producing melodies and still be bad at producing words—and therefore a bad singer (ibid., p. 23, n. 1; p. 20, n. 3).

Of the two terms, "lyric" and "melic," the first is the more elusive, in that it tends to be applied in contemporary academic usage to practically all archaic Greek poetry except for Homer and Hesiod. For my purposes, however, "lyric" is still

12. "Quand le divorce entre le texte et la musique sera consommé, la musique, paradoxalement, pourra prendre plus d'importance; elle sera développée pour elle-même et pour l'effet extérieur qu'elle produit, indépendamment des exigences internes du poème" (Zink 1972, p. 24).

the more useful term, since it is more general. As such, it is suitable for distinguishing the general notion of song from the more specific one of poetry, which is restricted to such recitative media as iambic trimeter. From here on, I shall be using the word "lyric" as a parallel to "song," excluding iambic trimeter.

It is instructive to notice one particular constraint, even in current usage, against the application of the term "lyric": we cannot say that the iambic trimeter of Athenian tragedy and comedy is lyric for the simple reason that it is patently *recited* as opposed to *sung*. As for what is sung, we call that "lyric" by way of opposition to what is recited. Thus the opposition of lyric meters and iambic trimeter in Athenian drama is that of song and poetry. We may note the dictum of Aristotle to the effect that iambic trimeter approximates, more closely than any other meter, everyday speech in real life (*Poetics* 1449a22–27; compare *Rhetoric* 1408b33). Thus the opposition of song and poetry in tragedy not only recapitulates an earlier opposition of song and speech; it also imitates the actual opposition of song and speech in "real life."

Needless to say, undifferentiated song as opposed to speech can be imagined as potentially having had features that ranged all the way from what we see in differentiated song to what we see in poetry. Thus, for example, song in any given society may or may not require melody. In other words, what counts as poetry for us may in another given society count as song if there are no melodic prerequisites. In this light, I cite a particularly useful formulation by Dan Ben-Amos, based on a wide cross-cultural variety of ethnographic data:

The existence or absence of metric substructure in a message is the quality first recognized in any communicative event and hence serves as the primary and most inclusive attribute for the categorization of oral tradition. Consequently, prose [what I have been calling speech] and poetry [what I have been calling song] constitute a binary set in which the metric substructure is the crucial attribute that differentiates between these two major divisions. It serves as the definitive feature that polarizes any verbal communication and does not provide any possible intermediary positions. A message is either rhythmic or not. However, within the category of poetry [in my sense of song], speakers may be able to perceive several patterns of verbal metrical redundancy which they would recognize as qualitatively different genres.[13]

This statement, useful as it is, can be made more precise with reference to the term "metric substructure." First, I turn to the cross-cultural linguistic evidence assembly by W. S. Allen, showing that all phraseology has built-in rhythm.[14] In line with this thinking, I would argue that the inherited words of song, as I have been calling it, *contain* the rhythm, from a diachronic point of view. In an earlier work on Greek and Indic metrics, I put it this way:

At first, the reasoning goes, traditional phraseology simply contains built-in rhythms. Later, the factor of tradition leads to the preference of phrases with some rhythms over phrases with other rhythms. Still later, the preferred rhythms have their own dynamics and become regulators of any incoming non-traditional phraseology. By becoming a viable structure in its own right, meter may evolve independently of traditional phraseology. Recent metrical developments may even obliterate aspects of the selfsame traditional phraseology that had engendered them, if these aspects no longer match the meter (Nagy 1974, p. 145).

Such a formulation, to be sure, presupposes that the traditional phraseology of song, generating fixed rhythmical patterns, is itself already regulated by principles of phonological, morphological, and syntactical parallelism and repetition that serve to differentiate song from speech.[15]

Granted, a factor like rhythm may become stylized to the point that it can become transferred from the words of song,

13. Ben-Amos 1976, p. 228. He quotes at this point Andrzejewski and Lewis, who note, as an example, that "the Somali classify their poems into various distinct types, each of which has its own specific name. It seems that their classification is mainly based on two prosodic factors: the type of tune to which the poem is chanted or sung, and the rhythmic pattern of the words" (1964, p. 46).

14. Allen prefers in the end not to use the word "rhythm" (1973, pp. 99–101). I shall continue to use it here in the sense of a system that operates in terms of stress (duration or intensity or both).

15. On the fundamental role of parallelisms and repetitions in differentiating what I am calling here song and speech, see Guillén 1985, pp. 93–121, esp. 103–104.

In this connection, I take note of the earlier theories of Curt Sachs, postulating three kinds of origins for melodic traditions: "logogenic," from language; "pathogenic," from motion; and "melogenic," from music (Sachs 1937, pp. 181–203; 1943, pp. 30–43). On the basis of what we have already noted about the relationship of language and motor activity, I consider the category "pathogenic" unnecessary. As for the category "melogenic," it may be useful for describing historically attested situations where a given melodic tradition has lost or at least outgrown its "logogenic" moorings, as it were, and where such a tradition is then recombined with or superimposed on originally unrelated phraseology.[20] Still, I would offer a formulation in the case of melody that parallels what I have already offered in the case of rhythm: that the primary situation is that of convergence and parallelism between the patterns of tone or intonation or both in the words of song on the one hand and the patterns of melody, dance, and instrumental accompaniment on the other hand.[21] I would also argue, conversely, that the secondary pattern is that of divergence and contrast.[22]

---

beginning musical phrases in Czech folk music, both vocal and instrumental; also his observation that, in English folksongs, the melodic contour "tends to descend at the end of a section, phrase, sentence, or song," corresponding to intonational patterns in the language.

20. Compare Herskovits and Herskovits 1947 on Trinidad melodies: "But not all melodies are rephrasings of old ones. Sometimes a tune heard, a European tune, can be 'swung' into a desired rhythm, with perhaps a change of a few measures, or no change at all. In this case, the words to a traditional song might be joined to the new melody, or a proverb might be used and to it added lines from older songs."

21. Note the description of "logogenic" melodies: they are "narrow of range, using small intervals," whereas corresponding dances are "tight, controlled, expressed through narrow steps" (Merriam 1964, p. 253). See Arnold Bake on the Indic tradition of the *bhāṣikasvara* (speech tone), which has the narrowest pitch compass and is employed, according to tradition, in performing the words of the (White) *Yajur Veda*. Note too the following formulation: "The melodic line follows the text in every detail; the words prescribe the rhythm and the flow; there is one note to each syllable, pitch is independent of duration. One might say that the melody only supports the words" (Bake 1957, p. 200). See M. L. West (1981, pp. 115–116), who draws particular attention to the old three-pitch and four-pitch patterns.

22. In the case of Balinese music lessons for the young, Merriam notes: "Those instruments which do not play the melody are ignored for the mo-

It should be stressed, however, that contrastive patterns between dance or instrumental accompaniment on the one hand and song on the other, even if they are diachronically secondary, are yet more effective than parallel patterns in marking off the language of song from the language of speech. Intensified contrast in form gives further marking to what is already marked in function. We should expect partial contrast, for example, in the patterns of melody in the song and of tone or intonation in the words of the song; or in the patterns of ictus in the verse and of stress (duration and intensity) in the words of the verse; or in the patterns of the colon in the stanza and of the clause or phrase in the words of the stanza; and so on.[23]

In light of these arguments, supported by the insights of ethnomusicologists, I now offer a broadened outline of possible developments, with special reference to the development of Greek music. Whereas song may or may not have required melody, song must be "plus melody" as opposed to poetry, which is "minus melody" or "reduced melody." Whereas song may or may not have required dance and instrumental accompaniment, given forms of song may be "plus dance" or "plus instrumental accompaniment" or "plus both."

Let us pursue further my earlier point, that the parallelisms between patterns of dance or instrumental accompaniment and patterns of rhythm or melody in song are diachronically primary and that the contrasts between them are secondary. If indeed song is marked speech, then such elements as dance and instrumental accompaniment can be viewed as ramifica-

---

ment, for the melody must be learned first" (1964, p. 152). On patterns of primary convergence and secondary divergence between song and speech, see the bibliography in Nettl 1964, pp. 290–291. See also the discussion of the factor of "tension" in Allen 1973, pp. 110–112.

23. Compare Allen 1973, p. 111: "one could envisage a form of which the pattern is determined by some prosodic feature x, such that there is another feature y whose distribution in the language is partially coincident with that of x. In such a situation one could speak of tension between x and y where the two factors failed to coincide in composition, and of 'concord' or 'harmony' where they coincided and so reinforced the metrical pattern; and such a 'counterpoint' between the patterns of the two features could arguably be manipulated by the poet for artistic ends."

tions of song that can in turn be further differentiated as either parallel to the song or contrasting with it or, even further, parting with it altogether, as in forms of dance or instrumental music that exist independent of song. This is not to say something altogether naive and pseudohistorical, such as "In the beginning there was song, which was both danced and instrumentally accompanied." Rather, it is to speak of the linguistic foundations of singing, dancing, and instrumental accompaniment. It is to speak of diachronic potential: song, as a marked form of language, is *structurally* capable of generating differentiated subforms such as dance and instrumental music. From a diachronic point of view, then, dance and instrumental music are optional realizations of the stylized speech act. From the standpoint of traditions where song, dance, and instrumental accompaniment happen to survive together, analogous forms where any of these consituents is missing are liable to be viewed as a tearing away of that constitutent from a unified whole, as we read in Plato *Laws* 669d–670a. In this connection, we may follow the formulation of A. M. Dale, who makes use of Milton's concept of Voice and Verse as uniting to form Song: "For the Greek lyric poet Voice and Verse were not a pair of sirens; Verse was merely the incomplete record of a single creation, Song" (Dale 1969, p. 166).

To set up language as the diachronic foundation of dance and instrumental music is in line with Dale's view that "song, with its dance, was a function of the words themselves when they were alive—that is, in performance."[24] More fundamentally, it is in line with Aristotle's view that the basis of musical rhythm is the syllable (*Metaphysics* 1087b33 and following).[25] Still, the fundamental function of dance and instrumental music, whether their patterns are parallel or contrastive with the patterns of language that they accompany, is to mark special speech as opposed to everyday speech, that is, song as op-

24. Dale 1969, p. 168. For reinforcement of this view of the level of testimony about the actual performance of song, see Pratinas *PMG* 708 (in Athenaeus 617b–f) and Plato *Republic* 398d.

25. See also Plato *Republic* 400a and *Cratylus* 424c. See the comments on these and other passages in Pöhlmann 1960, p. 30.

posed to speech.[26] An ideal example is Athenian drama, where the dancing and instrumental accompaniment further distances the words sung in the lyric meters by the *khoros* from the words recited in the iambic trimeter by the actors.

I close by highlighting Plato's vision of the medium of the chorus, as attested in Athenian drama, where song, dance, and instrumental accompaniment survive together. Wherever song has the capacity of being danced, as in the case of Greek choral lyric, dancing to the song is tantamount to dancing not only to its rhythms and melodies on the level of form but also to its words on the level of content. Hence the force of *pros* (corresponding to) in the expression *pros ta pathea autou* (corresponding to his sufferings [singular, *pathos*]) at Herodotus 5.67.5, describing the singing and dancing by *tragikoi khoroi* (tragic choruses) at Sikyon in the time of the tyrant Kleisthenes, in reenactment of the *pathea* (sufferings) of the hero Adrastos.[27]

From the standpoint of ritual, then, the activity of the chorus in an institution like Athenian drama, where, song, dance, and instrumental accompaniment can function as a unified whole, is a matter primarily of reenactment, insofar as the performers reenact the events of myth, and only secondarily of imitation, insofar as the performers at one given occasion imitate the performances of previous occasions.[28]

To sum up: an comparison of ancient Greek choral lyric with the Faroese traditions of ballad performance suggests that the coexistence of song and dance may be in both cases and an instance of archaism, not innovation. This observation may serve as a contribution to further research concerning the linguistic foundations of song and dance.

---

26. On patterns of primary convergence and secondary divergence between song and speech, I cite again Nettl 1964, pp. 281–292.

27. For cross-cultural parallels, see the discussion in Royce 1977, p. 73, including this interesting quotation from Franziska Boas (1944, pp. 14–15) concerning the dance traditions of the Kwakiutl: "In the Cannibal Dance, the women's War Dance, and some others, there is a fixed fundamental gesture like a basso ostinato that is broken at intervals by special gestures of pantomimic character which is descriptive of the text of the song."

28. For the perspective of a social anthropologist on the reenactment of myth in ritual, see Leach 1982, pp. 5–6.

References

Allen, W. S. 1973. *Accent and Rhythm: Prosodic Features of Latin and Greek: A Study in Theory and Reconstruction*. Cambridge: Cambridge University Press.

Andrzejewski, B. W., and I. M. Lewis. 1964. *Somali Poetry: An Introduction*. Oxford: Clarendon Press.

Bake, Arnold. 1957. "The Music of India," pp. 195–227 in *New Oxford History of Music*, vol. 1: *Ancient and Oriental Music*, ed. Egon Wellesz. London: Oxford University Press.

Ben-Amos, Dan. 1976. "Analytical Categories and Ethnic Genres," pp. 215–242 in *Folklore Genres*, ed. Dan Ben-Amos. Austin: University of Texas Press.

Boas, Franziska. 1944. *The Function of Dance in Human Society*. New York: The Boas School.

Bright, William. 1963. "Language and Music: Areas for Cooperation." *Ethnomusicology* 7: 26–32.

Burkert, Walter. 1979. "Mythisches Denken," pp. 16–13 in *Philosophie und Mythos: Ein Kolloquium*, ed. Hans Poser. Berlin and New York: de Gruyter.

———. 1985. *Greek Religion*, trans. John Raffan. Cambridge, Mass.: Harvard University Press. Originally published as *Griechische Religion der archaischen und klassischen Epoche*. Stuttgart: Kohlhammer, 1977.

Calame, Claude. 1977. *Les choeurs de jeunes filles en Grèce archaïque*, 1: *Morphologie, fonction religieuse et sociale*, 2: *Alcman*. Rome: Ateneo.

Comrie, Bernard. 1976. *Aspect: An Introduction to the Study of Verbal Aspect and Related Problems*. Cambridge: Cambridge University Press.

Dale, A. M. 1969. *Collected Papers*. Cambridge: Cambridge University Press.

Devine, A. M., and L. D. Stephens. 1985. "Stress in Greek?" *Transactions of the American Philological Association* 115: 125–152.

Guillén, Claudio. 1985. *Entre lo uno y lo diverso: Introducción a la literatura comparada*. Barcelona: Editorial Critica.

Herskovits, M. J., and F. S. Herskovits. 1947. *Trinidad Village*. New York: Knopf.

Herzog, George. 1934. "Speech Melody and Primitive Music." *Musical Quarterly* 20: 452–466.

Jakobson, Roman. 1939. "Signe zéro," pp. 143–152 in *Mélanges de linguistique, offerts à Charles Bally*. Geneva: Georg. Rpt. in Jakobson 1971, pp. 211–219, and Jakobson 1984, pp. 151–160.

————. 1957. *Shifters, Verbal Categories, and the Russian Verb.* Cambridge, Mass.: Department of Slavic Languages and Literatures, Harvard University. Rpt. in Jakobson 1971, pp. 130–147, and Jakobson 1984, pp. 41–58.

————. 1960. "Linguistics and Poetics," pp. 350–377 in *Style in Language,* ed. Thomas Sebeok. Cambridge, Mass.: MIT Press.

————. 1971. *Selected Writings,* 2nd. ed. The Hague: Mouton.

————. 1984. *Russian and Slavic Grammar: Studies 1931–1981,* ed. Morris Halle and Linda R. Waugh. The Hague: Mouton.

Leach, E. R. 1982. "Critical Introduction," pp. 1–20 in M. I. Steblin-Kamenskij, *Myth.* Ann Arbor, Mich.: Karoma Press.

Martin, Richard P. 1989. *The Language of Heroes: Speech and Performance in the Iliad.* Ithaca, N.Y.: Cornell University Press.

Merriam, Alan P. 1964. *The Anthropology of Music.* Evanston, Ill.: Northwestern University Press.

Nagy, Gregory. 1974. *Comparative Studies in Greek and Indic Meter.* Cambridge, Mass.: Harvard University Press.

————. 1976. "Formula and Meter," pp. 239–260 in *Oral Literature and the Formula,* ed. B. A. Stolz and R. S. Shannon. Ann Arbor: Center for the Coördination of Ancient and Modern Studies.

————. 1979a. *The Best of the Achaeans: Concepts of the Hero in Archaic Greek Poetry.* Baltimore: Johns Hopkins University Press.

————. 1979b. "On the Origins of the Greek Hexameter," pp. 611–631 in *Festschrift Oswald Szemerényi,* ed. Béla Brogyanyi. Amsterdam: Benjamin.

Nettl, Bruno. 1956. *Music in Primitive Culture.* Cambridge, Mass.: Harvard University Press.

————. 1964. *Theory and Method in Ethnomusicology.* New York: Free Press of Glencoe.

————. 1965. *Folk and Traditional Music of the Western Continents.* Englewood Cliffs, N.J.: Prentice-Hall.

Ong, Walter J. 1977a. *Interfaces of the Word: Studies in the Evolution of Consciousness and Culture.* Ithaca, N.Y.: Cornell University Press.

————. 1977b. "African Talking Drums and Oral Noetics." *New Literary History* 8: 411–429. Rpt. in Ong 1977a, pp. 92–120.

Pöhlmann, Egert. 1960. *Griechische Musikfragmente: Ein Weg zur altgriechischen Musik.* Nuremberg: Carl.

Royce, Anya P. 1977. *The Anthropology of Dance.* Bloomington: Indiana University Press.

Sachs, Curt. 1937. *World History of the Dance,* trans. Bessie Schönberg. New York: Norton.

Schneider, Marius. 1957. "Primitive Music," pp. 1–82 in *New Oxford History of Music*, 1: *Ancient and Oriental Music*, ed. Egon Wellesz. London: Oxford University Press.

Stern, T. 1957. "Drum and Whistle 'Languages': An Analysis of Speech Surrogates." *American Anthropology* 59: 487–506.

Tambiah, Stanley J. 1981. "A Performative Approach to Ritual." *Proceedings of the British Academy, London* 65: 113–169. Rpt. in Tambiah 1985, pp. 123–166.

————. 1985. *Culture, Thought, and Social Action: An Anthropological Perspective*. Cambridge, Mass.: Harvard University Press.

Waugh, Linda R. 1982. "Marked and Unmarked: A Choice between Unequals in Semiotic Structure." *Semiotica* 38: 299–318.

West, M. L. 1981. "The Singing of Homer and the Modes of Early Greek Music." *Journal of Hellenic Studies* 101: 113–129.

Wylie, Jonathan, and David Margolin. 1981. *The Ring of Dancers: Images of Faroese Culture*. Philadelphia: University of Pennsylvania Press.

Zink, Michel. 1972. *La pastourelle: Poésie et folklore au Moyen Age*. Paris: Bordas.

Zumthor, Paul. 1972. *Essai de poétique médiévale*. Paris: Seuil.

ALBERT B. LORD

Ring Composition in *Maldon;*
or, a Possible Case of Chiasmus
in a Late Anglo-Saxon Poem

Ring composition—the equation of which with the "chiasmus" of the rhetoricians will be explained in due course—and similar structural strategies in Anglo-Saxon poetry, especially *Beowulf,* have been much studied.[1] There is one instance of chiasmus in *The Battle of Maldon,* however, that has not been mentioned in any of the works that I have seen. The purpose of this paper is first to set forth that case, and second to comment on the important question as to whether such structures are

1. In 1934 John O. Beaty published "The Echo-Word in *Beowulf* with a Note on the *Finnsburg Fragment,*" *PMLA* 49: 365–373; 1935 saw the publication of Adeline Courtney Bartlett's well-known *The Larger Rhetorical Patterns in Anglo-Saxon Poetry* (New York: Columbia University Press), and in 1975 Constance B. Hieatt's seminal article "Envelope Patterns and the Structure of *Beowulf,*" came out in *English Studies in Canada* 1:249–265; in 1977 two pertinent studies appeared, H. Ward Tonsfeldt's "Ring Structure in *Beowulf,*" *Neophilologus* 61: 443–452, and James L. Rosier's "Generative Composition in *Beowulf,*" *English Studies* 58: 193–204; and more recently John D. Niles devoted a chapter to ring composition in his *Beowulf: The Poem and Its Tradition* (Cambridge, Mass.: Harvard University Press, 1983), pp. 152–162. In the notes to that chapter other references can be found, including those to the numerological studies of *Beowulf,* especially the investigations of Thomas E. Hart.

A¹	1.		stiðlice *clypode*	25
		wicinga ar,	*wordum mælde,*	
		se on beot *abead*		
A²	2.	Byrhtnoð *maþelode*		42
			wordum mælde	
			ageaf him andsware	
	[3.	Ongan *ceallian* þa		91
		Byrhtelmes bearn		
	4.		þa gyt *word gecwæð*	170
		har hilderinc,	hyssas bylde,	
		bæd gangan forð]		
B	5.	Swa hi bylde forð	bearn Ælfrices	
			wordum mælde	210
		Ælfwine þa *cwæð,*	he on ellen *spræc*	
C	6.	Offa *gemælde*		230
C	7.	Leofsunu *gemælde*		244
			he þam beorne *oncwæð*	
{B	8.	Dunnere þa *cwæð*		255
{A¹	9.		ofer eall *clypode*	
		bæd þæt beorna gehwylc	Byrhtnoð wræce:	
A²	10.	Byrhtwold *maþelode*		
			beornas *lærde.*	310

More briefly, noting the important verbs of speech, and omitting the two passages in square brackets with their special purpose:

A¹	clypode/abead	
A²	maþelode	bord hafenode
B	cwæð	
C	gemælde	æscolt asceoc
C	gemælde	and his linde ahof
{B	cwæð	daroð acwehte
{A¹	clypode/bæd	
A²	maþelode	bord hafenode

indications of oral-traditional or of nontraditional literary style.

There are several degrees, or levels, of ring composition, or chiasmus. The series of correspondences that have interested me in *Maldon* involves the verbs used to introduce speeches (see the accompanying table). They represent on a single-word level what is known in Anglo-Saxon studies as the "envelope pattern," as it was dubbed by Adeline Courtney Bartlett in 1935 and further investigated in respect to *Beowulf* by Constance B. Hieatt in 1975. The instance of chiasmus in *Maldon* with which I am concerned fits better the category of "envelope pattern" than it does John O. Beaty's "echo-word," which requires that the echo word should have the identical sound of the word echoed with a different meaning, connotation, or association, and must be within seventeen lines of it.

Stanley Greenfield's remarks on the introductions to speech in *Maldon*, especially those to the speeches by Byrhtnoð in lines 42–44 and by Byrhtwold in lines 309–311 (items 2 and 10 in the table) led me to a consideration of the patterning of the intervening speech introductions as well.[2] Here is the pair of speeches to which he first called attention:

> Byrhtnoð maþelode,   bord hafenode,
> wand wacne æsc,   wordum mælde,
> yrre and anræd   ageaf him andsware
>
> Byrhtwold maþelode,   bord hafenode
> (se wæs eald geneat),   æsc acwehte,
> he ful baldlice   beornas lærde.

Greenfield felt, with due caution, that the repetition of the first line must be more than coincidence and that it reflects the intention of the poet to make a special identification of the two speakers near the beginning and the end of the present fragment, thus rounding out its structure.[3] The verb *maþelode,*

2. See the chapter on "Expectations and Implications in Diction and Formula," in Stanley Greenfield, *The Interpretation of Old English Poems* (London and Boston: Routledge and Kegan Paul, 1972), pp. 56–59. His comments are well worth reading. I have myself made a study of introductions to speech and of sentences beginning in the b-verse in *Beowulf, Andreas, Elene, Guthlac, Christ,* and several other Anglo-Saxon poems, but the fullest investigation of *verba dicendi* in the older Germanic poetry is Teresa Pàroli's monumental *Sull' elemento formulare nella poesia germanica antica* (Rome: Università di Roma, 1975).

3. D. G. Scragg in the Introduction to his edition of *The Battle of Maldon* (Manchester: Manchester University Press, 1981, rpt. 1984), pp. 31–32, is also very cautious in noting Greenfield's claim that there is "deliberate echoing for stylistic effect" in lines 42 and 309. He comments that "there is a danger of the critic working harder than the poet."

known to us best from *Beowulf,* has a connotation of formal,
significant, even ceremonial address. Greenfield points out that
the poet could have used other verbs and that these are the
only two uses of the verb in the poem. The word fits admirably
the formal response by Byrhtnoð to the Viking spokesman
early in the poem, as well as the solemn gnomic statement of
Byrhtwold as the end draws near. When we look at the introductions to the speeches preceding those in which *maþelode*
appears (items 1 and 8) we see that the verb *clypode* (he cried
out) is used in both of them and, like *maþelode,* it is employed
in only those two passages in *Maldon.*[4]

> þa stod on stæðe,   stiðlice clypode
> wicinga ar,   wordum mælde,
> se on beot abead   brimliþendra
> ærænde to þam eorle,   þær he on ofre stod: (25–28)

> Dunnere þa cwæð,   daroð acwehte,
> unorne ceorl,   ofer eall clypode,
> bæd þæt beorna gehwylc   Byrhtnoð wræce . . . (255–257)

In short, the combination *clypode–maþelode* occurs in this
poem only in these two places.[5] One should add further that
clypode in both cases is followed by the preterite of either
abeodan or *biddan,* verbs that sound much alike, although
their meanings are not quite the same, so that one might ex-
pand the combination to *clypode–abead (bæd)–maþelode.*
There also occurs in the *clypode* passages one "unmarked"
verb of speaking, by which I mean a more common verb such
as *cwæð* or a somewhat more ordinary formula such as *wor-
dum mælde,* both of which mean "to speak," but do not have
any special coloring as do *clypian* (to call out, to shout) or
maðelian (to make a speech or a formal utterance).

---

4. It is worth remarking in passing that whereas *maþelode* carries overtones of the older heroic poems, *clypode* is used almost exclusively (except
once in *Andreas*) in later Christian poems such as the Lord's Prayer and the
Psalms.

5. In her extraordinary study of *verba dicendi* in the older Germanic poetry, Teresa Pàroli omits any reference to *clypode* in line 25, limiting references to that verb to its occurence in line 256.

It is true that Byrhtnoð's speech in lines 42ff follows the messenger's speech immediately and is in answer to it, whereas Byrhtwold's in lines 309ff is separated from Dunnere's by forty-nine lines. In fact, between Dunnere's speech and the final one of Byrhtwold comes a series of individual combats and deaths, a brief catalogue of action very reminiscent of the *Iliad.* Nevertheless, the correspondences between the two sequences are worth pointing out.

It seems to me quite possible that the poet of *Maldon* had an innate sense of what is now known as "ring composition" and that it may have come into play here. This type of formation, by no means uncommon in oral-traditional narrative poetry, including the Homeric poems and the South Slavic epics,[6] is one of the many manifestations of the general sense of balancing in poetic structure characteristic of oral composition on many levels.[7] In order to appreciate the possible presence of the "ring" here in *Maldon,* one must place the two introductions of speeches marked by Greenfield, plus the two preceding them, in their larger context.

I suggest that in the center of the "ring" are two passages in tandem, as it were, using the verb *(ge)mælde* (items 6 and 7);

6. For an example of ring composition in a South Slavic epic song, in this case "The Wedding of Smailagić Meho" by Avdo Međedović, see my article, "Words Heard and Words Seen," in R. A. Whitaker and E. R. Sinert, eds., *Oral Tradition and Literacy: Changing Visions of the World* (Durban, South Africa: Natal University Oral Documentation and Research Centre, 1986), pp. 11–12.

7. In chap. 7 of *Beowulf: The Poem and Its Tradition,* citing the work of Bartlett and Hieatt on "envelope patterns" in *Beowulf,* Niles discusses both small and large patterns, including those that might encompass the whole poem. The possible presence of "ring composition" in the Middle English *Alliterative Morte Arthure* has been suggested. See Jan Ziolkowski, "A Narrative Structure in the Alliterative *Morte Arthure* 1–1221 and 3150–4346," *The Chaucer Review* 22 (1988): 234–245, for bibliography and discussion of the term, as well as of important articles, such as Jean Ritzke-Rutherford's "Formulaic Microstructure: The Theme of Battle," in Karl Heinz Göller, ed., *The Alliterative Morte Arthure: A Reassessment of the Poem* (Cambridge: D. S. Brewer, 1981), pp. 83–95, and Valerie Krishna's review of that volume in *Speculum* 58 (1983): 178. Ziolkowski argues persuasively for an *abcd abcd* pattern in lines 1–1221 and 3150–4346, but he does not exclude the possibility of other patterns as well.

they follow one another in quick succession, and they too are
followed by martial brandishing of weapons and raising of
shields:

> Offa gemælde,   æscholt asceoc   (230)
>
> Leofsunu gemælde   and his linde ahof,
> bord to gebeorge;   he þam beorne oncwæð . . .   (244–245)

These two speeches are in turn enclosed by two others
(items 5 and 8), each containing three verbs of speaking:

> Swa hi bylde forð   bearn Ælfrices,
> wiga wintrum geong,   *wordum mælde,*
> Ælfwine þa *cwæð,*   he on ellen *spræc*   (209–211)
>
> Dunnere þa *cwæð,*   daroð acwehte,
> unorne ceorl,   ofer eall *clypode,*
> *bæd* þæt beorna gehwylc   Byrhtnoð wræce   (255–257)

The second, that by Dunnere, can be seen to serve two purposes: it pairs off with Ælfwine's speech with its three unmarked verbs of speaking, and it also pairs off with the first
speech in the poem with its use of *clypode* and *bæd.*

After Byrhtnoð's response to the Danish challenge given
above there follow two speeches before the first of those beginning with *cwæð.* They are special utterances, and I have
bracketed them, excluding them tentatively from the "ring."
The first is when Byrhtnoð calls over the cold water, telling
the Danes, as the men listen, that the way is open to them; it
is introduced as follows (item 3):

> Ongan ceallian þa   ofer cald wæter
> Byrhtelmes bearn   (beornas gehlyston)   (91–92)

The second is Byrhtnoð's dying words, which the poet introduces thus (item 4):

>   þa gyt þæt word gecwæð
> har hilderinc,   hyssas bylde,
> bæd gangan forð   gode geferan;
> ne mihte þa on fotum leng   fæste gestandan.
> He to heofenum wlat . . .   (168–172)

In them the story of Byrhtnoð's combat and wounding is enclosed. They fit another division of the speeches, namely: the
first four center upon Byhrtnoð and his death; the remaining
five treat the action following his death. Such overlapping or
interlocking of patterns is not uncommon in oral-traditional
style.

The diagrammatic picture as set forth in the table seems to
reveal a fine example of chiasmus, putting the *maþelode* passages into perspective and placing new emphasis on the central
speeches with *gemælde* and the heroic shaking of weapons,
which, in their turn, echo the outer circle. This is a typical
structure in oral-traditional poetics.

The style of *The Battle of Maldon* has been on occasion criticized as inept. In the introduction to his recent edition of the
poem D. G. Scragg has treated the critical writing with an even
hand. Some scholars have found that the style of *Maldon* has
anomalies when compared to "classical" Anglo-Saxon poetry.
They have pointed to puzzling metrical peculiarities, for example, and to the presence of rhyme in addition to alliteration.
Elizabeth S. Sklar in an article in 1975 found some characteristics of "popular poetry" in *The Battle of Maldon,* which she
felt that poem shared with Layamon's *Brut* and with the emerging Middle English tradition.[8] In spite of eloquent statements
by supporters of the poet's ability, I have found that some of
the well-attested characteristics of his style, which are acknowledged by all concerned, speak to a probable relationship
with the oral-traditional poetics of the earlier Anglo-Saxon
poetry.[9] I am thinking in particular of such a phenomenon as
the *Maldon* poet's fondness for end-stopped lines. Daniel
Donoghue reports that "seventy-eight percent of all clauses
that contain an auxiliary and verbal begin with the *a* verse,

8. Elizabeth S. Sklar, "*The Battle of Maldon* and the Popular Tradition:
Some Rhymed Formulas," *Philological Quarterly* 54 (1975): 409–418.

9. On the other hand, Fred C. Robinson, "Some Aspects of the *Maldon*
Poet's Artistry," *JEGP* 75 (1976): 25–40, pointed to a series of cases where
he felt that the poet's artistry came to the fore. More recently Daniel
Donoghue, in *Style in Old English Poetry: The Test of the Auxiliary* (New
Haven: Yale University Press, 1987), has risen again in defense of the poet.

which makes the syntax of the poem highly end-stopped" (p. 117). Some oral-traditional epic poetries have a strong tendency to what Milman Parry in his Homeric studies called unperiodic enjambement—that is, for the sense of a line to be completed by the end of the line.[10] We should not be surprised, therefore, to find in *Maldon* a typical oral-traditional structure such as ring composition.

Did the poet of *The Battle of Maldon* consciously plan this chiastic arrangement of verbs introducing speech? Can we conceive of him saying to himself: "Let me see. First comes *maðelode*, then *cwæð*, then in the middle *gemælde*, then *cwæð* again, and back to *maðelode*. Right? Looks good!"? I doubt it. That would assume that he was thinking in the same terms that modern literary scholars today employ and that he shared their mentality, a mentality that is the product of centuries of special development. It does seem reasonable to suppose, however, that such structures were inherent in the Anglo-Saxon oral-traditional style—as they were in the Homeric Greek oral-traditional style—and that the poet of *Maldon* expressed himself intuitively, unconsciously, through them, even as we use the structure of grammar and syntax without thinking about them.

In discussing "ring composition" in Homer, Samuel Bassett in his Sather Lecture of 1936, *The Poetry of Homer,*[11] wrote:

This principle—which is almost a law in Homer—may be stated thus: When two or more coordinate ideas are reported, the order, *ceteris*

10. Milman Parry, "The Distinctive Character of Enjambement in Homeric Verse," *Transactions and Proceedings of the American Philological Association* 60 (1929): 200–220.

11. Samuel Eliot Bassett, *The Poetry of Homer* (Berkeley: University of California Press, 1938). The whole of Bassett's discussion merits attention. The first use of the term "ring composition" in the study of ancient Greek literature is by W. A. A. van Otterlo, in *Untersuchungen über Begriff, Anwendung und Entstehung der griechischen Ringkomposition,* in *Mededeelingen der nederlandsche Akademie van Wetenschappen, Afdeling Letterkunde,* N. R. 7, no. 3 (Amsterdam, 1944). Special mention should be made of Cedric Whitman's analysis of ring composition in the *Iliad* in *Homer and the Heroic Tradition* (Cambridge, Mass.: Harvard University Press, 1958).

paribus, is inverted: ab ba. Aristarchus seems to have been the discoverer of the principle, and the Romans were familiar with it. . . . But Aristarchus makes perfectly clear the meaning of the Homeric hysteron proteron. . . . [He] says that Homer uses it "always," or "habitually," or "generally" . . . Unfortunately the scholia fail to give Aristarchus' explanation of Homer's reason for preferring the inverted order, but Eustathius seems to have known it. He notices the inversion, pointed out by Aristarchus, in the answers to the questions in the Catalogue (B 763), and says it is made to keep the *continuity of the thought* . . . In the carrying out of two commands or purposes Homer often inverts the order. When Zeus awakes on Mount Ida he bids Hera summon Iris and Apollo (O,55); she calls Apollo, then Iris (vss. 143ff.). They go to Zeus, who dispatches first Iris, then Apollo (vss. 157,221). The latter is given a two-fold command, (1) to take the aegis and with it to put the Achaeans to flight, and (2) to go to Hector and rouse his strength (vss. 229–232). Apollo goes first to Hector's aid, and it is not until verse 308 that we hear of the aegis, with which at verse 322 he makes the Achaeans forget their prowess. This fourfold inversion cannot be accidental. The poet must invert intentionally. (pp. 120–122)

A few pages later, Bassett continues:

Such is the "threaded speech" of Homer, the true λέξις εἱρομένη, because it continuously carries on the thought (Ar[istotle], *Rhet[oric]*, 3, 9, 2). Its opposite is the λέξις κατεστραμμένη of the orator . . . The Homeric hysteron proteron is not a rhetorical figure, but the unstudied, intuitive expression of intimate human discourse. Unfortunately, the rhetoricians denied this. Aristarchus, who discovered the hysteron proteron, said, "Let Homer speak for himself." [Aristarchus's] rival Crates [a Stoic, on the other hand], said: "Let Homer speak for rhetoric. The Homeric hysteron proteron is nothing but chiasmus." The *locus classicus* for this claim is in Eustathius, who was steeped in rhetoric . . . His comments are, in brief, as follows:

> This is a novel order. It is *chiastic* . . . A similar striving for effect is seen in "*Achilles* was chosen polemarch, and the *princes* tarried by the ships. *They* were to keep the Trojans within the walls, while *he* ravaged the country round about." This order is ornate because of the inversion of the thought.

These comments of Eustathius show that by the twelfth century the discovery of Aristarchus had been forgotten. To Eustathius the Homeric hysteron proteron is nothing more than chiasmus, an ornate, artificial figure of rhetoric.   (pp. 124–125)

We should be grateful to Bassett for his perspicacity in pointing out the obvious, that Homer *preceded* the rhetoricians, that the "Homeric" hysteron proteron and ring composition were in the ancient Greek oral-traditional style before the rhetoricians labelled them "chiasmus." They were not the inventions of the rhetoricians, but if Bassett, taking his cue from Aristarchus, is correct, a natural order of continuous thought.

Surely the Germanic oral-traditional poetic style preceded the teachings of the monastic schools, which derived from the classical rhetoricians. I wonder if the relationship of the traditional Germanic poetics to the later non-Germanic style taught in the monastic schools may be similar to that between Homer and the rhetoricians. Perhaps one can see an awareness of this difference in recent writings on Anglo-Saxon poetic style. A half-century after Bassett, in his book on the appositive style in *Beowulf,* Fred C. Robinson speaks of "calculated ambiguity" when discussing the boar's head image in *Beowulf* and the contribution of the appositive style to the appreciation of a possible layering of connotations.[12] If I understand him aright, he points to the possible survival in the apposed elements of older meanings and references merged with the contemporary. Near the end of his last chapter, however, he prefers to think of apposition as a "habit of mind"—a phrase, it seems to me, that hits the mark very well—rather than as a rhetorical device (p. 80). Literary scholarship can use more of such clear insight into the refinements of style through a developed sense of its history.

---

12. Fred C. Robinson, *Beowulf and the Appositive Style* (Knoxville: University of Tennessee Press, 1985), p. 69.

KARL REICHL

The Middle English Popular Romance: Minstrel versus Hack Writer

When Havelok is made king of Denmark, a splendid feast is organized with an abundance of food and drink and plenty of entertainment for all tastes, spear butting and stone throwing, wrestling and bowling, gambling and dancing, music and story-telling:

> Hwan he was king, ther mouthe men se
> The moste ioie that mouhte be—
> Buttinge with sharpe speres,
> Skirming with taleuaces that men beres,
> Wrastling with laddes, putting of ston,
> Harping and piping ful god won,
> Leyk of mine, of hasard ok,
> Romanz-reding on the bok.
> Ther mouthe men here the gestes singe,
> The glevmen on the tabour dinge . . .   (2321–2330)[1]

1. Quoted from Smithers 1987, p. 64. "When he became king one could witness the most splendid festivities imaginable: thrusting sharp spears, fencing with large shields carried by men, wrestling of young men, stone throwing, a great deal of harping and piping, games of dice and gambling, reading romances from a book. There one could hear the singing of *gestes* and minstrels beat the tabour [small drum] . . ." For parallels to this scene see ibid., pp. 168–169; for a comparison of the style of *Havelok* with that of the *chansons de geste* see Smithers 1988.

243

This passage is both revealing and enigmatic. It is clear from l. 2329 that narrative poems, *gestes,* were orally performed, indeed sung (the manner of performance characteristic of oral epic poetry all over the world), although it is not quite so clear whether the minstrels mentioned in the following line, the glee-men "dinging" their tabours, did the singing. And it is equally evident from l. 2328 that narrative poems, *romanz,* were read aloud from books to an audience, in the manner suggested by the famous illumination representing Chaucer reading to an elegant courtly circle (MS Corpus Christi Coll. Camb. 61, frontispiece).[2] Two ways of telling a tale, two modes of performance, perhaps two cultures, the literate and the oral. Where does the shorter Middle English romance belong, romances in octosyllabic couplets like *Havelok* and *King Horn* or tail-rhyme romances like *Octavian* and *Sir Isumbras?* Were they "read on the book" or orally performed by a professional entertainer?[3]

The answer to this question is not only of academic interest but also of relevance for our understanding and appreciation of the Middle English popular romance.[4] The same stylistic trait can assume different significance in a literate and in an oral tradition of poetry. If a particular scene is elaborated in an oral epic, this does not necessarily indicate its greater narrative importance; it might rather reflect the interest of the sing-

2. According to Albert Baugh this line "can only imply professional entertainment by minstrels and indicate that they sometimes read from a book" (Baugh 1967, p. 22). The illumination depicting Chaucer reading to a courtly circle of listeners must not be taken as a reliable historical document; it might rather be an expression of the illustrator's imaginative understanding of the text. See Pearsall 1985, pp. 38 and 45–46, n. 4.

3. The various Middle English terms for narrative poetry are notoriously ambiguous and often interchangeable. *Havelok* is referred to in the text as *tale, rym,* but also as *gest:* "Nu haue ye herd the gest al thoru / Of Hauelok and of Goldeborw" (Smithers 1987, p. 82). See the *MED* s.v. *geste* and *romaunce;* see also Hoops 1929; Strohm 1971.

4. To avoid circular arguments, by "popular" I shall intend "popular by destination" rather than "popular by origin" (for this distinction see Greene 1977, p. cxviii). The term "popular" is hence used essentially to describe a certain style and narrative technique (swift, action-oriented narrative pace, formulaic style, absence of a sophisticated narrating voice, and so on).

er's audience. "Decorate the man and the horse more pro-
fusely—you don't have to pay for it!" is a typical audience
intervention, reported by Matthias Murko for Yugoslavia (see
Braun 1961, p. 62). In a written text questions of proportion
and balance are of far greater importance for its interpretation,
even if the medieval canon of *proportio* does not coincide with
that of modern literature.[5] By saying this I am not implying that
oral poetry falls outside the realm of literary criticism and is
immune to critical evaluation. The Host's aversion to tail-
rhyme romances is certainly justified if they have the quality
of Chaucer's *Tale of Sir Topas*. Bad poetry is bad poetry—
written or oral. Nevertheless, the poetics underlying the interpretation of a literary text does not necessarily apply to an oral
text, and what might be bad from a literary point of view is not
necessarily bad from an oral point of view.

I have deliberately oversimplified the issue by talking glob-
ally of "bad poetry," because some of the most distinctive
traits of the Middle English popular romance—straightforward
action, minimally differentiated characters, commonplaces,
clichés, and formulas—have been interpreted as the very signs
of bad poetry by literary critics from Chaucer to the present
day. Lilian Hornstein remarks, for instance, on the various as-
sessments of the tail-rhyme romance *Sir Eglamour of Artois*
that "the poem has been condemned as insipid (Schofield), fantastic (Kane,) repetitious and lacking in invention (Hibbard)"
(Severs 1967, p. 125). But are some of the more questionable
popular romances simply bad poems or are they failures only
when evaluated according to the canons of written literature?

There are basically two types of arguments advanced by critics when they discuss these romances. For some authors a romance like *Sir Eglamour, Sir Degarre,* or *Sir Torrent of Portyngale* is simply a failure and hence the work of a bad poet, or
more likely a hack writer. A typical comment is the following:
"The extant version [of *Torrent of Portyngale*] abounds in trite

5. See the discussion of *amplificatio* and *abbreviatio* in Geoffrey of Vinsauf's *Poetria Nova,* in Faral 1924, p. 219–736, and Nims 1967, pp. 23–42.
Compare also Ryding 1971, pp. 66ff. On the need to distinguish between an
oral and a written poetics compare also Miletich 1986.

phrases, repetitive incidents, trivial details, and feeble elabo-
rations, all bespeaking the work of a crude hack-writer" (Severs 1967, p. 127). Others have argued that, although the extant
version of a romance might be trivial, this blame must be laid
not at the doorstep of the poet but rather at that of the transmitter. The first editor of *Torrent*, James Orchard Halliwell,
was of the opinion that the text we have is in all likelihood the
transcription of an oral performance: "It is very incorrectly
written, and the copy of the romance of Torrent of Portugal,
which occupies 88 pages of the book, contains so many obvious blunders and omissions, that it may be conjectured with
great probability to have been written down from oral recitation" (Halliwell 1842, pp. v–vi). The role of the minstrel in the
transmission of the Middle English popular romance has been
recognized by a number of writers, most clearly by Albert C.
Baugh in several important articles (Baugh 1950; 1959; 1967).
It has been variously addressed: as a basically detrimental and
corruptive force, as a factor responsible for textual variation
and fluctuation, but also as a more positive form of creative
transmission. There is only a short step from the view of the
minstrel as a creative transmitter of popular verse to that of
the minstrel was an improvising composer of traditional poetry. Minstrel versus hack writer, oral transmission versus
written transmission, oral creation versus written composition?

There is no space here for an extensive review of critical
opinion on this matter.[6] I will have to confine myself to a few
examples taken from a concordance of roughly 25,000 lines of
Middle English romance poetry, mostly of the tail-rhyme
type.[7] Let us first look at the transmission of a typical popular

6. Among recent studies of Middle English romance see in particular Stevens 1973; Wittig 1978; Ramsey 1983; Barron 1987; Fewster 1987.

7. I am grateful to the Institute of Phonetics and Communication Research of the University of Bonn for the use of their facilities for compiling
the concordance. The following tail-rhyme romances are included: *Sir Isumbras*, *Emaré*, *Sir Amadace*, *Sir Gowther*, *The Siege of Melayne*, *Octavian* (northern version), *King of Tars*, *Athelston*, *Sir Torrent of Portyngale*,
Sir Degrevant, *Libeaus Desconus*, *Sir Eglamour of Artois*, *Le Bone Florence de Rome*, *Sir Triamour*. In addition to these tail-rhyme romances, com-

romance such as *Sir Isumbras*. The romance comprises about 800 lines; it has come down to us in five MSS, all dating from the fifteenth century (Bodl. Ashmole 61, Caius Coll. Cambridge 175, BL Cotton Caligula A.2, Edinburgh Advocates 19.3.1, and Lincoln Cathedral 91 [Thornton MS]); there are furthermore three MS fragments (University Coll. Oxford 142, Gray's Inn 20, Naples Royal Library 13.B29), as well as various early printings and MS transcriptions of early printings (most of which are fragmentary).[8] Looking at a short sample from all available MSS, several conclusions can be drawn:

Caligula:

I wyll you tell of a knyghte
That dowghty was in eche a fyghte,
  In towne and eke in felde;
Ther durste no man his dynte abyde
Ne no man ayeyn hym ryde,
  With spere ne with schelde.

A man he was ryche ynowghe
Of oxen to drawe in his plowghe,
  And stedes also in stalle;
He was bothe curtey and hende,
Every man was his frende,
  And loved he was with all.

A curteys man and hende he was;
His name was kalled syr Isumbras,
  Bothe curteys and fre.
His gentylnesse nor his curtesye
There kowthe no man hit discrye:
  A ffull good man was he.

---

prising about 20,000 lines, the following romances have been concorded: *Sir Degarre* (octosyllabic couplets) and *Morte Arthure* (alliterative lines).

8. See Severs 1967, p. 279. In the following quotations I use the editions by Mills 1973 (for MS BL Cal.A.2), Michelson 1969 (for MS Caius Coll. Camb. 175), Brown 1914–15 (for the fragment in MS Univ. Coll. Oxf. 142), Kölbing 1880 (for the fragment in Naples), the facsimile edition of the Thornton MS by Brewer and Owen (1975) and microfilm for MSS Ashmole 61 and Adv. 19.3.1. For an edition of the Thornton version of *Sir Isumbras* see Halliwell 1844; for a critical edition (in the sense of Lachmannian textual scholarship) see Schleich 1901.

Naples:

Y wol you telle of a kynʒt,
That was douʒty in ilke a fight,
   In towne and eke in fielde.
Ther durst no man his dynt abide
. . . . .
   With spere ne with schilde.

Man he was riche ynowe,
Ox to drawe in his plowe
   And stedis in his stalle.
Man he was curteyse and hynde,
Every man was his frende,
   He was lord of alle.

Curteis and hynde he was,
His name was clepid sir Isombrase,
   Bothe curteis and fre.
The grettist of his curtesy
Ne couthe ther no man discry,
   A fulle good man was he.

Ashmole:

I wyll ʒou telle of a knyght
That was both herdy and wyght,
   A dughty mone he was.
Syre Isombras was his name,
A nobulle knyght of ryalle fame
   And stronge in euery cas.

He was a feyre mane and stronge
With schulderes brod and armes longe,
   That sembly was to se.
He was large man and hyʒe,
Alle hym louede that hym seyʒe,
   So hende a mane was he.

Thornton:

I wille ʒow telle of a knyghte,
That bothe was stalworthe and wyghte,
   [And worth]ily undir wede:

His name was hattene Syr Isambrace,
Swilke a knyghte als he was
    Now lyffes nowrewhare in lede.

He was mekille mane and lange,
With schuldirs brode and armes strange,
    That semly were to see;
So was he bothe faire and heghe,
Alle hym loffede that hym seghe,
    Se hende a mane was hee!

Advocates:

I wylle yow telle of a kny3t
That was bothe harde and wy3the
    And duxti in euery dede.
His name was callyd Sir Ysumbras,
Ffor seche a kny3the as he was
    Non leuys now in lede.

He was a myculle mone and stronge
With schulders brode and armes longe
    That semely was to se.
So was he bothe fayre and fre
That alle hym loued that hym se
    So fayr a mon was he.

Caius Coll. Cambridge:

I wold 3ow telle of a kny3t
That was bothe hardy and wy3t
    And dou3ty man of d[ede].
    Hys name was callyd Sere Ysumbras;
So dou3ty a kny3t as he was
    Ther leuyd non in lede.

He was mekil man and long
With armes grete and body strong
    And [f]air in was to se.
He was long man and hey3,
The ffayreste that euer man sey3;
    A gret lord was he.

University Coll. Oxford:

I woll ӡow tell of a knyӡt
That was herdy man and wyӡt
  And duӡty of hys dede.
Hys name was syr Isambras
So duӡty a knyӡt as he was
  Leuand none in lede

That myӡt with hym withoute fayll
I t[ur]nement ne in baytayll
  To usten opno a stede.
He was a man of muchel strang
With schulders brode and armis alang.
  Amen.

The first conclusion is that the texts agree so closely with one another that purely oral transmission is excluded. The close correspondence between MSS Caligula and Naples (st. 2) is particularly noteworthy, speaking quite clearly for a common written source (at some stage in the textual transmission of the poem). By the same token the other five MSS agree closely in stanza 2 (against stanza 3 in Caligula and Naples). Second, a number of variants are obviously the usual scribal errors in the course of copying; examples are variations like *will/wold* or the interchange of the rhyme-words *strong* and *long* in ll. 7–8 in MSS Ashmole, Thornton, Adv., Caius and in ll. 10–11 in MS Univ. Coll. Oxf. Note that once again this interchange is transmitted in writing, as the correspondence of MSS Ashmole, Adv. and Univ. Coll. Oxf. vs. MSS Thornton and Caius testifies. Third, there are variants which seem to have arisen through a faulty remembering of the text. A case in point is ll. 7–9 in MS Univ. Coll. Oxf., a short fragmentary passage which has most certainly been written down from memory on the final flyleaf of the MS.[9]

9. The Harvard University Percy Folio, MS Eng. 748, vol. 3, p. 52, reads:

    Ye shall well heare of a knight
    That was in warre full wyght
    And doughtye of his dede
    Hys name was Syr Isenbras

While textual variation in texts primarily transmitted in writing is normally explainable in terms of textual corruption, contamination and conscious change (sometimes resulting in new versions, as in the case of version B of Laȝamon's *Brut*), textual variation in texts which might have been memorized (such as lyrics, shorter verse legends, or popular romances) is partly caused by contaminations through oral transmission.[10] Typical for this kind of variation is a greater fluidity of the verse-line, with the rhyme-words comparatively fixed points in the line, as well as a greater variability of the text as a whole. Although the oral transmission of Middle English romances, parallel to

> Man nobler then he was
>   Lyved none with breade
> He was lyvely, large and longe
> With shoulders broade, and armes stronge
>   That myghtie was to se
> He was a hardy man and hye
> All men hym loved that hym se
>   For a gentyll knyght was he

This is a complete transcript (ca. 1761) of a printing by W. Copland and agrees with the fragments found in Harvard University *STC* 14280.7, p. 2:

> Ye shall well here of a knyghte
> That was in warre full wyght
> And doughty of his dede
> His name was syr Isenbras
> Man nobler than he was
>   Lyued none with brede
> He was louynge large and longe
> With sholders brode and armes stronge
>   That myghty was to se
> He was an hardy man and hye
> All men hym loued that hym se
>   For a gentyll knyght was he

As can be seen from the extracts, these texts belong basically to the Ashmole-Thornton-Advocates-Caius-Univ. Coll. Oxford Group against Caligula and Naples (*knyght : wyght; longe : stronge*).

10. This is not the place to go into questions of textual criticism. For a summary see Chaytor 1945, pp. 148–152; for more recent discussions see Kane 1960, pp. 115–149, and Allen 1984, pp. 24–72. For related problems in Middle High German literature see Heinzle 1978, pp. 56ff, 99ff.

their written transmission, is a well-established fact (and this applies even to longer romances such as *Richard Cœr de Lyon*), the precise part of the oral performer in this transmission chain is far from clear.[11] The basic question is not whether there were minstrels who performed romances orally; the question is rather whether these minstrels were more than transmitters of tales, creative or corruptive—whether they were also, at least in some cases, their authors. In other words, were romances like *Sir Isumbras* or *Sir Degarre* "minstrel romances," properly so called?

In order to answer this question other criteria than those of textual criticism are needed. Style is the most obvious candidate, in particular the extent to which the diction of a narrative poem is formulaic. Whatever the position one takes in regard to the oral-formulaic theory elaborated by Milman Parry and Albert B. Lord, it is clear that oral epic poetry, wherever it is found, is characterized by highly formulaic diction.[12] It is, however, equally clear that an epic poem written in a highly formulaic style is not necessarily of oral origin. Although such a style might have its roots in oral poetry, it can also become the style of written poetry, in particular in a period of transition from orality to literacy. This is true of Anglo-Saxon England, but also of other medieval and nonmedieval cultures.[13] Approaching the Middle English popular romance with this caveat in mind, we find first of all that "formulaicness" is indeed a general characteristic of this type of poetry. Various kinds and degrees of "formulaicness" have to be distinguished, however: formulaic phrases, content-oriented formulas, rhyme-

11. An often-quoted example of oral transmission is the variants due to auditory errors listed by Smithers for *Kyng Alisaunder*; see Smithers 1952–1957, vol. 2, p. 12. On *Richard Cœr de Lyon* compare Baugh 1967, pp. 30–31.

12. For a recent exposition and historiography see Foley 1988; Parry's contributions to the theory are collected in Parry 1971; the classic formulation of the theory is Lord 1960.

13. This has led to various critical comments on the oral-formulaic theory; see for instance Benson 1966; Smith 1977.

oriented formulas, and formulaic narrative patterns (on the level of both type scenes and story patterns).[14]

If we take Parry's famous definition of a formula as "a group of words which is regularly employed under the same metrical conditions to express a given essential idea" (Parry 1971, p. 272; originally published 1930), then a line like "Bathe with spere and with schelde" must be considered a formula. It appears in identical form seven times in *Sir Degrevant,* always in an appropriate context of fighting, and it is furthermore found, with variations, in other romances, a part of a formulaic system:

1. $\begin{Bmatrix} \text{(Bathe)} \\ \text{(. . .)} \end{Bmatrix}$ With spere $\begin{Bmatrix} \text{and} \\ \text{ne} \end{Bmatrix}$ (with) schelde

Degrevant 286, 330, 466, 1058, 1203, 1254, 1662; *Melayne* 43; *Isumbras* 12, 747; *Desconus* 1556, 1826

2. $\begin{Bmatrix} \text{(Bothe)} \\ \text{(Nother)} \\ \text{(. . .)} \end{Bmatrix}$ $\begin{Bmatrix} \text{(With)} \\ \text{(his)} \end{Bmatrix}$ schelde $\begin{Bmatrix} \text{and} \\ \text{ne} \end{Bmatrix}$ (with) spere

Melayne 619; *Torrent* 526, 549, 652; *Desconus* 416, 570; *Florence* 366, 465, 1016; *Octavian* 825, 883; *Triamour* 698

3a. $\begin{Bmatrix} \text{(Bothe)} \\ \text{(. . .)} \end{Bmatrix}$ With spere $\begin{Bmatrix} \text{and} \\ \text{or} \end{Bmatrix}$ $\begin{Bmatrix} \text{launce} \\ \text{knyffe} \\ \text{swerd} \end{Bmatrix}$

Melayne 102; *Torrent* 2192; *Desconus* 184

3b. (. . .) nothyr hors nor spere

Triamour 676

---

14. For a survey of studies on the formulaic nature of Middle English romances see Parks 1986; for the formulaic character of the alliterative romances in Middle English (which I am excluding from consideration here) see Finlayson 1963; Krishna 1982; Lawrence, 1966; Waldron 1957.

3c. $\left\{\begin{array}{l}\text{Bothe}\\ \text{With}\\ \text{That}\end{array}\right\}$ schyld and spere $\left\{\begin{array}{l}\text{then}\\ \text{in hond}\\ \text{all to-brase}\end{array}\right\}$

Torrent 1000, 1439; *Triamour* 836[15]

This example shows quite clearly the interconnection between a formulaic phrase and a formulaic line in Middle English. The expression "with scheld and spere" is on the phraseological level obviously a formulaic collocation which can be inserted into suitable contexts, as is shown in 3c. The same phrase can, on the other hand (with or without additional words such as *bothe*), also function metrically as a formulaic line. The usefulness—in the sense of the oral-formulaic theory—of this line consists in that it can be used for two rhymes, a rhyme in *-eld/ild* and one in *-ere* (1 and 2, respectively). (See Lord 1960, pp. 30ff.) Other variations are possible (compare 3), in particular the replacement of one of the lexemes by a synonym (3a).

The example also shows the correlation between content-oriented and rhyme-oriented formulas. The variants of this formulaic line are part of a set of expressions related to warfare and knighthood, but they are also representatives of definite rhyme patterns. The formulaic lines with *schelde* in rhyme position occur in various combinations with other rhyme words, forming "useful" groups of rhyming lines.[16] In *Isumbras*, *schelde* rhymes with *felde* (as in "In towne and eke in felde," l. 8, or "Whenne they mette in the felde," l. 750; see also the quotations from *Isumbras* above); the same applies to *Lybeaus Desconus* and *Sir Degrevant:*

> And rydeth yn-to the feld:
> My lord, wyth sper and scheld (*Desc.*, 1555–56);
>
> He lokede yn-to a feld,
> There he sawe, wyth sper and scheld (1825–26);

15. This schema has been simplified. For a discussion of formulaic systems see Riedinger 1985; for a detailed analysis of formulaic lines and phrases in Middle English romances see Baugh 1959, pp. 420ff.

16. See the analysis of *Havelok* and *King Horn* by Quinn and Hall 1982, and Reichl 1985c.

Now are thay mett in the felde
Bathe with spere and with schelde (*Degr.*, 285–286);

Bathe with spere and with schilde
How thay farede in the felde (330–331);

The knyghte houed in the felde,
Bathe with spere and with schelde (465–466);

"He es bown to the felde,
Bath with spere and with schilde (1057–58);

Thay prikkede fast thorow the felde,
Bathe with spere and with sch[el]de (1202–1203);

He fyndis the Duke in the felde,
Bathe with spere and with schelde (1253–54);

That fourty lay in the felde,
Bathe with spere and with schelde (1661–62).

What these examples show is that we have a combination of
two lines, of which only one is formulaic, while in the other
line the rhyme word only is fixed. Alternatively one might say
that a line ending in *felde* triggers off the formulaic line "with
spere and with schelde." Is "with spere and with schelde" then
a tag?

The line between a tag and a formula is not easy to draw.
One might differentiate the two terms by defining a tag as a
semantically redundant line whose presence is entirely conditioned by metrical considerations, and a formula as a possibly
equally cliché-like line of "low semantic load," which forms,
however, part of a "dynamic" set of formulaic expressions
used by the singer to "tell his tale."[17] This differentiation depends to a large degree on the view one takes of the composition and performance of a particular text. If we view a romance
like *Sir Isumbras* or *Sir Degrevant* as the work of an author
writing down the narrative with pen in hand, we are probably
more ready to speak of a tag when we encounter a line of "low
semantic load" than if we see the poems as basically works of

17. On this functional, not mechanical, aspect of formulaic diction see
Lord 1960, pp. 65–67; on the notion of "tag" in Middle English Romance
see also Smithers 1988, pp. 211–212.

oral poetry, their formal makeup conditioned by the exigencies of oral performance.[18] This twofold point of view is, incidentally, also possible on the content level of romance; while a combination of conventional motifs and the adherence to traditional story patterns might be seen as indicative of the work of a hack writer, the same structural characteristics can also be interpreted as a sign of popularity, in the sense of rootedness in folklore.[19]

A. C. Baugh, taking his cue from Jean Rychner's analysis of the *chanson de geste,* has also shown the formulaic nature of the Middle English popular romance on the level of theme and narrative pattern (Baugh 1959, pp. 440–454). Further investigations of the scenic and "thematic" (in the sense of oral-formulaic theory) composition of the Middle English romances have confirmed Baugh's findings, so that there is every reason to rank the Middle English popular romance with the Old French *chanson de geste* or the Middle High German *Spielmannsepos.*[20] But does this mean that the Middle English popular romance is, like the *chanson de geste* or the *Spielmannsepos,* essentially a genre of oral poetry, whatever the—secondary—contribution of the *clerici* as scribes, compilers, and authors? Critical opinion is as divided on this issue as it was in the eighteenth and nineteenth century. Thomas Percy conceded that "some of the larger metrical romances might come from the pen of the monks or others," but he also maintained that "the smaller narratives were probably composed by the minstrels who sang them" (Percy 1886, vol. 1, p. 347; orig-

18. On the function of lines like "with spere and with schelde" as tail-rhyme lines see Dürmüller 1975, pp. 71ff; on the syntactic analysis of the tail-rhyme lines in *Sir Isumbras* see Reichl, "Syntax and Style in *Sir Isumbras.*"

19. On a 'folkloristic view' of medieval literature see e.g. Rosenberg 1976; on the 'hack-writer hypothesis' see e.g. Slover 1931.

20. On the Middle English romance see in particular Wittig 1978; on the *chanson de geste* see Rychner 1955, and Duggan 1973; on the *Spielmannsepos* see Schröder 1967, and Curschmann 1968. Rychner's thesis has been critically scrutinized by Delbouille in an important article on the relationship between oral and written tradition; see Delbouille 1959, and compare also Riquer 1959.

inally published 1765). Joseph Ritson, on the other hand, is emphatic in his view of the minstrel as a mere performer, devoid of all poetic gifts and talents: "The minstrels were too ignorant, and too vulgar, to translate pieceës of several thousand lines; though such pieceës may have been translateëd or written for them, as many a minstrel, no doubt, could sing and play, what he had not the genius to compose, nor even the capacity to write or read" (Ritson 1802, p. cvi). Some modern editors of Middle English romances have assumed a minstrel authorship of individual romances, as for instance L. F. Casson has for *Sir Degrevant:* "Nothing of the author is known positively, but it is reasonable to infer that he wrote for minstrels, and even that he was a minstrel himself" (Casson 1949, p. lxxii). A positive view of the minstrel as a creative rather than just a destructive force is, however, on the whole restricted by qualifications such as Baugh's that "minstrel authorship of the Middle English romances was the exception, not the rule" (Baugh 1967, p. 5).[21] And there is, of course, no question of crediting the minstrel with any poetic sense if oral transmission as such (at whatever stage) is seen as leading only to textual corruption:

All the evidence we have suggests that oral transmission makes wretched what it touches, and that the longer the process the more debased the product. The range of evidence, from the Lincoln's Inn romance-manuscript to the Percy Folio, is complete, and confirms what we might, in common sense, expect. There is no mystery about oral transmission, and I should make it clear that I am not invoking the higher mysteries of oral formulaic composition, which are even more irrelevant to Middle English than to Old English alliterative verse. (Pearsall 1981, p. 6)

Although the application of oral-formulaic theory to medieval literature has met with opposition, some of it no doubt justified, the methodological basis of Parry's and Lord's investigations is in my opinion both sound and legitimate. If one wants to know what oral poetry was like one has to find out what oral poetry is like. Without fieldwork no qualified state-

---

21. Compare also Mehl 1967, pp. 7–13, and Burrow 1971, pp. 12ff.

ments about the probable or improbable oral nature of older poetry, transmitted only in writing, is possible. The adherents of oral-formulaic theory among medievalists have, however, possibly been somewhat one-sided in considering the South Slavic mode of oral composition by improvisation as the only genuine form of an oral epic tradition. There are other traditions of epic poetry more similar to the situation that must have prevailed in medieval Europe, and it is to one of these I want to turn to now, with the intention of probing its relevance for a better understanding of the minstrel's role as both performer and author. Within the scope of this essay, my remarks will have to be sketchy and the conclusions can hence be only tentative.

The tradition I want to discuss briefly is one variety of the epic traditions found among the Turks of Central Asia.[22] The rich epic traditions of the Turkic world have been known since Radloff, who, in his monumental *Proben der Volkslitteratur der türkischen Stämme Süd-Sibiriens,* had as early as 1885 stressed the relevance of Kirghiz oral poetry to the Homeric question (Radloff 1885, pp. xx–xxviii). The Kirghiz mode of oral composition is improvisational and in this way similar to the Serbo-Croatian epic tradition. There are, however, Turkic traditions which are closer to medieval minstrel poetry, among them the Chorezmian school in Uzbek oral poetry.[23] Oral epics are called *dåståns* in Uzbek; they are in verse and prose (somewhat like the *chantefable*), the prose parts being declaimed, the verse parts sung to the accompaniment of a musical instrument, most typically the two-stringed *dombra* of the lute family. There are two main genres of *dåstån,* the heroic epic and the lyrico-heroic epic or romance.

---

22. My arguments are based on various fieldtrips to Soviet and Chinese Turkestan sponsored by the Soviet and Chinese Academies of Science and on work carried out within the Research Project "Central Asia" of the Deutsche Forschungsgemeinschaft.

23. The classic account of Uzbek epic poetry is Žirmunskij and Zarifov 1947; for a summary in German see Fleischer 1958. For a discussion of Uzbek epic poetry see also Reichl 1985a and Reichl 1989a; for a description of various styles of Uzbek and Karakalpak epic poetry see Reichl 1985b; for a comparison between Serbo-Croatian and Turkic oral epic poetry see Lord 1987a.

The latter type of oral epic in particular flourishes in Chorezm, the area around Chiwa in northwestern Uzbekistan, south of Lake Aral, on the border with Turkmenistan. Whereas the tradition of epic poetry among the Uzbeks is basically improvisational, the Chorezmian tradition is clearly one of memorizing. This is to say that the singer has a strong sense of textual identity and feels constrained to adhere as closely as possible to the version of an epic poem handed down to him by tradition. The distinction between an improvising and a memorizing tradition in Turkic oral poetry is in many cases a matter of degree and must not be thought of as categorical. Memorization—or perhaps more correctly the emphasis on the preservation of textual identity—always entails the mastery of a traditional style and a formulaic technique.[24] It should be mentioned *en passant* that in Chorezm the singer or *bakhshi* is normally accompanied by a small ensemble and that the musical aspect of the epic, the singing of the lyrical parts of a text, is one of the most important elements of the performance.

This emphasis on verbatim recall is not limited to the Chorezmian school; it is also found among the Turkmenians, the Karakalpaks and the Kazakhs. Typical for this type of tradition is the close correspondence (in the verse parts) between various versions of a given epic. I have compared elsewhere a passage from one of the epics of the *Göroghlu* cycle in seven versions (two Uzbek, two Turkmenian, three Karakalpak) and have found just the kind of variants one finds among the different versions of *Sir Isumbras* or *Sir Degrevant*.[25] The conclusions one can reach from a study of these traditions are (1) that oral traditions can be based on memorizing (in the sense specified above) rather than on improvising and (2) that in the former case textual variation is precisely of the sort we encounter in medieval texts like the Middle English popular romances.

But this is not the whole story. In the case of the Chorezmian school the written text plays an important role in the transmission of epic poetry. It is also true of other Central Asian Turkic

24. For a recent discussion of the "memorizing oral poet" see Lord 1987b.

25. See Reichl 1985b, pp. 628–632; for similar variants in some (but not all) versions of the Kazakh epic *Qambar batïr* see Reichl, 1989b.

epic poetry that a purely oral tradition, a teaching of epic poetry by word of mouth, is sometimes paralleled by a written tradition. The latter consists either of manuscript copies of individual versions or of printed editions. There are, for instance, a number of popular editions of Kazakh epics which were prepared in Kazan in the nineteenth century. These chapbook-like editions had some influence on the transmission of epic poetry, just as modern, more scholarly editions have sometimes influenced a singer.[26] The manuscript versions of epic poems were used mainly by the *qissa-khåns,* professional storytellers and story-readers.[27] In one of the nineteenth-century manuscripts of an Azerbaijanian version of the *Göroghlu* cycle the next-to-last "branch" ends with the words: "In this way that loving couple realized their most sanguine hopes. God grant that likewise may be fulfilled the desires of all those who buy this tale, as well as of those who read or relate it!" (Chodzko 1842, p. 333). This close interrelationship between a written and an oral tradition, between the performance of an epic poem by a professional reader and by a singer, is underlined by the fact that the singer himself might possess a written manuscript version of his epic, which he might even make use of in the course of his performance: "It is well-known that in Chorezm the influence of the feudal urban centres, with which the life of the rural population of the small oasis was intimately connected, was particularly strong. Here singers who can read and write are not seldom. They do not improvise the verse parts of their *dåståns,* but learn them by heart, holding sometimes the manuscript of the poem in their hands as a help for their recitation" (Žirmunskij and Zarifov 1947, p. 55).

Although there is no space here to go into details and to provide textual evidence for this intermingling of oral and written

26. For the Serbo-Croatian heroic poems compare Lord 1967; for Uzbek epic poetry compare Mirzaev 1968, pp. 67ff.

27. The *qissa-khån* corresponds in many ways to the Turkish *meddah.* See Žirmunskij and Zarifov 1947, pp. 28ff; Jacob 1904. On the role of the *qissa-khån* in the Turkmenian and Uzbek, especially Chorezmian, narrative traditions see Mirbadaleva 1975, pp. 112ff. On the importance of the written text for the Iranian storyteller see Page 1979; on the interrelationship between written and oral transmission see also Finnegan 1974, pp. 56ff.

traditions in Chorezm, I hope that this particular situation does throw some light on what must have been the case in the Middle Ages. A great deal of research has gone into the definition of a medieval minstrel (*disour, jongleur, Spielmann,* or whatever the term might be); the one thing which is uncontroversial is that there must have been a great variety of minstrels in the Middle Ages, some certainly "only" acrobats or musicians, but some certainly also creative poets, such as Rutebeuf or Thomas Chestre.[28] It is also clear that those minstrels who performed narrative texts orally must have memorized their texts, the formulaic style of the poems "easing" their memory as well as providing a technique for rapid telling, or in the event that memory failed. In many cases the memorized texts might have come from manuscripts. There is little doubt that some of the extant Middle English romances were translated, pen in hand, from the French, although some romances closely corresponding to a French text could conceivably stem from an oral poet who was bilingual. An apt illustration of such a bilingual poet in contemporary Ireland can be found in Pat Linney of Rossport, Co. Mayo, who performs his "History of Ireland" in both Irish and English verse.[29] It might be of interest in this context that in the area of Turkic oral poetry many cases of bilingual singers (Uzbek/Tajik, Turkish/Kurdish, Azerbaijanian/Georgian, and so on) are known. Furthermore, as the quotation from *Havelok* above suggests, it seems fairly certain that professional entertainers read from manuscripts—that the class of minstrels, as far as they performed narrative texts, embraced not only the singer of tales but also the reader of tales, the *bakhshi* as well as the *qissa-khån*.

In spite of all the "written contamination" clearly discern-

28. For a discussion of the various definitions of the minstrel and approaches to minstrel poetry see Waremann 1951, pp. 11–58; Salmen 1960, pp. 12ff. On Rutebeuf see Faral 1910, pp. 159–166; on Thomas Chestre see Bliss 1960, pp. 12ff.

29. Baugh concedes that one would have to postulate a bilingual singer if one wanted to explain the origin of Middle English texts closely corresponding to a French original other than by translating in writing. See Baugh 1959, p. 432; see also Brandl 1910, pp. 879ff. On Pat Linney see McCrum et al. 1986, pp. 167–168.

ible in the Chorezmian tradition, there is not a shadow of doubt
that the *dåståns* performed by the Chorezmian *bakhshi* originate in an oral milieu. They are part of Turkic oral poetry, even
if in some cases the plot can be traced back to a Classical Persian verse epic or if many of the poetic devices (metaphors and
images, lyrical verse forms) have been influenced by Persian
and Turkic Classical poetry. It seems strange to suppose that
in medieval England a genre so clearly marked for oral performance as the popular romance, in particular the romance in
tail-rhyme stanzas, should always have originated in writing
and that the performers should have been capable only of remembering (and that only badly), but never of composing. Certainly, if we maintain a rigid dichotomy of oral vs. written, oral
singer vs. writing poet, the Middle English romances present
something of a puzzle. But maybe we should accept a less rigid
bipartition and allow for a greater variety of types. There might
have been the learned author writing in a popular style as well
as the less learned hack rapidly churning out popular fiction,
but there must have been also the minstrel performing the
works of others, with or without written help, as well as the
popular entertainer who had mastered the idiom of popular
storytelling to such a degree that he was capable of producing
his own works. There is no need to think that these produc-
tions must always have been second-rate simply because textual transmission through oral channels is often seen as corruptive. There are good and bad singers in oral traditions; and
what is true today was probably also true in the Middle Ages.
Despite the achievements of modern literary scholarship there
is still good sense in Bishop Percy, who, on the question
"whether every minstrel or harper composed himself, or only
repeated, the songs he chanted," answered in his "Essay
of the Ancient Minstrels in England" (1765): "Some probably
did the one, and some the other: and it would have been wonderful indeed if men whose peculiar profession it was, and
who devoted their time and talents to entertain their hearers
with poetical compositions, were peculiarly deprived of all
poetical genius themselves, and had been under a physical
incapacity of composing those common rhymes which were
the usual subjects of their recitation" (Percy 1886, vol. 1, p.
356).

References

Allen, Rosamund, ed. 1984. *King Horn: An Edition Based on Cambridge University Library MS Gg. 4.27(2), With an Analysis of the Textual Transmission.* New York: Garland.

Barron, W. R. J. 1987. *English Medieval Romance.* London: Longman.

Baugh, Albert C. 1950. "The Authorship of the Middle English Romances," *Annual Bulletin of the Modern Humanities Research Association* 22: 13–28.

———. 1959. "Improvisation in the Middle English Romance," *Proceedings of the American Philosophical Society* 103: 418–454.

———. 1967. "The Middle English Romance: Some Questions of Creation, Presentation, and Preservation," *Speculum* 42: 1–31.

Benson, Larry D. 1966. "The Literary Character of Anglo-Saxon Formulaic Poetry," *PMLA* 81: 334–341.

Bliss, A. J., ed. 1960. *Thomas Chestre: Sir Launfal.* London: Thomas Nelson.

Brandl, Alois. 1910. "Spielmannsverhältnisse in frühmittelenglischer Zeit," *Sitzungsberichte der königlichen preussischen Akademie der Wissenschaften, Philosophisch-historische Classe* 91: 873–892.

Braun, Maximilian. 1961. *Das serbokroatische Heldenlied.* Göttingen: Vandenhoeck & Ruprecht.

Brewer, Derek S., and A. E. B. Owen, eds. 1975. *The Thornton Manuscript (Lincoln Cathedral MS. 91).* London: Scolar Press.

Brown, Carleton. 1914–15. "A Passage from *Sir Isumbras*," *Englische Studien* 48: 329.

Burrow, J. A. 1971. *Ricardian Poetry: Chaucer, Gower, Langland and the 'Gawain' Poet.* London: Routledge & Kegan Paul.

Casson, L. F., ed. 1949. *The Romance of Sir Degrevant.* EETS 221. London: Oxford University Press.

Chaytor, H. J. 1945. *From Script to Print: An Introduction to Medieval Vernacular Literature.* Cambridge: W. Heffer.

Chodzko, Alexander, trans. 1842. *Specimens of the Popular Poetry of Persia, as Found in the Adventures and Improvisations of Kurroglou, the Bandit-Minstrel of Northern Persia; and in the Songs of the People Inhabiting the Shores of the Caspian Sea.* London: W. H. Allen.

Curschmann, Michael. 1968. *"Spielmannsepik": Wege und Ergebnisse der Forschung von 1907–1965; Mit Ergänzungen und Nachträgen bis 1967 (Überlieferung und mündliche Kompositionsform).* Stuttgart: J. B. Metzler.

Delbouille, Maurice. 1959. "Les chansons de geste et le livre," pp. 295–407 in *La technique littéraire des chansons de geste: Actes du Colloque de Liège*. Paris: Société d'Edition "Les Belles Lettres."

Duggan, Joseph J. 1973. *The Song of Roland: Formulaic Style and Poetic Craft*. Berkeley, Calif.: University of California Press.

Dürmüller, Urs. 1975. *Narrative Possibilities of the Tail-Rime Romance*. Schweizer Anglistische Arbeiten 83. Bern: Francke.

Faral, Edmond. 1910. *Les jongleurs en France au moyen age*. Paris: Champion.

———, ed. 1924. *Les arts poétiques du XIIe et du XIIIe siècle*. Paris: Champion.

Fewster, Carol. 1987. *Traditionality and Genre in Middle English Romance*. Cambridge: D. S. Brewer.

Finlayson, John. 1963. "Formulaic Technique in *Morte Arthure*," *Anglia* 81:372–393.

Finnegan, Ruth. 1974. "How Oral is Oral Literature?" *Bulletin of the School of Oriental and African Studies* 37: 52–64.

Fleischer, Wolfgang. 1958. "Das uzbekische heroische Volksepos," *Beiträge zur Geschichte der deutschen Sprache und Literatur* (Halle) 80: 111–156.

Foley, John M. 1988. *The Theory of Oral Composition: History and Methodology*. Bloomington: Indiana University Press.

Greene, Richard Leighton, ed. 1977. *The Early English Carols*. 2nd rev. and enlarged ed. Oxford: Clarendon Press.

Halliwell, James Orchard, ed. 1842. *Torrent of Portugal: An English Metrical Romance*. London: J. R. Smith.

———, ed. 1844. *The Thornton Romances: The Early English Metrical Romances of Perceval, Isumbras, Eglamour, and Degrevant. Selected from Manuscripts at Lincoln and Cambridge*. London: John Bowyer Nichols.

Heinzle, Joachim. 1978. *Mittelhochdeutsche Dietrichepik: Untersuchungen zur Tradierungsweise, Überlieferungskritik und Gattungsgeschichte später Heldendichtung*. Münchener Texte und Untersuchungen 62. Munich: Artemis.

Hoops, Reinald. 1929. *Der Begriff 'Romance' in der mittelenglischen und frühneuenglischen Literatur*. Heidelberg: C. Winter.

Jacob, Georg. 1904. *Vorträge türkischer Meddâh's (mimischer Erzählkünstler)*. Türkische Bibliothek 1. Berlin: Mayer & Müller.

Kane, George, ed. 1960. *Piers Plowman: The A Version. Will's Visions of Piers Plowman and Do-Well*. London: Athlone Press.

Kölbing, Eugen, ed. 1880. "Das Neapler Fragment von Sir Isumbras," *Englische Studien* 3: 200–202.

Krishna, Valerie. 1982. "Parataxis, Formulaic Density, and Thrift in the *Alliterative Morte Arthure*," *Speculum* 57: 63–83.

Lawrence, R. F. 1966. "The Formulaic Theory and Its Application to English Alliterative Poetry," pp. 166–183 in *Essays on Style and Language: Linguistic and Critical Approaches to Literary Style*, ed. Roger Fowler. London: Routledge & Kegan Paul.

Lord, Albert B. 1960. *The Singer of Tales*. Cambridge, Mass.: Harvard University Press.

———. 1967. "The Influence of a Fixed Text," pp. 1199–1206 in *To Honor Roman Jakobson: Essays on the Occasion of His Seventieth Birthday (11 October 1966)*, vol. 2. The Hague and Paris: Mouton.

———. 1987a. "Central Asiatic and Balkan Epic," pp. 288–320 in *Fragen der mongolischen Heldendichtung*, vol. 4, ed. Walther Heissig. Asiatische Forschungen 101. Wiesbaden: Harrassowitz.

———. 1987b. "The Nature of Oral Poetry," pp. 313–349 in *Comparative Research on Oral Traditions: A Memorial for Milman Parry*, ed. John Miles Foley. Columbus, Ohio: Slavica.

McCrum, Robert, William Cran, and Robert MacNeil. 1986. *The Story of English*. London: BBC Publications.

Mehl, Dieter. 1967. *The Middle English Romances of the Thirteenth and Fourteenth Centuries*. London: Routledge & Kegan Paul.

Michelson, Broh Charles, ed. 1969. "A Critical Edition of the Romance of Sir Isumbras." Ph.D. diss., Case Western Reserve University, Cleveland, Ohio.

Middle English Dictionary, ed. Hans Kurath, Sherman M. Kuhn, Robert E. Lewis, John Reidy. Ann Arbor, Mich.: University of Michigan Press, 1954–.

Miletich, John S. 1986. "Oral Aesthetics and Written Aesthetics: The South Slavic Case and the *Poema de Mio Cid*," pp. 183–204 in *Hispanic Studies in Honor of Alan D. Deyermond: A North American Tribute*, ed. John S. Miletich. Madison, Wis.: The Hispanic Seminary of Medieval Studies, Ltd.

Mills, Maldwyn, ed. 1973. *Six Middle English Romances*. London: Dent.

Mirbadaleva, A. S. 1975. "Obščie čerty i specifika turkmenskix i uzbekskix romaničeskix dastanov" [General traits and characteristics of Turkoman and Uzbek romance], pp. 110–127 in *Tipologija narodnogo èposa* [Typology of the folk-epic], ed. V. M. Gacak. Moscow: Izdatel'stvo "Nauka."

Mirzaev, Tora. 1968. *Alpåmïš dåstånïnïŋ ozbek variantlarï* [The Uzbek versions of the epic "Alpåmïš"]. Tashkent: "Fan" Našrijåti.

Nims, Margaret F., trans. 1967. *Poetria Nova of Geoffrey of Vinsauf.* Toronto: Pontifical Institute of Mediaeval Studies.

Page, Mary Ellen. 1979. "Professional Storytelling in Iran: Transmission and Practice," *Iranian Studies* 12: 195–215.

Parks, Ward. 1986. "The Oral-Formulaic Theory in Middle English Studies," *Oral Tradition* 1: 636–694.

Parry, Milman. 1971. *The Making of Homeric Verse,* ed. Adam Parry. London: Oxford University Press.

Pearsall, Derek. 1981. "The Origins of the Alliterative Revival," pp. 1–24 in *The Alliterative Tradition in the Fourteenth Century,* ed. Bernard S. Levy and Paul E. Szarmach. Kent, Ohio: Kent State University Press.

———. 1985. "Middle English Romance and its Audiences," pp. 37–47 in *Historical and Editorial Studies in Medieval and Early Modern English for Johan Gerritsen,* ed. Mary-Jo Arn, Hanneke Wirtjes, and Hans Jansen. Groningen: Wolters-Noordhoff.

Percy, Thomas. 1886. *Reliques of Ancient English Poetry,* ed. with an introduction by Henry B. Wheatley. 3 vols. London: Swan Sonneschein, Lebas & Lowrey.

Quinn, William A., and Audley S. Hall. 1982. *Jongleur: A Modified Theory of Oral Improvisation and Its Effects on the Performance and Transmission of Middle English Romance.* Lanham, Md.: University Press of America.

Radloff, Wilhelm, ed. and trans. 1885. *Proben der Volkslitteratur der nördlichen türkischen Stämme, 5: Der Dialect der Kara-Kirgisen.* St. Petersburg: Kaiserliche Akademie der Wissenschaften.

Ramsey, Lee C. 1983. *Chivalric Romances: Popular Literature in Medieval England.* Bloomington: Indiana University Press.

Reichl, Karl, trans. 1985a. *Rawšan: Ein usbekisches mündliches Epos.* Asiatische Forschungen 93. Wiesbaden: Harrassowitz.

———. 1985b. "Oral Tradition and Performance of the Uzbek and Karakalpak Epic Singers," pp. 613–643 in *Fragen der mongolischen Heldendichtung,* 3, ed. Walther Heissig. Asiatische Forschungen 91. Wiesbaden: Harrassowitz.

———. 1985c. Review of William A. Quinn and Audley S. Hall, *Jongleur: A Modified Theory . . . Anglia* 105: 175–178.

———. 1989a. "Uzbek Epic Poetry: Tradition and Poetic Diction," pp. 94–120 in *Traditions of Heroic and Epic Poetry,* 2, ed. J. B. Hainsworth and A. T. Hatto. London: Modern Humanities Research Association.

———. 1989b. "Formulaic Diction in Kazakh Epic Poetry," *Oral Tradition* 4: 360–381.

————. Forthcoming. "Syntax and Style in *Sir Isumbras*," in Alfred Bammesberger and Teresa Kirschner, eds., *Language and Civilization: A Groundwork of Essays and Studies in Honour of Otto Hietsch.*

Riedinger, Anita. 1985. "The Old English Formula in Context," *Speculum* 60: 294–317.

Riquer, Martín de. 1959. "Epopée jongleresque à écouter et épopée romanesque à lire," pp. 75–82 in *La technique littéraire des chansons de geste: Actes du Colloque de Liège.* Paris: Société d'Edition "Les Belles Lettres."

Ritson, Joseph. 1802. "A Dissertation on Romance and Minstrelsy," in *Ancient English Metrical Romances,* vol. 1, pp. v–ccxxiv. London: W. Bulmer.

Rosenberg, Bruce A. 1976. "Folklore Methodology and Medieval Literature," *Journal of the Folklore Institute* 13: 311–325.

Rychner, Jean. 1955. *La chanson de geste: Essai sur l'art épique des jongleurs.* Geneva: Droz.

Ryding, William W. 1971. *Structure in Medieval Narrative.* De Proprietatibus Litterarum, Series Maior, 12. The Hague: Mouton.

Salmen, Walter. 1960. *Der fahrende Musiker im europäischen Mittelalter.* Die Musik im alten und neuen Europa 4. Kassel: J. Ph. Hinnenthal.

Schleich, Gustav, ed. 1901. *Sir Ysumbras: Eine englische Romanze des 14. Jahrhunderts.* Palaestra 15. Berlin: Mayer & Müller.

Schröder, Walter Johannes. 1967. *Spielmannsepik.* 2nd ed. Stuttgart: J. B. Metzler.

Severs, J. Burke, ed. 1967. *A Manual of the Writings in Middle English, 1050–1500, 1. Romances.* New Haven: Connecticut Academy of Arts and Sciences.

Slover, Clark H. 1931. "'Sire Degarre': A Study of a Mediaeval Hack Writer's Methods," *Studies in English, The University of Texas Bulletin* 11: 6–23.

Smith, John D. 1977. *"The Singer or the Song?* A Reassessment of Lord's 'Oral Theory,'" *Man,* N.S. 12: 141–153.

Smithers, G. V., ed. 1952–1957. *Kyng Alisaunder.* 2 vols. London: Oxford University Press.

————, ed. 1987. *Havelok.* Oxford: Clarendon Press.

————. 1988. "The Style of *Hauelok," Medium Ævum* 57: 190–218.

Stevens, John. 1973. *Medieval Romance: Themes and Approaches.* London: Hutchinson.

Strohm, Paul. 1971. *"Storie, Spelle, Geste, Romaunce, Tragedie:* Generic Distinctions in the Middle English Troy Narratives," *Speculum* 46: 348–359.

Waldron, Ronald A. 1957. "Oral-Formulaic Technique and Middle English Alliterative Poetry," *Speculum* 32: 792–801.

Wareman, Piet. 1951. *Spielmannsdichtung: Versuch einer Begriffsbestimmung*. Amsterdam: Jacob van Campen.

Wittig, Susan. 1978. *Stylistic and Narrative Structures in the Middle English Romances*. Austin: University of Texas Press.

Žirmunskij, V. M., and X. T. Zarifov. 1947. *Uzbekskij narodnyj geroičeskij èpos* [The Uzbek heroic folk-epic]. Moscow: Gosudarstvennoe izdatel'stvo xudožestvennoj literatury.

STEPHEN A. MITCHELL

Gråkappan (AT 425) as Chapbook and Folktale in Sweden

The tale of Cupid and Psyche was in the air early in the Swedish nineteenth century. Visually, the Cupid and Psyche configuration was present in the form of a marble statue by Johan Sergell on display in Konungens Museum. This well-known sculpture had even inspired an anonymous poem in 1798 on Cupid and Psyche, as well as on the statue's ability to articulate the beauty of the story.[1] So well did the work reflect the mood of the times that a sketch of it formed the frontispiece to the first issue (December 1818) of *Svea: Tidskrift för Vetenskap och Konst,* one of the many publications connected with the Romantic movement (such as *Phosphoros, Poetisk Kalendar, Svensk Litteratur-Tidning*) to come from Vilhelm Palmblad's publishing house in Uppsala. The significance of the statue, and the tale it portrayed, for the Romantics and their program was underscored by the appearance in the subsequent issue of Anders Grafström's article on the history of the sculpture and its antecedents in the Classical tradition. And as could be expected, the lovers' situation was grist for the Romantics'

---

1. *Psyché: Saga, Tilägnad Hr Prof. och Ridd. Sergell* (Stockholm: Anders Jac. Nordström, 1798). The poem is attributed to Anders Fredrik Skjöldebrand.

mill, as exemplified by Euphrosyne's "dramatized fairy tale"
Psyche.[2]
Moreover, the themes central to the tale of Cupid and Psyche were celebrated in 1818 in an anonymous chapbook called
Gråkappan, published in Nyköping by P. E. Winge.[3] This "sor-
rowful and very delightful story about the beautiful Prince
Rosimandro, who is transformed in the most miserable fashion
by an evil troll-woman" but returned to his original state by
love (as the subtitle informs its audience), appeared regularly
throughout the early nineteenth century, with printings
in Stockholm, Jönköping, Lund, Kalmar, Linköping, and
Karlshamn, in addition to Nyköping.[4]
The story can be summarized as follows: While out hunting,

2. Anders Grafström, "Om Amor och Psyche, samt Faun, arbeten i mar-
mor af Sergell," *Svea 2 (1819): 313–26.* Treatments of the Classical representations of the theme available at the time included Børge R. Thorlacius,
Fabula de Psyche et Cupidine: Disqvistio mythologica (Copenhagen and
Leipzig: J. H. Schubothe, 1802) and Aloys Ludwig Hirt, *Ueber die Fabel
des Amor und Psyche* (Berlin: Akademie der Wissenschaften, 1812–13).
Euphrosyne [Julia Nyberg], "Psyche: Dramatiserad saga," in *Nyare dikter
af Euphrosyne* (Stockholm: Zacharias Häggström, 1828), pp. 37–101. It
should be noted that the author concludes her poem with Psyche's banishment after dripping the wax onto Amor's shoulder.
3. *Gråkappan* is one of several hundred eighteenth- and nineteenth-
century Scandinavian chapbooks of ballads and prose texts in the Harvard
Libraries whose acquisition is undoubtedly connected with Professor Francis J. Child's many years of service on the Library Committee in the 1880s
and 1890s; according to one of the Librarian's "waste-books" in the Harvard Archives, nearly one hundred of them arrived from Lyngbe's in Copenhagen on September 13, 1895, alone.
4. Many of the editions are listed in P. O. Bäckström, *Svenska folkböcker: Sagor, legender och äfventyr efter äldre upplagor och andra källor
utgifvne jemte Översigt af svensk folkläsning från äldre till närvarande tid*
(Stockholm: A. Bohlins, 1845–1848), p. 133. All subsequent citations to
Gråkappan are to the 1818 edition; there seem to be no substantive changes
in the various printings. In addition to *Gråkappan's* availability as a chapbook, Bäckström's lengthy précis and the reprintings of the story in Lénström's and Molbech's anthologies must also be reckoned with in considering its dissemination. Moreover, the possibility that *Gråkappan* was
reproduced in other formats, such as school textbooks, cannot be ignored.
Such a situation would not alter the widespread availability of the text, however, only the degree and character of its distribution.

a king and his driver are separated from the rest of the royal party. As they return to the castle, the carriage is blocked by a gray cape *(en grå kappa)*, which demands as its price for allowing the king to continue on his way the first living thing which greets him when he returns to his castle. Believing that his dog will fulfill this condition, the king agrees, only to find that it is his youngest and favorite daughter who meets him. The king attempts to deceive Gråkappan by sending his two other daughters into the forest by turns, but when his schemes fail, he ruefully sends the promised third daughter, Jucunda. She goes, pleased to be able to save her sisters and her father from "that troll." The princess falls asleep in the forest and dreams of a young prince, but awakens to find Gråkappan next to her. He escorts her to his castle and explains at length that everything in it is for her use and that she will not see him other than at meals; the only things she is forbidden are escape and opening a trapdoor in the floor of the drawing room. One night she again dreams of the young prince, with whom she falls in love. The days pass and eventually Jucunda opens the trapdoor and sees under it Gråkappan, who then comes to her and asks what it was she saw under the trapdoor. She swoons and when she awakens, the castle is gone. After wandering about, she meets a king who marries her. During the wedding service, however, the bridegroom feels himself slip into a stupor and can neither see nor speak, but no one else notices his condition. A year later Jucunda gives birth to a son and is visited by Gråkappan, who repeats his question, "What did you see under the trapdoor?" Fear and sorrow prevent her from answering, and Gråkappan takes the child from her and smears blood on her mouth and fingers. People believe she must be a troll when they find the child missing and Jucunda's mouth and hands all bloody, but they tell the king that she had a miscarriage. The same thing happens each of the following two years. When the third child disappears, however, the king declares that it must have been a *skogsrå* he met and determines to have Jucunda burned to death. As she is taken to the pyre, Gråkappan appears at her side and again asks what it was she saw under the trapdoor. Indignant and bitter, Jucunda shouts, "You, you damned gray cape, it was you I saw, you whom I hate with all my life and heart" (Jo just dig, din förbannade gråa kappa, war det som jag såg; dig, som jag hatar af lif och själ). At that moment the cape falls and reveals the prince she had seen in her dreams. The prince explains that he had in fact been the one she married, not the king, and that the three young princes are safe; they are his children, not the king's. The pair escapes from the king's men and the prince explains further that his name is Rosimandro and that he had been cursed by a witch whose affection he had spurned. He was to be nothing more than the cape with which she had covered him until he had found a princess who loved him with all her might, married him, and bore him three sons, but who at the same time hated him and cursed him, shouting that she hated him with all her heart and life.

While the history behind Sergell's famous statue is well known (he was responding to an interest in the Cupid and Psyche theme on the part of the mistress to Louis XV, the Countess du Barry), the history behind the chapbook remained a mystery for many decades. At the time of its publication however, Gråkappan's place as part of the Swedish legacy of the AT 425 repertoire appeared secure, especially with the publication a few years later (1822) of the third volume of the second edition of the Grimms' Kinder- und Hausmärchen. In it, Jakob Grimm thanks H. R. von Schröter for a copy of Der Graumantel which he had transcribed in the Swedish province of Östergötland from "the mouth of the people" (aus dem Mund des Volks aufgezeichnet hat).[5] Thus evidently verified as a genuine Swedish multiform of the AT 425 materials, Gråkappan was included in C. J. Lénström's collection of Swedish folktales (1842) and Christian Molbech's anthology of Nordic folklore (1843). In his monumental discussion of Swedish folkböcker (1848), P. O. Bäckström even goes so far as to proclaim the story as being of native origin, although he cautions that its tone and style have been influenced by earlier printed traditions, especially "La Belle et la Bête" of de Villeneuve's Cabinet des Fées.[6]

5. Kinder- und Haus-Märchen, gesammelt durch die Brüder Grimm, 2nd ed. (Berlin: G. Reimer, 1822), vol. 3, pp. 406, 407–08.
6. Bäckström, Svenska folkböcker, pp. 132–133. Printed Swedish-

Over time it has become clear that the chapbook text is the product not of folk tradition as the Grimms and von Schröter meant it, but of one of Sweden's preeminent writers and intellectuals, and one of its foremost Romantics, C. J. L. Almqvist (1793–1866). The first indication of Almqvist's role in the creation of the tale surfaced when he updated his biographical entry for the 1857–58 supplement to *Biographiskt lexicon,* which now included "Prins Rosimandro eller Gråkappan" among the expanded list of his works.[7] Certainly there is much in *Gråkappan* that bespeaks the young Almqvist, who only the year before the appearance of the chapbook had published *Parjamouf, en saga från Nya Holland,* which he called "an attempt to La Fontainize" (ett försök att Lafontainisera). Undoubtedly part of Almqvist's inspiration for *Gråkappan* was Per Daniel Amadeus Atterbom's *Fågel blå,* a reworking of folktale materials and medieval romance. *Fågel blå* was an undertaking Almqvist much admired, as he declared in 1816 at a meeting of Manhemsförbundet, a society devoted to reviving religiosity, patriotism, and the "Gothic" spirit in Sweden. Yet despite his proclaimed enthusiasm for the use of traditional materials as poetic resources, Almqvist's own reworking of the AT 425 theme remained unnoticed and unexamined until 1879. In that year, A. T. Lyssander documented that Almqvist was not merely the editor of *Gråkappan,* but the author of it (albeit using many traditional motifs); that the single most important confirmation of the story's indigenous and traditional character—von Schröter's transcription of *Der Graumantel,* of which the Grimms had published a précis—was nothing more than a fabrication based on a synopsis of Palmblad's review of *Gråkappan* in *Svensk Litteratur-Tidning* with occasional

---

language versions of AT 425 go back at least as far as M. Nyman's translation of Apuleius (1666), reprinted in 1690. Apuleius was translated into Swedish again in 1778.

7. *Svenskt biografiskt lexikon,* new ser. (Örebro: N. M. Lindhs boktryckeri, 1857–58), vol. 1, p. 131. Compare the revised list of publications (pp. 374–378) with the editor's remarks on Almqvist's role in the composition of the bibliography. A dated but still useful study of the relationship between folklore and Almqvist's authorship is provided by Ragnar Ekholm, "Folksaga och folkvisa i Almqvists diktning," *Samlaren* 40 (1919): 1–33.

references to the chapbook itself; and that at least some of
the folktales collected from oral tradition by Gunnar Hyltén-
Cavallius and George Stephens, among others, were heavily
influenced by Almqvist's text.[8]

The discussion of the Cupid and Psyche theme in Sweden
thus mirrors the situation which obtains for the AT 425 materials more broadly: analysis of the tale has often focused on
the question of how the folk traditions of AT 425 and AT 428
relate to the literary tales of Apuleius, Partenopeus de Blois,
and so on.[9] It is the view of many who work with these texts
that the folk traditions are secondary to (that is, based on) the
literary texts; indeed, it was only with Jan-Öjvind Swahn's
comprehensive study of the folktale in an international perspective that the persistence of the tale outside (or at least par-

---

8. A. T. Lyssander, "Tvifvel om en svensk folksagas äkthet," in *Chr.
Cavallin och A. Th. Lyssander: Smärre skrifter i urval samlade och utgifvna
efter författarnes död,* ed. Martin Weibull (Stockholm: P. A. Norstedt och
söners förlag, 1891), pp. 426–451 (originally published in *Ny Illustrerad
Tidning,* 1879). It is difficult to imagine that Atterbom's *Fågel blå* did not
play an important role in the creative life of the young Almqvist, with regard
to *Parjamouf* as well as to *Gråkappan.* Strangely, although Almqvist's admiration for Atterbom's medieval-clad retelling of AT 432—and his public
proclamation of these feelings at Manhemsförbundet—are well known (e.g.,
Ny illustrerad svensk litteraturhistoria, vol. 3, p. 312), the connection to his
own literary undertakings in the years following his pronouncement is
rarely made. Henry Olsson, *C. J. L. Almqvist före Törnrosens bok* (Stockholm: Bonniers, 1927), pp. 106–107, for example, cites La Fontaine, the
sentimental novel, medieval romance, and Spiess's *Hohenstaufen* as the
probable wellsprings of inspiration for Almqvist's creation of *Gråkappan,*
while Lyssander, "Tvifvel om en svensk folksagas äkthet," p. 446, suggests
that it was the Grimms, Beaumont, and E. T. A. Hoffmann who had been
Almqvist's models; both appear to ignore the influence of *Fågel blå.*

9. Jan-Öjvind Swahn, *The Tale of Cupid and Psyche (Aarne-Thompson
425 & 428* (Lund: C. W. K. Gleerup, 1955), pp. 371–410. Subsequent refer-
ences to this book are cited in the text. *Gråkappan* is based on subtypes of
AT 425, "The Search for the Lost Husband," and AT 707, "Three Golden
Sons" (compare Swahn's comment that it is based on AT 425 and AT 706,
"The Maiden without Hands"), whereas the traditional tales of Cupid and
Psyche fall into categories of AT 425 and AT 428, "The Wolf." A bibliog-
raphy of more recent publications of "Amor und Psyche" is provided in
Georgios A. Megas's entry in *Enzyclopädie des Märchens* (Berlin: Walter
de Gruyter, 1975), vol. 1, col. 464–472.

allel to) the literary realm was validated. Yet despite the energy which had been expended on studies of the older literary forms and the folktales, Swahn could still lament in the mid-1950s that "the indisputable cases of literary influence [on the oral tradition] which do exist have not been sufficiently closely examined" (p. 408). Restricting himself to traditional tales (those on which the printed *Gråkappan* exercised no discernable influence), Swahn lists over sixty multiforms recorded from Swedish oral tradition from 1840 to 1938. In addition, he mentions several texts which derive from the chapbook (p. 113). Since his is an essentially historico-evolutionary study with an international scope, Swahn follows the advice of Kaarle Krohn (see below) and purposefully sets these "hybrid" variants aside. But it is precisely these texts, which represent an assimilation of the printed tale into folk tradition, which are of interest here. With these thoughts in mind, I would like to take up the question of the printed *Gråkappan* and its relationship to the Swedish multiforms collected from folk tradition.

The question of these two realms—the oral and the written—and their interconnectedness is a thorny one, all the more so for an area such as Sweden, where a fairly high degree of literacy was already common at the turn of the century. Commenting on his trip through Sweden in 1798 and 1799, Joseph Acerbi observed that "there is certainly no country in the world in which greater provision has been made, and more pains taken for the advancement and diffusion of knowledge among all classes of society, than in Sweden."[10] So widespread was literacy that already in 1848 Bäckström could define "folk literature" as including both that which is created by and that which is read by the people ("hvad som *diktas* och hvad some *läses* af folket").[11] Therefore, we are not likely to be far wrong if we assume that a text such as *Gråkappan*—popular enough to have been published twenty times by 1870 and inexpen-

10. Joseph Acerbi, *Travels through Sweden, Finland, and Lapland to the North Cape in the Years 1798 and 1799* (London: Joseph Mawman, 1802), vol. 1, p. 158.
11. Bäckström, *Svenska folkböcker,* vol. 1, p. iii.

sively marketed for a mass audience—must have exercised some influence on the materials collected in the field.

An instructive example of the relationship between popular literature and the nineteenth-century Nordic folktale collections may be drawn from the Old Norse text *Auðunar þáttr vestfirzka* and the group of Norwegian folktales known as *Kjætten på Dovre*. Much research has been conducted on the tale-types to which the Norwegian narrative belongs, "The Christmas Visitors" (ML 6015) and "The Bear Trainer and His Bear" (AT 1161), including comments on the possible relationship of these migratory tales to the Old Norse saga.[12] The folktales, collected from oral tradition in the mid-nineteenth century, suggest that *Auðunar þáttr vestfirzka* is a reworked and localized version of a widespread folktale, and indeed, there seems to be every reason to believe that the folklore tradition played a role in shaping the theme and structure of the Old Norse text. But things are not so simple as this unilinear explanation would have us believe, for one of the Norwegian folktales collected by Peter Christian Asbjørnsen displays an almost preternaturally high degree of correspondence to the saga. This Norwegian multiform opens with "Det var engang en Mand oppe i Finmarken, som havde fanget en stor Hvidbjørn; *den skulde han gaae til Kongen af Danmark med*" (There was once a man up in Finnmark who caught a big white bear. *He intended to take it to the king of Denmark* [emphasis added]). The corresponding section of the Old Norse text reads: "Auðunn kaupir þar [in Greenland] bjarndýri eitt, gersimi mikla . . . ok *ætlar nú at fara suðr til Danmerkr á fund Sveins konungs ok gefa honum dýrit*" (Auðunn bought there [in Greenland] a bear, a great treasure . . . and *now intends to take it south to Denmark and give it to King Sveinn* [emphasis added]).[13]

12. See especially Reidar Th. Christiansen, "The Living and the Dead," *Studia Norvegica* 2 (1946): 1–96, and *Kjætte på Dovre: Et bidrag til studiet av norske sagn* (Kristiania: J. Dybwad, 1922); and Knut Liestøl, "Kjetta på Dovre," *Maal og Minne* 24 (1933): 24–28.

13. *Norske Folkeeventyr*, coll. and ed. P. Chr. Asbjørnsen and Jørgen Moe, 2nd rev. ed. (Christiania: John Dahls Forlag, 1852), p. 354; *Vestfirðinga sögur*, ed. Björn K. Þórólfsson and Guðni Jónsson (1943; rpt. Reykjavík: Hið íslenzka fornritafélag, 1972), p. 361.

In the Old Norse text, Auðunn's plans direct the tale's central action; in the Norwegian tale, however, the comment has absolutely nothing to do with the rest of the story. This fact, coupled with the astonishing degree of verbal correspondence between the texts, leads to the conclusion that the opening of this variant has been reworked under the influence of the written text, that is, that elements of the Old Norse story have been reintroduced into oral tradition. In fact, there is good evidence to support the supposition that something along these lines has taken place: *Auðunar þáttr* was published in modern translations throughout the early nineteenth century (1818, 1821, 1832, 1849).[14] Apparently, someone who knew or had read the published text incorporated part of the translation into the traditional folktale also dealing with a bear and thus a new form of the tale arose and was collected in the field.

The symbiotic relationship evidenced over time by the written and oral AT 1161 and ML 6015 materials is important, as it underscores the fact that the flow of communication between the oral and written cultures is by no means one-way. In fact, the general relationship between the two kinds of tradition has come under scrutiny in recent years, although there is as yet no clear solution to the questions of how to draw a completely satisfactory distinction between the two categories of art or how to describe the synergism which may exist between them.[15] In the case of the modern *Kjætten på Dovre* variant, the influence is more or less incidental and of little significance,

---

14. "Om Auden den vestfjordiske: En islandsk Fortælling oversat udaf Hr. Prof. Ridder Thorlacii Program [ved K. L. Rahbek]," *Dansk Minerva* (1818): 88–93; rep. in *Nordiske Fortællinger,* trans. K. L. Rahbek (Copenhagen: Dorothea Schultz, 1821), vol. 2, pp. 21–30; "Auden fra Vestfjord," *Oldnordiske Sagaer udg. i Oversættelse af Det nordiske Oldskrift-Selskab* (Copenhagen: Popp, 1832), vol. 4, pp. 242–251; "Ødun med Bjørnen," *Sagaer,* trans. Brynjólfur Snorrason and Kristian Arentzen (Copenhagen: Chr. Steen og Søner, 1849), vol. 2, pp. 213–225.

15. See, for example, Kirill Čistov, "Zur Frage der theoretischen Unterschiede zwischen Folklore und Literatur," *Studia Fennica* 20 (1976): 148–158; Carl Lindahl, "On the Borders of Oral and Written Art," *Folklore Forum* 11 (1978): 94–123; and Albert B. Lord, "The Merging of Two Worlds: Oral and Written Poetry as Carriers of Ancient Values," in John Miles Foley, ed., *Oral Tradition in Literature: Interpretation in Context* (Columbia: University of Missouri Press, 1986), pp. 19–64.

but in other cases, and *Gråkappan* is certainly one, the synergism between the written and oral traditions can result in a kind of narrative calque which earlier generations of folklorists decried as untraditional or impure. Kaarle Krohn's views are typical: he pillories the results of literary tales taken up in oral tradition and admonishes scholars to use such hybrid forms (*Mischformen*) only when real folklore materials are unavailable.[16] The fate of *Gråkappan* provides an interesting window on this process, in particular on the different ways in which a printed text can evolve in folk tradition, for Swedish folklore archives possess four highly variegated versions of the tale. Two of these tales may confidently be called oral multiforms, while one was written down by the narrator herself. The conditions under which the fourth multiform were recorded are unclear. Fortunately the circumstances surrounding some of the transcriptions of *Gråkappan* are richly documented and provide us with an unusual opportunity to speculate on the results of the transition from the printed medium to the oral medium.

In an era when the discussion of contextualizing folklore was still far distant, August Bondeson's *Historiegubbar på Dal* (1886) stands out as a work remarkably ahead of its time.[17] The author of several collections of Swedish folktales, Bondeson gravitated over time toward more and more faithful transcriptions of the tales he heard.[18] This process culminated in *His-*

16. Kaarle Krohn, *Folklore Methodology,* trans. Roger L. Welsh (Austin: University of Texas Press, 1971), p. 47. It should be noted that Krohn has the effects of chapbooks very much in mind as he makes this remark, and while he admits that literary versions can go back into the folk tradition, he expresses the view that such a process "hastens the disappearance of oral tradition from the folk mind" (p. 47). Compare the excellent, if somewhat differing, discussions of the influence of popular printed literature on folk narrative in Linda Dégh, *Folktales and Society: Story-Telling in a Hungarian Peasant Community,* trans. E. M. Schossberger (Bloomington: Indiana University Press, 1969), pp. 146–153, and Bengt Holbek, *Interpretation of Fairy Tales: Danish Folklore in a European Perspective* (Helsinki: Suomalainen Tiedeakatemia, 1987), pp. 250–258.

17. *Historiegubbar på Dal: Deras sagor och sägner m.m.,* coll. August Bondeson (Stockholm: Albert Bonniers förlag, 1886). All subsequent references to this book are given in the text.

18. See the review of Bondeson's development in this direction under the

toriegubbar på Dal, in which he also provides frame-stories portraying the character and circumstances of his informants, and it is worth noting that in contrast to most published collections from the period, which typically convey the notion of tales (or other narrative items) from a certain province, Bondeson entitles his collection after the *tellers* of these tales (*historiegubbar,* "story fogies").

In sketching the evolution of folklore studies in Scandinavia, Axel Olrik reviews Bondeson's work appreciatively and comments prophetically that the frames he provides for his tales will undoubtedly be of value to future generations of researchers.[19] Among Bondeson's primary informants was the crofter (*backstusittare*) Anders Backman, a self-educated man in his late fifties who claimed to have read through the Bible three times.[20] In addition to friendliness and a love for folktales, what most struck Bondeson about Backman was his uncanny memory: he states that Backman could repeat word-for-word (*ordagrant återgifva*) most of the chapbook tales he had ever read (p. 15). Bondeson was no stranger to the *folksaga-folkbok* phenomenon, and he recognized that many of Anders Backman's narrations derived from such publications (p. 5).[21] Apparently, however, he did not un-

---

influence of Asbjørnsen, Lundell, and others in Albert Sandklef, *August Bondeson: Folklivsforskaren—Författaren* (Lund: C. W. K. Gleerup, 1956), pp. 50–87. In a letter to Djurklou, Bondeson claims that he will not change a word of his informants' narratives (p. 75).

19. Axel Olrik, "Til nordiske Folkemindesforsknings Historie," *Danske Studier* 13 (1916): 106–108.

20. Bondeson gives a very full account of Anders Backman (pp. 4–16). Although he was the first person residents of the village thought of when asked by Bondeson to identify talented storytellers, some of his neighbors believed that his narrative abilities were responsible for his financial failings, insofar as these talents demonstrated that he was lazy: "'Hå,' tyckte bonden, 'prata lort och önska bort i väder och vind, det kan fella Backmans Anders, men ta sig för något som ger bröd, det har han aldrig velat. Det har varit en äkta lathund, och därför har han det ock som han har det'" (p. 15). Sandklef (*Bondeson,* pp. 75–79) provides some further remarks on Backman, including transcriptions of some of his letters to Bondeson.

21. As a separate result of his research in Dal, Bondeson published *En saga från Dal och hännes källa* (Uppsala: Almqvist och Wiksell, 1885), in which he provided a comparison of a printed chapbook text with a tale he had collected in the field. See Sandklef, *Bondeson,* pp. 71–72.

derstand *Gråkappan* to be one of them (surprisingly, since Lyssander's article had appeared five years earlier in the popular *Ny Illustrerad Tidning*).

It is not difficult to understand Bondeson's admiration for Backman's memory, for he does indeed have remarkable recall, occasionally echoing phrases from the published *Gråkappan* with astonishing fidelity. When, for example, the princess curses Gråkappan in Backman's narration, she says it *exactly* as Jucunda does above. But it is only rarely that Backman, as in this case, uses precisely the same words and phrases as those found in the chapbook; more often, key phrases or words are common to the two tales, with similar but by no means identical wordings. When the princess first dreams of the prince in the forest, for example, he is described by Almqvist as having "mournful gestures" (*sörjande åtbörder*, p. 9) and by Backman as having "melancholy gestures" (*sorgliga åtbörder*, p. 43). When the king returns to his castle and sees that it is his daughter who first greets him, the king in the chapbook says, "How happily you leapt into my arms without knowing that you leapt down into Hell!" (huru sprang du mig så glad i armarne, och wisste icke, att du sprang neder i helwetet! p. 7). Backman's king says, "You cause me great sorrow, for you do not know that you have jumped into the arms of Hell" (du gör mig stor sorg, ty du vet ej, att du hoppade i helvetets armar, p. 42).

While some portions of Anders Backman's tale mirror with remarkable clarity the story of the chapbook, it is by no means the case that he has memorized the entire text, or simply shifted the printed *Gråkappan* into an oral medium. Few of the events of Backman's story differ from Almqvist's, but the treatments diverge radically, as may be gathered from the fact that the oral multiform is only about one-third the length of the printed text (ca. 1600 words to ca. 4500 words). There are no quasi-philosophical ruminations in Backman's *Gråkappan*, no florid descriptions of emotions; his is a *story,* in which action dominates. When Gråkappan takes the princess to his castle, Backman's version says merely that Gråkappan shows her how beautiful and magnificent it is (p. 43); Almqvist, on the other hand, has Gråkappan describe the gardens of the castle, what sorts of reading materials she will find in it (religious and historical texts, tales of love, and tales of perserverance), what materials she will find to paint with, and so on, for two and a half pages. Likewise, Backman has the princess dream about the "very lovely prince" just once, without taking her emotional temperature at all (p. 43). In Almqvist's *Gråkappan,* she dreams of him twice, and on both occasions the reader is told in minute detail of her reactions to the vision and of her feelings for the prince (p. 9, p. 14). And whereas Almqvist has the king fall into a stupor in order to explain away the fact that it is Rosimandro who marries the princess, Backman says simply that the king has a wedding ("Då gjorde konungen straks bröllop," p. 44) and when the prince is revealed to the princess, he says that he is really married to her ("att han var värkligen vigd vid hänne," p. 45). Moreover, Backman does away with proper names and makes Jucunda and Rosimandro "prinsässan" and "prinsen," the classic protagonists of the folktale. This is not to suggest that Backman could not have given attention to these issues if he had wanted to, or, in the fashion of those who mistakenly believe that the oral raconteur is by nature cruder and less capable of such elaboration, that it was beyond his artistic means: oral literature has shown itself to be capable of great complexity and subtley and from what we have of Backman's repertoire it is clear that he was a narrator of considerable skill.[22] Backman does not ape the written text, he improves on it; from this point of view, the greatest weakness of Almqvist's *Gråkappan* is its purple prose and what Backman lends it, not as a passive but as an active member of the tradition, is concentration.

Bondeson also collected "Hvitebjörn i skogen går" from Backman, one of the traditional Swedish multiforms of AT 425, and thus provides us with an opportunity to understand how

---

22. Examples of how complex prose narration can be are provided by Dégh (*Folktales and Society,* pp. 105–106), who discusses a telling of "I don't know" which lasted from sundown to sunrise, and by Éamon a Búrc's *Eochair, Mac Rí in Éirinn: Eochair, a King's Son in Ireland,* ed. Kevin O'Nolan (Dublin: Comhairle Bhéaloideas Éireann, 1982), an Irish prose epic recorded over the course of three evenings.

the two tales functioned in the repertoire of a single *historie-gubbe*. "Hvitebjörn i skogen går" belongs to the AT 425A group, and opens with AT 621 "The Louse-Skin" (that is, with the motifs B873.1, "Giant louse"; F983.2, "Louse fattened"; H511, "Princess offered to correct guesser"; H522.1.1, "Test: Guessing nature of certain skin—louse-skin"). This multiform is a frequently encountered type in the Swedish corpus (compare Swahn's subtype B); and comparison of Backman's version with these other multiforms (such as those in Hyltén-Cavallius and Stephens) indicates that his knowledge of *Gråkappan* had little influence on his rendition of "Hvitebjörn i skogen går" with respect to style, phraseology, or content.[23]

Another multiform of *Gråkappan* was recorded in 1919 by Anton Olofsson, a schoolteacher in Halmstad.[24] It was taken from the narrated version of Ester Gullander, born in 1890 in Blekinge, where her father, Adrian Lundén, had been a shoemaker. She had learned many of her tales from her father, who had become an itinerant shoemaker at fifteen (in 1882), when he apprenticed himself to "Elias i Piggesmåla," from whom he learned many of his tales. Olofsson's notes strongly imply that Gullander learned *Gråkappan* from her father's narrations, but whether or not it was one of the tales he had learned from Elias is uncertain.

Perhaps most striking about Gullander's version is that she tends to emphasize the horror of the princess's situation: when she sees Gråkappan behind the trapdoor, she is frightened ("kände sig hemsk till mods") by the fact that she has just seen him leave, and yet he is at the same time behind the trapdoor. The princess does not immediately meet and marry a king as in Almqvist's original, but instead spends the next three years in Gråkappan's castle, bearing him one child after another, despite the repeated grisly episodes with the babies. These scenes have become even more terrifying because Gråkappan comes to her and without asking what she saw behind the trap-

23. *Svenska folk-sagor och äfventyr efter muntlig öfverlemning*, coll. and ed. Gunnar Hyltén-Cavallius and George Stephens (Stockholm: A. Bohlins förlag, 1844), vol. 1., pp. 325–350, 350–351.
24. Lunds universitet, Folkminnesarkivet, MS no. 2140, pp. 20–24.

door simply takes the babies away and smears her hands and mouth with blood. It is only *after* he has done so that he puts the question to her. In Gullander's version, the princess is given no opportunity to save herself from her fate; she must simply endure it. And, of course, rather than believing that it is the king's children she is bearing, it is clear that they are the children of her persecutor. In the meanwhile, she is becoming known among the servants as a "maneater" *(människoätare)*. Perhaps most telling is that the servants' distress and subsequent desire to burn the princess do not derive from their repugnance at what they believe her to have done to her children, but rather because they fear being eaten by her themselves ("De kunde ju själva frukta för att bli uppätna av princessan"). Gullander's version intensifies the somewhat dark tone of the original, making her telling of the tale much more horrifying than any of the other versions.

In the main, Gullander's version of *Gråkappan* is like Backman's, in that it is a very full account, yet unlike his in that Gullander has made numerous changes to the plot of the printed versions of *Gråkappan*. Indeed, compared to Backman, she alters the tale dramatically. Thus in Gullander's version, there are not three daughters, but one, and the king now attempts to fool Gråkappan by sending the dog to him instead of the princess. The complicated explanation behind the prince's plight as stated in the original *Gråkappan* and retained by Backman has been trimmed in Gullander's version to a simple spell, without the personal motivation of the witch. Nor in Gullander's tale does the princess dream about the prince. Consequently, the question of how an individual can both love and hate the same person plays no role in this version. Most markedly, when the princess opens the trapdoor and sees Gråkappan, she is not banished from the castle, nor does she subsequently meet and marry a king; rather she continues to live in Gråkappan's forest castle. It is the reaction of the servants there after the disappearance of her third baby with Gråkappan which brings about the demand for her to be burned. And when the liberated Gråkappan and the princess celebrate their relationship at the end of the tale, it is Gråkappan's three sisters who come bearing the lost children, specifically said to be two boys and a girl. While the ample descriptions and narrative richness of Gullander's version can make her multiform seem close to Almqvist's original and Backman's tale, in fact it is substantially different with regard to its treatment of the plot.

A third multiform of *Gråkappan,* recorded in the mid-nineteenth century on Gotland, forms part of Per Arvid Säve's collection of Gutnish folklore. The sheer size of Säve's collection (over four thousand folio pages of materials from over seven hundred informants) tends to obscure exact knowledge of how and from whom the tale comes. Quite clearly this *Gråkappan* multiform is connected with Elisabeth Bolin, but whether it comes through her or from her is uncertain.[25] Born in Visby in 1828, she was the daughter of a merchant and could boast lengthy priestly lineages on both sides of her family. She never married and became a teacher at the girl's school (Fruntimmerssamfundets skola) in Visby. Despite her short life (she died in 1866), Bolin was an active participant in Säve's project, being responsible in one way or another for some seventy folktales, as well as several legends, a ballad, and a proverb. In some cases, Bolin recorded materials from her students, but many of the other texts (around thirty), possibly including *Gråkappan,* are assumed to have been her own.[26] The two very

25. On the complex question of Elisabeth Bolin's contributions to the collection, see Ragnar Bjersby, *Traditionsbärare på Gotland vid 1800-talets mitt: en undersökning rörande P.A. Säves sagesmän* (Uppsala: Almquist och Wiksell, 1964), pp. 153–156. It is clear that Bolin often acted as a collector (for instance, "Charlotta Börjesson, g[enom] Elisabeth Bolin"), but the situation is somewhat more complex, as many of the tales, including *Gråkappan,* originally bore the annotation "Johanna Bolin," with "Johanna" crossed out and replaced by "Elisabeth." Elisabeth had a sister named Johanna, but there was also a student at Fruntimmerssamfundets skola named Johanna Bolin. Bjersby believes that the confusion derives from the fact that Säve was not well acquainted with the sisters and for a time got their names confused. He also suggests that Elisabeth Bolin may have been working independently before her materials were made part of Säve's project.

26. *Gotländska sagor upptecknade av P.A. Säve,* ed. Herbert Gustavson (Uppsala: Almqvist och Wiksell, 1955), pp. 78–79. Knowledge of *Gråkappan* may also have affected Elisabeth Bolin's work as a transcriber of Gut-

different scenarios which may account for the recording of the Gutnish tale, one in which Bolin transcribed a narrated version of *Gråkappan* by someone else and another in which she simply wrote out a version she knew, must be borne in mind. Unlike Anders Backman's version of *Gråkappan,* which despite its generally independent character maintains many of the contours of Almqvist's tale and even some of his words, the terse rendering of the Gutnish story bears little stylistic resemblance to Almqvist's *Gråkappan.* The Gutnish *Gråkappan* is short (ca. 450 words) and now no longer has a princess as its heroine, but rather a poor girl who lives in the forest by herself. (Elisabeth Bolin lost her father when she was ten and her mother in 1849, two years before she began as a teacher at Fruntimmerssamfundets skola.) Thus the introductory matter is entirely different from Almqvist's, Backman's, and Gullander's tales, lacking the promise to give away the first thing which greets the king on his return home, and says simply, "Once upon a time there was a poor girl who lived alone in the forest. Then a Gray Cape came and took her with him to where he lived in the forest" (Det var en gång en fattig flicka, som bodde ensam i skogen. Då kom der en Grå Kappa och tog henne till sig der han bodde borta i skogen). Moreover, like Gullander in her account of the princess's time with Gråkappan, Bolin (or her informant) does not wince at allowing the story to conclude with the girl becoming the prince's consort *(gemål),* without any of Almqvist's elaborate explanations about stupors and implications of shape-shifting or even Backman's simple explanation that the prince was really her husband. Nor does she hestiate to have the prince return the three young princes to *their father, the king,* before leaving with the girl ("dem han nu återlemnade åt deras fader, Konungen"). And the Gutnish version is the only one of the col-

---

nish tradition: item [115] 3:23, collected "genom Elis. Bolin," bears the title "Liten Hans (eller Grå Kappan)" (p. 26). The cape in question makes the wearer invisible and is one of three magical objects which assist the protagonist in defeating the Devil. It in no way resembles the gray cape of Almqvist's or Backman's tales, nor does it play a role of greater significance than the other magic objects.

lected materials to have the princess respond to Gråkappan's question ("What did you see under the trapdoor?") with his name, but *without* cursing him or saying that she hates him.

Obviously a story only one-tenth the length of another will treat its materials quite differently, yet the astonishing fact is that the Gutnish *Gråkappan* has by no means suffered from the process. In fact, the events of this rendition, the introductory matter and some details aside, are more or less the same as those of the other tales: the heroine is abducted by a supernatural being; she is allowed the freedom of her abductor's home; his interdiction against opening a particular trapdoor is violated; his question "What did you see under the trapdoor?" goes unanswered; she is found by a king to whom she bears a child; the heroine's failure to answer Gråkappan's question results in his taking away the infant and smearing her mouth with blood; the episode is repeated twice; the king decides to burn her; her answer to Gråkappan's question releases him from the curse; and she goes to live with him in his castle. Where this version of the tale differs, and differs dramatically, from the printed *Gråkappan* and both Backman's and Gullander's multiforms is with respect to style; this version adheres almost maniacally to what Max Lüthi characterizes as the common style of all European folktales, a "love of action, clarity, precision, and compactness."[27] To an extent, this rule governs all the *Gråkappan* multiforms from tradition—they are all much more concentrated than the printed original—but in the case of the Gutnish *Gråkappan,* the tendency is taken to an extreme. Furthermore, the "problem" of Almqvist's original (how a person can both love and hate the same individual), retained by Backman but not by Gullander, is missing in this version, since this *Gråkappan* no longer has the heroine dream about the prince, or even see her captor in his true form, before the curse has been lifted.

In addition to the Dalsland, Blekinge, and Gotland multiforms, a fourth Swedish account also exists. The narrative is

---

27. Max Lüthi, *Once Upon a Time: On the Nature of Fairy Tales,* trans. Lee Chadeayne and Paul Gottwald (Bloomington: Indiana University Press, 1976), p. 72.

by Lotten Landersholm of Eskilstuna, who claims to have
known the tale from her childhood in Södermanland, and
forms part of the collection Walter Liungman assembled in
1925–26.[28] Landersholm has clearly handwritten the text herself and seems to imply that she has not told a full version: in
a postscript, she comments that she could remember more, but
that she does not have time and furthermore finds it tiresome
to write, as she is over sixty years old ("Ja [!] kunde nog min-
nas mer men ja hinner inte ock det är tröttsamt att skrifva. Jag
är öfver 60 år så ja vill slippa litet"). Given the position of the
comment (following directly after *Gråkappan,* which is itself
the last of several tales she has written out) and the ungram-
matical character of the phrase "Nu är det här minnen [!] från
min barndom", it is not entirely clear whether she means she
could remember more about this tale or remember more tales
in general, although the latter seems to be the more probable.
In either event, she has clearly tired of the process; because of
these circumstances, and the resulting unanswerable question
as to whether the changes derive from artistic decisions or
from fatigue, the Landersholm tale must be used cautiously.
Obviously this concern applies more to reductions in the plot
than to amplifications and other alterations which increase the
length of the story. In fact, despite her objections that she has
tired, Landersholm tends to add copious details: when the
older daughters are sent to Gråkappan, they receive golden
bracelets and diamonds; when she describes Gråkappan's castle, it has mechanical dolls that can walk by themselves and a
silver bathtub in the bathroom. There is also, as in Backman's
tale, notable fidelity to Almqvist's printed version: Landersholm gives the king's dog the same name (Gratiana) it bears in
the chapbooks and in Bäckström's précis, and her version of
the witch's curse is remarkably like those of the printed versions. On the other hand, she condenses the main plot considerably: in her story, the princess responds to Gråkappan's
question and breaks his curse after nothing more than the com-

28. Västsvenska folkminnesarkivet, Dialekt-, ortnamns-, och folkminnesarkivet i Göteborg. Liungman, MS no. 177, pp. 5–10.

ment that she was asked constantly what it was she saw under
the trapdoor. There is no mention of the king or the lost children ("hon vänder sig bort, så får hon den frågan ideligen hon
blef utledsen beslöt att svara fick bli hur det ville när sen frågan
kom så sade prinsessan, 'Jo just du din förb, Grå kappa var
det som ja såg dig som ja hatar af lif ock själ' "). Given Landersholm's remarks, it easy to imagine that she might under
other circumstances have related a fuller version, but has tired
of writing out the story and has telescoped this portion of the
tale.

What these four multiforms of the tale make clear is that
Gråkappan does not belong solely to the realm of printed literature. Although the tale may have been initially fashioned as
written art, its legacy is much broader than its publication history, large as it is, implies: the Swedish tales collected from
folk tradition demonstrate that the story took on a life of its
own in the repertoires of various narrators. Moreover,
Almqvist's chapbook may have had further ramifications for
the character of Swedish folktale collections. Thus, for example, one of the traditional AT 425 tales collected by Hyltén-
Cavallius and Stephens from Västergötland, a multiform of
"Prins Hatt under Jorden," opens with a king out hunting who
is separated from his party and then met by a dwarf who blocks
his path, a motif (F402.1.2, "Spirit blocks person's road")
known in Irish and Swiss tales, but not attested in other Nordic
folktales—other than at the beginning of *Gråkappan,* of
course, and in the various oral multiforms of it.[29] But facts of
this sort lend themselves to two interpretations: it is perhaps
as likely that Almqvist was using a traditional motif as it is that
the device became traditional in Swedish oral literature
through him, although the concatenation is suspicious. However this specific example may have developed, Lyssander is
no doubt correct when he suggests that the "literary" style of
Swedish folklore collections, which Jørgen Moe so decried,

---

29. Hyltén-Cavallius and Stephens, *Svenska folk-sagor,* p. 379. But compare some Swedish multiforms of "King Lindorm" (AT 433B).

resulted from a widespread familiarity with inexpensive literature, such as chapbooks.[30]

Trekking along what Carl Lindahl calls "the borders of oral and written art" allows us to draw certain conclusions about the relationship between Almqvist's popular chapbook *Gråkappan* and the various traditional accounts for which it formed the basis. It is perhaps not so surprising that the results conform to what Linda Dégh found in the case of the Hungarian folktale, namely, that although the raw materials may derive from a printed text, the form comes from oral tradition.[31] In a very similar vein, Albert B. Lord concluded with regard to the Serbo-Croatian oral epic that the influence of a fixed text on an oral raconteur can vary tremendously, from nearly complete reliance on the written text to virtual independence of it.[32] As we have seen, *Gråkappan* in Swedish tradition also spans a very great range, from Backman's carefully crafted version, which retains some very specific verbal echoes of the printed text, to Gullander's rich but quite altered text, to the much more concentrated Gutnish multiform, which has maintained the essential plot of the printed version but otherwise has very little in common with it. Incomplete though it probably is, even Landersholm's version provides ample evidence of diversity and authorial control.

The relationship between folklore and literature in Sweden has, in general, only rarely been examined. And when scholarship has taken up the question at all, it has typically been left to literary historians to ferret out instances of traditional materials being used by famous authors, such as Erik Johan Stagnelius, Selma Lagerlöf, Jan Fridegård, or, as in Ragnar

---

30. Lyssander, "Tvifvel om en svensk folksagas äkthet," p. 447. Moe complains about what he calls an "untraditional narrative style" (ufolkelig fortællemåde) in the published Swedish folktales which results in a stiff and pompous tone.

31. Dégh, *Folktales and Society*, p. 154.

32. Albert B. Lord, "The Influence of a Fixed Text," in *To Honor Roman Jakobson: Essays on the Occasion of His Seventieth Birthday* (The Hague and Paris: Mouton, 1967), vol. 2, pp. 1199–1206.

Ekholm's study, C. J. L. Almqvist.[33] Such an enterprise makes sense for literary history, where the focus of interest is often on individual writers and their materials ("source studies"). On the other hand, such studies say little about the synergism between oral and written literature that existed in the nineteenth century, where it may be surmised that the relationship typically did *not* involve the publications of famous authors. Rather, the dynamic interchange between the two narrative forms much more frequently involved anonymous, inexpensive, widely circulated, and much prized chapbooks. But if examinations of folklore's role in the creation of written literature are uncommon, even rarer are attempts by folklorists to vent the question of how the Swedish oral prose tradition may be informed by the written record.[34] That scholars are disinclined to treat materials from oral tradition which have a demonstrably untraditional basis no doubt proceeds from a dread that the "pure" folklore tradition sometimes imagined as flourishing among the "illiterate" peasantry has been contaminated, poisoned even, by the written word.[35]

Comparison of Almqvist's *Gråkappan* and its multiforms from tradition demonstrates that such is not the case: each of the traditional narrators considered here has taken, either directly or at some remove, the same tale from the printed record and fashioned it according to his or her tastes. In some cases the results display greater adherence to the printed form of the tale than in others, yet in no instance is there any indication that the narrative tradition has stagnated or declined because of the written origins of the materials. In fact, the testimony of the published *Gråkappan* transformed into traditional tales directly contradicts the negative assessment of written art's in-

33. See Bengt af Klintberg, "Kvinnan som inte vill ha barn: litterära utformningar av en nordisk folksaga," in Ebbe Schön, ed., *Folklore och litteratur i Norden* (Stockholm: Carlssons, 1987), pp. 102–33, for examples of this sort of investigation, as well as note 7 above.

34. By narrowing the field to prose traditions, I specifically want to exclude Swedish ballad scholarship from this generalization. Ballad scholars have, in general, been at the forefront of this kind of research.

35. See Krohn's remarks in note 16 above concerning the decline which results when written works are taken up in oral tradition.

fluence on oral art, even if we limit our considerations to the two undisputedly oral forms of the tale. Despite their origins in a printed medium, the traditional multiforms of *Gråkappan* give ample testimony to the durability and vitality of the Swedish oral tradition, to the synthesizing capacity of that tradition, and to the sustained artistry of its raconteurs, as well as to the continued diversity of their artistic designs.

DWIGHT REYNOLDS

The Interplay of Genres in Oral Epic Performance: Differentially Marked Discourse in a Northern Egyptian Tradition

The epic is, so to speak, a supergenre that encompasses and harmoniously fuses together practically all genres known in a particular culture.

Daniel Biebuyck

It has been noted by a number of scholars that in cultures possessed of an epic tradition, the epic poem functions as a metagenre including, referring to, and alluding to other genres of poetry, song, and ritual from within the culture.[1] The encompassing nature of certain epic poems—I am not fully certain that it is a general characteristic of epics throughout the world—is realized through rather different means, however, in different cultures, and often to different ends.[2]

In some epic traditions, when specific genres (prayers, lullabies, lamentations, wedding songs, rituals, and so on) occur within the epic, the performer renders a facsimile performance, abandoning temporarily the strictures of the epic poetic mode. This seems particularly true of some African and

1. See for example Christiane Seydou, "The African Epic: A Means for Defining the Genre," *Folklore Forum* 16 (1983): 47–68, in particular pp. 50ff. for the epic as "meta-society."

2. See Daniel Biebuyck, "The Epic as a Genre in Congo Oral Literature," in Richard Dorson, ed., *African Folklore* (Bloomington and London: Indiana University Press, 1972). The epigraph to this essay is from p. 266.

292

Asian traditions which in some cases reach full dramatization, so that the poem becomes a string of performances of various genres linked by, or embedded in, an epic narrative mode. In European oral and literary epic traditions, however, a different aesthetic commonly reigns, and references to different genres of poetry and song within the epic do not break out of the form of the epic itself; formalistic continuity is maintained and exterior genres are subjugated to epic form.[3] In this paper I propose to examine examples from Arabic oral epic tradition, a tradition which displays several different techniques of allusion and reference, and one in which, as a living tradition, we may observe performative processes unavailable to us from written traditions.

Poets in the Nile Delta region of Egypt who sing the *Sîrat Banî Hilâl* oral epic often mark passages in performance in such a way as to key them to other genres of performance without, however, completely breaking the form of the epic poem.[4] For lack of a more widely accepted term, I shall refer to this as "differentially marked discourse," that is, passages within the epic itself which are (1) marked in performance so as to direct the attention of the listener to the differential re-

3. Excellent explorations of this aspect of Homeric texts can be found in Richard Martin, "Hesiod, Odysseus, and the Instruction of Princes," *Transactions of the American Philological Association* 114 (1984): 29–48, and Gregory Nagy, *The Best of the Achaeans: Concepts of the Hero in Archaic Greek Poetry* (Baltimore: Johns Hopkins University Press, 1979).

4. *Sîra,* which literally means a journey or a traveling, is the genre of Arab oral literature closest to the western concept of folk or oral epic. The Banî Hilâl were a Bedouin tribe who from the tenth to twelfth centuries C.E. migrated from the Arabian peninsula across North Africa where they eventually conquered and ruled Tunisia. They were destroyed in the mid-twelfth century by a Moroccan dynasty, and had ceased to exist as a major tribe by the end of that century. Their name literally means "children of Hilâl" (Hilâl is a personal name which means "crescent moon"). For a general introduction to this tradition see Susan Slyomovics, *The Merchant of Art: An Egyptian Hilali Oral Epic Poet in Performance* (Berkeley and Los Angeles: University of California Press, 1987); a generally less reliable treatment of the material is also found in Bridget Connelly, *Arabic Folk Epic and Identity* (Berkeley and Los Angeles: University of California Press, 1986). See also my "*Sîrat Banî Hilâl:* Introduction and Notes to an Arab Oral Epic Tradition," *Oral Tradition* 4:1–2 (Arabic Oral Traditions) (1989): 80–100.

lationship between the passage in question and the surrounding
material, and (2) marked in such a way as to direct the listener's attention to the relationship between the passage and a
body of material external to the epic.

In what follows, I shall explore two sample types of differentially marked discourse taken from texts of *Sîrat Banî Hilâl*
oral epic performances recorded in the village of al-Bakâtûsh
in 1986–87.[5] Since performative aspects of this folk epic vary
a great deal from region to region, I shall restrict my observations to the poets of al-Bakâtûsh and the immediate surrounding area of the Nile Delta in Northern Egypt.[6] My first type
focuses on the relationship between an independent genre of
poetry, the *mawwâl*, and passages within the epic which are
similar to it in tone and style. The second type is a passage
which we shall examine in renditions by three epic poets to see
how they mark it as a separate genre of song, and perhaps as
"feminine" discourse.

Perhaps the most ubiquitous and enduring theme in Egyptian
folk poetry is that of *shakwa*, literally "complaint," but specifically complaint about the vicissitudes and injustices of fate
and destiny. These are not complaints dealing with or addressed to the real, quotidian world, for this would be anti-
thetical to the cultural ideal of stoic, patient endurance.
Rather, *shakwa* is wrenching, passionate complaint addressed
to Time *(al-zaman)*, the Days *(al-ayyâm)*, the Nights *(al-*

5. My year of research as an apprentice poet in a community of heredi-
tary epic singers in 1986–87 was funded by a Fulbright-Hays doctoral dissertation grant. Additional periods of fieldwork in al-Bakâtûsh were under-
taken in 1983 and 1988.

6. Though the *sîra* of the Banî Hilâl tribe is known and performed
throughout much of the Arab Middle East, poetic and musical dimensions
of the performances vary widely. In many areas such as Tunisia, Chad, and
the Sudan, the *sîra* is no longer sung in verse, but rather narrated in prose
tale cycles. Even in Egypt there are several regional differences: in Upper
Egypt, quatrains are used in singing the epic, to the exclusion of the *qasîda*-
form (mono-endrhyme odes) which dominates the rest of the tradition. In
an unpublished paper, 'Abd al-Ḥamîd Ḥawwâs and Muḥammad 'Umrân of
the Folklore Institute and Centre for the Folk Arts in Cairo have, in addition, distinguished over a dozen regional musical traditions of *sîra* performance.

layâlî), the Era *(al-awân),* Fate *(al-dahr),* Destiny *(qadar),* the World *(al-dunyâ),* and Separation *(al-bên;* CA *al-bayn).*[7] Though it is accepted that all things take place by the will of God, complaint is not addressed directly to the Almighty—that is the domain of prayers, pleas, and invocations. In addition, though the poet, or any person who sings or recites poems or songs of *shakwa,* may have specific troubles in mind, in poetic form these must be expressed in the abstracted imagistic world of folk symbols: the camel *(jamal)* is a stalwart man, the crow *(ghurâb)* is an omen of death and separation, the eye *(al-'ên;* CA *'ayn)* is the soul, the doctor *(ṭabîb)* is the source of spiritual cures or the beloved who alone can cure the yearning lover, the camel's burdens *(aḥmâl,* sing. *ḥiml)* and wounds *(ajrâḥ,* sing. *jarḥ)* are human troubles and woes, the lion *(asad,* also *sab')* is a figure of authority, the mosquitoes *(nâmûs)* are pretty interlopers. The foregrounded virtues in both the real and poetic world are patience and endurance *(ṣabr),* the ability to be someone who conceals *(mughaṭṭî)* one's worries and troubles, one who does not babble *(halwas),* grumble *(fatfaṭ,* also *faḍfaḍ),* who empties his mind of whisperings *(wiswâs)* and thought or brooding *(tafâkîr),* and who, above all, submits to the will of God *(ḥukm allâh).*

Shakwa represents a poetic discourse in which one may express feelings and emotions which it would be dishonorable to express in action or in everyday speech. It is a poetry which constructs a world of unacted-upon impulses, unspoken voices, unrealized desires. The poetic form, by social convention, allows the speaker to disavow actual responsibility for the contents expressed; the process of symbolization within the tradition allows statements to be couched in a language one level removed from the real world and yet completely comprehensible.[8]

---

7. The transcription of colloquial Arabic and the oftentimes cognate classical Arabic terms poses a number of difficulties. In this article all references are to Egyptian colloquial Arabic unless otherwise marked as "CA," Classical Arabic. More detailed notes about transcription are found in the Appendix.

8. See Lila Abu-Lughod, *Veiled Sentiments: Honor and Poetry in a Bedouin Society* (Cairo: American University in Cairo Press, 1987) for a fas-

In the Delta region of Egypt, the most common poetic form used as a vehicle for the expression of *shakwa* is the *mawwâl;* the two are in fact almost inextricably tied together. Although *mawwâls* are composed and sung about a number of themes, a significant percentage of the *mawwâl* repertory deals exclusively with *shakwa*.[9] When moments of *shakwa* arise within the epic, poets at times turn to the "ready-made" *mawwâl* as a means of expressing their theme; at other times they use the images, tone, and style of the *mawwâl* while remaining firmly within the epic verse form.

The *mawwâl* and the epic *(sîra)* are distinct from one another in both formal and performative terms. The epic is narrated in mono-endrhyme verse with medial caesura; the *mawwâl* is constructed most often on a pattern of five, seven, or nine verses involving at least two different rhymes, and often three or more, for example *aaabbba*.

In musical terms the two genres are equally distinct; the *mawwâl* possesses a sound and ethos quite separate from that of epic verse. Epic verse is in general rhythmic, the same melody often being used for dozens of lines before a change occurs, and, while the poet may throw in a large number of devices such as holding certain notes, accenting the line differently, adding musical embellishments, and so on, these rarely become the focus of the audience's attention. The overall effect is one of regularity. The *mawwâl* on the other hand is a genre used to demonstrate vocal virtuosity. It has no reg-

---

cinating description of the interaction between poetic discourse and the social codes of honor in an Egyptian Bedouin setting.

9. For more on the Egyptian *mawwâl,* see Pierre Cachia, "The Egyptian Mawwâl," *Journal of Arabic Literature* 8 (1977): 77–103; Serafin Fanjul, *El Mawwâl Egipcio: expressión literaria popular* (Madrid: Instituto hispano-arabe de cultura, 1976), "Le mawwal blanc," *Mélanges de l'Insitut Dominicain d'études orièntales du Caire* 13 (1977): 337–348, and "The Erotic Mawwâl in Egypt," *Journal of Arabic Literature* 8 (1977): 104–122; Sami A. Hanna, "The Mawwâl in Egyptian Folklore," *Journal of American Folklore* 80 (1967): 182–190; Aḥmad ʿAlî Mursî, *al-ughniyya al-shaʿbiyya: madkhal ilâ dirâsatihâ* [The folksong: an introduction to its study] (Cairo: Dâr al-Maʿârif, 1983); Nada Tomiche, "Le mawwâl égyptien," *Mélanges Marcel Cohen* (The Hague: Mouton, 1970): 429–438.

ular rhythm and is often sung with a great deal of melisma, heavy rubato, and in an emotionally heightened style; it is essentially freesong.

Example 1: *(aaaabca)*

qâl: il-'ajab 'alâ jamal majrûḥ wi-mighaṭṭî
He said: "What a wonder is the camel who is wounded but *conceals it!"*

yifût 'alâ 'l-i'âd [= a'âdî] miḥammil ghulb wi-mighaṭṭî
He passes by enemies bearing misfortune and is *covered by it*

yiqûl: anâ fî zamânî kunt ashîl aḥmâl wi-axâṭî
He says: "I in my time used to bear burdens and *travel on."*

yâ 'ênî xudî lik rafîq zên min xiyâr il-nâs wi-law xadtî
O my eye, take for yourself a fine companion from the best of people, if you must *take one*

yibqâ da xêra wi-law
This will be good and if

ḥakam il-zaman wi-mâl
Fate judges and "leans,"

yuq'ud yidamdim 'alâ 'l-'ibâd wi-yighaṭṭî
He will sit with you and say only "hmmmm" and *hurrumph"* to others (concealing your troubles).[10]

This example encapsulates much of the worldview and style of the *mawwâl* complaint. The voices are detached, nameless; we must fill in the unspecified subject of the third-person verb which introduces the first and third lines. The ideas are expressed in depersonalized symbols, terms with no specific antecedents. The virtue extolled is that of concealing pain and worries in the presence of enemies and rivals. If possible, troubles and concerns should not be expressed to anyone; failing that, the *mawwâl* exhorts us to choose a companion to confide in only with great care, someone who will conceal our secrets from others. The result of a bad choice is in fact another major

---

10. *Ghaṭṭ/yighuṭṭ* is literally to snort or snore, which I have tried to capture with "hurrumph"; *ghaṭṭâ/yighaṭṭî* is to conceal, as in the first line. On paranomasia in the *mawwâl,* see below.

theme of *mawwâls*—deception and betrayal by friends and trusted companions.

The *mawwâl* has an additional feature which distinguishes it from other forms of Arabic folk poetry: an extremely artful and complex technique of paronomasia and double-entendre. Very briefly, the final words of all the lines which share one rhyme are pronounced almost exactly the same in performance, leaving the listener to choose between the various similar-sounding possibilities, and to select those meanings being foregrounded by the poet. Providing a written transcription of a *mawwâl* often conceals much of the artistry of the genre. In Example 1, for instance, the final words in lines 1, 2, 3, 4, and 7 (italicized in the translation) are very close puns, not only because the words themselves are similar (standard puns) but because the poet often deliberately obscures differences in pronunciation.

In Example 2, the final word of lines 1, 2, 3, and 9 (pronounced *khaṭâbî* and *ḥaṭâbî* in performance), can be broken down into several possibilities:

Sung pronunciation	Common spoken pronunciation(s)	Translation(s)
khaṭâbî	khaṭâ biyya [CA khaṭi'a]	he/it wronged me
	khaṭâ biyya	he/it walked with me (carried me) he/it walked on me (trod on me)
	khaṭa biyya [CA khaṭâ']	a fault in me
ḥaṭâbî	ḥaṭabî	my kindling
	ḥaṭṭ biyya	he/it pushed down on me (humbled, abased me)
	ḥâṭṭa biyya	he/it is pushing down on me (humbling, abasing)

In performance the poet can sing *kh* and *ḥ* so that they are almost indistinguishable, which means that in theory all of the

listed translations are possible interpretations for each of the
lines. In the translation that follows, when more than one possibility functions with ease in a line, I have bracketed and retained all of them.

Example 2 *(aaabcccda)*

wi-yikûn jamalî 'ind shêl il-himl khatâbî
And my camel at the carrying of the burden   { *wronged me*
                                              { *carried me*

mâ kân ghurâb il-naya shâlnî wa-khatâbî
In spite of the crow of separation, [Fate] bore me and
                                              { *carried me across*
                                              { *trod on me*

yâ nâr qalbî 'alêhum qidînî hatâbî
O Fire of my heart, against them light *my kindling*

anâ as'alak yâ rabb, anâ as'alak yâ rabb
I ask you O Lord, I ask you O Lord,

yâ mugrî 'l-laban fî 'l-bizz
O you who cause milk to flow in the breast!

tita'ta' il-bakr min taht il-himûl wi-yifizz
You stir the young camel beneath his loads and he springs up!

wi-tisaltan il-'izz
And you have authority over all prosperity!

wi-layâlî il-'izz bitdûmlî
Let the nights of prosperity continue for me;

lakin il-layâlî ma'a 'l-ayyâm hatâbî
But the nights, along with the days,   { *push down on me*
                                        { *(humble me)*

Paraphrase (based on the singer's interpretation):

As a strong man, when the time comes, I should shoulder life's
burdens,
Yet Fate seized me, despite my intentions, and bore me away from
what I had hoped my life would be,
O my heart, strengthen yourself against the difficulties of life (or:
against your enemies),

I ask you, O Lord, I ask you, O Lord,
You who cause milk to flow in the breast,
You who give the young hope despite their troubles,
You have the power to grant me prosperity,
Let me continue to prosper—
Yet all the forces of the world try to overcome me!

The *mawwâl* is an independent genre of poetry which possesses its own contexts for performance separate from the
epic, but in the Nile Delta region of Egypt it is a genre intimately associated with the singing of epic at several levels.
First, it is one of several genres of poetry which are often included in a night's performance *(sahra)*. Other such auxiliary
genres include *madîḥ* (praise songs to the Prophet Muhammad), *ḥitat baladî* (literally, "bits of country stuff"—a type of
comedy routine in which the poet tries to mention all of the
listeners present in a joking manner through allusions to their
names, families, relatives, or land), and *salâmât wa-taḥayyât*
(sung greetings and "toasts" to audience members).

Second, a *mawwâl* occasionally appears within the epic narrative itself. Of the genres listed above only the *mawwâl* actually occurs in full form *within* the epic; the others are all
associated with epic performances because they occur in con-
junction with the epic.

By far the most common occurrence of the *mawwâl* in *Sîrat
Banî Hilâl* performances by the al-Bakâtûsh poets, however,
is in its third context, at the moment of transition from spoken
scene-setting into sung epic verse, that is, when it acts as a
lyric, nonnarrative pause occupying the halfway point between
the outside world and the world of the epic.

When a poet is beginning to sing, either at the commence-
ment of a performance or after a break of any sort, he follows
a rigid series of steps in order to move into epic verse. First,
he sets the scene in spoken rhymed prose *(saj')*; this is referred
to by the poets as *kalâm al-râwî* (literally, the words of the
reciter) or the *qâ'ida* (base or foundation). This often involves
a brief recapitulation of the plot, a reminder of who is about to
speak, and a phrase enjoining the listeners to wish God's blessings on the Prophet Muhammad. Second, he plays a short passage of music and begins to sing in rhymed verse, moving, in

the poets' terminology, to *kalâm al-shâ'ir* (the words of the poet). His first lines must be in praise of the Prophet Muhammad (this is in addition to any full *madîḥ* he may sing at the very beginning of an evening gathering); according to the situation he may stretch this theme out for several lines. Next, in a highly formulaic phrase, the poet calls upon the audience members to listen to the words of So-and-so, naming the character whose utterance we are about to hear. And then, in the voice of the character, we hear several lines of *shakwa*. This *shakwa* may be either in the form of a *mawwâl* or in epic verse. At the conclusion of the *shakwa,* the poet proceeds with the tale in epic verse and we have moved fully and completely into the epic world.[11] The movement into sung epic verse therefore comprises:

1. Beginning of performance or end of break in ongoing performance
2. Spoken rhymed prose scene-setting *(saj'; kalâm al-râwî)*
3. Music
4. Beginning of singing *(kalâm al-shâ'ir):* brief praise of the Prophet Muhammad
5. Formulaic announcement of speaker
6. *Mawwâl* or *shakwa*
7. Epic verse

11. A suggestive parallel can be found in the heroic songs of the Mande hunters, which Charles Bird breaks down into three separate modes: proverb-praise, narrative, and song. The proverb-praise mode acts as an introduction, establishes the singer's veracity and authenticity, and is often found at major divisions in the story. See Charles Bird, "Heroic Songs of the Mande Hunters," in Richard Dorson, ed., *African Folklore* (Bloomington and London: Indiana University Press, 1972), pp. 275–293. An even closer parallel is found in the opening passage of "The Wedding of Smailagić Meho" as sung by Avdo Međedović. The epic poet, a Muslim, first invokes God's assistance, then sings a series of aphoristic sentiments ("Rain will fall and the year will bear its fruits, and the debtor will free himself of his debt, but never of a bad friend, nor yet at home of a bad wife . . . Roof over your house and it will not leak. Strike your wife and she will not scold . . ."), then addresses his listeners, sets the scene, and finally begins the narrative itself. *Serbo-Croatian Heroic Songs Collected by Milman Parry,* vol. 3: *The Wedding of Smailagić Meho,* trans. Albert B. Lord (Cambridge: Harvard University Press, 1974). My thanks to Albert Lord for directing me to this parallel.

The poets of al-Bakâtûsh are quite conscious of some of the functions of these steps. They are quick to point out that beginning with praise to the Prophet Muhammad is not only proper, but also serves to focus the audience's attention and forces them to settle down in preparation for extended audition of the epic. In Islamic countries it is traditional to respond to any mention of the Prophet by name or epithet with either the phrase "May God bless him and preserve him" (sallâ allâhu 'alayhi wa-sallam) or "Upon Him be blessings and peace" ('alayhi al-salâtu wa-'l-salâm). During any extended madîh or praise to the Prophet, repetition of these phrases occurs quite frequently, and eventually subverts any ongoing conversations.

The moment of breaking through from rhymed prose into epic verse is always one of highly charged emotions. Each time the poet moves back into the epic, he must do so through the vehicle of a character within the epic who is moved to speak. Once in the epic verse mode, different voices may occur, including extensive passages in a narrator's voice, but the moment of movement into epic verse must occur with the speaking of a character and this must take place for clear emotional motivations. Thus typical transitions are at moments of grief, fear, joy, or anxiety.

To clarify this process, let us examine two examples of the same text, which concern the first breakthrough into epic verse in the opening episode of the epic "The Birth of Abû Zayd," as sung by two different poets. The emotional motivation is expressly laid out by both poets: King Rizq of the Hilâlî tribe has no male heir and is moved to lament this state. The first poet, Shaykh Biyalî Abû Fahmî, renders the obligatory *shakwa* in a *mawwâl;* the second poet, Shaykh Ṭâhâ Abû Zayd, renders his in epic verse. The translations have been purposefully kept close to the Arabic, with the loss of some fluency in the English, so that comparisons may be made between the phraseology of the two texts.

Example 3 (Shaykh Biyalî Abû Fahmî, 2/11/87)

[Music]
[Praise song of twenty verses to the Prophet Muhammad, recounting an episode from the Prophet's life]

[Music stops]
[Spoken:]
We have praised the Prophet, no blame is upon us, O lords, O generous ones. The Râwî ["reciter"] says of the Arabs who were called the Hilâl Arabs: their Sultan in that time and that era was named Ḥasan, the child of Sarḥân. The judge of the Arabs was Badîr son of Fâyid . . . [poet corrects himself][12] The judge of the Arabs, his name was Shaykh Fâyid. The guardian of the daughters of the Arabs, his name was Zayyân. The guardian of the Zaghâba [clan], his name was Ghânim. I say to you that Diyâb had not yet appeared, nor had Abû Zayd appeared, nor had Zaydân appeared—those young ones had not yet appeared. They will appear during this story, O lords, O listeners. And the great [warrior] of the Hilâlî Arabs was Rizq the Valiant, son of Nâyil. And the number of the [Hilâlî] Arabs was four times ninety thousand. And Rizq the Valiant, son of Nâyil had married of women eight. He sired by them eleven maidens. But of male offspring he had sired none. Rizq began to lament his state and the lack of siring boys, in these verses. I and you, we wish God's blessings on the Prophet, Lord of Miracles:
[Music begins]
[Sung *mawwâl:*]

And my camel at the carrying of the burden	{ *wronged me* { *carried me*

In spite of the crow of separation,

[Fate] bore me and	{ *carried me across* { *trod on me*

O Fire of my heart, against them light *my kindling*
I ask you O Lord, I ask you O Lord,
O you who cause milk to flow in the breast!
You stir the young camel beneath his loads and he springs up!
And you have authority over all prosperity!
Let the nights of prosperity continue for me;

But the nights, along with the days,	{ *push down on me* { *(humble me)*

12. The poet has begun on the wrong foot, so to speak, in that he started to list the epic heroes who occupy these respective posts throughout most of the epic. At the opening of this episode, however, it is still the fathers of the main heroes who are sultan, judge, and so on. The sultan should be Sarḥân, for Ḥasan has not yet been born. It is in order to rectify this false start that the poet interrupts his list of characters and inserts the sentence beginning, "I say to you that Diyâb had not yet appeared . . ."

[Sung Epic Verse:]
The nights are greeted with our wishes for God's blessings on the
Prophet!
　　Our Prophet of Guidance, His light from the Tomb shines forth.

Now listen to what sang Rizq the Valiant, son of Nâyil,
　　Come now Salâma [= Rizq], time only brings struggles!

"I have married of women, O my Eye, eight:
　　I sired with them eleven maidens,
　　No profit comes from siring only daughters."

Example 4 (Shaykh Ṭâhâ Abû Zayd, 6/1/87)

[Music]
[Music stops]
[Spoken:]
After praise for the Prophet of the clan of 'Adnân, and we do not
gather but that we wish God's blessings upon Him, for the Prophet
was the most saintly of the saintly, and the Seal of God's Messengers,
on the Day of Resurrection he shall smile on the faces of those who
wished God's blessings upon Him. The author of these words tells of
Arabs known as the Banî Hilâl Arabs; and their Sultan at that time
and that era was King Sarḥân, and their Warrior was Rizq the Valiant,
Son of Nâyil, for every age has its nation and its men. The guardian
of the women was a stalwart youth, his name was Prince Zayyân. And
the protector of the Zaghâba clan was the courageous Ghânim, warrior of warriors. Rizq had married of women eight maidens, but had
not sired a male heir. He sat in his pavilion and some lads passed by
him (that is, the lads of the Arabs, the lads, that is to say the young
boys, if you'll excuse me).[13] His soul grew greatly troubled over the
lack of an heir, so Rizq sat and sang, of the lack of a male heir, words
which you shall hear, and he who loves the beauty of the Prophet
wishes God's blessings upon Him:
[Music begins]
[Sung epic verse:]
I am the servants of all who adore the beauty of Muhammad,
　　Ṭâhâ, for whom every pilgrim yearns.

Listen to what said Rizq the Valiant, Son of Nâyil,
　　a tear from the orb of his eye did flow.

---

13. Shaykh Ṭâhâ here uses an archaic word for young men, *ghilmân,*
which he then glosses with the more common word for young boys or children *'ayyâl.*

Ah! Ah! the World and Fate and Destiny!
All I have seen with my eyes shall disappear.

I do not praise among the days one which pleases me
but that its successor comes along stingy and mean.

O Fate make peace with me, 'tis enough what you've done to me,
I cast my weapons at thee, wrongfully it is clear.

My wealth is great, O men, but without an heir;
wealth without an heir after a lifetime disappears.

I look out and find Sarḥân when he rides,
his sons ride [with him], princes and prosperous.

I look out and find Zayyân when he rides,
his sons ride [with him] and fill the open spaces.

I look out, ah! and find Ghânim when he rides,
and his sons ride [with him] and are princes, prosperous.

I am the last of my line and my spirit is broken,
I have spent my life and not seen a son, prosperous.

I have taken of women eight maidens,
and eleven daughters followed, princesses true.

This bearing of womenfolk, ah! has broken my spirit,
I weep and my eyes' tear on my cheek does flow.

What is of interest to us here is the similarity in style and
material between Shaykh Ṭâhâ's *shakwa* (particularly lines
2–6) rendered in epic verse and Shaykh Biyalî's *mawwâl*. The
two passages function in the same manner as both plot elements and structural elements; that is, they express Rizq's
grief at not having a son and they serve to move us through the
pivotal moment between the prose world and the world of epic
poetry. Given the great disparity between the two forms, it
would be nearly impossible for the two texts to share any formal characteristics such as rhyme or verse structure. The epic
verse *shakwa,* however, shares images and terms from the
mawwâl repertory: fate, destiny, the world, the days. It also
maintains the depersonalized discourse of the *mawwâl* and introduces the motivating circumstances only in stanza 6. This
is noteworthy, for there are many moments when characters in
the epic moved by grief, joy, or other emotions sing passages

filled with the specifics of their situation. The epic verse
shakwa in Example 4, however, alludes to the aphoristic tone
and the stylized emotional content of a *mawwâl*.

This is common practice among the al-Bakâtûsh poets. At
the structural juncture between scene-setting and epic narrative, all of the poets utilize either a *mawwâl* or an epic verse
passage reminiscent of the *mawwâl* such as the example
above. While *mawwâl*s occur at times within the body of the
epic, epic verse passages which allude to the *mawwâl* form,
such as those we have examined here, occur only in the transitional passages leading into sung epic verse.

The rigorous mechanism by which the poets introduce us
into the epic itself clearly functions in pragmatic terms to draw
and focus the attention of the audience members; at each stage
full entrance into the epic mode is deferred slightly. It is particularly noteworthy that the formal poetic features of the performance complex are introduced, or reintroduced, one at a
time: first rhyme (in the rhymed prose scene-setting), then music (without voice), then rhymed verse sung to music without
narrative thread, and finally the totality of song, verse, music,
and narrative in the full epic mode—an ascending process from
mundane to heightened expression, from quotidian existence
to the larger-than-life existence of epic heroes. A series of
boundaries is successively marked and crossed by the changing texture of presentation, as well as by the changed content
at each stage. Recapitulation prepares us for concentration,
mention of the Prophet frames what follows as a serious endeavor, and exposition of the hero's *shakwa* induces us to em-
pathy, to the essential recognition of the epic hero as a human
struggling with the higher forces of fate and destiny, without
which his exploits would be meaningless.

The examples above illustrate a process of allusion to an external genre through the use of evocative imagery and style
reminiscent of that genre. Our second set of examples involves
a process of differential marking by performative means such
as changes in melody, tone of voice, tempo, and so on. The
passage which I will use to illustrate it is one sung by the hero

Abū Zayd's mother upon his first victorious return from the battlefield.

In the examples of *shakwa* we were introduced to King Rizq, who yearned for a male heir. Later, while hunting in the desert, Rizq and a companion meet a dervish, a mystic, who instructs Rizq to marry Khadra the Noble, daughter of the Sharīf of Mecca, who will bear him a son.[14] Rizq obeys, but for seven years there is no child. Khadra and her companions one day go down to a pool of water in the desert where they see birds drinking. At the sight of a beautiful white bird, one woman wishes for a son equally as handsome. A large black bird lands and frightens the other birds away, and Khadra wishes for a son as powerful as this bird, even if he be just as black. She bears a son who is indeed black, for which Khadra is accused of adultery by the elders of the tribe. Rizq wishes to kill the child but is prevented; Khadra and her child are banished, with the assumption that she will return to her father. She instead seeks refuge with an enemy tribe, the Zahlân, and raises her son among them. Her son grows up thinking he is the son of the king of the Zahlân tribe.

A larger and more powerful tribe arrives, the 'Uqayla, and demands tribute from the Zahlân; according to the law of the desert, Khadra should pay no tribute since she is a refuge-seeker. The head of the 'Uqayla tribe wrongfully seizes her livestock despite her protests. Abū Zayd, now an adolescent, engages the kings of the 'Uqayla tribe in combat. After the first battle, having killed one of the 'Uqayla kings, he returns with the livestock to the encampment of the Zahlân. It is at this moment that we first hear Khadra's song of joy and vengeance, which she sings as her son comes into sight, clearly victorious, with the livestock.

Abū Zayd goes on to fight a series of battles against the other

---

14. The Sharīf of Mecca is the ruler of the Holy Sanctuary of Mecca. The term literally means "noble" and is one of Khadra's epithets throughout the epic; she is referred to perhaps even more often as al-Sharīfa ("the Noble One") than as Khadra within the epic. The term is also an honorific applied to anyone who is a descendant of the Prophet Muhammad.

kings of the 'Uqayla tribe, killing seven of them. Depending
upon the amount of summarizing or expansive detail the poet
feels the audience is in the mood for, Khaḍra's song may be
repeated at his return from each battle or left out. It is an integral part of the epic, however, and no version among the al-
Bakâtûsh poets omits this passage entirely.

Abû Zayd eventually fights the heroes of the Banî Hilâl tribe,
unaware that he is in reality fighting his own tribesmen. In the
climactic moments of this section of the epic, he fights and
nearly slays his own father. Abû Zayd's sister deduces that
only Rizq's own son could be powerful enough to defeat him
in combat, and brings about Khaḍra's confession that Abû
Zayd is indeed the son of Rizq the Valiant. Their subsequent
reconciliation completes the tale. This narrative, encompassing the birth of Abû Zayd, his battles first against the 'Uqayla
tribe and then against his own tribe, and culminating in the
reconciliation between father and son, is but the first of the
nearly thirty episodes of the *sîra,* and is known as "The Birth
of Abû Zayd" *(mîlâd abû zayd).*

The monorhyme for the sequence we are about to examine
is /â/ or /âh/, and the brief text of the song we are to explore
here consists in its most basic form as a single line of epic
verse, complete with medial caesura and endrhyme. The verse
is ornamented, however, with three internal rhymes, creating
in effect a miniature quatrain. This duality of form can be seen
in Shaykh Ṭâhâ's rendition which I have laid out in Example 5
in both epic and quatrain form. Here Khaḍra is addressing
those elders of the Banî Hilâl tribe who wrongly accused her
of adultery many years before. The epithet "Requested of
God" *(ṭulba min allâh)* in various forms indicates Abû Zayd
throughout the epic and refers specifically that fact that he is
black because of his mother's request from God. Khaḍra refers
to her son as "the request of my eyes" as we might in English
say "my heart's desire."

Example 5 (Shaykh Ṭâhâ Abû Zayd, 6/1/87)

As epic verse:

qâlit:

yâllî sabitûnî [= sibtûnî] ta'âlû zurûnî
ṭulbit 'uyûnî min il-karîm ṭalbâh

She said:
O you who forsook me, come [now and] visit me,
The request of my eyes, from the Most Generous One [i.e. God]
I requested him.

As quatrain:

qâlit:
    yâllî sabitûnî
    ta'âlû zurûnî
    ṭulbit 'uyûnî
    min il-karîm ṭalbâh

She said:
    O you who forsook me,
    Come [now and] visit me,
    The request of my eyes,
    From the Most Generous One I requested him.

This doubling of form, quatrain and epic verse, is exploited by
poets to create a memorable passage in the epic. The use of
internal rhymes occurs fairly often in the epic as an embellishment, but only a handful of passages receive the same attention
in performance as Khaḍra's song.

Shaykh Ṭâhâ (above) normally eschews any repetition or
embellishment. This is typical of his performance style in general. In this performance, in fact, he describes only four of the
initial six battles, and in one line, between battles three and
four, recounts that Abû Zayd killed off two other kings, as
well. Shaykh Ṭâhâ is, however, one of the master poets of the
village, and his no-nonsense, stark performance style is considered by at least one group of aficionados in the village to be
superior and more authentic than more dramatized versions
such as those we are about to examine. Shaykh Ṭâhâ does,
however, frame this passage very clearly by completely stopping the music and then singing Khaḍra's song on a distinctive
melody, which he drops as soon as the verse is completed.

Shaykh Biyalî, who sang the two examples which follow, is
known in al-Bakâtûsh as a lively performer, much more of an

entertainer, a showman. He is the favorite poet of younger audiences in the village. It is not unusual for him to swing his
rabâb (spike-fiddle) high into the air as he plays, to employ
comic voices (particularly when representing women and religious figures), and to use a large number of techniques such as
rapping the bow on the side of the instrument to create battle
sounds in order to dramatize his renditions. Shaykh Biyalî in
this performance of "The Birth of Abû Zayd" sings Khadra's
song twice, after the first and second battles. Each time, he
expands the text with repetitions and substitutions:

Example 6 (Shaykh Biyalî Abû Fahmî, 2/11/87)

[After the first battle]
khud bâlak min aQwâl khadra min farḥithâ hâtqûl êh?
   yâllî sabitûnî taʿâlû shûfûnî
   yâllî sabitûnî taʿâlû shûfûnî
   yâllî taraḍtûnî taʿâlû shûfûnî
   yâllî sarashtûnî[15] yallî sabitûnî
   taʿâlû shûfûnî addî ṭulbit ʿuyûnî
   ṭulbit ʿuyûnî wi-raḍânî fîhâ 'llâh!"

Take note of the words of Khadra! From her joy what will she say?
   O you who forsook me, come [now and] see me
   O you who forsook me, come [now and] see me
   O you who cast me out, come [now and] see me
   O you who abused me, O you who forsook me,
   Come see me, this was the request of my eyes,
   The request of my eyes, and God granted it to me!

Example 7 (Shaykh Biyalî Abû Fahmî, 2/11/87)

[After the second battle]
yâ mâ zaghratit khadra al-sharîfa al-munassiba:
   yâllî sabitûnî taʿâla shufûnî
   yâllî yâllî yâllî yâllî sabitûnî
   yâllî yâllî yâllî . . . sabitûnî
   taʿâlum shufûnî ṭulbit ʿuyûnî
   wa-raḍânî fîhâ 'llâh

---

15. Metathesis of *sharasa*.

yâddî 'l-hinâ! balaghnâ 'l-munâ!
il-sa'd gêh linâ! min 'ind illâh!

O how she ululated, Khaḍra the Noble, the Highborn:
   O you who forsook me, come [now and] see me
   O you O you O you O you who forsook me
   O you O you O you . . . who forsook me
   Come see me; the request of my eyes
   And God granted it to me!

   O what joy! Our desire has reached us!
   Happiness has come to us from God!

In each case it is the phrases ending in the internal rhyme /ûnî/ which are expanded, reiterated, and substituted; the final rhyme /â/ marks the end of the expanded or dilated text and a return to epic verse. In Shaykh Biyalî's second rendition (Example 7) he further strengthens the passage from Khaḍra's song to the narrative voice of the epic by adding an unexpanded verse with internal rhyme similar in form to Khaḍra's song, but in which the quadruply repeated rhyme is /â/, our anchor to the epic verse.

This type of expansion of text from a much simpler, shorter "citation form" is a common performance process at all levels of Arab culture. The following two instances are from very different social contexts, but they demonstrate a single performance principle.

Lila Abu Lughod has published a meticulous study of a form of poetry *(ghinnâwa)* common among Bedouin women in Egypt that consists of two phrases when spoken; when sung, however, the text is greatly expanded. In the text quoted below, a refrain is created with the phrase "in the time" and the whole expanded to seventeen phrases:

   [Spoken:]
   Tears increased, oh Lord
   the beloved came to mind in the time of sadness . . .

   [Sung:]
   In the time
   in the time
   in the time of sadness

in the time
beloved in the time of sadness
in the time
in the time
beloved in the time of sadness
in the time
in the time
in the time tears
tears increased oh Lord
in the time
in the time
beloved came to mind
the beloved came to mind
in the time of sadness . . .[16]

The second instance is Egypt's most famous singer, Umm Kulthûm (d. 1975), who often sang poetic texts of less than a page, which, when expanded through repetition and reinterpretation using different embellishments, became concerts of several hours' length. She would regularly sing one or more verses of a song first to the precomposed melody of the song, and then would backtrack to repeat each verse several times, embellishing and varying the melodic line at each repetition. She would then begin to vary the text itself, adding her own interjections and at times altering the order of phrases. The culmination of this process was reached by abandoning the precomposed melody completely, at which point she would improvise the melody while at the same time reworking verses and fragments of the text with great freedom before finally returning to the precomposed melody and text. The resulting performance, much as the Bedouin text cited above, derives from a set, citable form (in this case a song with precomposed text and melody); however, the process of expansion through repetition and embellishment creates an entity far less structured, and far less controlled, in performance.

This process represents an aesthetic which is recognizable and understood by the listening audience. Its application to Khakra's song (and to only a handful of other passages within

16. Abu-Lughod, *Veiled Sentiments*, p. 179.

the *Sîrat Banî Hilâl* epic) marks the passage first of all as song. The passage is differentially marked; that is, lifted out from the surrounding epic background and highlighted. The salient features here, however, are not the contents or the imagery, as in our first example of the *mawwâl*, but rather the performance process applied to it, for the original text, at least in its "citation form," is indistinguishable from the surrounding material.

An additional series of renditions of Khadra's song, sung by a third epic poet, Shaykh 'Abd al-Wahhâb, further demonstrates the relationship between the expanded and "citation form" of the passage. In this performance, Shaykh 'Abd al-Wahhâb sings Khadra's song twice in expanded form, and then, because the performance was briefly interrupted, recapitulates Khadra's song in the rhymed prose scene-setting which initiates the continuation of the performance. In the prose scene-setting he gives Khadra's song in citation form as a single line. After the next battle, however, he again sings Khadra's song in expanded form.

Through this performance process Khadra's song is clearly being marked for emotional weight, an impact it would not otherwise possess. In the dynamic of oral performance, wherein a listener cannot call back a line he or she has not heard or understood properly, any repetition creates emphasis. This passage is in fact so well known that members of the audience often sing along with the poet and even throw their arms into the air and begin swaying back and forth. The celebratory mood in the epic as a result of a long-awaited victory (and the beginnings of anticipated vengeance) is translated into the form of the text and into the performance situation. The emotional outburst within the story of the epic (through the character of Khadra) occasions a change not only in the *form* of the poetry, with the insertion of densely occurring rhymes and highly repetitive phrases, but in the *texture* of the performance as well. This provokes a visible and audible change in audience behavior.

In musical terms, all of the poets, whether or not they dilate the verbal text, mark the passage with melodies that emphasize the four-part construction of the line created by the internal rhyme, rather than melodies which emphasize the two-part balance straddling the medial caesura. Quite simply, rather than a melody which, for example, rises in the middle (at the caesura) and then descends to the tonic center at the end of the line (at the rhyme), they choose melodies which consist of four short parallel phrases closing on the tonic at the end of the line. This process of creating a strongly rhythmic, tightly rhyming passage, and then applying an expansive or dilatory process of performance through repetition and substitution, marks the passage as song; I suspect the process also marks it as feminine. Although the idea is speculative, and one which I shall not have room to justify properly here, there is, I believe, a male stereotype about women's poetry and song at work here, one which sees female poetry as simple in form (such as is connoted by our term "ditty") and highly charged emotionally. Connotations of emotionality and formal triviality are also found in male testimonies about women's funeral lamentations and wedding songs.

In the al-Bakâtûsh epic repertory there are only a few passages which receive the specialized treatment I have just described; and all those which I have located so far are either sung by female characters or are comic texts sung by men. This female/comic mode should not be understood as being simply mimetic of the way women speak or sing; instead it seems most decidedly to have been created by male poets for their male listeners, providing a moment in which the audience may cheer, sing, laugh, and practically dance about, activities that are normally unacceptable in a male-dominated performance situation. These highlighted passages allow for emotional release, and, just as comic release functions in the service of epic seriousness, the temporary deployment of a "female" mode may function to articulate and display the masculinity of the epic endeavor.

The use of *dilatio* as a rhetorical figuration of the feminine has been examined in some detail in a series of articles by Patricia Parker.[17] Using sources primarily from European Clas-

---

17. Patricia Parker, *Literary Fat Ladies: Rhetoric, Gender, Property* (London and New York: Methuen, 1987), especially chap. 2, "Literary Fat Ladies and the Generation of the Text"; also, "Deferral, Dilation, Différ-

sical and Renaissance texts, she argues for a figurational complex which correlates delay, deferral, and dilatory expansion of texts with connotations of female physicality. Some of these connections may also be true for Arabic literature. Just as Circe, Calypso, and Penelope are figures of delay in the *Odyssey,* holding men back from their world of action, deferring any conclusion, any coming to a "point," so surely Scheherezade subverts the teleological thrust of the frame tale in the *1001 Nights* through deferral and the dilation of text.

The concept of the dilated text as figuration of the feminine in Arabic tradition, and specifically in the oral epic tradition, must remain, as I have stated above, a speculation, but it is tempting to read Khaḍra's songs as instances of dilation, moments of delay in the otherwise forward movement of the epic.

The *mawwâl* and Khaḍra's song thus demonstrate allusion to external genres by differing means and for somewhat different purposes. The *mawwâl* may actually be performed as *mawwâl* within an epic performance, or it may be alluded to by introducing its imagery and voice into the epic, though the formal characteristics which define the external, independent genre are lost and subjugated to those governing epic verse. Here the differentially marked material constructs a bridge, a transitional space, between the outer world and the world of epic.

Khaḍra's song demonstrates a double level of formal organization (as epic verse and as quatrain) which may be expanded by the performing poet so as to key the text as song, and perhaps specifically as women's song. It does not represent a specific form of song, but this is not surprising. Much of the folk poetry and song of Egypt is occasional poetry. There is no folk taxonomy for most types of folk poetry

---

ance: Shakespeare, Cervantes, Jonson," in Patricia Parker and David Quint, eds., *Literary Theory/Renaissance Texts* (Baltimore and London: Johns Hopkins University Press, 1986), pp. 182–209; and "Shakespeare and Rhetoric: 'Dilation' and 'Delation' in *Othello,*" in Patricia Parker and Geoffrey Hartman, eds., *Shakespeare and the Question of Theory* (New York and London: Methuen, 1985), pp. 54–74. My warmest thanks to Juliet Fleming for having introduced me to this set of ideas.

in Egyptian Arabic other than labels which indicate the occasions at which they are sung ("wedding songs," "circumcision songs," and so on). Only a few poetic forms are individually labeled (such as the *mawwâl, dôr,* and *sîra*). Even researchers who have attempted to classify the folk poetry of Egypt by form have inevitably fallen back on content and contextually defined characteristics.[18]

Men no longer ride back to camp from mounted desert raids and battles; in the case of the Nile Delta peasantry they have never done so. The genre of women's song sung upon the return of a victorious son can now be keyed only to a sense of what women used to sing, or might have sung on such occasions. This, I believe, is precisely the effect the epic poets of al-Bakâtûsh do create in this passage. But this contact with the feminine, even if only in stereotyped, male-perceived form, contrasts with the listeners' own male project of association and identification with men of action, epic heroes—men who, when they do pause to handle words, do so in carefully controlled ways, creating utterances bound by rhyme and caesura, subjugating emotion to the constraints of form.

These examples serve, I hope, to demonstrate not only the differing means by which poets allude to external genres, but also, in part, the power they wield in doing so, and the importance of the interplay of genres to our own understanding of the performed text.

18. See for example ʿAlî Mursî, *al-ughniyya al-shaʿbiyya.*

Appendix

All texts are in colloquial Arabic unless marked "CA" (Classical Arabic). The transcription system is that of the *International Journal of Middle East Studies* with the following exceptions.

1. The dialect spoken in al-Bakâtûsh uses three distinct forms for the phoneme /q/. In these transcriptions *Q* represents the Classical Arabic pronunciation, *q* represents the pronunciation /g/ which is most common in the region, and *q'* represents Cairene-style glottal stop. The phoneme /j/ fluctuates between /j/ and /g/ and has been transcribed as it occurs. The transcribed sounds *q* and *g* thus represent the same sound, but are derived from two separate CA phonemes.

2. Assimilation of the definite article has not been marked, though preceding vowels appear as sung.

Contributors

JOSEPH HARRIS
Harvard University

FLEMMING G. ANDERSEN
Odense University

HUGH SHIELDS
Trinity College, Dublin

DAVID BUCHAN
Memorial University, Newfoundland

SIGRID RIEUWERTS
University of Kent, England

WILLIAM B. MCCARTHY
Pennsylvania State University

EMILY LYLE
School of Scottish Studies, Edinburgh

VÉSTEINN ÓLASON
Institute for Nordic Philology, Oslo

BENGT R. JONSSON
Swedish Folksong Archive, Stockholm

NATASCHA WÜRZBACH
University of Cologne

JAN ZIOLKOWSKI
Harvard University

GREGORY NAGY
Harvard University

ALBERT B. LORD
Harvard University

KARL REICHL
University of Bonn

STEPHEN A. MITCHELL
Harvard University

DWIGHT REYNOLDS
Amherst College